D1268776

Israel's United Monarchy

Israel's United Monarchy

Leon J. Wood

Baker Book House
Grand Rapids, Michigan

ISBN: 0-8010-9622-7

Printed in the United States of America

Preface

The time of Israel's united monarchy has well been called Israel's glory period. During this time the boundaries stretched further, the influence in world affairs was more pronounced, and the kings carried a wider-reaching prestige than at any other. This was not true of the first king, Saul, but it became true of David and reached its zenith at the midpoint of Solomon's reign. Before the monarchy, the people had been fractionalized into twelve quite independent units and presented little united strength; and, after Solomon, the kingdom came to be divided into two parts, with neither part able to rival the power of the former period. The in-between years, when the kingdom took on actual empire status, were the outstanding years, as Israel's name came to be known and respected through all the Middle East.

This means that the period of united monarchy is especially important for study. What made this time so outstanding? Did contemporary world conditions contribute? Were the kings who ruled unusually talented? What sort of government did they establish and how well organized and equipped were their armies? What place did they give to religious matters and how diligent were they in their personal conduct and attitude before God?

Another area of question concerns the theocratic relationship between God and the monarchy. During the preceding period of the judges, the relationship intended had been a pure theocracy. God was to be the sole supreme King, with but a minimum of human government between Himself and His people. With the introduction of a monarchy, an earthly sovereign, having numerous subordinate officers, was instituted. Did this mean that the idea of theocracy was abandoned? If not, in what way did God intend for the idea to continue, and, as history developed, to what degree was this divine intention realized?

These and many other questions are investigated in the following pages. Part One focuses on matters of a general nature, seeking answers to questions that pertain to the period as a whole. Part Two pursues a study of each of the three kings concerned, their kingdoms, and the events in their times of rule. Several chapters are devoted to each king, with the first chapter in each instance presenting an overall survey of the kingdom that ruler established. The following chapters take up the biblical texts that portray events from his reign. First the events are analyzed and then specific points to notice concerning them are set forth. These points take up the underlying significance of the recorded events—either their relevance to the world of that day or their practical lessons for the Christian life today.

The King James Version is regularly used for biblical quotations. Occasionally I use my own translation where greater clarity is needed. Because the King James uses "LORD" for the name of God, rather than the more literal *Yahweh,* this form has been employed.

I wish to add that I am greatly indebted to my dear wife for typing the manuscript and making numerous suggestions.

Contents

List of Maps

PART ONE
Backgrounds

1

Source Material

The period of the united monarchy was the most significant in all Israel's history.[1] The prior period—that of the judges—had the potential of being the most significant, for it was the time of pure theocracy, with God as sole King. As such it held the highest possibilities for God's people in terms of prosperity and world importance. Due to the people's sin, however, it ended in weakness, confusion, and frustration. During the period following the united monarchy, that is, the period of the divided kingdom, there were a few times when extensive power was displayed, but none that could match the reigns of David and Solomon. Never again did Israel reach the zenith of influence in world affairs that she achieved during their combined time of rule.[2] Accordingly, this period is most significant for study.

Initial questions concern source material regarding the period. Where does one look for information, and is this information ample? The answer is that it is remarkably ample. Though little is found in extrabiblical

[1]Cf. John Bright, *A History of Israel,* p. 179.

[2]The widest sphere of influence was attained during the reigns of Jeroboam II (793-753 B.C.) in the north and Uzziah (790-739 B.C.) in the south, when the total area controlled did approximate that of David's and Solomon's day.

materials, the Bible itself has more to say of this period than of any other.[3] The information is found in I and II Samuel, the first eleven chapters of I Kings, I Chronicles, and the first nine chapters of II Chronicles. In contrast, the divided empire, when no fewer than nineteen kings of Israel and nineteen kings of Judah ruled, is set forth in only the last eleven chapters of I Kings (12-22), II Kings, and the last twenty-seven chapters of II Chronicles (10-36). It is true that it was during the divided kingdom that all the writing prophets penned their books, and these contain considerable historical information in addition; but in respect to pure history the divided kingdom is reported in much less detail than is the united monarchy.

Because one's source of information for any study is of prime importance, it is well to devote the few pages of this first chapter to a consideration of the materials here involved.

A. I AND II SAMUEL AND I KINGS 1-11

1. NAME

The two books of Samuel and the first eleven chapters of I Kings call for discussion together, for they provide one continuous history. The two books of Samuel were originally considered one book, and the same is true also of the two books of Kings. The division of both Samuel and Kings into two books occurred when the Old Testament was translated into Greek (the Septuagint).[4] The names then given to the two Samuels were the First and Second Books of Kingdoms, and to the two Kings the Third and Fourth Books of Kingdoms. With the Latin version (Vulgate)[5] occurred the change of Kingdoms to Kings for all four books; and when English translations were made, the first two were again called by the name *Samuel,* as in the Hebrew, while the distinction *First and Second* was retained. The designations *I and II Samuel* and *I and II Kings* are now standard for almost all translations.

2. AUTHORSHIP

a. I and II Samuel

Jewish tradition ascribes to Samuel the two books that bear his name, but he could not have written more than a part of what they contain for his death is recorded already in I Samuel 25:1, and events are described that took place some time later. The author is unknown. Because I Samuel 27:6 refers to the kings of Judah, it appears that the books were not completed in their present form until after the kingdom was divided. The author,

[3] Cf. Bright, *A History of Israel,* p. 179.

[4] The Septuagint was probably completed about 180 B.C.

[5] The Vulgate was completed by Jerome in A.D. 405.

whoever he was, used other sources. He directly mentions "the book of Jasher" (II Sam. 1:18), and he probably used also "the book of Samuel," "the book of Nathan," and the "book of Gad" (I Chron. 29:29) in order to gain firsthand information. This would account for the fact that much of his material reads as if it were written by an eyewitness.

b. I and II Kings

Jewish tradition points to Jeremiah as the author of Kings, and it is likely that this is correct. At least the author certainly lived about the time of Jeremiah, for the history recorded extends until the time of the captivity. And a factor in favor of his authorship is the absence of any mention of him in the books. This would otherwise be quite strange in view of his prominent role at the time of Jerusalem's fall to the Babylonians. If he was the author, however, the Spirit of God must have used someone else to write the closing chapter, which speaks of Jehoiachin's release from prison in Babylonia (II Kings 25:27-30). Jeremiah would have had no way of knowing about this, since he had gone down into Egypt well before it occurred (see Jer. 43:1-8).

3. TEXT OF I AND II SAMUEL

For some reason the text of I and II Samuel appears to have been more poorly preserved than that of I and II Kings, or of any of the other Old Testament books for that matter. There are a few problem areas in the text as preserved in the Masoretic recension, and there are more than the usual number of variants from texts of Samuel found in the Dead Sea Scrolls. Some of these variants point to an original text appreciably closer to the Septuagint than the present Masoretic text. One possible explanation is that the present text depended at some time on an early text that had become worm-eaten or frayed from wear and age, and the result was occasional losses of letters.[6] It should be understood, however, that such variants are not of sufficient number or importance to harm the present text in any significant degree. It remains a reliable and excellent source of information as the Word of God.

4. CONTENT

a. I and II Samuel

The first book of Samuel covers history concerning Eli and Samuel, the establishment of the monarchy under Saul, and then the events of his unhappy rule until his tragic death. David became involved with Saul in the

[6]Cf. Gleason Archer, *A Survey of Old Testament Introduction,* p. 273.

later years of his reign; recall, for example, that when the "evil spirit" came upon the king David played his instrument in Saul's presence. So David is introduced in the latter chapters and the years of his flight from Saul are there described. The second book of Samuel takes up the reign of David, so different in terms of success from that of Saul, and traces it through to its conclusion.

b. I Kings 1-11

It is only the first eleven chapters of I Kings that are of concern here. These chapters tell of the reign of Solomon. Since fewer chapters tell of Solomon than of the first two kings, it follows that less detail is given regarding Solomon than regarding the first two rulers.

B. I CHRONICLES 10-29 AND II CHRONICLES 1-9

1. NAME

The two books of Chronicles were also treated originally as one book. This book was called "The Words of the Days." The title carried the thought of "annals." The one book was divided into two by the Septuagint translators, and they gave the name *Things Omitted* to both. The thought behind this name was that these books contained many details that were omitted from the earlier books of Samuel and Kings. It was the translator of the Vulgate, Jerome, who first used the name *Chronicles* for both books, and almost all translations since have retained this title.

2. AUTHORSHIP

Jewish tradition assigns the authorship of I and II Chronicles to Ezra. This could be correct. At least the author was of his approximate date, for the history is carried down until the close of the captivity. Edward J. Young sees one difficulty in this view: he points out that the closing verses of II Chronicles (36:22, 23) and the opening verses of Ezra (1:1-4)—both of which give a record of Cyrus' decree permitting Jews to return to Judah —do not use identical words in stating the decree. Young believes that one can legitimately ask why the same author would not have used the same words.[7] However, the argument is not conclusive (as Young himself admits), and Ezra remains the most likely author.

[7] *An Introduction to the Old Testament,* p. 381.

3. THE TRUSTWORTHY CHARACTER OF CHRONICLES[8]

The trustworthiness of Chronicles has been seriously attacked by liberal scholars. Robert H. Pfeiffer, for instance, believes the books contain little of historical value and sees them as polemics in defense of the Levites.[9] W. O. E. Oesterly and T. H. Robinson state bluntly that "not much importance can be attached to the history as presented in Chronicles."[10]

a. Numerous source materials

It may be maintained, however, that both books of Chronicles are fully trustworthy and accurate, as are all parts of the Bible. There are some problem areas involved (these will be discussed next), but it is also true that actually the books of Chronicles give more attention to source material than do any of the other historical books. The list of materials noted is impressive: I Chronicles 29:29, "the book of Samuel the seer . . . the book of Nathan the prophet . . . the book of Gad the seer"; II Chronicles 9:29, "the book of Nathan the prophet . . . the prophecy of Ahijah the Shilonite . . . the visions of Iddo the seer"; II Chronicles 13:22, "the story [midrash] of the prophet Iddo"; II Chronicles 16:11 (cf. 25:26; 27:7; 28:26; 32:32; 35:27; 36:8), "the book of the kings of Judah and Israel"; II Chronicles 20:34, "the book of Jehu the son of Hanani . . . the book of the kings of Israel"; II Chronicles 24:27, "the story [midrash] of the book of the kings"; II Chronicles 26:22, a work written by "Isaiah the prophet, the son of Amoz"; and II Chronicles 33:19, "the sayings of the seers."

b. Problem areas

One problem area noted by liberal scholars concerns what are called incredibly high numbers that are cited in the Chronicles.[11] For instance, in I Chronicles 22:14 David is said to have amassed for the temple no less than a "hundred thousand talents of gold, and a thousand thousand talents of silver"; and in II Chronicles 14:8, 9 Asa of Judah is said to have had as many as "three hundred thousand" in his army and Zerah the Ethiopian who faced him a "thousand thousand." These numbers are very large; no one could say otherwise. But this in itself is insufficient reason to say they are not accurate. It is possible that errors in transmission crept into the text regarding such numbers, but it should also be remembered that David gave enormous effort to gathering materials for the temple—since he was very interested in it—and it has become clear in recent years that ancient armies

[8]Ibid., pp. 384, 394.
[9]*Introduction to the Old Testament,* pp. 781-801.
[10]*Hebrew Religion,* p. 118.
[11]See Samuel R. Driver, *Introduction to the Literature of the Old Testament,* p. 500.

were often of very large size. It may be added that numbers given in Chronicles are sometimes actually smaller than corresponding numbers in Samuel or Kings. For instance, compare II Samuel 23:8 with I Chronicles 11:11, or I Kings 9:23 with II Chronicles 8:10.[12]

A second problem area also concerns numbers; namely, that numbers cited in Chronicles sometimes differ from corresponding numbers in Samuel and Kings and are usually higher. It is alleged that by making the numbers higher the chronicler was attempting to glorify Israel's history by deliberate exaggeration. In reply, it may be pointed out that in the great majority of instances there is exact agreement between Chronicles and Samuel or Kings. Gleason Archer points out that actually "there are only eighteen or twenty examples of discrepancy," and that in as many as one-third of these the corresponding number in Chronicles is smaller than in Samuel or Kings.[13] This fact alone shows the fallacy of seeing the chronicler as one intent on exaggeration. What discrepancies there are have to be studied individually, for one answer will not account for all. In general the solutions concern various types of errors in transmission. Ancient times saw different and often unusual (in terms of today's methodology) ways in which numbers were designated, and, because of this, inaccuracy in transmission of the text became quite possible. The wonder is that more errors did not creep in than did, in view of the many years involved in the transmission and the many copies made.[14]

A third problem area concerns the omission in Chronicles of events in the lives of David and Solomon which were derogatory to their character. Nothing is said, for instance, of David's sin with Bathsheba or of Solomon's idolatry late in his life, events which are set forth in Samuel (II Sam. 11) and in Kings (I Kings 11:1-8). This omission, it is alleged, was due to an apologetic interest in presenting these two kings in their finest light. Young points out, however, that in view of the chronicler's pains to list his sources (as we have already noted), one can hardly make such a charge successfully; for these sources did give the full story, as is made clear by the reports of Samuel and Kings. Rather, one should attribute the omissions to the fact that inclusion of these shortcomings did not fit into the chronicler's purpose in writing the books, a purpose which will be noticed shortly.

A fourth problem area concerns what is called the apologetic nature of Chronicles in a defense of Judah. It is observed, for instance, that Chronicles—in contrast to Kings—is almost totally silent regarding the northern nation of Israel. Reasons alleged for this silence are that Israel's history was irrelevant to the history of Jerusalem and Judah, and that

[12]See also p. 314, n. 11.
[13]*Survey,* pp. 394-395.
[14]See Young, *Introduction,* pp. 389-390.

possibly there was an actual bitterness toward the northern nation on the part of the author. In response, it may be said that such thinking comes only from reading into the mind of the author something for which the book gives no evidence. The real reason for the omission is once more that a history of the northern kingdom did not fit into the chronicler's purpose in writing.

4. PURPOSE

It is important, therefore, to set forth the purpose of the book. Written following the Babylonian exile, the book was intended to show the returned exiles the true greatness of their nation and especially the place and importance of the Davidic dynasty in its history. The people had come back from having been away from home for many years. A new generation, which had not known the former days of the kingdom, now lived. They needed encouragement. A major means of giving this encouragement, and an incentive to carry on in a way pleasing to God, was to acquaint them with Israel's past history. They needed to hear that they were God's chosen people. They needed to be instructed to safeguard their glorious heritage by the forms of worship prescribed in the Mosaic law, forms of worship administered by the priesthood under the authorized *Davidic* dynasty. For such a purpose, the northern nation was of little use; thus there was no reason to mention its past. Jerusalem and its temple, and the all-important Davidic dynasty that ruled there, were the important matters; and, accordingly, these were the factors that received stress in Chronicles.

5. CONTENT

The Book of I Chronicles begins with genealogies, running from Adam to David. The intent is to lay a foundation for the more important monarchial history. Then David's story is told in the remainder of the book, with continual stress on priestly and sanctuary-oriented matters. It may be observed that Saul's story is by-passed, but this is because it is not a part of the continuing *Davidic* history. The Book of II Chronicles then tells the story of Solomon, again with a stress on priestly matters and especially on the construction of the temple. Following this comes the story of the nineteen kings of Judah, closing with the edict of Cyrus permitting the Jewish return from captivity. Our interest, then, will concern all of I Chronicles following the genealogies, and then II Chronicles 1-9.

2

The Need for the Monarchy

The question now in point concerns the need or reason for the monarchy. Since this form of rule had not been instituted for the tribes when they had first entered Canaan, it is reasonable to ask why it was introduced after more than three centuries had elapsed. The question becomes more pointed when one realizes that actually a higher form of government had been in existence during these prior three centuries; in other words, a higher form was now replaced by a lower form. That higher form had been a pure theocracy.[1] God had been the supreme King, with the people expected to render allegiance directly to Him. Now there would be an earthly ruler, to whom, as an intermediary between the people and God, allegiance would be rendered. Why did God permit this substitution in form of rule?

The Bible indicates that an immediate reason lay in a poor performance by Samuel's two sons, Joel and Abiah, as judges in the area of Beersheba (I Sam. 8:1-5). Samuel had appointed them, but they did not follow in the upright ways of their father. Instead, they accepted "lucre, and took bribes, and perverted judgment" (I Sam. 8:3). When a request for the inauguration of a monarchy was given to Samuel, it was their conduct that was presented

[1]See C. D. Press, "King, Kingdom," *International Standard Bible Encyclopedia,* p. 1800.

as the reason (I Sam. 8:5). Behind this reason, however, there must have been other, more basic motivations, to account for such a major request. And a study of the time reveals that there were; indeed, there were at least three that carried prime importance.

A. FEAR OF ENEMY POWERS

One that is probably the most obvious, and on which practically all scholars are agreed,[2] is that the people were fearful of enemy powers. Two were particularly menacing at the time, the Philistines and the Ammonites.

1. THE PHILISTINES

a. Type of people

The Philistine menace was the most serious. Philistines had inhabited southwest Canaan since the days of Abraham (Gen. 21:32, 34; 26:1, 8, 14, 15, 18; Exod. 13:17), but the big influx, that brought about this menace, came with the movement of the Sea Peoples in the early part of the twelfth century. One group among these roving people was the Philistines (the *prst* as identified by Egyptian notices of the time), and these came to settle in the same area occupied by their ancestors. Once there, they quickly established themselves as a people to be reckoned with by all surrounding peoples.[3]

Their manner of government took the form of a pentapolis, with the leaders (*serens*) of their five major cities (Gaza, Ashkelon, Ashdod, Gath, and Ekron) sharing the rule. They were warlike, geared to military occupation, and had in mind no less than the conquest of all Palestine and probably Syria.[4] An important factor in their expansionist plans—and certainly a reason for the measure of success they achieved—was their monopoly in respect to iron. The Hittites had known the secret of smelting iron for centuries, and it may be that the Philistines had learned it from them, as they had earlier migrated across Hittite territory in Anatolia, pillaging as they went. Now in Canaan, they were careful to keep this knowledge from the Israelites (and probably Canaanites), as indicated in I Samuel 13:19-21. The monopoly gave them a significant advantage in war, for an iron sword could completely sever one made merely of bronze.

[2]Ibid.; also John Bright, *A History of Israel,* p. 180.

[3]Regarding Philistine entry into Canaan, see Kenneth Kitchen, "The Philistines," *Peoples of Old Testament Times,* ed. D. J. Wiseman, pp. 57-60; and for discussion of Philistine language, religion, architecture, material culture, society, and cultural assimilation see the same article, pp. 67-70.

[4]In this their menace was more serious than that of earlier oppressors of Israel whom Eugene Maly (*The World of David and Solomon,* p. 17) calls only "nomadic raiders."

b. Previous history in Canaan

Prior to the beginning of Israel's monarchy, Philistines had held the Israelites in bondage for no less than forty years (Judg. 13:1).[5] A correlation of chronological factors shows this to have extended from approximately 1095 to 1055 B.C.[6] This was the sixth and last oppression during the period of the judges. God permitted the oppressions to come on His people as measures of discipline for sin, and this last one was the longest and no doubt the most severe. It began about the same time as a contemporary oppression by the Ammonites (Judg. 10:7), but that one lasted only eighteen years (Judg. 10:8), when it was brought to a close by the mighty warrior Jephthah (Judg. 11:32, 33).

The Philistine oppression had been marked by two major battles. The first was the battle of Aphek,[7] when Israel was soundly defeated twice by the enemy and, most significantly, the ark of God was seized (I Sam. 4:1-18). The other came twenty years later (I Sam. 7:2),[8] the battle of Mizpeh. In this battle, Israel was victorious and the forty-year oppression came to an end. Because this battle shortly preceded Saul's inauguration as king in 1050 B.C.,[9] its date is best placed about 1055 B.C., making the Aphek battle about 1075 B.C. Correlations work out well for locating Samson's twenty years of judgeship (Judg. 15:20; 16:31) in the twenty years separating these battles, and a major part of Samuel's work fits best into these same twenty years.[10] By the time that the people made their request for a king to Samuel, the oppressive days of the Philistines were past (by about five years), but they were fresh enough in the people's minds to remember well how near to complete destruction they had come. Also, the Philistines, though defeated at Mizpeh, were in no way permanently hurt, and therefore could be expected to renew an attack on Israel at almost any time—as indeed they soon did (I Sam. 13:3-18). Accordingly, the people wanted a ruler who could lead in assembling an army and commanding it in battle.

2. THE AMMONITES

a. The people

The Ammonites were named after their progenitor, Ammon, a half brother of Moab. Ammon and Moab had been born to Lot from incestuous

[5]For pictures of plaster casts of Philistine soldiers see R. D. Barnett, *Illustrations of Old Testament History,* pp. 25-27.

[6]See my discussion, *A Survey of Israel's History,* p. 225.

[7]Aphek was in the Sharon plain, about ten miles northeast of Joppa.

[8]The twenty years indicated in I Sam. 7:2 do refer to this span of time and not to the period in which the ark was at Kirjath-jearim, for it was there about seventy years.

[9]Saul began to reign forty years (Acts 13:21) before David, who began in 1010 B.C.

[10]See my discussion, *The Distressing Days of the Judges,* pp. 341-342.

relationships with his two daughters (Gen. 19:33-38). The Ammonite land lay east of the Jordan, at the edge of the Arabian desert (Deut. 2:37; Josh. 12:2; 13:10, 25), and their capital was Rabbath-Ammon (present day Amman, capital of Jordan). Because of the arid condition of the land, their lifestyle must have been seminomadic, though they did have a few cities (in addition to their capital) which appear to have served as border fortresses.[11] One distinctive advantage enjoyed by the Ammonites was their control of a portion of the "king's highway" (the international road joining Syria with southern Transjordan), which gave them political power and taxation benefits from caravan travel.

b. Relation to Israel

As has been observed, the Ammonites had brought one of the six oppressions on Israel, in the early part of the same century in which Saul was crowned king. This oppression had been largely confined to the Transjordan area (Judg. 10:8, 9) and, after eighteen years, had been brought to a close by Jephthah's victory over them (Judg. 11:32, 33). The date of that victory can be fixed at approximately 1078 B.C. The time of Saul's inauguration as king was twenty-eight years later, in 1050 B.C. But, as will be seen, a major factor in making that inauguration possible was another victory over these people effected by Saul at Jabesh-gilead (I Sam. 11:1-15). This means that, during the few intervening years, the Ammonites had recovered from their losses suffered at the hands of Jephthah and had become strong again.

In passing, it should be noted that in the southern Transjordan area, where the Ammonites lived, there was a basic relationship among the several peoples living there which is important to keep in mind. This relationship is that, when one of these peoples was strong, the others quite necessarily had to be weak. The reason is that available land simply was not sufficient to permit more than one group to be strong at the same time. Moab lay immediately to the east of the Dead Sea. Reuben had been allotted land along that eastern edge also, north of the Arnon River, but clearly had not kept it, for during much of the Old Testament time Moab is seen controlling territory as far north as the northern tip of the Dead Sea. The Reubenites apparently were pushed up into the territory of Gad, at least in major part. And then Ammon lay further east of both Moab and the allotted land of Reuben, on the edge of the desert. Sometimes the Midianites also came into the region, as was true in the time of Gideon (Judg. 8:1-12). All this made for very crowded conditions, so that, if any one of these

[11]See Abraham Malamat, "The Period of the Judges," *The World History of the Jewish People,* pp. 156-157, for discussion.

groups became stronger than usual and expanded their territory, the others were thus made smaller and weaker.[12]

In view of Ammon's ability to recover quickly after Jephthah's victory, one must conclude that this general period was a time of strength for Ammon. The king must have been a capable leader so that, though defeated, he was able to maintain his position of power and leadership, and by Saul's time to make offensive strikes once again.[13] Israel was aware of this, as Samuel himself gave indication (I Sam. 12:12), and so they were afraid of another general invasion by this foreign power, in addition to their fear of the Philistines. Both enemies had attacked at about the same time a half century before, and there would have been a strong desire that this not be repeated.

B. DEVELOPING DESIRE FOR MONARCHY

Besides this fear of enemy oppression, a second reason behind this call for a monarchy, as voiced to Samuel, was really a long-standing desire for this form of government. The request to Samuel, then, was not an expression of a new thought. It was the re-emergence of an old thought, which had come to notice in various ways several times before.

1. OCCASIONS OF MONARCHIAL EXPRESSION

The first occasion when a desire for monarchy was expressed came in the time of Gideon's judgeship. Following his victory over the invading Midianites—including his challenging pursuit of them across 150 miles of difficult Transjordan terrain (Judg. 8:1-12)—"men of Israel," meaning no doubt people of his home area of Ophrah (Judg. 6:11), offered him a continuing kingship over them, both for himself and his posterity (Judg. 8:22). Gideon properly refused, for this was not God's will in the days of the pure theocracy.

A second occasion came with the actual kingship of a son of Gideon, Abimelech, immediately after Gideon's death (Judg. 9). He was crowned at Shechem[14] and probably never ruled an area much larger than the immediately adjacent territory. The fact, however, that a few people had been

[12]See Malamat, "The Period of the Judges," pp. 152-153.

[13]This strength of the Ammonites testifies to the remarkable ability of Jephthah in defeating them.

[14]Shechem was about twenty-five miles south of Gideon's home region. Gideon had apparently exerted influence this far south because he had taken a concubine from there who became Abimelech's mother (Judg. 8:31).

willing to make a person king suggests that the thinking of others was of a similar nature. There is no reason to believe that Shechemites constituted an island of thought to themselves. Then, besides this, a question Abimelech put to the Shechemites at the time of his negotiations with them may be significant to the same end. He asked them, "Whether is better for you, either that all the sons of Jerubbaal, which are threescore and ten persons, reign over you, or that one reign over you?" (Judg. 9:2). It is possible, of course, that Abimelech intended to convey a totally false impression by these words, but there may have been some truth involved. That truth would be that Gideon's other sons had the same thing in mind as Abimelech and possibly were already at work in setting up a type of monarchy in the Ophrah region, just as Abimelech was at Shechem. The fact that Gideon had been offered the rule, and then possibly had conducted himself as judge in quite a kingly manner—at least his having seventy sons indicates that he had a large harem of wives in the manner of kings of the day—could have led both them and Abimelech to take what may have seemed a logical next step.

A third indication of monarchial thinking comes from what appears to have been a kingly lifestyle, in the pattern of Gideon, followed by several of the following minor judges. These also had large families: Jair with thirty sons, who apparently ruled over thirty cities called Havoth-jair (Judg. 10:3, 4); Ibzan with thirty sons and thirty daughters (Judg. 12:9); and Abdon with forty sons and thirty grandsons (Judg. 2:14).[15] Such a number of children speaks again of several wives, after the manner of kings of the day. It is quite clear that these judges did not pose as kings, but their lifestyle could well have been in that pattern as a reflection of current thinking concerning the need for a strong central ruler.

It may be that God, to keep this manner of thinking from crystallizing sooner than it did, made use of the poor performance by the one man that had thus far actually served as king—Abimelech. He had not benefited the people who crowned him, but instead, within three years, had quarreled with them and finally destroyed them utterly, including their city. People would have learned of this and remembered it for many years. It would certainly have had a deterrent effect.

2. THE REASONS FOR THIS GROWING DESIRE

There were at least two reasons for the growing desire for a king. One was the continuing threat of outside oppressions, the same basic fear that motivated the final request for a king to Samuel. By the time of Gideon, there had been four of these oppressions, counting the one of his time (the

[15]The KJV reads "nephews," but the Hebrew says "sons of sons," meaning "grandsons."

Mesopotamians, the Moabites, the Canaanites, and the Midianites). Quite clearly, when the people had asked Gideon to rule them, following his remarkable victory over the Midianites, they had done so thinking that it would be good to have a monarch, so that further incursions of the kind could be avoided.

The other reason was the continuing increase in sinful activity and the resulting harmful effects for the country. The two stories that bring the Book of Judges to a close illustrate several aspects of this sin. The one story concerns the private sanctuary of Micah and the movement of Danites from their allotted territory to new land in the far north (Judg. 17-18); the other concerns an outrageous action against a Levite's concubine by the people of Gibeah and a civil war that resulted among the tribes (Judg. 19-21). Both stories occurred early in the period of the judges[16] and show that sin had already become serious at that time. Sins involved in the stories include the following: the movement of a tribe from its God-assigned territory, the establishment of private sanctuaries, the making of images, the establishment of priests from other than the family of Levi, the movement of a Levite from his designated city of residence, the stealing of other people's property, sexual atrocities of an outrageous kind, protection of guilty people, a low respect for human life, and the violation of personal rights. And in back of most of these sins—indeed, responsible in large part for them—was the most serious sin of all, the worship of the Canaanite god Baal (Judg. 2:11-13; 3:7; 6:25-32; I Sam. 7:3, 4).

The sin of the people had not been abating, but increasing. Judges 10:6 indicates that by the time of Jephthah, the people had come to serve not only the Canaanite Baal, but also "the gods of Syria, and the gods of Zidon, and the gods of Moab, and the gods of the children of Ammon, and the gods of the Philistines." And when people come to engage freely in such sinful activity, the very fact that it thus becomes widespread—with no one really doing anything to curtail it—becomes a reason in itself for general frustration and depression. In this light, the four-time repetition of the statement that this sin occurred because "there was no king in Israel" (Judges 17:6; 18:1; 19:1; 21:25) becomes significant. People were increasingly recognizing that a firm hand at the helm was needed if these sinful excesses were to be controlled. People at a given time may think they enjoy sinning, but those who practice it eventually become disillusioned by it and wish for something better.

[16]Earliness is indicated for the first story in that the Danite move is mentioned in the Book of Joshua (Josh. 19:47) and that book was written while Rahab yet lived (Josh. 6:25). It is indicated for the second story in that Phinehas, son of Eleazar, was yet active (Judg. 20:28) and he had been active already before the conquest (Num. 25:7, 11; Josh. 22:13, 31f.).

C. REJECTION OF PURE THEOCRACY

Still a third reason for the monarchy request can be discerned by considering Israel's situation from God's supreme point of view. The high form of government instituted by God at the time of the entrance into Canaan, the pure theocracy, had not worked to the benefit of either God or the people; therefore, there was need for a change. This really was what God told Samuel when the prophet brought the request for a king to Him. God's words were:

> Hearken unto the voice of the people in all that they say unto thee: for they have not rejected thee [as Samuel thought], but they have rejected me, that I should not reign over them. According to all the works which they have done since the day that I brought them up out of Egypt even unto this day, wherewith they have forsaken me, and served other gods, so do they also unto thee. (I Sam. 8:7, 8)

The government God had given His people, on their first entering the Promised Land, was a pure theocracy; God was their sole supreme Ruler. They were given no earthly king or governor, in fact almost no earthly government at all, apart from the priests and Levites. They did have local elders who served in a juridical capacity (Deut. 19:12; 21:2, 18f.; 22:15; 25:7), but probably only on a part-time basis since no provision is given in the law for their support. And the Israelites had courts, both local (Deut. 16:18) and one central (Deut. 17:8f.). But they had no central authority, not even over the local tribes. God was their King. He had given them His regulations in the Mosaic law and He had provided the high priest with the Urim and Thummim for determining His will on matters not covered by it (Exod. 28:30; Num. 27:21). The government was a theocracy in the full sense of the word.

1. THE IMPORTANCE OF OBEDIENCE

A vital aspect in this theocratic arrangement was obedience on the part of the people. God had laid down His requirements, but the people had to obey them. The people knew, or had ways of knowing, what God wanted them to do, but, if the arrangement was to work, they had to comply with this knowledge. If they had done so, everything would have functioned well. Most important, God would have been given the place of centrality and honor He deserves and desires. The people too would have greatly benefited, for there was no expensive government to support with high taxes.

2. OBEDIENCE NOT GIVEN

This vital element of obedience, however, had not been rendered. Instead, sin had come to abound in blatant rebellion. This had begun already in Israel's early days, directly after the death of Joshua (Judg. 2:7-11). In this way, the people almost immediately showed their rejection of God as King; or, as God Himself said, "According to all the works which they have done since the day that I brought them out of Egypt even unto this day, wherewith they have forsaken me, and served other gods, so do they also unto thee [Samuel]" (I Sam. 8:8). The nature of this sin in Israel's early days has already been seen in the stories from Judges 17-21.

3. DISOBEDIENCE STILL WORSE AFTER THE JUDGES

a. Disobedience at the tabernacle

Sin was serious enough in the early days, but it became worse. An obvious and shocking evidence of this comes from the conduct of Hophni and Phinehas at the central tabernacle. The tabernacle had been instituted to be representative of God's presence among His people, and it was to serve as a common meeting point for Israelites at least three times a year (Exod. 34:23). It was also to provide for the people a center of instruction in God's divine requirements, and those who conducted its ceremonies were to provide the finest examples of God-approved conduct before the people.

Hophni and Phinehas, however, did not provide such examples. They were sons of the high priest Eli. All three of them lived and died at the close of the period of the judges, just before the people presented their request for a monarchy to Samuel (I Sam. 4:11, 18; cf. 8:1-5). Not only did these sons not provide good examples, but they became actual leaders in disobedience. When people brought their offerings to be sacrificed, Eli's sons would insist on more meat from those offerings for themselves than the law prescribed (I Sam. 2:12-16),[17] and so made people to abhor the thought of bringing "the offering of the LORD" (I Sam. 2:17). Besides this, "they lay with the women that assembled[18] at the door of the tabernacle" (I Sam. 2:22), thus copying the sensual practices of Baal priests and priestesses. The degree of God's displeasure with all this is indicated by the significant words, "Notwithstanding they [Hophni and Phinehas] hearkened not

[17]From animals brought as peace-offerings, the law stipulated that the priest could have the breast and upper part of the right rear leg, though only after the fat portions of the animal had been sacrificed (Lev. 7:30-34). Hophni and Phinehas, however, wanted in addition all that a three-pronged fork could bring up when plunged into the remaining meat being boiled for the sacrificial meal. And, besides this, they demanded from the offerer raw meat that was not cooked at all.

[18]The Hebrew word for "assembled" is *tsaba',* which here could well mean "served." The women in view were probably those in reference in Exodus 38:8, who performed service around the tabernacle.

unto the voice of their father, because the LORD would slay them" (I Sam. 2:25).[19]

When such conduct was carried on right at the central sanctuary, the people of the land experienced a serious negative influence on their lives. If the leading priests of the day were so misbehaving, why should they conduct themselves any better? Besides this, there would have been an added sense of frustration and hopelessness. If the leaders were so bad, then what hope did the country have at all?

b. Disobedience seen in the increase of judgeships

A second indication of disobedience is less obvious but just as significant. It is that God saw fit, during the closing years of the period of the judges, to raise up many more judges than during the earlier years. Since one of the reasons for the judges clearly was to restrain people from engaging in sin, it follows that this increase in judgeships was indicative of a corresponding increase in sin that made them necessary.

That judgeships did increase in number can be seen by a look at the chronology of the period. Admittedly, problems do exist, but a view that takes the chronology given in Judges seriously—and such a view can be defended with significant argumentation[20]—sees the total period, from Joshua's death to Saul's crowning, as lasting from approximately 1390 B.C. until 1050 B.C., or about 340 years. Now during this number of years, five judges (Othniel, Ehud, Shamgar, Deborah, and Gideon) served through the first 271 years,[21] and nine judges (Tola, Jair, Jephthah, Ibzan, Elon, Abdon, Samson, Eli, and Samuel)[22] served during the remaining 69 years. Or, put differently, during one-fifth of the total time, nearly two-thirds of the judges did their work.

This striking statistic suggests that God was indicating to the people—even as they were coming themselves to believe—that more governmental control was becoming necessary as the period progressed. In this light, it is not surprising that God gave His approval to the people's request for a king when it was presented. Sometimes it is held that God gave His permission reluctantly. In one sense, this was true: God was disappointed that the people had not obeyed Him during the period of the judges, and it

[19]The basic nature of the sin committed was in discouraging the people from worshiping God as God had commanded, and this is probably one of the most serious sins in the sight of God; cf. Paul's statement in I Tim. 1:13. Paul did essentially the same thing when he persecuted the church.

[20]See my discussion, *The Distressing Days of the Judges,* pp. 10-17.

[21]Ibid., pp. 32-33.

[22]Eli and Samuel are correctly classified as judges (see I Sam. 4:18 and 7:15). Eli, then, was both high priest and judge, and Samuel both prophet and judge.

was this disobedience which made the permission appropriate.[23] In view of the disobedience having been rendered, however, it was indeed best that the people have a continuing earthly ruler. In this sense, the permission was not reluctant.

4. THE MONARCHY LONG ANTICIPATED

In keeping with God's granting of the people's request is the fact that years before God had predicted the time when a king would reign over His people. In fact, He had even given instructions relative to the qualifications of such a ruler. A prediction regarding kings was voiced already to Abraham (Gen. 17:6, 16), and then to Jacob (Gen. 35:11), and later on to Moses (Deut. 28:36). To Moses, instructions were also set forth (Deut. 17:14-20). These instructions included the following points: the king should be one of Israel's own number, and not a stranger; he should not "multiply horses to himself," nor "return to Egypt" for this purpose, meaning apparently that he should not put his trust in earthly strength but in God; he should not "multiply wives to himself" or "silver and gold," for these would turn his heart away from God; and he should take care to study God's law, a copy of which was to be given him that he might "learn to fear the LORD his God." These regulations may well have been included in "the manner of the kingdom" which Samuel wrote up and gave to the people at the time of Saul's selection as their first king (I Sam. 10:25).

The point to notice is that God had long before anticipated the day when the people would bring the request they did. It was not that He wanted the situation to develop that would bring them to do this, but only that in His perfect foreknowledge He knew that it would come and gave these words of preparation accordingly.

[23]This is the significance of Hosea 13:11, "I gave thee a king in mine anger."

3

The World of the Day

The question now before us concerns the nature of the world of the day. At the time that Israelite representatives came to Samuel and asked for a king, what were the conditions in the world about them? Since they asked for a "king to judge us like all the nations," the question might be asked in the form: what were the nations like that they wanted to emulate? Another question, to be considered in the following chapter, is: how near to these nations did the resultant kingdom come?

But the question now to be considered is of two parts: what was the world like politically, and what was it like ideologically, so far as kingship is concerned?

A. THE WORLD POLITICALLY

Israel's world was composed of peoples close at hand and far away. Those nearest were the Canaanites; next were the nations that bordered Palestine, which were all comparatively small; and farthest away were larger nations, including especially Assyria and Egypt. It is well to consider these peoples in that order.

1. THE CANAANITES

The progenitor of the Canaanites was Canaan, one of the four sons of Ham (Gen. 10:6). The Canaanites quite clearly had been in the land for some time when Abraham arrived among them (Gen. 12:6). The ethnic line of those among whom the Israelites settled, when they later arrived in the land under Joshua, however, was not of pure descent from Ham's son. There had been two major migrations into the region, which had resulted in an intermingling of races.

a. The Amorite migration

The first was a migration of Amorite people from Upper Mesopotamia. They came at the close of the third and the beginning of the second millennia B.C. The time of their migration is marked by a wide destruction of Canaanite cities after 2200 B.C., among which were Megiddo, Jericho, and Ai.[1] The cities first affected lay west of the Jordan, but later (after 2000 B.C.) there was similar destruction on the east.[2] The incoming people spoke West Semitic and were seminomadic, adjusting to a sedentary lifestyle after arriving in Canaan. That they were Amorites is indicated both by the pottery they made and the names they bore.

It would appear that, in some areas of Canaan, a rather complete intermingling between these migrants and the native Canaanites took place and that, in others, a rather distinct separation was maintained. In Numbers 13:29, for instance, "Amorites" (along with other named peoples) are said to have inhabited the mountain areas of Canaan, while Canaanites proper lived by the sea. Also, in Transjordan, both Sihon and Og were kings of the Amorites (Num. 21:21, 26; Josh. 2:10; 24:8), indicating that Amorites remained relatively distinct there. On the other hand, a general amalgamation is indicated for most of the country by the fact that the people of the land could be called by the broad term *Amorites* (Josh. 24:18), when one would expect the more customary term *Canaanites.*

b. Hurrian migration

The second was a migration of Hurrians, with probably some Indo-Aryan people included, both non-Semitic. This movement of people oc-

[1]For discussion, see G. Ernest Wright, *Biblical Archaeology,* pp. 41-42; or William F. Albright, *From the Stone Age to Christianity,* pp. 118-120. More recently M. Liverani, "The Amorites," *Peoples of Old Testament Times,* ed. D. J. Wiseman, pp. 100-133, accounts for the presence of Amorites in the Palestinian area in a different manner. He believes they were there along with, if not identical with, Canaanites from earliest historical times.

[2]Indicated both by excavation in Palestine and by the Execration Texts of Egypt, which date to the twentieth and nineteenth centuries B.C.; see William F. Albright, *Archaeology of Palestine,* pp. 82-83, for description.

curred during the eighteenth and seventeenth centuries B.C., coming again from Upper Mesopotamia. Hurrian and Indo-Aryan people settled the kingdom of Mitanni about the same time, the latter becoming rulers for the most part and the former the basic population. In southern Canaan, these migrants no doubt intermarried in many cases with the native populace, but once more there is indication that some groups remained relatively distinct. For instance, the people called Horites in the Bible (Gen. 14:6; 36:20, 29; Deut. 2:12, 22) are probably to be identified as Hurrians. Then some scholars believe that the Hivites, mentioned as many as twenty-four times in the Old Testament (e.g., Gen. 34:2; Josh. 9:7), are also to be identified with them, and possibly even the Perizzites, who are mentioned nearly as often (e.g., Gen. 13:7; Judg. 1:4), since the element *izzi* appears in connection with Hurrians at Mitanni.[3] Hurrians must have been well known in southern Canaan for the Egyptians occasionally referred to the area as Huru.[4]

A major significance of this twofold migration into Canaan is that both groups, coming from Mesopotamia, brought with them Mesopotamian ways and ideas. This means that the people who lived in Canaan at the time of Joshua's conquest brought their cultural impact on the Israelites during the period of the judges—since Israel did not exterminate them from the land as God had commanded (Exod. 23:33; 34:11-16; Deut. 7:1-5)—were characterized by this eastern influence. Consequently, in order to grasp all the factors that played on Israelite thinking from contacts with the Canaanites, one must be knowledgeable of the ways and ideas of Mesopotamia as well as of Canaan proper. Or to put it differently, if one is to appreciate fully the Canaanite influence on Israel, he has to use not only the comparatively few texts from Canaan proper, but also the much larger number extant from the Mesopotamian region.

c. Area of land occupied

At the time of Saul's inauguration as Israel's first king, these Canaanites still occupied substantial portions of the land, especially the lowland areas which were the best for farming. This included the fertile Mediterranean sea coast, which had not been taken by Joshua in the initial conquest (Josh. 13:1-6) and had not been occupied by the tribes later on (Judg. 1:19, 27-36).[5] It may also have included parts of the upper Jordan Valley and the Esdraelon Plain, though the decisive battle of Deborah and Barak against

[3]See John Bright, *A History of Israel,* p. 107.

[4]See Yohanan Aharoni, *The Land of the Bible,* pp. 175, 246, for discussion; see *Ancient Near Eastern Texts,* ed. J. B. Pritchard, p. 261, for the name in a text.

[5]The Danites are directly said to have failed to occupy their land along the Mediterranean, and all identified cities that the other tribes are said to have failed to take are also known to have been in the lowlands.

the Canaanites had done much to remove the latter from Canaanite control.[6] And certain highland areas—for instance, the region of Shechem—held significant Canaanite populations.[7]

2. NATIONS AROUND CANAAN

a. The Edomites

Among the nations that surrounded Canaan proper was Edom. It lay directly south of the Dead Sea. Edom, often called "Seir" or "Mount Seir" in the Old Testament (e.g., Gen. 32:3; 36:20, 21, 30), stretched for about 100 miles from the Dead Sea to the Gulf of Aqaba (Deut. 2:8-13). It lay on both sides of the rugged mountain range of Seir and included the low Arabah Valley on the west of that range. It was less fertile than Palestine, but did boast fields, vineyards, and wells in Moses' day (Num. 20:17, 18).

The earliest inhabitants were Horites (Gen. 14:6; Deut. 2:12), or, as we have just seen, Hurrians. The name *Edom,* however, comes from one of Isaac's sons, Esau (Gen. 36:1), who moved to the region and whose descendants apparently absorbed the Horites into their number. The land was first ruled by tribal chiefs (Gen. 36:15-19, 40-43; I Chron. 1:51-54), but later by kings (Gen. 36:31-39; I Chron. 1:43-50). An extrabiblical reference to Edom occurs in Papyrus Anastasi VI of Egypt (dated in the late thirteenth century), which speaks of desert people moving from Edom to the rich Nile Delta.[8] Another reference is found in the Amarna Letters (no. 256): Edom (*Udumu*) is cited as an enemy of a prince from the Jordan Valley.[9]

The period of the judges witnessed a minimum of contact between Edomites and Israelites. Edom was the first country that Moses asked for permission to pass through (Num. 20:14-21).[10] Upon being refused, Israel was forced to take a long and tedious circuit around Edom (Num. 21:4; Judg. 11:17, 18).[11] Following that time however, no contact between the two peoples is recorded until after Saul's inauguration. Apparently, then,

[6]See my discussion in *The Distressing Days of the Judges,* pp. 189-193.

[7]Ibid., pp. 242-245.

[8]See Benjamin Mazar, "The Exodus and the Conquest," *The World History of the Jewish People,* vol. III, p. 71.

[9]See *Ancient Near Eastern Texts,* p. 486.

[10]Similar permission was asked from Moab (see Judg. 11:17, 18) and later still from Sihon, king of the Amorites (Num. 21:23-23); both gave negative replies.

[11]Some scholars believe Israel reversed directions after leaving Mt. Hor (Num. 20:23) and marched north to by-pass Edom at its north end rather than its south. This view is based largely on identifying Punon and Oboth (Num. 33:42-44; 21:10, 11) with modern Feinan and el-Weibah, both of which are on Edom's west side rather than the east. These identifications are not sure, however, and Deut. 2:8 says that the turn was made at Elath and Ezion-geber, which are at the head of the Gulf of Aqaba. See Aharoni, *The Land of the Bible,* p. 51, for the opposing view.

all during the period of the judges, the people of Judah and Simeon (Simeon had been given cities in southern Judah; see Josh. 19:1-9) had not bothered, or been bothered by, Edom. The country was probably a more formidable rival at the time of Saul than at the time of Moses and Joshua.

b. The Moabites

Immediately to the northeast of Edom lay Moab. Its principal area was confined between the Zered and Arnon rivers, on the east side of the Dead Sea (Num. 21:12, 13), but for much of Old Testament time its people also occupied land north of the Arnon, as far as the northern tip of the Dead Sea. This additional land constituted the territory that had been allotted to the tribe of Reuben (Josh. 13:15-23), but apparently Reuben had not held it well, with its people probably being forced north into Gadite territory.[12] The land Moab occupied was mainly plateau, averaging a height of about 3,000 feet.

The name *Moab* comes from the progenitor of the people, Moab, born to Lot by an incestuous relationship with his oldest daughter (Gen. 19:33-37). Descendants of the son evidently came to live among, enter marriages with, and then take leadership over the original inhabitants of the area. These original inhabitants were Emim (Deut. 2:10, 11), related to the Anakim, both groups being characterized by large stature. Excavation has revealed that these earlier people had numerous villages, which were largely destroyed toward the close of the twentieth century by the invading Amorites, as we have seen. By the time of this destruction, Lot's descendants would have just begun to intermingle with them; this indicates that most of the intermarriages occurred following that time, when the people had assumed a more nomadic form of life. Quite clearly, in view of the name employed, the bloodline from Lot's son had become dominant by the time of Israel's journey from Egypt to Canaan.

Three major contacts between Israelites and Moabites had occurred prior to the beginning of Israel's monarchy. The first was at the time of conquest, when Moses had by-passed Moab, and then Balak, the Moabite king, had summoned Balaam all the way from Mesopotamia to curse Israel (Num. 22-24). The second was the occasion of Moab's direct invasion and oppression of Israelite people, and Ehud's arising as Israel's champion to effect deliverance (Judg. 3:12-30). And the third was the ten-year sojourn of Naomi in Moab, when her husband and two sons died and she returned to

[12]Whenever the Bible mentions cities of this area allotted to Reuben, especially Heshbon and Medeba, they regularly are shown to be under the control of either Moab or Ammon (Isa. 15:4; 16:8, 9; Jer. 48:2, 45; I Chron. 19:7); Reuben is seldom even mentioned (only in Judg. 5:15, 16; II Kings 10:33; I Chron. 5:6, 26; 12:37; 27:16) after the Moabite oppression and never in a way to show that it controlled its allotted land.

Judah a widow, along with her widowed daughter-in-law Ruth (Ruth 1-4). This last occasion, which occurred about the middle of the twelfth century,[13] or about one century before the beginning of Israel's monarchy, shows that peaceful relations existed then between Israel and Moab, and the same seems to have been true at the time of Saul. It is significant that David, somewhat in the pattern of Naomi and her husband, took his father and mother to Moab for safe-keeping, while he was a fugitive from Saul (I Sam. 22:3-5).

The fact that Moab was comparatively weak as a country at the time of Saul is further in line with this idea of peaceful relations between Moab and Israel. That Moab was weak at this time was suggested in Chapter 2. It was noted that more than one of these compacted countries could not be strong and expansive at the same time and that Ammon was the Transjordan country that was now strong.[14] This weakness of Moab could also have existed as early as Naomi's day, for the Book of Ruth refers to the country not as a kingdom, but only as "the fields [KJV, country] of Moab" (1:1). This manner of reference would be surprising if Moab were a strong country at the time.

c. The Ammonites

To the northeast of Moab, and directly east of Reuben-Gadite territory, lay Ammon. Chapter 2 has already discussed this power, which was one of the enemies threatening Israel at the time of Saul's inauguration. The country had not been touched by the Israelites at the time of their approach to Canaan under Moses, for God had commanded that Israel not distress or bother its people (Deut. 2:19). Since Ammon bordered Moab, and since both countries were by-passed, it must be that Moses moved along the border that separated the two countries. The Ammonites brought the fifth oppression on the tribes during the period of the judges, as has been observed, and were still very strong. It was their threat against Jabesh-gilead that provided Saul with his opportunity to display his ability before the people of Israel and so make himself acceptable to them as king (I Sam. 11). Later on, David would have a major clash with the Ammonites, following an occasion when he had intended to show kindness to their new and young king (II Sam. 10:1-19). This would result in a complete victory for David and the incorporation of Ammon into the Israelite kingdom.

d. The area of Damascus

The group of people now to be considered did not enjoy a unified status during the period of the judges nor even at the beginning of Israel's mon-

[13]On the basis of David's genealogy given in Ruth 4:18-22.

[14]See pp. 24-25.

archy. The people consisted of several tribal groups that lived in the general area of Damascus, reaching as far south as the Manassite territory east of the Jordan. Damascus itself is one of the oldest continuing cities of the world, located to the northeast of Mount Hermon. An early nonbiblical reference to the city occurs in a list of enemies that confronted Thutmose III of Egypt at the famous battle of Megiddo; the form of the name used is *Timasku.*[15] Also, in the Amarna Letters the city is mentioned in the form *Timasgi* and spoken of as maintaining loyalty to Egypt during troubled times.[16] The area around Damascus constitutes a fertile plain known for its gardens and orchards and watered by the Abana (modern Barada) and Pharpar rivers.[17]

1) ***Period of greatest power.*** The period of greatest power for Damascus came in the ninth and eighth centuries B.C. By this time, Aramaeans from the northeast had come to control the city and to build for themselves a formidable state. The state is first noticed in the Bible when Asa, king of Judah, sent to Ben-hadad I of Damascus to ask for assistance against Baasha, king of Israel, then oppressing Asa in Jerusalem.[18] Ben-hadad, desirous of enlarging his sphere of influence anyway, did as requested, and from then on for more than a century his kingdom remained a continual threat to Israel. During the reigns of Jehu and Jehoahaz of Israel, in fact, when Hazael was the Aramaean ruler, Israel was brought to a position of extreme humiliation before Damascus. Hazael was able actually to dictate how many horses, chariots, and infantry Israel's king could have in his army (II Kings 13:7).[19]

2) ***Condition when Israel's monarchy began.*** This day of power still lay in the future, however, when Saul became Israel's first king. At this early time, the city was relatively unimportant in world affairs, as was the area around it. During the period of the judges, the region was being infiltrated by Aramaean people, but they did not yet become sufficiently numerous or consolidated to exert the strength they did later. Prior to this infiltration, Amorite people had inhabited at least the southern portion of the area, and at the time of Moses' conquest of Transjordan, Og was their ruler. The Aramaeans apparently first lived among the Amorites and then became numerous enough to supplant them as the people of greatest influence.

[15]For discussion, see Merrill Unger, *Israel and the Aramaeans of Damascus,* p. 15.

[16]Ibid., p. 21.

[17]Damascene pride in these rivers is reflected in Naaman's response to Elisha at the time Naaman came to the Israelite prophet to be healed of leprosy (II Kings 5:12).

[18]In an economic warfare centered at Ramah just north of Jerusalem, apparently to stop trade from entering or leaving Jerusalem (II Chron. 16:1-4).

[19]For discussion, see my *Survey of Israel's History,* pp. 322-323.

They increased in number greatly following the invasion of the Sea Peoples in the early twelfth century, when so many changes in political power took place. Shortly after this time specific Aramaean states come to be mentioned in texts of the period.[20]

The most powerful of these states was Zobah, to the north of Damascus. At the time of David, Zobah's king was Hadadezer; his power reached all the way to the Euphrates River (II Sam. 8:3) and probably as far south as Damascus. Damascus at this time does not appear to have had a king of its own,[21] and the people of Damascus were obliged to come to Hadadezer's aid, when he was pressed by Israel's advance under David (II Sam. 8:3-5). The kingdom of Zobah was already existent in Saul's time, for it is listed as one of his military foes (I Sam. 14:47); it is mentioned only once after David's victory over it. Solomon is said to have made conquest of Hamath-zobah at the time he built Tadmor (Palmyra) in the desert to the east (II Chron. 8:3, 4). The reason for the hyphenated form *Hamath-zobah* in this late context may be that the two powers, Hamath and Zobah, had now come to be interrelated or allied with each other.[22]

Another important state was Beth-rehob,[23] probably located just north of the city of Laish that later was called Dan. Judges 18:28 states that Laish was located "in the valley that lieth by Beth-rehob" (literally, "in the valley which was to Beth-rehob"). The state was so strong in the days of David that the Ammonites appealed to it, along with Zobah and others, to supply troops in their battle with David (II Sam. 10:6-8). The state may have included all Coele-Syria, thus succeeding the early state of the region, Amurru.[24]

Other states that are known were Maacah, Geshur, and Tob. An exact location for each, however, is impossible to determine. They appear to have been somewhere on the east of the Jordan River and south of Mount Hermon. Maacah and Geshur are often mentioned together, as though near each other; they probably were farther north than Tob (see Deut. 3:14;

[20]See a recent discussion of these states by Abraham Malamat, "The Aramaeans," *Peoples of Old Testament Times,* ed. D. J. Wiseman, pp. 141-142.

[21]In II Sam. 8:5, 9, both Zobah and Hamath are said to have had kings, but there is no mention of a king of Damascus.

[22]For discussion, see Unger, *Israel and the Aramaeans,* pp. 44-45. J. Lewy ("Hamat-Zobah and Subat-Hamatu," in *Hebrew Union College Annual* 18 [1944], pp. 443-454) equates the names *Zobah* and *Hamath* and identifies them with modern Baalbek. Scholars have not taken the view very seriously, however, because of its forced argumentation.

[23]Probably there is no connection with the city of Rehob, listed as belonging to Asher (Josh. 19:28, 30; Judg. 1:31), which clearly was nearer the Mediterranean since Rameses II refers to it as having been near Dor (on the Mediterranean); see Aharoni, *Land of the Bible,* p. 241, n. 101.

[24]Regarding Amurru, see Benjamin Mazar, "The Historical Development" *The World History of the Jewish People,* vol. III, pp. 10-11.

Josh. 12:4, 5; 13:11). Unger places Maacah as the farthest north, between Mount Hermon and Geshur, since the city of Abel (identified at times as Abel Beth Maacah—I Kings 15:20; II Kings 15:29), somehow linked to Maacah, quite clearly was located northeast of Dan.[25] This would place Geshur on the east side of the Sea of Galilee. Tob was probably south of Geshur, or possibly southeast. Tob was the land to which Jephthah of Gilead fled when driven from home by his brothers (Judg. 11:3-5), and so may have been just north of Gilead near the Yarmuk River. Since it is called only "land of Tob" (Judg. 11:3, 5) and its inhabitants only "men of Tob" (II Sam. 10:6), it may not have been as well organized as the other states.

The land south of Tob, as far as the region of Ammon and Moab, was occupied, of course, by Israel's own tribes.

The people around Damascus had not been able to oppress Israel's tribes during the period of the judges because they lacked the strength of unification. They were only a fragmented group and not a unified people as later in the days of Ben-hadad and Hazael. The small Aramaean states that came to be formed, however, would become involved with Israel's monarchy.[26]

e. The Phoenicians

The next area to notice is Phoenicia, lying north of Palestine along the Mediterranean.[27] It was squeezed between the Lebanon Mountains and the Mediterranean, and it stretched from the city of Acco on the south of Arvad on the north, a distance of about 150 miles. Its people were of the same ethnic stock as those of Palestine; namely, Canaanite with an intermixing of Semitic blood from the migrations of the early second millennium B.C. The principal occupation was trading. There was little land to farm, but there was excellent wood for building ships and to offer in trade,[28] and the coastline boasted splendid harbors.

1) ***Biblical references.*** Only in the New Testament does the Bible refer to the area as Phoenicia (Mark 7:26; Acts 11:19; 15:3; 21:2). The Old Testament commonly designates simply either (or both) of the principal cities of

[25]Unger, *Israel and the Aramaeans,* p. 45.

[26]Besides David's involvement with Zobah, Beth-rehob, Maacah, and Tob (II Sam. 10:6), the land to which Absalom fled was Geshur, where his mother had been born (II Sam. 13:37, 38).

[27]For helpful information regarding Phoenicians see D. R. Ap-Thomas, "The Phoenicians," *Peoples of Old Testament Times,* ed. D. J. Wiseman, pp. 259-286.

[28]Both David and Solomon contracted with Tyre to supply cedar for building (II Sam. 5:11; I Kings 5:6-10). Centuries earlier, Gudea, ruler of Lagash in southern Mesopotamia, had acquired cedar from this region; and the Egyptian Wenamon came to Lebanon for cedar around 1100 B.C.; see G. A. Barton, *Archaeology and the Bible,* pp. 449f., 455.

the land, Tyre and Sidon. These two cities, both prominent in trade, continue to the present day and are only twenty miles apart. They seem never to have enjoyed true political cohesion, however; it is likely, then, that the country did not either. In keeping with this is the fact that the boundaries of the country at any given time are difficult to determine. Another way of designating the country in the Old Testament is the term *Sidonians* (e.g., Deut. 3:9; Josh. 13:4, 6; Judg. 3:3; 18:7; I Kings 5:6). This is because historically the more important city was Sidon, with Tyre becoming dominant later on. Jezebel, for instance, who married King Ahab of Israel, is identified as the daughter of Ethbaal, "king of the Sidonians" (I Kings 16:31), even though Ethbaal probably lived and ruled in Tyre.[29]

2) ***Extrabiblical references.*** Phoenicia is first mentioned in recorded history by Thutmose III. He speaks of having secured it as a necessary avenue for communicating with his homeland, Egypt, and he states that he severely punished the city of Arvad, at its extreme north, for not cooperating with him. Several of the Amarna Letters were written by kings of Phoenician cities, and these testify to a confused condition within the country during the fourteenth century. The country continued under the nominal control of Egypt during the time of both the eighteenth and nineteenth dynasties of Egypt. But that it considered itself quite independent by the middle of the twelfth century is indicated by the story of Wenamon. This Egyptian was sent to do business with Byblos (as well as Dor farther south) and was treated with distinct discourtesy.[30] At the beginning of the twelfth century, the country was severely jolted by the Sea People's movement, with both Arvad and Byblos suffering destruction and the people of Sidon fleeing to Tyre for safety.

3) ***Contact with Israel.*** Phoenicia had little contact with Israelite tribes during the period of the judges. It had been under Egyptian domination for most of the period, keeping it from independent action, and it experienced the crippling blow of the Sea Peoples shortly after 1200 B.C. Besides this, the people never became strong militarily and did not attempt any conquests. Even after Israel became a nation, when so many neighboring countries met her in conflict, no military encounter with Phoenicia is recorded. The significant contact at that time was to be in trading, the principal activity of the area. Both David and Solomon would contract with its king, Hiram, to obtain its prized cedar.

[29]Homer too refers to the Phoenician king as "king of the Sidonians" (*Od.* 6.618).

[30]For the story with discussion and references, see *Ancient Near Eastern Texts,* pp. 25-29.

f. The Philistines

The last neighboring country to consider is Philistia, but this land, like Ammon, was discussed in Chapter 2. It was one of the two countries fear of which contributed to Israel's desire for a monarchy. It had held Israelite tribes under oppression for forty years, and this period had ended probably not more than five years before Saul began to reign. The Philistines constituted a strong, formidable enemy, consequently, when the monarchy began, and Saul was to experience their power during much of his time of rule. In fact, his years on the throne would be brought to a close by a tragic battle with the Philistines near Mount Gilboa (I Sam. 31:1-10). David would encounter the Philistines also, but would decisively defeat them twice at the very beginning of his rule and then keep them well subdued from that time on.

3. THE LARGE NATIONS

We come now to look at the larger nations of the day, those more powerful and also at a greater distance from southern Canaan. The study of these nations is particularly significant because their strength and activity, at any given time, had a major impact on the activity of the smaller nations that lay between them. These smaller nations included those that surrounded Israel, which have just been considered, and also Israel itself. Since David was able to expand Israel's borders so extensively, it follows that these outside powers must have been comparatively quiet at the time, and this was indeed the case. It will be well to consider first the powers that lay to the north of Israel and then Egypt to the south.

a. Powers to the north

We begin with a few general statements regarding the powers to the north. There were two powers that would affect life in Israel during the monarchy period, though not yet in the time of the united monarchy; they were Babylonia and Assyria.

Babylonia had first been strong in what is called the Early Babylonian Period (ca. 1900 B.C. to ca. 1600 B.C.), ruling at the time from the Persian Gulf to the region of Mari well north on the Euphrates River.[31] It lost this position of power, however, when it was invaded by the Kassites.[32] Kassite domination continued for four centuries, and when the country recovered from the dark ages that resulted, other nations were pre-eminent in power.

[31]For a helpful discussion of Babylonian history and culture, see W. G. Lambert, "The Babylonians and Chaldaeans," *Peoples of Old Testament Times,* ed. D. J. Wiseman, pp. 179-196.

[32]Kassite origin is unknown, but it is believed that they came south out of the Luristan Mountains, possibly pushed by Indo-Aryan pressure.

Further days of glory for Babylonia were far in the future, when the great Nebuchadnezzar (605-562 B.C.) would reign, a time at the close of the divided monarchy of Israel. Babylonia was not to be reckoned with by Saul, David, or Solomon.

Assyria lay to the north of Babylon and was correspondingly nearer to Israel, that is, as one follows the Fertile Crescent. During most of the second millennium B.C., Assyria did not assume the importance of a major power, due in large part to the rival nations of Upper Mesopotamia and Anatolia. When these nations were removed, Assyria became Israel's greatest menace (and conqueror in time). Had the rival powers not been there as long as they were, this situation might well have developed before it did. And if it had, Israel's history for the period of the united monarchy could have been seriously affected. Therefore, before looking further at Assyria itself, there is reason to look at the two principal nations that served to hinder Assyrian expansion.

1) ***Mitanni.*** The country of Mitanni was located between Assyria on the east and Hatti on the west, mainly north of the Euphrates River. Its exact boundaries are hard to define, both because of lack of information and because of frequent change of boundaries. The country was founded late in the sixteenth century B.C., with a population predominantly Hurrian. The rulers, however, were mainly Indo-Aryan, as is indicated by their names (e.g., Shuttarna, Saushsatar, Artatama, Tushratta, etc.). They worshiped the Vedic gods, Indra, Mithra, and Varuna. An honored class were the patrician chariot-warriors, called *maryannu.* The name of the capital city was Wasshugani, which probably lay near the upper Khabur River, though the site is uncertain. The height of Mitannian power was reached under Saushsatar (ca. 1450 B.C.), contemporary with Thutmose III of Egypt. His territory probably extended all the way from the Tigris on the east to northern Syria and possibly even the Mediterranean on the west. In this day of Mitannian strength, Assyria was actually a dependency of Mitanni, giving rich booty to Saushsatar.

Had an enemy nation not risen to stop the expansion of Mitanni at this time, the country could have become an oppressor of Israel, during Israel's tribal days. One did arise, however, namely, Egypt, under the mighty Thutmose III. By means of several campaigns, this powerful Egyptian was able to push the Mitannian holdings back to the Euphrates and then make terms with the king. Following this agreement, a period of peace ensued between the two countries, which proved to be mutually beneficial in view of another rising power to the west, the Hittites of Hatti. In fact, this Egyptian-Mitannian alliance probably served to hold back for at least a generation the wide influence later achieved by the Hittites. Mitanni never was able to bring direct influence on the Israelites, both because of Egypt and because of this Hittite power. The nation of Hatti brought Mitanni to a complete cessation even before the beginning of Israel's united monarchy.

2) ***Hatti.*** The country of Hatti is more often referred to by the name of its people, the Hittites. Hatti was located to the west of Mitanni, across the Taurus Mountains in Anatolia (Asia Minor). The origin of the Hittite people is not clear.[33] The evidence points to an amalgamation between a native populace and migrating Indo-Aryans, about the beginning of the second millennium B.C. The name *Hittites* comes from the name of the Hittite capital city, Hattusas, better known by the modern name, Boghazkoy, located ninety miles east of present-day Ankara.[34] The history of the nation can be divided into three parts: the old Kingdom Period (1800-1450 B.C.), a brief Intermediate Period (1450-1400 B.C.), and the Empire Period (1400-1200 B.C.). Only the last is significant here.

The great builder of Hatti's empire was Suppiluliuma (ca. 1375-1340 B.C.). He pushed the Hittite boundaries beyond the Taurus Mountains and southward as far as the Dog River (*Nahr el-Kalb*), which flows into the Mediterranean just north of modern Beirut. This was the nearest that Hittite power ever came to Israelite territory, however. Even Suppiluliuma apparently did not dare to challenge Egyptian power any farther from home, for this was the day of Egyptian control over much of the eastern Mediterranean seaboard.

The Hittite ruler also challenged Mitanni, which until this time had enjoyed Egypt's protection. Tushratta, the Mitannian king of the day, appealed to the Egyptian court for help, but none was forthcoming. The Egyptian ruler was now Amenhotep IV (Akhenaten) and he was more interested in furthering his new departure in religion[35] than in helping frantic nations. The result was that Tushratta was assassinated, and his son appealed to Suppiluliuma for mercy and help. The great Hittite conqueror took the opportunity to seize control over Mitanni. He married his daughter to the young man and then aided him in gaining the throne. His price, however, was that Mitanni become a vassal state to Hatti. This brought Mitanni to an end as a separate entity, and clearly established Hatti as the strongest nation of the north.

[33]For an excellent study of Hittites, see O. R. Gurney, *The Hittites;* for a brief, more recent study see H. A. Hoffner, "The Hittites and Hurrians," *Peoples of Old Testament Times,* ed. D. J. Wiseman, pp. 197-221.

[34]For a discussion of the city, see Philip Hitti, *History of Syria, Including Lebanon and Palestine,* pp. 154-155.

[35]An innovative monotheism that centered in the god Aten; for discussion see John A. Wilson, *The Burden of Egypt,* pp. 221-228. See *Ancient Near Eastern Texts,* pp. 369-371, for the Hymn to Aten.

Following the death of Suppiluliuma, the prestige of Hatti declined. This was due in part to a long siege of fighting with two Egyptian kings, Seti I (1316-1304 B.C.) and Rameses II (1304-1238 B.C.). Finally a peace treaty was signed in Rameses's twenty-first year (1283 B.C.), copies of which are extant in both its Hittite and Egyptian forms.[36] Hattusilis III, who signed for the Hittites, was the last great king of the country. Soon after the treaty was made, the former country of Mitanni was seized from Hittite control by the Assyrians. Then the successors of Hattusilis III encountered increased offensive strength from the western states of Anatolia; finally, near the end of the thirteenth century, the Sea Peoples overran the capital and the country of Hatti was no more. By the time of Israel's monarchy, then, the Hittites, like the Mitannians, no longer existed as a nation.

3) ***Assyria.*** It is appropriate now to take a more detailed look at the history of Assyria.[37] The kings of Assyria ruled at the city of Assur, on the Tigris River, for most of its history. The early history of Assur is little known. Quite clearly it was at one time under the control of the third dynasty of Ur (ca. 2130-2030 B.C.), and then following this period it was ruled by independent kings for a number of years. These rulers established trade relations with Cappadocia (ca. 1920-1870 B.C.).[38] During the height of power of the Early Babylonian Empire and then later when the Hurrian and Mitannian peoples became strong, Assyria was a comparatively weak nation. As indicated above, under Saushsatar the Mitannian power probably reached as far east as the Tigris River.

With the eclipse of Mitanni, however, in the days of the Hittite Suppiluliuma, Assyria again began to assert itself. It is known that its king, Ashur-uballit I (ca. 1365-1330 B.C.), considered himself sufficiently important to engage in correspondence with Amenhotep IV of Egypt and even had an ambassador accepted at the foreign court. Then Adad-nirari I (ca. 1307-1275 B.C.) through military action was able to bring Shatturara I of Hanigalbat (name of Mitanni at this time) to the status of a vassal. The successor of Shatturara revolted, but he was conquered in turn by Shalmaneser I (ca. 1275-1245 B.C.), and Hanigalbat came fully under Assyrian control. Tukulti-Ninurta I (ca. 1245-1208 B.C.) continued this expansion of Assyrian power and conquered all northern Mesopotamia as far west as the Euphrates, and he also moved south and made conquest of

[36]See *Ancient Near Eastern Texts,* pp. 199-203, for both forms.

[37]The reader will find helpful a recent survey of Assyrian history by H. W. F. Saggs, "The Assyrians," *Peoples of Old Testament Times,* ed. D. J. Wiseman, pp. 156-166.

[38]Information regarding this trade has come from no fewer than 3,000 tablets found at Kultepe and Alishar in modern Turkey. The tablets show that Assyria was strong enough to guarantee safety for caravans traveling between Cappadocia and Assur. Trade was mainly in metals and raw materials.

Babylonia.[39] And most significant, less than a century after this, Tiglath-pileser I (ca. 1118-1078 B.C.) actually made conquest all the way to the Mediterranean, where he received tribute from Arvad, Byblos, and Sidon. He was not able to conquer the Aramaean states of the region, however, and so was not able to move on south to have possible contact with the Israelite tribes.

It is of high significance for Israel's united monarchy that the successors of Tiglath-pileser were not able to maintain the holdings he had gained, much less expand them any farther. Had Assyrian conquests continued as they had started, the story of Israel's expansion could have been far different. One may say that God in His providential control saw to it that they did not. In fact, not only did the conquests not continue, but the kings that followed Tiglath-pileser were contrastingly weak so that almost nothing is known about them. Assyrian power, having risen so far, went into eclipse for a time, until the emergence of the powerful Ashur-nasir-pal II (883-859 B.C.) two centuries later. By this time the reigns of Saul, David, and Solomon were completed and the Israelite kingdom was divided. Assyria thus was kept from interfering with David's wide-ranging conquests.

b. Egypt to the south

A change had also taken place in Egypt, prior to the beginning of Israel's monarchy, and this too helped in the building of Israel's empire. Somewhat similar to the situation in Assyria, Egyptian rulers came to have less vision and capability than their predecessors, and foreign conquest was quite forgotten.

During the time of the eighteenth dynasty (sixteenth to fourteenth centuries), the great Thutmose III had extended Egypt's border as far as the Euphrates. Then during the nineteenth dynasty (thirteenth century), both Seti I and Rameses II had sought to reaffirm this border, though the Hittites had stopped them from fully doing so. At the beginning of the twelfth century, Rameses III of the twentieth dynasty still showed strength in successfully resisting the Sea Peoples, but after his rule, Egypt's power suffered a marked decrease. The continuing rulers of the twentieth dynasty, all named Rameses (IV to XI), were much weaker, and any semblance of an Egyptian empire ceased. The twenty-first dynasty, beginning about 1085 B.C., was actually a divided rule. The king of Upper Egypt was the high priest of Amun, while the king of Lower Egypt ruled at Tanis. The two came to an agreement on general policy and ideas, which gave some unity to authority for Egypt itself, but no interest was shown in foreign affairs. It was this dynasty and these conditions that existed at the time of Saul's crowning as Israel's first king. The same situation prevailed while David

[39]For several centuries there was almost constant rivalry between Assyria and Babylonia.

ruled, thus bringing no resistance to his extensive expansion, and also for most of Solomon's reign, thus giving no hindrance to his maintenance of Israel's far-flung borders.[40]

B. THE WORLD IDEOLOGICALLY

The discussion of the chapter thus far has shown what Israel's neighbors were like politically. A principal benefit has been to see an important reason why Israel's expansion during the united monarchy was physically possible. It is necessary now to consider these neighbors ideologically, to see how people thought of their kings and kingship in general. This will give information as to what Israel's leaders had in mind when they asked Samuel for a king that they might be "like all the nations."

There are two parts to the question: what was the relation of kings and people politically? and, what was the relation between kings and the deities worshiped? It will be well to consider both questions as the various countries are surveyed once more. First, however, a few general observations regarding kings and kingship are in order.

1. GENERAL OBSERVATIONS

The basic derivation of the word *melek* ("king") is not clear. It may be from an Arabic root meaning "possess" or "reign," or it may be from an Assyrian and Aramaic root meaning "counsel." The first would suggest strength and prowess, while the latter would suggest intellectual superiority.

The earliest known king was Nimrud, said to have ruled over an extensive territory in Mesopotamia (Gen. 10:8-12). Later the Bible speaks of four kings who came all the way from lower Mesopotamia to southern Canaan in the time of Abraham and Lot, and were encountered by five kings of the Jordan plain (Gen. 14:1-12). These five kings were rulers over individual cities; many early kings seem to have followed this pattern. This was true in ancient Sumer of the third millennium B.C.,[41] and it was true in Canaan, as will soon be noted at greater length. Kingship usually operated on the basis of hereditary lineage, but this was not always true, as is indicated by a listing of successive kings of Edom (Gen. 36:31-39). In general, kingly authority was believed to come from the god worshiped, who was considered the divinity-king; this is illustrated in the *Legend of Keret* from Ras Shamra.[42]

[40]For a recent survey of Egyptian history of this general time see Ronald J. Williams, "The Egyptians," *Peoples of Old Testament Times,* ed. D. J. Wiseman, pp. 94-95.

[41]For discussion and references, see John Bright, *A History of Israel,* pp. 34-35.

[42]For text and discussion, see *Ancient Near Eastern Texts,* pp. 142-149.

2. COUNTRIES SURVEYED

a. Canaan

1) ***People and king.*** Southern Canaan, where Israel's tribes came to dwell, knew only city-state kings. The region had never been united under one general authority, but each city and surrounding territory had its own ruler. This is evidenced continually in the biblical record. Jericho, encountered by Joshua after crossing the Jordan, had its own king (Josh. 2:2, 3); Ai's king was taken alive in the next main battle (Josh. 8:23); Canaanite kings (plural) are said to have been frightened by these events (Josh. 9:1); five kings from five leading southern Canaanite cities banded together to punish the Gibeonite confederacy for making peace with Joshua (Josh. 10:1-5); a host of kings from across northern Palestine assembled under the leadership of Jabin, king of Hazor, to fight Joshua (Josh. 11:1-5); and no fewer than thirty-one kings of individual cities are listed in Joshua 12:9-24 as having been killed by Joshua's forces.

The fact that this was the situation in Canaan no doubt contributed measurably to making Joshua's task easier in effecting a conquest of the country. Twice numerous city-kings banded together in a temporary confederacy to fight him, but for the most part the task consisted of taking city and king, one by one.

2) ***King-deity relationship.*** The Old Testament is all but silent on the Canaanite concept of the relation of earthly kings to the gods they worshiped. Canaanite kings were certainly devoted to their gods, especially to Baal, the god of storm and rain. If it had been otherwise, Israelites would not have been drawn to Baal worship to the extent they were, and Jezebel, daughter of the Phoenician-Canaanite ruler of the Sidonians, would not have been so intent on bringing her Baal religion into Israel (I Kings 16:31; 18:18, 19; 19:2; 21:25, 26).

Perhaps the most helpful information comes from the extrabiblical *Legend of Keret,* noted above and found at Ras Shamra by French excavators in 1930-31. The text dates from the fourteenth century, and the king (Keret) in reference is thought to be fictional, though it is believed the story contains a core of history. In respect to the question here in point, King Keret is addressed by the god in three significant ways: "lad of El" (e.g., lines 40, 61), "servant of El" (e.g., lines 153, 155), and son of El (actually El is called his "father"; e.g., lines 60, 169). None of these identify Keret as a god, to establish the idea of divine kingship, but they do show Keret's ancestry as being divine. Such ancestry would at least give divine authority for his rule.

b. Nations near to Canaan

1) ***People and king.*** Nations around Canaan may be treated as a group, for they appear to have been similar in their ideas, with the exception of the Midianites and the Philistines. Kingship among these similar nations was different than in Canaan. They all had state-kings, not city-kings. Kings of Edom, listed already in Genesis 36:31-39, are presented as kings of the entire nation of Edom, not of merely separate Edomite cities. Also, when Moses asked for passage through Edom, he sent his request to the king of Edom (Num. 20:14). Both Sihon and Og, whom Moses defeated before Israel crossed the Jordan, were kings of states: Sihon, king of the Amorites (Num. 21:21), and Og, king of Bashan (Num. 21:33).

Later on, the Aramaean state of Zobah is said to have had Hadadezer as its king (I Sam. 14:47; II Sam. 8:3-10; 10:16, 19); Hamath had Toi as its king (II Sam. 8:9); Moab had Nahash followed by Hanun as its king (II Sam. 10:1, 2); the Amalekites had Agag as their king (I Sam. 15:8). And Phoenicia had Hiram as its king at one time (I Kings 5:1) and Ethbaal at another (I Kings 16:31).[43]

The Midianites appear to have differed from this general pattern, though they do not evidence the idea of city-kings like the Canaanites either. They seem to have been divided into five subtribes, with a king over each. The mention of five sons of Midian (Gen. 25:4—Ephah, Epher, Hanoch, Abidah, and Eldaah) suggests this, and five Midianite kings were slain at one time by the Israelites, prior to crossing the Jordan (Num. 31:8—Evi, Rekem, Zur, Hur, and Reba). By the time of Gideon, however, this number may have been reduced to two, for only two kings, Zebah and Zalmunna, are mentioned as being slain by the Israelite leader (Judg. 8:5, 6, 10). On the other hand, it is possible that Oreb and Zeeb should be added to these two, for a total of four. At least they are described as army commanders for the Midianites at the time (Judg. 7:25) and are classed as Midianite leaders along with Zebah and Zalmunna in Psalm 83:11.

The Philistines were ruled as a pentapolis, having five leading cities, each with a "lord" or "tyrant" (*seren;* e.g., Josh. 13:3; Judg. 3:3; 16:5). These five cities were more than city-states, however, for these five lords are regularly presented as supervising all Philistia, as a sort of joint council.

2) ***King-deity relationship.*** Really nothing more can be said regarding the thinking in these countries concerning the relation of king and deity

[43]Though Hiram is called "king of Tyre" and Ethbaal "king of the Sidonians" (cf. above, p. 42), this does not mean that they were kings only of Tyre and Sidon, respectively. Hiram was in a position to contract with both David and Solomon for cedar which belonged to all Lebanon, and Ethbaal probably lived actually at Tyre and not Sidon, since Tyre had been made capital of the country ca. 1050 B.C. (see William F. Albright, *Archaeology and the Religion of Israel,* p. 131).

than has been said in respect to the Canaanites. Because these nations all occupied areas close together, it is at least possible that a common viewpoint was held. The Philistines may have differed in their view, for they were immigrants who did not have a long history in the region, but nothing is known concerning their ideas.

c. The large nations

1) ***People and king.*** All the larger nations, at the time of Israel's beginning monarchy, had national kings. It is true that early Sumeria had city-kings, but this had changed when the lower Mesopotamian cities had been brought under one head in the Akkadian period, instituted by Sargon (ca. 2130 B.C.).[44] Since at least the twenty-ninth century B.C., Egypt had been united under one rule. Apparently this was first accomplished by King Narmer, whom Henri Frankfort identifies with the legendary Menes.[45] About the time of the beginning of Israel's monarchy, Egypt became separated again into Upper and Lower Egypt, with a king over each, but this still was far from a city-state form of rule. The Assyrian King List shows that kings ruled the full country of Assyria from at least the third millennium on. Mitanni had only national kings for all its history, and the same appears to have been true for the Hittites.

2) ***King-deity relationship.*** Civilization was born in Mesopotamia and in Egypt. These two centers continued to dominate thinking in the Middle East for centuries. The two were quite different, however, in their view of the national community and its relation to the divine, otherworldly realm. Both centers believed that the basic function of kingship was to maintain a harmonious relationship between people and this otherworldly realm, but saw the function from two points of view.

In Mesopotamia the function was viewed as a faithful observance of ritual and festival ordained by the superrealm and intended to relieve the people of anxiety. The people feared lest this realm—identified in substantial part with nature—not provide conditions conducive to prosperity. In Egypt, on the other hand, the function was seen as an observance of ritual and festival to celebrate the regularity of natural processes, concerning which the people did not have cause for anxiety. There was good reason for this difference in viewpoint. In Mesopotamia, the land was dependent on rainfall; thus the gods could be thought of as treating the people well if rainfall was ample, but harshly if it was sparse. In Egypt, however, the land

[44]The region had actually been united already through a general conquest by Lugal-zaggisi of Uruk, but Sargon defeated him shortly thereafter.

[45]*Kingship and the Gods,* p. 7.

depended on the ever-flowing Nile, which yearly and almost without fail brought abundant water and enriching soil.

The basic idea of the relationship between king and gods differed in the two regions according to this variant philosophical viewpoint. In Egypt, the king himself was considered a god; he was "of divine essence, a god incarnate," to whom (in theory) all the land of Egypt belonged.[46] He was actually born a god and never had to become one; he never had to be deified. By this belief the Egyptians freed themselves of fear and uncertainty, for all life processes would continue in regular pattern because a god was over the land. In holding this view they sacrificed liberty, for this god ruled absolutely and his word was law, but they gained an assured harmony between the superrealm and themselves.

In Mesopotamia, however, the king was but a member of the community. The Sumerian word for this ruler was *lugal,* meaning "great man." As the "great man," the ruler was the agent of the gods, and therefore was the accepted mediator between man and the gods for keeping necessary harmony. He was divinely chosen and this endowed him with a power greater than that of ordinary men, though it did not constitute him a god. Frankfort states that this view continued in Mesopotamia from the Sumerian period until the end of the empire.[47]

In Hatti the kings were thought of as high priests. They were held responsible for religious conditions in the land and, accordingly, had more cultic duties to perform than did the kings of either Mesopotamia or Egypt. Numerous festivals called for their attendance and could not be observed if they were absent. They were not considered gods so long as they lived, but were declared so on their death and then had ancestral sacrifices offered to them. In this way the people did not think of their king as dying but rather as becoming a god.

In summary, one must say that the world of Samuel's day presented a variety of viewpoints concerning kings and kingships. The nations did not present a common ideology, though there were basic similarities. Complex as the thinking was, however, this was the world in which the Israelites asked Samuel for a king, and the nature of their request must be judged in view of it.

[46]Ibid., p. 5.
[47]Ibid., p. 295.

4

Israel's Kingdom

Our interest now turns to the kind of monarchy Israel became. In the world of the monarchies of the day, as they have now been viewed in their many variations, what type did Israel become? How did it compare with the others?

It is appropriate to inquire, first, what type of monarchy the Israelite leaders had in mind when they made their request of Samuel. As noted in Chapter 3, they said they wanted to be like all the nations, but, we ask, in what way did they want to be like the nations? Since kingship differed so much among the nations, one can well ask which of the nations the Israelites wanted to be like. And did they really want to be like any of them in all respects?

A. THE REQUEST FOR A KING

The story of the people making their request, and the several significances involved, will be investigated in the following chapter. Our interest now lies in the nature of the request. What did the people want? And this involves the opposite question: what did they not want?

1. WHAT THE PEOPLE WANTED

The people voiced their request two times, the second of which is more relevant for our purpose. The first request is given in I Samuel 8:5: "Now make us a king to judge us like all the nations." Here only the element of judging is cited. This element is important, for it involves the same word (*shaphat*) that is used for the work of the judges of the preceding period (see, e.g., Judg. 10:2, 3; 12:7, 8, 11, 13). The significance is that the people were asking for a "king" (*melek*) to "judge" (*shaphat*) them; in other words, they wanted the judging activity of past days to continue but to have this carried on now by kings rather than judges.

The second occasion is given in I Samuel 8:19, 20, after Samuel has heard from God in respect to the request. The people then make the request again, and at greater length: "Nay; but we will have a king over us; that we also may be like all the nations; and that our king may judge us, and go out before us, and fight our battles." Five matters call for notice.

a. The repeated element of judging

The people repeated the fact that they wanted a king to judge them. It is appropriate to ask what the people meant by this term. What was the particular function of the preceding judges that they wanted continued? In brief, that function had been "the service of a leader." In normal parlance, the idea of judging means simply to make a decision between alternatives; and the office of a judge, whether of today or ancient time, is to decide cases of disagreement in the varied relationships of a community (see, e.g., Deut. 16:18). Israel's judges, however, had been more than arbitrators; they had been true community leaders, who no doubt served in part to decide cases, but carried on numerous other functions as well.[1]

A prime aspect in this service as leader certainly had involved efforts to curtail sin among the tribes. Sin had become rampant during the period of the judges, and this had called for a marked increase in the number of judges toward the close of the period. Just how the judges with their limited degree of official authority—not being elected or officially appointed as were the later kings—may have accomplished this goal is not clear, but the evidence is too convincing to doubt that it constituted a major part of their work. Supporting this theory is the fact that four times the significant note is sounded: "In those days there was no king in Israel, but every man did that which was right in his own eyes" (Judg. 17:6; 21:25—and a shortened form, 18:1; 19:1). The fact that sin abounded, then, was related to the idea that there was no king. It follows that, when the people made their request for a king, they had this thought in mind. The fact that the people actually

[1]For discussion with evidence, see my *Distressing Days of the Judges*, chap. 1, pp. 4-6.

mentioned the sins of Samuel's sons, Joel and Abiah, when they first voiced their request (I Sam. 8:5), ties in further with this conclusion.

It may be noted also that one of the reasons observed in Chapter 2 for this request by the people was that for some years there had been a growing recognition of the need for a king. It was indicated that a major factor in this recognition had been a dissatisfaction with moral conditions. So then, in asking for a king the people were also voicing a request for the curtailment of sin.

b. The element of fighting

A second element to notice in this request for a king is that the people referred to fighting battles. They wanted a king to go out before them and fight their battles. The verbs "go out" (*yatsa'*) and "fight" (*nilham*) should be taken together as a combined thought. The expression "go out" is commonly used in reference to battle engagements (see I Sam. 23:15; II Sam. 2:13; I Kings 20:17, 39; II Kings 5:2). Though the people would have had in mind any enemy power that might encroach on their land, the immediate enemies were the two noted in Chapter 2, the Philistines and the Ammonites.

c. The element of permanence

Not directly stated in this request, but clearly implied, is the fact that the people wanted a permanent, continuing head of their nation. The judges had served to curtail sin and also to fight battles, but they had not been continuous in this activity. They had ministered only when and as long as God had desired. The people now wanted an uninterrupted service in these capacities. Though the idea of permanence is not intrinsic in the term *melek* ("king"), it is involved historically. Kings do not rule for a while and then quit. They serve for life and, when they die, another takes their place.

d. The element of loss of freedom

A fourth element comes also by way of implication. It is a definite concession on the people's part. They said, "We will have a king over us." The word *over* is here in point. It implies a subjection of the people's will to this requested leader. It is noteworthy that the people did not express this thought in their initial request. At that time, they said only that they wanted a king to judge them. Before they brought the second form of the request, Samuel had meanwhile spoken to God and returned with divine instructions regarding the price they would pay if their request was granted. The king would make heavy demands of them.[2] These instructions were in mind,

[2]See Chapter 5 for an analysis of these demands.

then, as the people now declared, "We will have a king over us." In other words, they were ready to have these demands imposed; they were prepared to give up some of the freedom they had enjoyed under the judges for what they believed were the offsetting benefits of having a king.

e. A continuation of theocracy

A fifth element calls for notice, not as something the people requested, but as something which the overall story shows God desired. This element pertains to the type of rule anticipated. God wanted a rule as near to the pure theocracy of the period of the judges as possible.

The meaning of theocracy was presented in Chapter 2, as was also the fact that this highest form of rule had not worked because of the people's sin. God was now permitting a substitution in form of rule, but He was in no way abandoning the basic principles of theocracy. He still desired to be King in the final sense. The earthly monarch was to be only an earthly representative, a vicegerent, who would take all his orders from God. This was why one of the specific requirements for a king—when and if one should become necessary—had been that "a copy of the law" should be provided for him so that he might "learn to fear the LORD his God" and to keep all the words of the law and its statutes (Deut. 17:19).

This was also the reason for Samuel's ominous words at the time that Saul was anointed at Gilgal (I Sam. 12:15-25). He warned the people that if they would "not obey the voice of the LORD, but rebel against the commandment of the LORD," God would be against them as He had been against their fathers. Then to stress the importance of this warning Samuel called on God to send a thunderstorm. The time of year was the wheat harvest; this is the dry season when any storm at all is most unusual. The people, therefore, were extremely impressed when it came and asked that Samuel pray for them so that they would not die. They even admitted that they had sinned in asking for a king. Samuel's response was that they had no reason to fear providing they simply served the Lord with all their heart; he reminded them that God had specially chosen them and so desired their best welfare. Furthermore, he promised that he would be faithful in praying for them. He closed, however, by warning again that if they persisted in sin God would consume both them and their king.

2. WHAT THE PEOPLE DID NOT WANT

The question now to consider concerns what the people did not want.[3] An identification of these factors may be made by surveying the nature of

[3]It should be observed that, even though the fifth matter noted as to what the people wanted was really what God wanted, there is no implication that the people had any objection to having this approximation to theocracy continue.

monarchies around Israel. One may conclude that the factors in these monarchies, which the Israelites either did not ask for or did not include as an aspect in their monarchy, were factors the Israelites did not want.

a. A city-state form of rule

One clear factor not wanted was a city-state form of government. This is noteworthy because the city-state was the form of rule the Canaanites had. The Israelites, however, were not interested in this form. This is clear, first, because the request for a king was voiced by "all the elders of Israel" (I Sam. 8:4), and they asked for a "king" (singular), not for "kings" (the plural would have been necessary if every major city was to have one). It is clear also from the fact that Samuel anointed Saul to be ruler over God's "inheritance," meaning Israel (I Sam. 10:1). And, of course, Saul in due time was acclaimed king of all Israel (I Sam. 10:17-25; 11:14, 15).

In this regard, then, the people were thinking more of kingship as observed in lands outside Canaan than in Canaan proper. For the lands outside Canaan also had national kings.[4]

b. A divine kingship

It is just as clear that the people did not have in mind a divine kingship, that is, a deified king. Nothing in the request of the people implies such thinking, and surely they would not have broached such an idea to Samuel, who, regarding political forms, would accept nothing but theocracy. God, of course, would not have approved the request if it had included such thinking, nor would He have offered guidance in the selection of Saul (I Sam. 9:15, 16). A divine-king concept would have been diametrically opposed to the idea of theocracy, making the human ruler a deity when God wanted him only as a vicegerent. Moreover, God is a wholly-other Being, infinite as over against finite man; He alone is God, not even permitting His people to make images of Him, let alone to claim equality with Him.

In this, Israel was unique among the nations. Though Egypt was alone at the time in claiming outright deity for its ruler, other countries saw their rulers as god-related, often as a descendant. The reason for this difference lay in the contrasting views of God. With the exception of Israel, all countries believed their gods were in some way a part of nature—usually identified with the deeper and mysterious aspects of nature—and really not far removed from the human level. Like men they were regarded as being subject to limitations, desires, and passions. On such a basis, it was not a great step for a king to claim either to be, or to be descended from, a god. In Israel, however, God was supreme above nature, the universal God,

[4]See Roland deVaux, *Ancient Israel: Its Life and Institutions,* p. 92.

Creator of all. On this basis, it was unthinkable for Israel to regard a human mortal as identified with, or even as descended from, God.

B. THE KINGSHIP THAT RESULTED

Now that we have in mind the concept of kingship which the Israelites had as they voiced their request, it is appropriate to inquire what sort of kingship resulted. Did the people get what they wanted? Did they get more than they wanted? And how did Israel's kingship compare with others of the day in respect to fundamental features? Though many of the aspects now to be considered will be treated at length later on, it is appropriate to speak of them here in brief.

1. THE CONTROL OF SIN

The logical initial inquiry concerns whether or not sin came to be better controlled under the monarchy than it was under the judges. The implication of the four references from Judges (17:6; 18:1; 19:1; 21:25), attributing the extent of sin to the fact there was no king, is that the situation did become better. The Book of Judges certainly was written after the monarchy began.[5] These passages, then, would not have been included unless matters had improved. Actually conditions had become better even before Saul was inaugurated. The very fact that the people asked for a king to judge them shows this, for, as has been observed, judging meant especially the control of iniquity and sin. If the people wanted such control enough to ask for it, they already had recovered enough to see their sin in better perspective than before. It should be remembered, too, that there had been a meaningful revival at Mizpeh not long before (I Sam. 7:3-6), and this no doubt contributed substantially to the improvement implied in their request.

As for Saul's own rule, his beginning as a king was auspicious, and this would have inclined people to give heed to his directives. The fact that he made spiritism illegal is stated directly (I Sam. 28:9), and if he took this concrete measure it is likely that he took others. In Saul's later life, after he came under the influence of an "evil spirit," this effort to curtail sin no doubt became less, but certainly the overall impact would still have been positive. Then with the rise of the godly David, measures for proper conduct would have been set forth in greater degree than at any time in Saul's reign. When David himself set a high standard of behavior, it is only to be expected that he required the same from the people. And after David's reign, Solomon would have continued in this good path during his early

[5]Written probably in the early reign of David, since Judges 1:21 speaks of Jerusalem as still being in Jebusite hands and 1:29 of Gezer as still belonging to the Canaanites. Pharaoh was able to give Gezer to Solomon early in Solomon's reign (I Kings 9:16).

years, when he also set a fine example (though standards would have been lowered when his own spiritual condition deteriorated in later years).

2. THE PURSUIT OF WARFARE

The establishment of the kingdom also gave the people what they wanted with respect to military activity. It was noted that there were two enemy powers that were particularly menacing when the people voiced their request. One was the Ammonites, and Saul had defeated them soundly even before he became king (I Sam. 11:1-15). It is significant that the Ammonites are not heard from as a threat to Israel again until the time of David (II Sam. 10:1-14; 12:26-31).

The other enemy was the Philistines, but Saul did not do as well with this source of danger. It was David that brought a full defeat. On coming to the headship of both Judah and Israel (II Sam. 5:1-5), David met and decisively defeated the Philistines twice in the valley of Rephaim, just south of Jerusalem (II Sam. 5:18-25), and from that time on the Philistines remained a subdued people. Besides this, of course, David went on to defeat many other nations and establish an actual empire, which was something far beyond anything the people could have dreamed about when they made their request for a king. On this count, then, the monarchy was eminently successful.

3. THE ACHIEVEMENT OF PERMANENCE

Continuation or permanence of rule was also achieved. It is true that Saul did not begin a dynasty, due to his rejection as king (I Sam. 13:13, 14; 15:28), but David took over directly after his death and God promised that he would have a continuing dynasty that would be established forever (II Sam. 7:16). Permanence of rule was thus assured to the people; they would not have to be concerned about being left without an earthly ruler as during the period of the judges.

4. THE LOSS OF FREEDOM

Along with these benefits realized, however, the people did lose a substantial part of the freedom they had enjoyed under the pure theocracy. It was observed that they agreed to this loss when Samuel warned them that it would be experienced, and one may be sure that it did become a part of their life. Under the judges they had enjoyed almost complete freedom, with little civil government to impose regulations or high taxes, but this now changed. The change was probably not pronounced under Saul,[6] but it became so under David and still more under Solomon. The reigns of both were strong

[6]For discussion, see pp. 110-112.

and dominant, and this means both rigid controls and high taxes. The people came to chafe under them, especially in the time of Solomon, and when he died they approached his son Rehoboam and petitioned for relief (I Kings 12:1-15). At that time, certainly, the people recognized the truth of what Samuel had told their fathers and how good life could have been under the theocracy had their fathers rendered the required obedience.

5. FAILURE TO ACHIEVE THE IDEAL OF THEOCRACY

Loss also was experienced in respect to the theocratic ideal. In permitting the monarchy, God had wanted a government that would be as little removed from pure theocracy as possible; the king should serve only as His vicegerent. This called for perfect obedience by the king to God's directives. This, however, was not rendered.

The concept of theocracy suffered most under the first king, Saul, as matters got off to a poor start. After only two years of rule, Samuel at God's instructions already came to Saul and told him that God was rejecting him as a suitable ruler (I Sam. 13:13, 14). Then a second time, following a battle with the Amalekites when further blatant disobedience was shown, Samuel spoke similarly to Saul (I Sam. 15:28). God's ideal, therefore, had not been fulfilled by this first ruler, and God was indicating that a new start would be made, a new ruling family would be tried.

The new ruling head was David, and now much greater success was achieved. David followed in the ways of God carefully and God spoke of him as a man "after his own heart" (I Sam. 13:14). As a result, God's words to David were quite different from those to Saul: David's family would continue on the throne without cessation (II Sam. 7:16; Ps. 132:11-18). God had found His man in David; David approached close enough to the ideal that his family could continue as God's earthly representatives.

But David's son, Solomon, did not do as well. He began on a high plane (I Kings 3:5-14) and maintained a righteous life until at least his twenty-fourth year,[7] but then he began to feel the influence of foreign contacts and fell into grievous sin. The result was that a message from God similar to that given to Saul was soon spoken regarding him (I Kings 11:31-33). Though all of his kingdom was not taken away—because of God's promise to David—most of it was; ten of the tribes began a new kingdom in the days of Rehoboam. God had wanted an earthly viceroy that would follow His will in ruling, and once again the chosen representative had failed. This means that in the period of the united monarchy, two out of three kings fell seriously short of the theocratic ideal. This was far from what God had desired when He gave His approval to the idea of a monarchy.

[7]For evidence and discussion, see pp. 323-328.

6. A NATIONAL TYPE OF KINGSHIP

It was observed that the people did not want a city-state type of rule, but a national type, and this clearly is what did come to existence. Saul, David, and Solomon all became kings of the entire land, not merely one city. Even when David became king at Hebron, immediately after Saul's death, he was ruler of far more than merely Hebron and its environs. Hebron was his official center, but the whole tribe of Judah was his kingdom. Then, when seven years of rule there had been completed, all the other tribes sent representatives to ask him to reign over them. He was then anointed king over all Israel (II Sam. 5:3).

7. NO DIVINE KINGSHIP

It was also indicated that the people did not want a divine-kingship form of rule, and the record is clear that this too was realized. Some scholars have attempted to maintain otherwise. Evidence is taken especially from the so-called enthronement psalms, which are believed to depict the enthronement of Israel's king as a deified ruler.[8] Proper exegesis of these psalms, however, reveals no hint of this idea. Most of the passages cited are messianic, referring to Christ in His divine enthronement (see Ps. 2:7; 45:6; 110:1). None of them carry any reference to an enthronement of an Israelite king as a god.[9] And when one looks at the history recorded in the historical books, one looks in vain for any idea of divine kingship. The idea of a king as divine would have been diametrically opposed to the concept of theocracy, so much desired by God.[10]

8. MAINTENANCE OF DISTINCTION BETWEEN KING AND RELIGIOUS PERSONNEL

The suggestion has been offered that David assumed "something of the role of priest-king" when, wearing a linen ephod, he danced before the ark as it was brought into Jerusalem, and also "sacrificed oxen and fatlings"

[8]See George Fohrer, *History of Israelite Religion,* pp. 142-148. For refutation along with bibliography see Edward J. Young, *The Book of Isaiah,* vol. III, appendix II, pp. 550-552.

[9]Evidence is sometimes taken from God's statement regarding David, "I will make him my firstborn" (Ps. 89:27). In the verse preceding, however, God says, "He shall cry unto me, Thou art my father, my God, and the rock of my salvation." Furthermore, the word *firstborn* as here used is defined in the same verse: David would be "higher than the kings of the earth." The thought is that God would exalt David over all other kings, as indeed He did.

[10]For further refutation of the idea of divine kingship being found in the Psalms, see Kenneth A. Kitchen, *Ancient Orient and Old Testament,* pp. 102-106.

(II Sam. 6:13-19).[11] This episode is unusual, but it need not be interpreted in this way, and to do so is contrary to other factors soon to be noticed. David's dancing should be thought of only as an expression of holy enthusiasm for the bringing of the ark to Jerusalem, and as an attitude of humility as king before almighty God. David's first attempt at bringing the ark had ended in failure (II Sam. 6:1-11), and he did not want this to happen again. He was now ready to give himself in whatever way was appropriate, no matter the extent of exertion or humiliation, if God would be pleased to permit a safe transportation.

That David wore a linen ephod—which was ordinarily worn only by priests, true enough (see I Sam. 22:18)—can be explained as a way of showing his association with the priests and Levites who were officiating in carrying the ark and in performing the sacrifices. It may also have been a further way of showing humility, since a linen ephod was a modest dress in comparison with David's ordinary royal robes. As for the sacrificing of oxen and fatlings, one need not think that David offered these himself. It was he who ordered this done, but the work certainly was performed by priests and Levites that he had invited to be on hand. After all, considerable work is involved in sacrificing, and a large number of animals were sacrificed. The work of many men would have been required.

There is ample evidence that the kings of Israel did not usurp priestly duties. It is true that Saul attempted to do so, at the time he became impatient in waiting for Samuel and offered a sacrifice himself (I Sam. 13:8-10), but for this sin he was severely reprimanded and his descendants rejected as a royal dynasty (13:11-14). Saul's action was in no way approved by God. It may be that Saul did not recognize beforehand the true character of the sin, for he readily accepted Samuel's rebuke. Never again is he seen engaging in such an action, and neither is David or Solomon. It is true that Solomon is said to have offered sacrifices at Gibeon (I Kings 3:4), but, again, the evidence is clear that he did not offer these with his own hands. As in the case of David, this would have been physically impossible, for no less than a thousand sacrifices were offered.

Further indication may be found in the high respect Israel's kings held for religious personnel, recognizing them to be God's spokesmen to them as well as to people generally. Saul still sought out the counsel of Samuel after Samuel had died, when Saul made his improper visit to the woman of Endor (I Sam. 28:7-25). David desired to build the temple in Jerusalem, where the

[11]For a recent statement of this viewpoint by a conservative scholar see Carl E. Armerding, "Were David's Sons Really Priests?" *Current Issues in Biblical and Patristic Interpretation,* ed. Gerald F. Hawthorne, pp. 75-86. Armerding believes that the Old Testament reflects a concept of royal priesthood which began with Melchizedek, continued through the nonroyal figures of Moses and Samuel, and came to full fruition in the time of David. Though the evidence Armerding sets forth is worth noting and thought-provoking, it is inconclusive.

priests might minister, but readily accepted the prophet Nathan's word that God did not want him to do so (II Sam. 7:1-13). It is significant, too, that God communicated this word to David through a prophet, and not to David directly; had David been considered a priest or prophet himself there would have been no reason for this indirect manner of contact. And Solomon, in turn, had both the high priest Zadok and the prophet Nathan present at the time of his coronation (I Kings 1:38, 39). Later he built the temple for the priesthood (I Kings 5-8); he never entered it to perform sacrifice himself.

It is noteworthy that prophets actually became more prominent and influential during the time of the monarchy than under the judges.[12] Samuel, who lived on for most of the reign of Saul, was almost certainly the one responsible for the companies of prophets mentioned during his time. Samuel also served in anointing both of Israel's first two kings (I Sam. 10:1; 16:13). And Nathan and Gad played a prominent role in the reign of David. Following the time of the united monarchy, prophets took on still greater importance, especially when the outstanding writing prophets began their work. The authority of both priest and prophet was continually recognized by Israel's kings; they did not try to take their place or serve in their designated roles.

9. A TRUE KINGSHIP

One might think that, because the kingship was instituted as a replacement for the judges and not established at the beginning of Israel's history, it was something less than a true kingship. It may be asserted definitely, however, that it was a true kingship. This can be demonstrated in various ways, but one of the clearest is the manner of installation of the king. There are two accounts of installations that are especially revelatory. One is the installation of Solomon (I Kings 1:38-40, 47) and the other of Joash (II Kings 11:12, 17), about a century-and-a-half later. Though Joash was not a king of the united monarchy, there is no reason to think that the pattern of coronation was basically different.[13]

a. The crown and the testimony

One of the official acts in the coronation of Joash was the presentation to him of the "crown" (*nezer*) and the "testimony" (*'eduth*).[14] The mean-

[12]It is clear that prophets did exist during the period of the judges; see Judg. 4:4; 6:8; I Sam. 2:27-36; 9:9; and cf. Deut. 18:9-22.

[13]The coronation of Saul, who was the initial king, and of David, who ruled first over Judah and then over Israel, may have been somewhat simpler in form, but probably carried the same essential elements.

[14]For a discussion of the identity and significance of the *'eduth* see Kitchen, *Ancient Orient and Old Testament,* pp. 106-109.

ing of *nezer* as crown is well-established (II Sam. 1:10; Jer. 13:18). The crown has long been a central royal accouterment. The meaning of *'eduth* is best related to Deuteronomy 17:18, 19, where one of the requirements laid down regarding future kings is that a special copy of the law was to be provided for them (cf. I Sam. 10:25).[15] Though only seven years old at the time, and crowned in the midst of well-planned intrigue, Joash was invested with these two basic emblems.

b. The anointing

Both Solomon and Joash, as well as many others (e.g., Saul—I Sam. 9:16; 10:1; David—I Sam. 16:13; II Sam. 2:4; 5:3; Jehu—II Kings 9:3, 6; Jehoahaz—II Kings 23:30), are declared to have been anointed as kings. The procedure was to pour oil from a container over the head of the person (I Sam. 10:1; I Kings 1:39), as was done also in respect to the priests (Exod. 28:41; 29:7; 30:30). This anointing quite clearly symbolized the person's endowment with the Spirit of God (see Isa. 61:1), and it constituted him as especially chosen by God (see I Sam. 24:6, 10; 26:9, 11, 16, 23; II Sam. 19:21).

Some have held that this anointing of the king empowered him "to perform certain religious acts";[16] this, however, was not the purpose. The king was not made a priestly person thereby, so that he could perform priestly-type functions. Through the rite he was only set aside as a person who was chosen of God for a particular task in God's kingdom. To perform this work properly, he needed the Holy Spirit's power.

c. The acclamation

At the anointing came the public acclamation of the new ruler. This apparently involved the sounding of a horn and the clapping of hands by the assembly, as they shouted, "God save the king" (I Kings 1:34, 39; II Kings 11:12). Quite clearly it was this loud cry that first alerted the wicked queen, Athaliah, that Joash had been crowned in her place (II Kings 11:13, 14). This acclamation did not signify that the people believed they had themselves chosen the new king, but that they recognized him as the one God had chosen. As Roland de Vaux says, it was not a wish, but an acquiescence.[17]

d. The establishment of a covenant

In the case of Joash, a "covenant" (*berith*) was established between "the LORD and the king and the people" (II Kings 11:17). Whether this was a

[15]Some scholars suggest the change of *'eduth* to *tse'adoth,* meaning "bracelets" (cf. II Sam. 1:10), but this is unwarranted (see Norman H. Snaith, "The First and Second Books of Kings," *The Interpreter's Bible,* ed. George A. Buttrick, vol. III, p. 247).

[16]See de Vaux, *Ancient Israel,* p. 105.

[17]Ibid., p. 106.

customary action or peculiar to this one time is not indicated. The coronation of Joash was unique, because of its having to be effected through intrigue, but still there is no reason to think of this ceremony as different from others in basic respects. The covenant is described as having been between the king and people, to the end that the people "should be the LORD's people." This clearly was a gesture in recognition of the theocratic character of the kingdom. The king should serve as God's representative to govern the people according to God's dictates, so that they would be truly God's people.

e. The homage

The final action involved due homage by officials of the kingdom (I Kings 1:47). Though this aspect is indicated only regarding Solomon's coronation, it is likely that it was done on each occasion. The officials declared their obeisance, and the king confirmed them in their positions. This was done in other countries and there is no reason to think that it was otherwise in Israel.

10. THE OFFICIAL PERSONNEL

Little is said regarding Saul's administrative personnel, but more concerning those of David and Solomon. Officials under David are listed twice, once at the beginning of his rule (II Sam. 8:16-18; I Chron. 18:14-17) and again at its close (II Sam. 20:23-26). Solomon's officials are listed (I Kings 4:1-6) at the beginning of his rule. These officials need not be presented or discussed here, for this will be done at some length in Part Two. The only point to notice here is that these kingships had their appropriate officials even as did other countries. In this they followed the pattern of the other nations.

5

The Establishment of the Kingdom

The discussions thus far have considered Israel's kingdom in the most general sense. We have treated source material, the need for the kingdom, the world of the day in which this need existed, and the kind of kingdom that resulted. It is time now to become more specific. In this chapter we consider the establishment of the kingdom, and in the next a general comparison of the particular kingships of Saul, David, and Solomon. These two chapters still logically fall under Part One of the book, however, for in intent they are introductory to the more detailed studies of all three kingships in Part Two.

A. THE REQUEST FOR A KING

The first historical factor in the actual establishment of Israel's monarchy was the request for it voiced by elders to the prophet-judge Samuel.

1. THE OCCASION

a. The immediate reason

Three matters that prompted this request were presented in Chapter 2. These were all imbedded in past history. Frequently, when matters of this kind have been a long time in developing, some one incident, possibly of little comparative importance, is required to bring them to a head and impel action. The trigger in this instance was the poor performance of Samuel's two sons, Joel and Abiah, whom he had appointed as judges in the area of Beersheba. Samuel was growing old by this time and was confining his work to the relatively small area of Bethel, Gilgal, Mizpeh, and Ramah (I Sam. 7:16, 17). Through these sons, apparently, he had sought to supplement this activity by assigning them to the southern region. Thus assigned, however, the sons did not conduct themselves in the pattern of their father, but took bribes in their perversion of judgment (I Sam. 8:3). Learning of these actions, the people reacted and the request was made.

b. Those who made the request

The people who presented the request are identified as "all the elders of Israel." "Elders" were the logical people to do this, for they were the principal civil office holders. They held jurisdiction over local communities (Deut. 21:18-21; 22:17, 18; I Sam. 11:3).[1] Apparently in this instance they had banded together from many cities to bring their request as a group. Though the phrase does not necessarily mean that every elder in all the land came (which would have been a very large number), it suggests that elders from all parts of Israel were included.[2] The desire for a king, then, was widespread. It follows, too, that the elders of the Beersheba area, where the triggering actions of Samuel's sons had occurred, had done some work in soliciting support for the effort they apparently initiated.

c. The one to whom the request was addressed

This sizable group of people came to Samuel to voice their request. This fact should not be overlooked. They might have simply gathered and agreed on a choice of a king without consulting Samuel, for Samuel, after all, was not an elected official. He was not a king or a governor; he was only a prophet and a judge. There are three implications in this that call for notice.

One implication is a commendable recognition of God's authority. These leaders, in spite of the shocking extent of sin in the land, still came to God's recognized leader to make the request. Apparently the same inner sense that told them there was need for a king told them also that divine approval was necessary if the king was to accomplish what they had in mind. The significance of this should not be missed: it shows that the moral and spiritual climate was indeed better than it had been a few years earlier.

[1]Elders had been active since the days of Egypt (see Exod. 3:16-18; 19:7; 24:9). Even other countries of the day had their elders (e.g., Moab and Midian—Num. 22:7).

[2]Cf. the same expression in Exod. 18:12; Deut. 31:9; I Kings 20:7.

Another implication is that the office of judge was a respected office. It was to Samuel as the leading judge of the day that the people went with their request. This suggests that at the time the judge was considered the representative of God's authority. It is true that Samuel was a prophet as well as a judge, but it is likely that the elders went to him primarily in his capacity as judge, a civil office of the day.

A third implication is that Samuel himself was well respected. The elders would not have gone to just any judge. It is doubtful, for instance, that they would have consulted one of the minor judges; possibly they might not have consulted an Othniel or an Ehud. Samuel was the greatest of the judges and the people apparently did not hesitate in going to him. Samuel had been of great importance for the country, and the people held him in high esteem.[3] Though Samuel at first took the request as a direct rejection of himself (I Sam. 8:6, 7), God assured him that it was not. Probably Samuel himself later on recognized that the elders really had honored him.

d. The nature of the request

As noted in Chapter 4, the nature of the elders' request was that the country might now have a "king" (*melek*) to "judge" (*shaphat*) them. This use of *melek* with *shaphat* (the work of the preceding judges) indicates that they wanted a king to do the work formerly done by the judges. They wanted a substitute: kings for judges. Several implications in this request have already been investigated.

It remains to be observed here that the people did not ask for another judge, or a different sort of judge—one, for instance, that was continuous in his position and would be regularly followed by another on his death. This means they were through with judges; they wanted a "king-form" of rule instead. In this connection it is necessary to note distinctions between a king-form of rule and a judge-form.

The main distinction is that features of the judge-form made possible its immediate cessation, while those of the king-form did not. One feature that made this possible was the unofficial nature of judgeship. The judge was not elected or humanly appointed; he was a leader because people recognized him as such. Another feature was that the office was not continuous; time gaps actually occurred between some of the judgeships. A third was that there was no involvement of government personnel to whom notice of resignation had to be given. And a fourth was that the office was not subject to prescribed rules and responsibilities. All this made the cessation of a judgeship possible almost at a moment's notice.

[3]Conrad von Orelli (*International Standard Bible Encyclopedia,* vol. III, p. 1518) is quite correct when he says of Samuel, "What his activity meant for the uplift of the people cannot be estimated too highly."

In contrast, the opposite was true regarding the king-form of rule. It could not be brought to a close quickly or easily. The elders certainly knew this, and the fact that they requested this form shows that they wanted this particular change. What they hoped to gain, of course, was greater stability as a people and an increase in strength against threatening powers from outside.

2. SAMUEL'S REACTION

Samuel's reaction to this request was displeasure. The text says, "But the thing displeased Samuel" (I Sam. 8:6). Probably three factors contributed to this displeasure.

a. An imagined personal rejection

For one thing, as the text implies, Samuel took the request as a personal rejection of himself. He thought the elders were saying that they did not want him as judge any longer. This implication is evident in God's response to Samuel: "They have not rejected thee, but they have rejected me" (I Sam. 8:7). It is also evident in Samuel's last words to the people: "Witness against me before the LORD, and before his anointed: whose ox have I taken? or whose ass have I taken? or whom have I defrauded? whom have I oppressed? or of whose hand have I received any bribe?" (I Sam. 12:3).

Actually, the people were not rejecting Samuel. God indicated this to Samuel, and other matters give witness to the fact. It has already been noticed that it was to Samuel that the elders came; they did not proceed with a selection of a king by themselves. Later they responded to Samuel's call to come to Mizpeh for the purpose of witnessing God's selection of the first king (I Sam. 10:17-25). And later still they looked to Samuel for the actual installation of Saul as first king (I Sam. 11:14, 15).

Another indication that Samuel was not being personally rejected comes from the keen interest Saul's uncle[4] displayed one day in what Samuel had told his nephew. Saul had just seen Samuel and been told the remarkable news that he was to be Israel's king. When Saul returned home, even though he did not speak of this incredible piece of information, his uncle quickly urged, "Tell me, I pray thee, what Samuel said unto thee." Here the uncle used an imperative form of the verb along with the enclitic *na'* to indicate unusual interest in what Samuel had told the young man. That Saul had not spoken of the prediction that he was to be king shows this interest to have been only in Samuel himself as a spokesman.

At the same time, Samuel's hurt feelings can be readily understood. He had performed a task of immense significance for Israel, which probably

[4]Possibly Ner, father of Saul's army commander Abner (see I Sam. 14:50).

few Israelites really understood or appreciated.[5] He had been thrust into his place of leadership following the disastrous battle of Aphek, when the ark had been taken by the Philistines and when the two leading priests, Hophni and Phinehas, had died. Eli, the high priest, had also died on hearing the tragic news. At the time, public morale could hardly have been lower. The Philistines constituted a terrible military threat, and many people no doubt believed that the days of the tribes were near an end.

However, instead of being finished, the people actually gathered at Mizpeh for revival just twenty years later (I Sam. 7:2-13). There the people resolved to cease in their worship of the Canaanite gods and follow their own God truly. And before the revival was over a genuine defeat had been inflicted on the feared Philistines, who had thought the occasion opportune for an attack. Such a turnabout in conditions—from complete despair to actual victory—could not have just happened. There had to be a reason, and that reason under God surely was Samuel. Evidently he had worked very hard to bring a change in people's thinking and a sense of guilt for their sin. At Mizpeh his work had come to a climax. And now with the people voicing this request for a king, it seemed to Samuel that, not only were they showing no appreciation for his work, but they were actually rejecting him as their continuing judge. Indeed, Samuel's reaction, though mistaken, is understandable.

b. A rejection of God's theocracy

A second factor contributing to Samuel's displeasure can also be inferred from the statement in I Samuel 8:6: "But the thing displeased Samuel, when they said, Give us a king to judge us." Not only is Samuel's sense of rejection of himself implied, but also his recognition that the people were at the same time rejecting God's theocratic rule of the country. The people were asking for an earthly king and, therefore, rejecting God in heaven as their only Sovereign.

It is to be expected that Samuel would have recognized this. His own hurt would not have been so great that he would have missed it. He was of keen mind and had been trained in theocratic thinking by Eli himself. He would have understood that God wanted to be the sole Head of His people; and therefore any earthly ruler, no matter how good his qualities might be, could only hinder that ideal. Samuel must have had this in mind—along with his own sense of rejection—when he brought the people's request before God. Though the words of his presentation at the time are not given, one may guess that they included two items: "Lord, the people have re-

[5]For a discussion of the importance of Samuel see F. F. Bruce, *Israel and the Nations,* pp. 22-23.

jected me from being their judge; and they have rejected the theocratic form of government you graciously gave them."

c. Recognition of his sons' failure

The third factor follows only from force of logic, but one may be sure that it was involved. Samuel was displeased also because his own sons had proved to be poor judges. The elders had made this fact clear in their statement to him, "Behold, thou art old, and thy sons walk not in thy ways" (I Sam. 8:5). It may well be that this was the first indication Samuel had of the sad truth. And, even if he had known it before, the statement would have been a reminder of something that must have burdened him terribly. He had given his life for a revival in Israel, so that sin would be lessened and God would be pleased to grant blessing again. Now here his own sons were working against all he had given so much effort for. Rather than helping, they were hindering. No doubt when he had placed them in Beersheba, he had done so with high anticipation that they would carry on in the pattern he had set. Now it was clear that they were not.

This sinful behavior of Samuel's sons is difficult to understand given the fact that Samuel had seen firsthand the harm Eli's sons had done. One would think that he would have taken extra precautions to make sure his own sons would behave differently. That they did not is probably best attributed to the enormous effort Samuel had put forth in Israel's behalf. He had simply given himself so much that he had not saved sufficient time for his family.

3. GOD'S RESPONSE

Quite frequently the nature of God's response to the urgent cry of His people is surprising to them; this is clearly the case with Samuel. God's response comes in three parts.

a. Solace for Samuel

One part is the gracious solace God gave to Samuel in this time of hurt feelings. He told Samuel, "They have not rejected thee, but they have rejected me." Though Samuel should not have been hurt, God knew that he had been and met him in that need. Samuel should have recognized that the people were really doing him honor by coming to him with their request, but he was only human in seeing it otherwise. God quite clearly recognized this and evaluated his attitude accordingly. This is one more example of God's understanding of man's frailty and His grace in meeting a servant's need in that frailty.

b. Approval of the request

The second part of God's response must have surprised Samuel. This was God's directive: "Hearken unto the voice of the people in all that they say unto thee." So, then, Samuel was to do what the elders had asked. The story is quite clear that Samuel had expected another type of response. For more than three centuries God had worked through a theocratic manner of rule; it would have seemed, then, that He would continue to do the same and deny this request. God recognized that Samuel was not prepared for this answer and quickly moved on to tell His servant the reason.

In substance, the reason was that the theocratic manner of rule had not worked well, and therefore it was better that a monarchy be instituted. God's actual statement was: "According to all the works which they have done since the day that I brought them up out of Egypt even unto this day, wherewith they have forsaken me, and served other gods, so do they also unto thee" (I Sam. 8:8). The force of the statement is that the people had rejected God and the theocracy not merely by this present request, but they had been doing so ever since the theocracy had started. A vital factor for making theocracy work is obedience, and the people had not given it. For this reason, the theocracy had not proven beneficial, and therefore it was better that the substitution be made.

In passing, it may be observed that actually God had been gracious in permitting the people as much as three centuries and more to have opportunity for making the theocracy work. The theocratic form of rule, after all, was for their benefit, as much as for God's, as will be seen. Since by their disobedience the people had already begun to forfeit this benefit three centuries before, God could have withdrawn the theocracy from them then. He had not done so, but had employed discipline—through repeated attacks by other countries (Mesopotamians, Moabites, Canaanites, Midianites, Ammonites, Philistines)—so that the people might still turn and render the necessary obedience and thus receive the benefit. Now, however, time had run out; the final occasion of discipline had not yielded the desired result and it was appropriate to make a change. In this light, the petition of the people, rather than being something contrary to God's will, was a way of accomplishing what God saw to be necessary.

c. Warning for the people

A third part of God's response was instruction to Samuel to give the people due warning as to what they were really asking for. God said, "Protest solemnly unto them, and show them the manner of the king that shall reign over them." Before God granted the new form of king-rule to the people, He wanted them to be aware of how much better their situation had been under the judge-rule He had first given them. In other words, the people were definitely asking for a second-best form of rule, and God wanted them to recognize that it was indeed second-best.

The details of why king-rule was only second-best are presented in Samuel's reply to the people (I Sam. 8:10-18). They will be treated at length presently, but the essence is that the people would now lose the freedom they had long enjoyed under God's rule. The people had not realized nor appreciated how good their status had been, and now, before the new form of rule was granted, God wanted this fact made clear to them.

4. SAMUEL'S REPLY TO THE ELDERS

With God's response given, Samuel returned to the elders to tell them what God had said. He spoke to them first concerning the "manner of the king" (I Sam. 8:11-17), and second, he warned them that, as a result of this manner, they would cry out in regret for their request (I Sam. 8:18). The second part, calling for briefer consideration, will be noted first.

a. The warning

Samuel's warning consisted of two parts: the warning proper, that the people would cry out as a result of having a king, and then the assertion that, when they did, God would not hear them to give relief.

The full reality of Samuel's warning was experienced under Solomon's rule. Saul did not impose great hardship and, though certainly David became a much stronger ruler, no indication is given that his demands were excessive either.[6] Solomon, however, did impose severe measures that resulted in the northern tribes' demanding relief when his son Rehoboam came on the throne (I Kings 12:1-19). Relief was not given at the time, and this fulfilled the second part of Samuel's warning.

One might ask whether Samuel in so warning them may not have wanted the people to withdraw their request. Note the words he used, and also the statement that follows: "Nevertheless the people refused to obey the voice of Samuel." If Samuel wanted them to withdraw their request, however, a question immediately arises: would this not have been contrary to what God had just told him? The answer is clear that it would have been. To counteract God's word would have been out of keeping with Samuel's character. It seems better, then, to think of him speaking in this way not to cause the people to change, but to shame them for letting conditions become so bad that the request was voiced and God had acceded. They should realize that they had committed a great wrong in refusing God's better way—theocracy.

[6]An indication to the contrary might be thought to exist in Absalom's ability to steal "the hearts of the men of Israel," pretending to be more their friend than was David. No hint is given in the account, however, that the people were overly taxed. Reference seems to be only to possible social injustice (II Sam. 15:1-6).

b. The "manner of the king"

The "manner of the king" that Samuel set before the people can be divided into four parts. These parts summarize what the king that had been requested would be like. Because the summary is so accurate in respect to the monarchy that did eventuate, it has been common for liberal expositors to believe it was added to the story by someone who lived after the kingdom had been in existence for some time.[7] Discoveries of texts at both Ugarit and Alalakh, however, dating from the eighteenth to the thirteenth centuries B.C., have shown that all of these burdens placed on the people were characteristic of kings long before the time of Samuel. These discoveries are described well by I. Mendelsohn and his material is reflected in parts of the following discussion.[8]

1) ***Recruitment of manpower for military, agricultural, and manufacturing purposes.*** The first point that Samuel made was that the king would recruit the sons of the people to man his chariots and horses, to serve as commanders of thousands and fifties, to "reap his harvest, and to make his weapons of war" (I Sam. 8:11, 12). All this was done in Canaanite city-states of the day. Men from lower classes were conscripted as foot soldiers, and those from the aristocracy as charioteers. This latter group was called *maryannu* and occupied an honored position in Canaanite society. Their status as *maryannu* was hereditary, and only the king could elevate a commoner to this status. Even these honored soldiers, however, were not exempt from personal service to the king, in addition to their military duties. They were responsible also for agricultural and manufacturing activity. They were required to pay the king a tithe of their income as a tax.

2) ***Confiscation of private land.*** The king would take the best fields, vineyards, and oliveyards of the people and give them "to his servants" (I Sam. 8:14). The first point noted concerned seizure of people; this one concerns seizure of land. Canaanite kings engaged in commercial and industrial enterprises, as well as military, and for this needed extensive land. One source of this land was confiscation of property. Texts from Ugarit are particularly revealing concerning confiscation of land and the fact that land so taken would often be granted to members of the king's own family, to high officials, and to others, under the condition that the recipient perform certain service for the king and pay designated taxes. The texts even specify

[7]See Eugene Maly, *The World of David and Solomon,* pp. 21-22; also G. B. Caird, "The First and Second Books of Samuel," *The Interpreter's Bible,* ed. George A. Buttrick, vol. II, p. 922.

[8]"Samuel's Denunciation of Kingship in the Light of the Akkadian Documents from Ugarit," *Bulletin of the American Schools of Oriental Research* 143 (1956), pp. 17-22.

that this land would include fields, vineyards, orchards, and oliveyards (just as designated by Samuel).

3) ***Taxation on the basis of the tithe.*** The king would take a tenth of the people's seed, vineyards, and sheep, and give it "to his officers and to his servants" (I Sam. 8:15, 17a). Evidently, this would be in addition to actual confiscation. Some land, then, would be taken outright, while a tenth of the produce from other land would be demanded as tax. One of the main sources of royal income for Canaanite kings was the demand of a tenth in just this fashion. This tenth (called *ma'sharu, meshertu*) was imposed on both field and livestock. It is noteworthy that the principle of the tithe was observed in other lands besides Israel. It may be that this principle was laid down by God soon after man's creation (well before its first mention in Scripture—Gen. 14:20) and then carried along in the taxation imposed by various kings, as here in Canaan.

4) ***Imposition of corvée labor.*** The king would take the people's daughters to be confectionaries, cooks, and bakers, and he would take their menservants, maidservants, and goodliest young men, as well as asses, to do his work (I Sam. 8:13, 16). It is not likely that paid employees are here in view, for being a paid employee is not a hardship; it must be, then, that the unpaid service of the corvée system is in mind. Mendelsohn comments on Canaanite practice: "That the common people were subject to *corvée* labor (consisting of the construction of roads, the erection of fortresses, the building of temples, and the tilling of crown lands) in Syria and Palestine in the middle of the second millennium B.C. we know from the reference to it in the alphabetic texts from Ugarit (*msm*) and from the Amarna letters."[9] Corvée labor was despised by the people, for it required unpaid service for the king, over a set length of time, and this usually brought severe economic hardship on a family while the breadwinner was away. Working conditions also were often very disagreeable.[10]

This, then, is the information God wanted Samuel to tell the people. They should know that for which they were asking, that they might be prepared for these demands when they came and that they might be reminded of how good life could have been under the theocratic rule God had granted them in prior years.

[9]Ibid., p. 22.

[10]Mendelsohn's concluding word is, "In view of the evidence from the Akkadian texts from Ugarit it seems obvious that the Samuel summary of 'the manner of the king' does not constitute a 'rewriting of history' by a late opponent of kingship but represents an eloquent appeal to the people . . . not to impose upon themselves a Canaanite institution alien to their own way of life" (ibid.).

B. SAMUEL'S ANOINTING OF SAUL

After Samuel had delivered God's message to the elders, and they still maintained that they wanted a king (I Sam. 8:19, 20), Samuel told them, "Go ye every man to his own city" (I Sam. 8:22)—and they did. This is significant. The elders had come to Samuel to ask permission for a king; now that they had received it they were willing to return home and wait for developments. Their action shows again that they did have respect for God, for in going home they were really leaving the matter in God's hands. It further shows that they had respect for Samuel. On being told to go home, they might have replied to Samuel, "Look, we came for a king and we want one now before we leave." They did not, however, but left the matter with God and Samuel.

It was important that the people so responded. If God was to have the form of monarchy He desired—as little removed from pure theocracy as possible—it was indispensable that He choose the king to serve. It is also to be observed that, when the choice was left with God, He promptly did something about it.

1. A SEARCH FOR LOST DONKEYS

The means God employs to work out His will are often surprising. In His interest of choosing a king now, He employed the loss of donkeys. The animals belonged to the father of Saul, the young man of God's choice. Kish, the father, sent the young man, along with a servant, to find the donkeys, but they could not do so until they had come in contact with Samuel, whom God planned to use to anoint the future king. The two looked for three days (I Sam. 9:20) and were ready to quit when the servant suggested they inquire of "an honorable man" in a city nearby, since "all that" this man said "cometh surely to pass." The man was Samuel. At first Saul hesitated, showing a natural timidity, but, because of the urging of the wise servant, did agree to the suggestion. Coming to the city, the two were directed to Samuel, and the important encounter took place.

2. THE ANOINTING

The day prior to this encounter, God had told Samuel, "Tomorrow about this time I will send thee a man out of the land of Benjamin, and thou shalt anoint him to be captain over my people Israel" (I Sam. 9:16). Therefore, when Saul arrived, God told Samuel, "Behold the man whom I spoke to thee of" (I Sam. 9:17). Samuel first reassured the young man that the lost donkeys had already been found and then told him that it was on him that all the desire of Israel rested. To this Saul protested that he was unworthy of such honor, but Samuel paid little attention as he now took him to a prepared feast where he seated him in a place of honor. This was no doubt to fortify the young man's confidence.

Then the following morning Samuel actually anointed Saul for the office of king.[11] He took a "vial of oil and poured it upon his head," and informed him that God had anointed him "to be captain over his inheritance" (I Sam. 10:1). Having done this, he told Saul of three events that would take place as he walked home: he would meet "two men by Rachel's sepulchre at the border of Benjamin,"[12] who would tell him that the lost donkeys had been found; he would meet three men carrying three loaves of bread, three kids, and a bottle of wine, who would share these food items with him; and he would meet a "company of prophets coming down from the high place" and playing musical instruments. This last group would be prophesying[13] and he should join in prophesying with them. The reason for telling Saul all this was to assure the young man that Samuel's anointing had been authentic. All these events did occur, and no doubt Saul was thereby assured.

3. THREE MATTERS OF SIGNIFICANCE

Three matters should be noticed relative to this occasion of anointing. First, it was God who made the selection of Saul; no man or any group of men had any part in the matter. Even Samuel was only God's representative to make the selection known. Second, God's perfect wisdom is evident. Saul was of the comparatively small tribe of Benjamin, wedged between Judah on the south and Ephraim on the north. If the choice had been from either of these two important tribes, jealousy could have been aroused. Then there was wisdom in choosing a person of commanding stature. Saul stood head and shoulders above other people (I Sam. 10:23), and this was important for making him more acceptable to the people. Acceptance of the first king would be difficult at best, and every advantage would help.

[11]Apparently Saul (and maybe his servant) slept on a roof. It had been on a roof (roofs of that day were flat; cf. II Kings 4:10) that Samuel had talked with Saul the prior evening, and I Sam. 9:26 is best translated, "And they arose early; and it was as the dawn arose that Samuel called to Saul on the roof, 'Arise and I will send you away.' So Saul got up and both of them went outside."

[12]The city where Saul met Samuel can hardly have been Ramah, as is often supposed, for he would not have passed Rachel's grave (cf. Gen. 35:16-19) in going south from Ramah to Gibeah, Saul's home town. The city in question must have been in the general vicinity of Bethlehem, from which he would have gone north as he passed into the territory of Benjamin. The traditional site of the grave, being just outside Bethlehem, is probably too far south, but it could not have been very far north of this either.

[13]Not engaging in ecstatic frenzy, as commonly believed, but probably singing in praise to God, a meaning illustrated in I Chron. 25:1-3, where Levites "prophesied in giving thanks and praising" God; see my discussion, "Ecstasy and Israel's Early Prophets," *Bulletin of the Evangelical Theological Society* 9 (Summer 1966), pp. 125-137. Cf. pp. 157-158.

The third matter concerns the fact that Saul was anointed well before his time of rule. This gave the naturally timid man time to think and adjust emotionally to the idea of one day being king. The initial reaction of one of Saul's temperament is to hesitate and refuse an assignment of a demanding nature. And the assignment Samuel spoke of was indeed demanding. Saul needed time to adjust, and God gave it to him by having him anointed privately well before the day when he would begin his duties.

C. PUBLIC SELECTION AT MIZPEH

A second and public selection of Saul to be king is now presented (I Sam. 10:17-25). The record of this selection has sometimes been called a second account that conflicts with the first one, and, therefore, is believed to have come from another author's hand.[14] This view must be rejected, for the two accounts actually fit together nicely.[15] There was a definite need for this public selection: the people needed to know whom God had chosen. It was one thing for Samuel to know, but it was another for the people to be informed. They had been sent home by Samuel after presenting their earlier request (I Sam. 8:22), and now they needed to be told the identity of the one God had chosen. One may be sure that they had been waiting for just such an occasion.

1. THE ASSEMBLY AT MIZPEH

No indication is given of the amount of time that had intervened since the presentation of the request for a king until this public assembly at Mizpeh. One must realize that travel took considerable time, when one had to walk or go by donkey; therefore, just for the elders to have returned home after the request was granted and then to have come to Mizpeh for the present occasion would have occupied a number of days. The only recorded event that had occurred in the interim was the private anointing of Saul, though apparently there had also been a later meeting between Samuel and Saul at Gilgal, when Samuel had given Saul further instructions (I Sam.

[14]See Caird, "Books of Samuel," pp. 935-936; John Bright, *A History of Israel,* pp. 182-183.

[15]Heinrich Ewald, *The History of Israel,* vol. III, p. 23, says that this story "exhibits nothing but the great truth that, for the full and auspicious acknowledgment of Saul as king, his mysterious interview with the Seer did not alone suffice; publicly, in solemn national assembly, must the Spirit of Jahve choose him out, and mark him as Jahve's man."

10:8).[16] Further instructions would have been necessary, if only to prepare the young man for the Mizpeh meeting, for, among other things, he would have had to be told to be on hand. One may think of at least a few weeks having elapsed.

The place of assembly is important to notice. It was Mizpeh and not, for instance, Samuel's home town of Ramah, which would have been more convenient for him. Mizpeh is best identified with Tell en-Nasbeh, about two miles north of Ramah.[17] It was a comparatively central location, but this was not the most significant feature. Mizpeh was where the people had gathered a few years earlier for revival and where a decisive victory had been won over the Philistines (I Sam. 7:1-14). For the people to come here for the selection of a king, then, would at the same time remind them of that occasion and give corresponding encouragement. The people can be imagined gathering over a matter of days, as they came from varying distances with their donkeys, wagons, and provisions.

2. THE SELECTION OF SAUL

When all were assembled, Samuel assumed charge, in keeping with his role as judge. His first words were again a rebuke, as he reminded the people that they had rejected the rule of the true God (I Sam. 10:18, 19). Then Samuel had each of the tribes (as represented by their elders) pass before him, and "the tribe of Benjamin was taken." Then the family clans of Benjamin passed by and "the family of Matri was taken." Finally members of this family passed by and "Saul the son of Kish was taken" (I Sam. 10:19-21).

This procedure in selection is reminiscent of Joshua 7:16-18, where Achan was found to be the one who had sinned and caused Israel's defeat at Ai. Probably both selections were accomplished by use of the Urim and Thummim, the divinely assigned device by which God had chosen to reveal His will (Exod. 28:30; Num. 27:21). For so many people to pass by Samuel as the selection was made would have taken a substantial portion of the day. In the end, however, Saul was designated.

Why did Samuel go through this process when he already knew whom

[16]C. F. Keil and F. Delitzsch, *Biblical Commentary on the Books of Samuel.* pp. 101-103, see the "seven days" of I Sam. 10:8 in I Sam. 13:8-10, when Saul did not wait for Samuel for seven days; but this view must be rejected. There is no reason for Samuel to have been anticipating that occasion, which did not come until at least two years later (I Sam. 13:1). Though there are certain similarities in the occasions, these are insufficient to offset this time factor. Samuel R. Driver, *Notes on the Hebrew Text of the Books of Samuel,* 2d ed., pp. 81-82, finds objection also on the basis of the Hebrew employed.

[17]See Yohanan Aharoni and Michael Avi-Yonah, *The Macmillan Bible Atlas,* maps 81, 85, 123.

God had chosen? The answer is quite clear: he wanted these elders,[18] who were no doubt the very men in large part who had brought the earlier request for a king, to see for themselves that God had indeed made the selection. Samuel might have simply told them of the earlier private anointing, but this would not have been as forceful as a demonstration by God's approved method of communication. In this way, no one could possibly charge Samuel with somehow having chosen Saul himself.

3. SAUL IN HIDING

Not only did Samuel know beforehand who would be chosen, but so did Saul. No doubt a part of Samuel's previous instruction to the young man had been to be present at this public occasion. Saul was there all right, but he had hidden himself among the "stuff," meaning the wagons and provisions brought by the people. Here is another indication of Saul's timidity.[19] If Saul had been an ambitious person, he would have been at the center of activity; and, even if he had been only an average person, he would at least have been available on the fringes of the crowd. Saul, however, had hidden himself, so that he would not be found.

As a result the people could not find Saul to acclaim him as the king. Probably Samuel told them that the young man should be there some place, and so another inquiry of God was made. This revealed his hiding place and he was now brought forth. Seeing his imposing stature—"higher than any of the people from his shoulders and upward" (I Sam. 10:23)—"the people shouted and said, God save the king" (v. 24). Saul's size, therefore, held him in good stead. It is implied further that he was a handsome person, for Samuel declared, "There is none like him among all the people," as he presented him to the assembled throng.

4. CONCLUDING NOTES

Three matters should be observed as concluding notes to the occasion. First, "Samuel told the people the manner of the kingdom." He wrote this information "in a book" which he then "laid up before the LORD" (I Sam. 10:25). Heinrich Ewald calls this book the "new constitution" of the

[18]Though the term *elders* is not used here, one may be sure that these were the ones assembled. They were the logical representatives of the people, and surely the people in general did not assemble, for the number of elders alone would have been sizable. Moreover, it was the elders who would have been especially desirous of coming, for they had constituted the group that presented the request for a king.

[19]Ewald, *The History of Israel,* vol. III, p. 231, does not understand Saul's action this way but sees it as showing only that he was not forcing himself into office and therefore is to be commended. A person hardly has to hide, however, to show that he is not forcing himself into office.

kingdom.[20] It probably had been written beforehand by Samuel for this occasion, no doubt in accordance with revelation from God and certainly in keeping with, if not including, the regulations laid down in Deuteronomy 17:14-20. That he laid it up "before the LORD" probably means that he placed it in the tabernacle, now located at Nob (I Sam. 21:1; 22:19), along with the law of Moses, which was the constitution of the theocracy and still much in force.

The second note is that Saul now went home to Gibeah and was accompanied by a "band of men whose hearts God had touched." Gibeah was Saul's home town (I Sam. 11:4), and this group of men apparently were those who were particularly favorable to him. They might have thought in terms of instituting proceedings immediately for installing the new monarch. This, however, was not to be for a time yet.

The third note is that there were also a few dissenters present. Rather than admiring Saul, they "despised him" and asked, "How shall this man save us?" Seldom are people unanimous in their approval of leaders, and they were not in this instance, even though God had made the selection. The most likely factor that prompted the disapproval was the apparent timidity of Saul. That he had been in hiding at the time of his selection could have made them think he was hardly kingly material. They no doubt had thought in terms of a self-confident, easy-speaking person and not one who would hide from notice. They did not realize, however, that if God chooses a man for a position, He will also grant him all the necessary ability to perform it.

D. GENERAL ACCEPTANCE AFTER THE BATTLE OF JABESH-GILEAD

It is one thing to be selected for an office and it is another to enjoy the general acceptance of people at large for that office. Saul now found that out. Though the elders had witnessed his divine selection, the people generally had not, and Saul quite clearly found actual reign impossible until they accepted him. Thus he did not immediately proclaim a kingdom after the events at Mizpeh, but went home and continued what apparently had been his normal work on his father's land (I Sam. 11:5). The people that followed him home may have soon left when they also realized an actual establishment of a kingship was not yet possible. Money was needed for buildings and salaries, and people would not be willing to pay taxes until they were ready to accept the king. Saul really had quite a task before him in beginning a kingdom.

[20]Ibid., p. 23.

1. THE BATTLE AT JABESH-GILEAD

God, however, knew how to bring the necessary public acceptance. To arrange for Saul's first anointing, He had employed lost donkeys; now He used a threat against a Transjordan city by enemy Ammonites. Certainly, when the people of this city encountered the threat they could not see how any good could be involved in it, but God did.

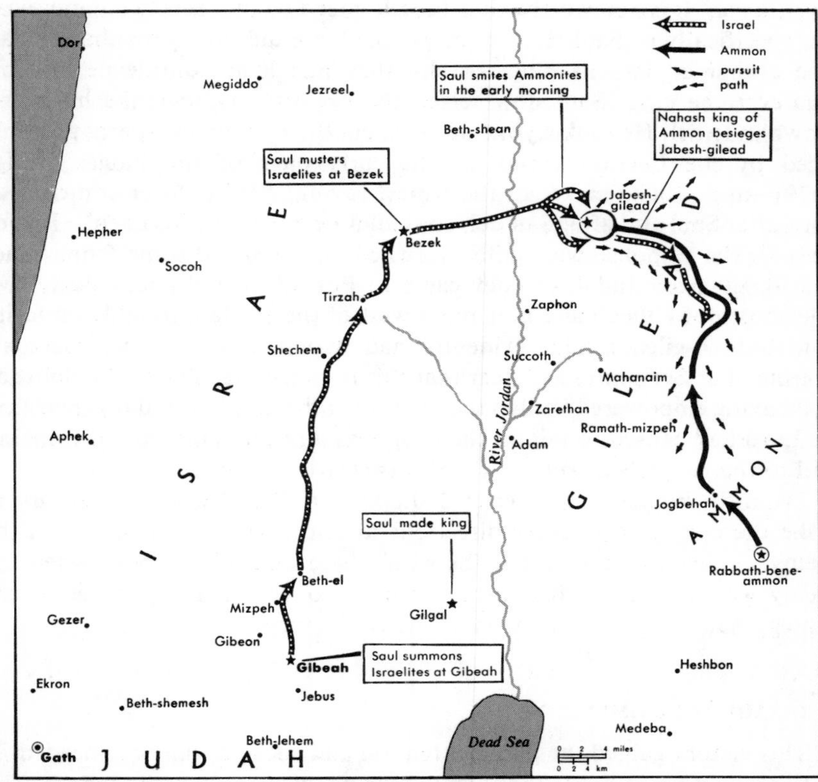

Map 1. The Jabesh-gilead Battle

The city was Jabesh-gilead, identified with Tell el-Maqlub, about six miles east of the Jordan River and eighteen miles south of the Sea of Galilee.[21] It was roughly thirty miles north-northeast of Rabbath-ammon, capital of the Ammonites. In laying siege to the city, then, this enemy power

[21]See Yohanan Aharoni, *The Land of the Bible,* p. 116; also Aharoni and Avi-Yonah, *The Macmillan Bible Atlas,* map 87.

had extended its domain far from home, and apparently was attempting to establish the same control that it had held prior to its defeat by Jephthah. Jabesh-gilead feared the Ammonite king, Nahash, sufficiently to sue for peace, but the price Nahash demanded was the right eye of all the city's inhabitants. Jabesh-gilead asked for seven days respite to seek help from the other tribes; apparently Nahash thought he had little to fear from this request and consented.

Jabesh-gilead sent messengers to all the tribes and one came to Saul's city, Gibeah. It is noteworthy that Jabesh-gilead did not send a communication specifically to Saul. Either the people there did not know that he had been acclaimed Israel's king, or else they had little confidence in him. Whatever the case, Saul now seized the opportunity to make his name known in Israel. He took a yoke of oxen, cut them in pieces—perhaps influenced by the Levite's action in the early days of the judges (Judg. 19:29)—and sent them to all the tribes, saying, "Whosoever cometh not forth after Saul and after Samuel, so shall it be done unto his oxen" (I Sam. 11:7).[22] The response was quite overwhelming: 300,000 came from Israel and 30,000 from Judah.[23] They came to Bezek, located about thirty-five miles north of Gibeah and nine miles west of the Jordan, roughly opposite from Jabesh-gilead; Saul evidently had assigned this as the place of meeting. The Scriptures are clear that this response was due to the Spirit of God having empowered Saul in the sending of the message and to a fear that the Lord had caused to fall on the people as a result. This way of bringing Saul to the people's attention, then, was clearly of God.

From the immense number of 330,000 men, Saul chose three groups to strike the enemy from three directions at once. The groups came on the enemy in the morning watch (between three and six o'clock) when the enemy was little expecting them. Though no details are given as to the strategy Saul employed, he won a decisive victory.

2. SAUL ACCLAIMED KING

This victory gained the public attention and acclaim that Saul needed. It had been victory in battle that had led the people to follow the judges. The same held true now. Moreover, one of the motivating reasons for the request in the first place, as noted in Chapter 2, had been fear of both Ammonites and Philistines. Saul had now not only shown his ability to alleviate such fear, but had actually destroyed the ranks of one of those enemies. Indeed, he was satisfactory as Israel's king.

[22]That Saul here included Samuel in the notice again shows his high regard for the man.

[23]Here already was an indication of the basic division in the land between Judah and the other tribes, which finally issued in the division of the kingdom in the time of Rehoboam.

One of the first reactions of the people was a desire to take vengeance on those who had earlier expressed dissatisfaction with Saul, but Saul magnanimously rejected the idea (I Sam. 11:12, 13). Then Samuel, who evidently had accompanied Saul in the crucial battle, urged the people to assemble at Gilgal for the official establishment of the kingdom. This was done, and sacrifices and peace-offerings were presented before the Lord, with great rejoicing by all that were present. And no doubt many were there, in view of the 330,000 that had come to Bezek.

3. SAMUEL'S ADDRESS

No details are given regarding the nature of Saul's coronation ceremony, but an entire chapter is devoted to an address that Samuel gave to the people at the time.[24] This means that in God's view the most significant part of the occasion was this address.

Samuel began by defending his own judgeship. This is understandable, for Samuel had served hard and well, and, as noted earlier, the people did not realize the greatness of their debt to him. Moreover, this was Samuel's last official act as judge, for now the people had their king. It was fitting that he refer to the past as well as to the future.

Then Samuel reviewed some of the major deliverances God had worked for Israel, speaking of Egypt, the Canaanites under Sisera, the Philistines, and the Moabites as enemy countries. He also referred to several of the judges, including himself, who had been used to bring deliverance from the foreign oppressors (I Sam. 12:6-11). Then he came to the menace of the Ammonite Nahash, reminding the people that this enemy had constituted an important reason for their request for a king.[25] He continued, "Behold the king whom ye have chosen . . . and behold, the LORD hath set a king over you," thus viewing the situation from two sides: in making the request, the people had chosen Saul, and God had now answered that request by giving them the man they had just acclaimed.

Now Samuel came to his main point: the land needed more than a change of government if matters were to improve; it needed a change of attitude toward God. If the people would do what God wanted (as they should have done all during the period of the judges), they would be

[24]Caird, "Books of Samuel," p. 941, sees the address as following naturally after Saul's public selection in I Sam. 10:24, but at that time there was no recognition by the general public to make the actual coronation possible.

[25]The very recent threat of Nahash against Jabesh-gilead cannot be in mind here. The threat depicted in I Sam. 12:12 served to motivate in part the people's request for a king, whereas at the time of the latest threat (I Sam. 11) Saul had already been selected as king (I Sam. 10). Samuel's reference must be to earlier campaigns of Nahash, which had made the Ammonites a threat along with the Philistines, as noted in Chapter 2.

blessed; if they would not, however, the Lord would permit trouble for them just as He had for their fathers (I Sam. 12:14, 15).

To stress the truth of the point, Samuel requested a miraculous sign; he asked for a display of "thunder and rain" in the dry season of wheat harvest.[26] God heard, and thunder and rain indeed came, with the result that "all the people greatly feared the LORD and Samuel." This led the people to ask that Samuel intercede for them that they "die not" (I Sam. 12:16-19).

Samuel responded by telling them that they had nothing to fear if only they obeyed their God. Furthermore, he promised that he—though no longer their leading official—would not cease to pray for them and would continue to teach them "the good and the right way." He ended with another admonition that they "fear the LORD, and serve him in truth," remembering all that God had done for them, and with the warning, that, if they did not, both the people and their king would be consumed (I Sam. 12:20-25).

Thus, Israel had its first king; the last judge had given his parting admonition, and a new day had dawned for God's chosen people. The period of the united monarchy had become a reality.

[26]The dry season runs from early April to early November. Wheat harvest comes between Passover and Pentecost, following immediately after barley harvest.

6

Three Reigns in Summary

We now come to a general comparison of the reigns of Saul, David, and Solomon, the three kings of the united monarchy. It is important to have this general survey in mind before taking up each reign in detail, so that one may understand and evaluate the detail in terms of the general overview. It is well first to note broad comparisons and then to look somewhat more into particulars, though still in a general manner.

A. BROAD COMPARISONS

1. THE REIGN OF SAUL

Saul's rule began with promise but ended in dismal failure. His story is a sad one. He had imposing challenges and the finest opportunity upon being crowned at Gilgal; but when he died on Mount Gilboa, defeated by the Philistines, the country was really worse off than when he began to reign. A main reason why the people had earlier asked for a king was that they might meet and ward off enemy attacks, particularly from the Philistines; when Saul died, however, the Philistines not only had not been defeated but were more in control of the land than at his accession. The people also were divided in loyalties, so that Judah took David as its king, and the northern tribes took Saul's son Ish-bosheth. Significantly, Ish-bosheth did not try to set up a capital west of the Jordan, where the Philistines were in control, but in Transjordan at Mahanaim. And from there he could have done little in terms of actual control of the main part of the country during his brief and unhappy rule of two-and-a-half years.

2. THE REIGN OF DAVID

David's rule, on the other hand, started with serious problems and ended with an empire formed. The country was divided when he began. From Hebron he ruled over only Judah; the northern tribes gave at least lip service to Ish-bosheth, while at the same time their land was available to and extensively controlled by the Philistines. After seven years, however, these tribes came to ask David to rule them as well. David's first task concerned the Philistine problem, and he solved it in two quick battles. Then he organized the country into a true unity, and, after this, David's army continued to win battles until an empire had been built. It extended roughly—in accordance with God's promise to Abraham—from the "river of Egypt to the . . . Euphrates" (Gen. 15:18). David had problems with his own family, but his reign was a story of unbelievable success.

3. THE REIGN OF SOLOMON

Solomon was as unlike Saul or David as the first two kings were unlike each other. Neither of the first kings had been raised in a palace, but Solomon was. From earliest days he knew only luxury and wealth. The court was always his home. Nor did he have the same problems that his predecessors had. Not only was his inherited kingdom united, it was an empire that could compare with any power of the day. This led Solomon to have expensive tastes, which in turn led to numerous foreign entanglements. For one thing, he married many foreign women, who had a serious influence on him religiously, and for another he became involved in an extensive trading activity. He began well in pleasing God, but ended poorly. Accordingly, whereas his empire was strong when he started, it gradually became weaker and when he died was far from what his father had left him. Problems with other countries pressed on him, and his own people were dissatisfied because of high taxes. Solomon, like Saul, ended in failure, though not to the same degree.

B. OVERVIEW OF EACH REIGN

1. THE REIGN OF SAUL

a. His task

Saul's main task, apart from warding off outside enemies, was uniting his country. There was also the need to curtail sin, but his measure of success in this was greatly dependent on how well he could unite the tribes, first in working together with each other and second in having confidence in him as their common head. If he could implant this confidence, the people would listen to his words and conform to his regulations. But if he could not, they would still go their own way, whether or not he spoke fine words and made strong regulations. This task was not a small one. The tribes had been disunited for too many years. They had remained quite to themselves, as indicated by even a difference in dialect—recall the Ephraimites' inability to pronounce the "sh" sound.[1] The natural topographical barrier of the Jordan had separated the Transjordanian tribes from the rest of the land during the period of the judges, and the Esdraelon Plain had done the same with respect to the northern tribes, until at least the time of Deborah and Barak. Civil war had actually broken out twice—once between a collection of the tribes and Benjamin (Judg. 20), and again between Jephthah's troops and the Ephraimites during the occasion just noted.

b. His problem

An immense problem that faced Saul at the beginning of his rule was setting the kingship into motion. He had no government buildings, no palace, no army, no administrative personnel, no taxation program by which to raise money, and not even a capital city. After his selection he did have a nucleus that was ready to follow his leading, and this helped; but the actual task of getting a monarchy started presented a very challenging problem.

c. His manner of rule

Saul began his rule simply and modestly—no doubt purposely so—and wisely. There had been time for Saul to plan, as he had awaited the opportunity for public acclaim, and he had apparently recognized that the people were in no mood for an elaborate government. It would not be easy to impose rigid controls when the people had never had them; and, though Samuel had warned that taxes would come, it would require time and education before the people would accept them.

The capital Saul established was at Gibeah, his home town.[2] He may have appropriated a used building as his palace to reduce expense, for excavation has revealed that the palace was of simple design, actually more of a fortress than a lavish residence.[3] There is no suggestion that he gave the capital city any special privileges, something that could have stirred

[1]They could not say "Shibboleth" but only "Sibboleth" when tested by Jephthah's troops at the Jordan (Judg. 12:6).

[2]Well identified as Tell el-Ful, located at the northern outskirts of present-day Jerusalem. The heinous crime of Judges 19, which ignited civil war, had occurred here.

[3]See pp. 111-112.

criticism if done. Neither was an elaborate court established. The Bible actually names only one officer, Abner, captain of the army and cousin of Saul (I Sam. 14:50). For discussing problems and planning strategy there may have been monthly meetings at the time of the new moon (I Sam. 20:24-27).

There is no indication that Saul instituted many policies that caused appreciable change in people's lives. Old tribal borders, for instance, remained as ever. No indications are given regarding an imposed taxation program, though certainly some money must have been collected for even a simple government. Probably the people were pleased to have matters that way. Like other nations they had a king but they did not suffer irritating interference in their lives. Saul had been able to raise an army, for he often fought with enemy powers—especially the Philistines. This would have pleased the people for it gave them a sense of security against the outside invasions they feared so much. Thus Saul's approach to beginning a kingship was commendable, though it may be that he should have introduced controls of a more stringent kind later on, in the interest of national unity and strength.[4]

d. His military episodes

Saul has been called—and perhaps correctly—"primarily a military king."[5] By this is meant that he did not build a strong state and governmental organization as such, but held the country together by an active army that engaged frequently in battle. For this reason, sometimes the phrase *transitional stage* is used regarding his reign; that is, his rule was merely a transitional time between the period of the judges and the true monarchy. In a sense this is true, for Saul surely did not stress organization but did fight many battles. This fact was likely one of the main reasons for the people's remaining as loyal to him as they did. On the other hand, as has already been seen, the people had in mind a monarchy from the beginning, and certainly Saul sought to institute one, though he seems to have accomplished something less than he had hoped for.

The military encounters Saul had were important for his rule. His main enemy was Philistia, but he fought other countries as well. His first encounter was with the Ammonites, whom he apparently defeated severely. Other enemies included Moab, Edom, Zobah (far to the north—see Chapter 3), and the Amalekites (see I Sam. 14:47, 48). Only the encounter with the last group is described in detail (I Sam. 15).

As for the Philistines, they were encountered many times. Saul fought them already in his second year, and because of outstanding bravery on the

[4]That laws for the control of sin had been made, however, is evident from the words of the woman of Endor that people such as herself had been declared illegal (I Sam. 28:7-25).

[5]George Fohrer, *History of Israelite Religion,* p. 124.

part of his son Jonathan, won a clear victory (I Sam. 13:1—14:46). The next engagement was the time David fought Goliath and won the day for Israel (I Sam. 17). After this, numerous battles transpired, with David serving as Saul's military commander and apparently winning on every occasion (I Sam. 18:5-7). One encounter occurred while David was in flight from Saul, though the outcome is not indicated (I Sam. 23:27, 28). The last time was the tragic encounter at Mount Gilboa, when Saul was killed, the army destroyed, and all Israel abandoned to this enemy power (I Sam. 31:1-10). For much of his reign, Saul apparently did quite well against the Philistines, especially through the time when David served as his commander, but in the end things were different and finally the tragic defeat was suffered.

e. His twofold rejection

Saul was selected by God as Israel's king but during his reign he was told twice that he had been rejected. The reason was that Saul had not fulfilled God's requirement of obedience, the main requisite for the modified form of theocracy to work as God desired.

The first rejection came in connection with the Philistine encounter two years after the beginning of Saul's reign (I Sam. 13:8-14).[6] Saul had arranged with Samuel to meet him prior to the struggle so that sacrifice to God might be made, but Samuel delayed in coming. Having waited seven days, the impatient Saul assumed the priestly office and offered the sacrifice himself, showing that he had a proud, self-sufficient heart. Samuel arrived shortly after and pronounced the divine rejection.

The second rejection came in connection with a battle with the Amalekites, about twenty years later (I Sam. 15).[7] Samuel, at God's direction, gave Saul specific directions regarding this battle: he was to destroy the people completely and all their livestock. Saul carried out the mission in almost every respect, but spared the Amalekite king and some of the finest sheep and oxen. Samuel rebuked Saul for disobedience and conveyed God's second rejection.

f. His decline as a king

With Saul thus rejected twice, David was anointed as his replacement (I Sam. 16:1-31), and God's Spirit ceased His empowerment of Saul for proper kingship (I Sam. 16:14). Following this, Saul's actions as king degenerated rapidly. Under the influence of an "evil spirit" he was given to periods of fear and depression, and a musician was sought to help soothe him. The musician proved to be David, whose prior anointing was unknown to Saul. In time, Saul became jealous of the young man and numerous times

[6]See pp. 125-136.
[7]See pp. 137-142.

attempted to take David's life. Finally David fled from him. Saul now made the further mistake of spending his time in pursuing the righteous David, rather than in governing his country. This seems to have lost him much of the respect the country had for him.

Finally came the deciding battle with the Philistines. The Philistines had been able to move north to the Esdraelon Plain and then eastward through the plain as far as Shunem[8] near Mount Gilboa. Saul moved to meet them at that place, but his force was evidently small, probably due to the loss of confidence in him on the part of the people. The battle was joined and Israel was severely defeated (I Sam. 31:1-10). Saul's three sons including Jonathan were killed. Saul himself was hard pressed and took his own life. This left the country without a king or army, and the Philistines were free to move in and take control almost at will.

Saul's last moments, as he came to fall on his own sword, must have been as regretful as any could be. He had started with so much potential those many years before; he was now dying, having accomplished really nothing of lasting value, with his country having fallen to the very enemy he had been raised up to defeat.

2. THE REIGN OF DAVID

a. His task

In a real sense, David had a still greater challenge and task than did Saul. The tribes still needed to be united and the Philistine problem had become accentuated, with all northern Israel in the virtual control of this enemy. One may assume that David wondered why God permitted the conditions to be so difficult when he took over as ruler. He had been anointed about fifteen years earlier, when matters were much better.[9]

b. The seven years at Hebron

David began his reign at Hebron, the leading city of Judah, where he stayed for seven years and six months (II Sam. 5:5). During these years he was not bothered by the Philistines for they probably felt he was not a great threat to them, since he ruled only Judah. In the north, Ish-bosheth, the one remaining son of Saul, served as king, but living in Transjordan at Mahanaim, he was far away and little contact resulted. Abner, who had taken the lead in making him king (II Sam. 2:8-10), finally deserted him to

[8]Identified with modern Solem in the territory of Issachar at the eastern foot of "Little Hermon" (hill of Moreh, Judg. 7:1), about eight miles from where Saul would have camped at Mount Gilboa. This is doubtless the town where the Shunammite later provided a special room for Elisha (II Kings 4:8-10).

[9]See p. 138.

go to David, promising David at the time the rule of all Israel. Abner started to effect a union, but Joab, David's commander, murdered him before he could complete the task (II Sam. 3:6-27).

c. The tribes united under David

Abner had done enough, however, and the northern tribes recognized their need sufficiently anyway, so that soon a union was effected in spite of Joab's deed. Ish-bosheth in Mahanaim was assassinated shortly after Abner's death, and this made the way clear for the northern tribes to act. They remembered David's former ability against the Philistines, and they wanted that ability demonstrated in their behalf now.

Accordingly, elders from all the northern tribes came to David at Hebron to ask him to be their king. Since the record states specifically that a league or covenant was made at the time, it is likely that some negotiation transpired. The people wanted David as king, but he would have wanted some commitments in return. Agreement was reached between the parties, and David was anointed for the third time in his life.

d. The Philistine problem solved

A main reason for the coming of the northern tribes to David was that he might solve their problem with the Philistines. They may have been somewhat taken aback, then, when David solved the problem very quickly.

When the league between the north and south was ratified, the Philistines moved to thwart it. They had left David to himself until now, but apparently they did not want a united Israel under his leadership. Therefore, they marched in strength to the valley of Rephaim just south of Jerusalem. Here David met them in two decisive battles, winning both times. The result was that the Philistines made no further problem through all of David's reign.

e. Jerusalem made the civil and religious capital

David's choice of Jerusalem as a capital has often been called a stroke of genius, and it was.[10] The city was located at the border between Judah and the northern tribes—thus obviating any undue jealousy between the tribes—and it occupied a strong position topographically, able to withstand enemy attacks.

David first had to conquer Jerusalem from the Jebusites, but he masterminded this without great trouble (II Sam. 5:6-9). David set up his center of operations in the city, and he soon brought the ark there as well (II Sam. 6; I Chron. 13). The ark had been at Kirjath-jearim since the time of its return

[10]William F. Albright, "The Biblical Period," *The Jews: Their History, Culture and Religion,* ed. L. Finkelstein, p. 51.

to Israel by the Philistines, some seventy years before.[11] David erected a tent for it and located it there amid great rejoicing and offering of sacrifices (II Sam. 6:17).[12]

f. Consolidation of the tribes

Little is said regarding David's consolidation of the tribes, but much regarding his foreign conquests. Since the latter could not have been accomplished without a strong nation at home, however, it is certain that he did achieve true unity. This tribal consolidation would have involved acquiring control of land originally allotted to the tribes but never occupied. Until this time the Israelites had been confined mainly to the hill country, but this situation now changed. The Philistines were not driven from their land to the southwest, but they were confined to a comparatively small region and no longer made their vigorous attacks. David thus ruled a continuous and unbroken region from north of the Sea of Galilee to south of Beersheba and on both sides of the Jordan. As a result, Israelites could know for the first that they did exist as a true nation.

g. Foreign conquests

With the home country firmly united, David was in a position to wage war on foreign soil as need arose. There is no indication that he intentionally sought conquest, however, or that he gave himself to creating an empire. For the most part, he merely entered battle situations as they arose. He was invariably victorious; as a result the country's borders and influence were continually enlarged.

The first war was with Moab, across the Dead Sea (II Sam. 8:2; I Chron. 18:2), and the second with Edom, south of that body of water (II Sam. 8:13, 14; I Chron. 18:12, 13). A third involved Ammon, and when Ammon's king hired soldiers from the northern areas of Beth-rehob, Zobah, Maacah, and Tob, these states also became involved.[13] A later war resulted with these northern states; they were defeated and David established control in Damascus and Hamath (II Sam. 8:3-12; 10:1-19). Some of these defeated areas came directly under Israelite supervision, others had governors appointed by David, and still others (particularly Hamath) kept their own government, but acknowledged Israelite sovereignty. With varying degrees of control, David's power came to extend all the way from Egyptian territory to the Euphrates, just as God had promised to Abraham.

[11]That had been shortly after the battle of Aphek (ca. 1075 B.C.) and it was now about 1002 B.C.

[12]This "tent" was not the "tabernacle" (as KJV translates) for the tabernacle was now at Gibeon (II Chron. 1:3).

[13]Cf. pp. 39-41.

h. The problem of succession

As David's outstanding reign drew to a close, the problem of who should succeed him became increasingly acute. In that the ruling family had changed following Saul, no pattern of succession had been established.[14] With David having been so strong, certainly most people expected him to make the selection, but apparently no public announcement was issued. Actually David had made his choice, having designated Solomon at the time of his birth, but for some reason he had not made this generally known. The result was that a serious struggle for the throne ensued, involving especially two sons.

One of these sons was Absalom (II Sam. 13-18). He was David's third son, born of an Aramaean princess of Geshur.[15] Amnon, the eldest, had been killed by Absalom in revenge (II Sam. 13:23-29), and Chileab the second son probably had died while still young. On the basis of age this left Absalom the next claimant in line. Apparently, he did not believe David would follow this pattern, however (probably because he knew of Solomon's selection), for he made his play for the throne while David was still vigorous. He first curried favor with the people, winning the allegiance of many, and then moved on Jerusalem with a military force he had been able to assemble. David was taken by surprise and found the situation serious enough to flee.

An ensuing battle took place near Mahanaim, the former capital of Ishbosheth. David's forces were fewer than those of Absalom, but under the skillful guidance of Joab, they were victorious; and Joab, against the wishes of the king, killed the young aspirant king. This left David free to return to Jerusalem, apparently as strong as ever on the throne.

The other son who struggled for the throne was Adonijah (I Kings 1:1-9). He was the fourth son, and therefore next in line after Absalom. It probably was not long after David returned to Jerusalem that Adonijah made his try for the throne. He assembled a military force, after the pattern of his older brother—though much smaller in number—and persuaded key people to help him. He assembled all these at the well of En-rogel, to proclaim him as Israel's next king.

News of this clandestine gathering came to Nathan the prophet, however, and he quickly took steps in favor of Solomon. He somehow knew of David's desire regarding the young man, and therefore, through Bathsheba, Solomon's mother, brought the situation to David's attention. Immediately the king gave orders, and the coronation of Solomon took place. The ceremony was performed at the spring of Gihon, slightly north of En-rogel.

[14]Most countries adopted the custom of a continued dynasty, with the oldest son becoming king; but there were exceptions. Note Edom's kings (Gen. 36:31-39).

[15]See pp. 40-41.

When the assembled people shouted in acclaim of the new king, the sound traveled as far as En-rogel, and Adonijah's people quickly dispersed. Solomon thus became king.

David spent his few closing months—as coregent with Solomon—in preparing the new king and the people for Solomon's reign. Finally he died "full of days, riches, and honor," the greatest king that Israel would ever know (I Kings 2:10, 11; I Chron. 29:26-28).

3. THE REIGN OF SOLOMON

a. His task

Solomon's task was quite different from that of either Saul or David. He did not have to start a kingdom or unite a people; neither did he have to defeat a menacing enemy. He inherited a well-organized kingdom, with outside enemies not only subdued but under control. Israel was easily one of the stronger powers of all the Middle East. His task was mainly just to keep the status quo. This does not mean the work was to be easy, however, for an empire the size of Israel would have had many facets to supervise and responsibilities to care for. Moreover, the countries David had conquered would be looking for ways of regaining their independence, and Solomon was not the warrior his father had been.

b. Early problems

When David died, Solomon had a problem first of consolidating his position against potential opposition within his own kingdom. Adonijah continued to be a rival, and Solomon had him killed. Then Solomon dispensed with the two major supporters of Adonijah, Abiathar and Joab. The former he deposed from office as high priest and the latter he had killed, as Joab fled for safety to the altar at the tent David had erected (I Kings 2:28-34).

Another potential enemy was Shimei, who had cursed David at the time he had fled from Absalom (II Sam. 16:5-14), for he still maintained loyalty to the house of Saul. Solomon believed he had nothing to fear as long as Shimei stayed in Jerusalem, where he would be under surveillance, but when the man left one day Solomon had him killed also (I Kings 2:36-46).

c. Manner of rule

Solomon's approach to rule was to maintain conditions militarily, and to devote himself primarily to building activity and international relationships. He was a statesman, not a military figure. Accordingly, he did not give himself to offensive battles, but built defensive fortresses (I Kings 9:15-19). He also employed the chariot as a defensive measure, something David had never done (I Kings 10:26; II Chron. 9:25).

Solomon differed also in that he maintained a lavish court. He had been raised in luxury and had a taste for extravagance. His official personnel numbered more than David's, and his own family included as many as 700 wives and 300 concubines (I Kings 11:3). He evidently entertained extensively, for the amount of food required for one day was incredible.[16]

d. Building activity

David had wanted to build a temple for God, but God had denied this to him in favor of his son. Solomon, therefore, undertook the task. He first contracted with Hiram of Lebanon for cedar wood, and actual building operations began in his fourth year (ca. 966 B.C.—I Kings 6:1) and continued for seven years (I Kings 6:38). The location was on Mount Moriah (II Chron. 3:1), immediately adjacent to David's city on the north.

Other buildings erected—probably in the same general area—were Solomon's personal palace, which took thirteen years to build (I Kings 7:1), the "house of the forest of Lebanon" (which might be the name of the palace), the hall of the pillars, the hall of judgment, and a special house for Solomon's honored wife, the daughter of Pharaoh. The implication is that Hiram of Lebanon continued to help with material, workmen, and gold for all these buildings, which left Solomon heavily in debt to him (I Kings 9:10-14).

e. Revenue sources

Defensive fortifications, food and equipment for personnel to man them, provisions for such a lavish court, and the building activity called for considerable revenue. One source of revenue was taxation, for which Solomon divided the country into twelve districts. Each district was to furnish provisions for the court for one month of the year (I Kings 4:7-28). Another source of revenue was tribute and gifts received from foreign countries. Details of amounts received are not given, but the indication is that many countries sent silver, gold, fine garments, valuable spices, and animals (I Kings 10:24, 25). Solomon also developed extensive trade relationships. One avenue was through the Red Sea to the south. Another was directly by land, involving especially horses and chariots. Solomon purchased horses and chariots not only for himself, but took advantage of his geographical position to act as middleman between Egypt to the south and the Hittites and Aramaeans to the north (I Kings 10:28, 29). In addition to collecting all this revenue, Solomon saved on expenses by means of labor conscription or the corvée. Though some Israelites were involved, the majority of labor conscripts were foreigners (I Kings 5:13-15; 9:21).

[16]See p. 286.

f. Foreign alliances and marriages

In addition to trade, Solomon also made foreign alliances which involved God-displeasing marriages. The most important alliance was with Egypt, which was sealed by Solomon's marriage to a daughter of Pharaoh (I Kings 3:1). Solomon no doubt considered this a great honor, for Egypt had long been a leading world power.[17] Another alliance was with Hiram of Lebanon. Solomon's wife of the Zidonians (I Kings 11:1) was probably a daughter of this ruler.[18] As noted in Chapter 3, this northern area was advanced in merchandising, and Solomon wanted to share in the income.

A serious result of these alliances was that many foreign wives were brought into the country, and they in turn brought an increasing influence on Solomon religiously. Gradually, he was led away from his commendable obedience to God.

g. Enemy opposition

As soon as Solomon turned away from God, the divine law of retribution began to work. The Scriptures are clear that, as long as people obey God, they are blessed, but when they do not they suffer trouble. Three sources of enemy opposition arose for Solomon.

One source of opposition was from within the country—Jeroboam (I Kings 11:26-40), who later became the first king of the northern kingdom. Evidently a capable man, Jeroboam had been placed in charge of a work force. One day when on leave, he was met by the prophet Ahijah, who tore a new garment into twelve pieces and gave Jeroboam ten. He explained that these ten represented ten tribes over which Jeroboam would rule when Solomon was dead. Solomon learned of Ahijah's words, and immediately sought to take Jeroboam's life, with the result that Jeroboam fled to Egypt.

A second source of opposition was from Edom to the south (I Kings 11:14-22). The central person involved was Hadad, whose activity served to diminish Solomon's control in this southern country. Hadad was the sole survivor of Edom's royal family at the time of Joab's extensive slaughter there during David's reign (II Sam. 8:13, 14; cf. I Kings 11:15, 16). Following that occasion, he sought asylum in Egypt, much as Jeroboam did later. On learning that David was dead, Hadad returned to Edom and probably became head of the country. He continued as a bitter enemy of Israel all during Solomon's rule.

A third enemy was Damascus to the north (I Kings 11:23-25). The main trouble this time came from Rezon, who effected a lessening of Solomon's control in the north much as Hadad in the south. Rezon had been a supporter of Hadadezer, king of Zobah, whom David had defeated early in his

[17]See pp. 305-306.
[18]See p. 42.

reign (II Sam. 8:3-9). Rezon apparently had escaped unharmed from that battle and then formed a small army of his own to further his personal desire for power. His main prize had been Damascus, and he succeeded in becoming ruler there, making it a strong center. He clearly was a man of ambition, and he worked to the end of freeing Damascus from all Israelite control.

h. Israel's status at Solomon's death

A general survey of Solomon's closing years reveals an unhappy picture. The country, while not in complete disarray as when Saul died, was far from the condition in which Solomon had inherited it. Religiously, there was an actual worship of foreign deities. Solomon, who had started so well, ended with God's severe condemnation and punishment upon him. Politically, he knew that as a result God would rend his kingdom into two parts after his death, with Jeroboam receiving ten of the twelve tribes. And as to foreign relations, the empire had so dwindled that little control remained either south in Edom or north in Damascus. Solomon was one of the grand kings of the Middle East, so long as he remained true to God, but he fell well below this exalted position before he died. Sin took its toll with him, as it does in every such case.

PART TWO
The Monarchies of Saul, David, and Solomon

7

Saul's Kingdom

We come now to Part Two of our study, where we look at the kingships of Saul, David, and Solomon at close range. Background and general survey information have been the concern in Part One; here there is need to consider the rule of each of these kings in some detail. The general view has been necessary first, because the details can be rightly understood only when seen in the light of the larger picture. These details are important, because they provide the evidence for general conclusions already reached. The details are important also because they provide a rich source of lesson material for the reader's profit. One must always remember that the Bible is God's book for people of any day. When biblical history is studied, therefore, the benefit is more than an intellectual learning experience; it is also a behavioral learning experience. Accordingly, the approach to be followed, in several of the ensuing chapters, will be to consider first the historical facts of a given period or situation and then "points to notice" regarding those facts. These points will concern practical lessons for the Christian life today and also underlying significances pertaining to the historical period involved.

Each of the kings of the united monarchy will be considered in turn, with several chapters devoted to each. We begin with Saul, and a first concern will be to look at him as king. We want to consider what sort of a man he was, what kind of government he instituted, the nature of his task, and how well he fulfilled it.

A. SAUL THE MAN

1. HIS FAMILY

Saul was of the tribe of Benjamin, a son of Kish. Kish was a son of Ner (I Chron. 9:39) and grandson of Jehiel (I Chron. 9:35, 36). The lineage given in I Samuel 9:1 omits Ner, designating Kish as the son of Abiel (who may be identical with Jehiel). Since Hebrew genealogies often omit generations, it may be that both Ner and Jehiel (Abiel) were not immediate ancestors, but at least the information given shows that the line ran: Jehiel (Abiel), Ner, Kish, and Saul. It should be realized that the name *Ner* was also given to a brother of Kish (I Chron. 9:36) who, then, was Saul's uncle (I Sam. 14:50). To him, Abner was born, cousin of Saul, who served as Saul's military commander (I Sam. 14:50, 51; 17:55, 57).

Saul married Ahinoam, daughter of Ahimaaz, and they had four sons, Jonathan, Malchishua, Abinadab, and Eshbaal (Ish-bosheth) (I Chron. 8:33; cf. II Sam. 2:8). They also had two daughters, Merab and Michal (I Sam. 18:19, 20). At some time, Saul in addition took a concubine, Rizpah, daughter of Aiah (II Sam. 3:7), and she bore him two sons, Armoni and Mephibosheth (II Sam. 21:8). This Mephibosheth was not the man honored by David in memory of Jonathan (II Sam. 9).

The family in prior days had dwelt in Gibeon (I Chron. 9:35), but by the time of Kish, they were in Gibeah (I Sam. 10:26), about four miles southeast of Gibeon. Kish is described as a "mighty man of power" (*gibbor hayil*), which probably means he was affluent and prominent in his community. He is said to have had servants and numerous donkeys. When the donkeys ran away, Saul was sent to find them (I Sam. 9:3). The family burial plot was at Zelah (II Sam. 21:14), an unknown site, but it is listed in Joshua 18:28 as one of fourteen cities assigned to the Benjamites. No indication is given as to what ancestral tie the family of Kish had with this city.

2. THE MAN HIMSELF

a. His physical appearance

Saul is described as a "choice young man, and a goodly" (*bahur watob*), so that "there was not among the children of Israel a goodlier person than he" (*tob mimmennu,* "better than he"). One aspect in his striking appearance was that "from his shoulders and upward he was higher than any of the people" (I Sam. 9:2). The reference to "choice" and "goodly" is probably to a handsome appearance, which certainly was enhanced by his large stature. David referred to him as swift and strong in his eulogy at Saul's death (II Sam. 1:23), and Samuel earlier had said that there was "none like him" (I Sam. 10:24). Saul would have made a strong physical impression wherever he went. A striking, pleasing appearance is always helpful to those seeking public office.

b. His character

In character, Saul had some advantageous points also, though at the same time he had some that were not so helpful.

1) ***A regenerated person.*** For one thing, Saul was a regenerated person. He had numerous failings as a king and eventually disobeyed God, but it is clear that he was truly regenerated. Several matters so indicate. First, and perhaps foremost, he was picked by God as Israel's king; and a basic factor in the concept of the new monarchy was that the king serve merely as a human intermediary between God and the people. Under the judges, God had not used any permanent go-between, but had served as Israel's supreme Ruler directly. Now, God still wanted this basic theocratic ideal to continue, with the variation of the human ruler acting as intermediary. But if the king were to be an appropriate intermediary, he surely had to be a man of God. It is unthinkable that God would have picked a person who was not right in his heart with Him.

A second evidence is found in the words God used regarding Saul when He first told Samuel concerning His choice. He said, "Thou shalt anoint him to be captain [*nagid*] over my people Israel, that he may save my people out of the hand of the Philistines" (I Sam. 9:16). God definitely designated Saul to be Israel's *nagid* ("leader"), and entrusted him with the task of fighting off the menacing Philistines. It is implied that God would be pleased to use and prosper the man in accomplishing this goal. Such a man surely had to be a child of God.

A third indication is that the Spirit of God was given to Saul to enable him for his task as Israel's king. The Spirit was given to him temporarily at the time of his meeting a company of prophets (I Sam. 10:6, 10), with the result that he prophesied along with this company,[1] and then on a continuing basis just before the battle of Jabesh-gilead (I Sam. 11:6). That this latter instance did mark the beginning of a continuing presence of the Spirit within Saul is evidenced by the fact that there is no further indication of the Spirit coming on him and by the statement from many years later that the Spirit left him (I Sam. 16:14). If the Spirit left him, He must have been with him since the last indication that He came upon him. This coming of the

[1]See p. 78, n. 13.

Spirit was for the purpose of empowering Saul for service as king, and such empowerment, though given to numerous individuals at different times (see, e.g., Exod. 31:3; Judg. 3:10; 13:25; II Chron. 20:14), was never given to one who was not a child of God.

In view of this evidence, a question rises in respect to the names Saul gave his sons, one of which incorporated the name *Baal*—Eshbaal (I Chron. 8:33; 9:39). Does this not counter what has been said and show that Saul gave some allegiance to Baal? The answer is that it does not, and the following evidence is cited in support.

First, Saul's other sons were all given names fully in keeping with a respect for God. They were Jonathan, Malchishua, and Abinadad (I Chron. 8:33; 9:39). Jonathan, meaning "Yahweh has given," is thus built on the very name of God. Malchishua means "the king of salvation," and "king" here probably refers again to God. It might refer to Saul as Israel's leader, but at least the name has no reference to Baal. And Abinadad means "father is generous," which also could have either God or Saul in mind as "father." Once more there is no reference to Baal. Since these three older sons all were given names in keeping with Saul's respect for God, it would be unusual if a contrasting type of name were given to the youngest.

Second, the name of the youngest, Eshbaal, more likely means "Fire of Baal," rather than "Man of Baal," or "Baal exists," as conjectured by some.[2] The element "Esh" (*'esh*) is the word for "fire"; the pointing has to be changed to get "man" (*'ish*), or to get "exists" (*'ish*), which is really basically *yesh*. And "Fire of Baal" could well carry the same basic thought as "Jerubbaal" (the name given to Gideon when he tore down Baal's altar; cf. Judg. 6:27-32), or of "Meribbaal" (the name given to Jonathan's son Mephibosheth). Both Jerubbaal and Meribbaal come from the root idea "contend" (*rib*), and each means "Baal-contender." Gideon earned his name because he did contend with Baal and emerge the victor. As a result of the reputation he earned, as many as 32,000 men responded to his call to fight the Midianites (Judg. 7:3). No doubt, Jonathan, whose own name was built on the name of Israel's God, called his son by the name *Meribbaal* from a similar point of view. The idea of "Fire of Baal" fits nicely with this thought. Saul's youngest son was seen as one who would be a "fire" in combating the forces of the Canaanite Baal.

A third matter to notice is not a further argument, but a pertinent observation. All three of these names, Eshbaal, Jerubbaal, and Meribbaal, were eventually changed, and in the same manner. Eshbaal, which so appears twice in I Chronicles 8:33 and 9:39, was changed to Ish-bosheth ("man of shame"). This form is found twelve times in II Samuel 2-4. Jerubbaal, which so appears fourteen times in Judges 6-9 and I Samuel 12:11, was

[2]See William F. Albright's discussion in favor of "Baal exists"—*Archaeology and the Religion of Israel,* p. 113.

changed to Jerubbesheth and is so used once in II Samuel 11:21. Meribbaal, which appears twice in I Chronicles 8:34 and 9:40, was changed to Mephibosheth and is so used fourteen times in II Samuel 9, 16, 19, and 21.

The element "bosheth" or "besheth" means "shame." Apparently, in time the three names with the element "Baal" were seen to be offensive to Israel's religion (even though they were given for the proper reason noted) and the element "shame" was substituted for the name of the offending foreign deity. Hosea (9:10) and Jeremiah (3:24) seem to use the element "shame" as a disdainful manner of reference to the Canaanite deity also. A point to notice is that, though the names were eventually changed, this is insufficient reason for believing that their original bestowal was an endorsement of Baal worship. As has been seen, this was not the case with Gideon and Jonathan's son, and therefore very likely not with Saul's son either. These changes in names could have been made well after their original bestowal when the reason for giving them no longer seemed sufficiently significant to offset possible misunderstanding.

2) ***A humble man.*** A second admirable characteristic is that Saul, at the time of his call, was a humble person. Samuel spoke of him in I Samuel 15:17 as having been little in his own eyes when he was made king. Saul gave evidence of this by his reply to Samuel at the time of Samuel's indication to him that he was to be king. Samuel said: "On whom is all the desire of Israel? Is it not on thee, and on all thy father's house?" (I Sam. 9:20). And Saul replied, "Am not I a Benjamite, of the smallest of the tribes of Israel? and my family the least of all the families of the tribe of Benjamin? wherefore then speakest thou so to me?" A proud man would have responded quite differently. Actually, though Benjamin was one of the smaller tribes, the family of Kish may well have been quite prominent in light of the indication of wealth noted above.

Then, tying in with this characteristic is the unmistakable spirit of timidity that Saul evidenced. When his servant suggested going to see Samuel regarding the lost donkeys, Saul hesitated (I Sam. 9:6-10). The servant had to produce a quarter shekel to give to Samuel before his master could be persuaded. Later, when Saul was chosen by God in the presence of Israel's elders—gathered at Mizpeh for the purpose—Saul was found hiding among the wagons with which these elders had come (I Sam. 10:17-27). They had to look for the king that had just been selected. Afterward, there were a few people who remained unconvinced that this man could lead Israel—in spite of his fine appearance (I Sam. 10:23)—and the reason may well have been the apparent timidity displayed. How could such a man provide the strong leadership Israel needed?

Admittedly, timidity and humility are not the same thing, but in this case they seem to go together. Saul was not one to push himself forward. On reaching home after he had been anointed by Samuel, he did not even tell his uncle (probably Ner) that anything unusual had happened (I Sam. 10:14-16). Even if Saul had not been proud but merely an average person, he would at least have given some hint about such an event. That he did not says much concerning his humble, retiring spirit.

3) ***A magnanimous man.*** Saul was also a magnanimous man, at least at first. Following his brilliant victory over the Ammonites at Jabesh-gilead, when the people were ready to make him king, the cry went up concerning those who had earlier despised Saul, "Who is he that said, Shall Saul reign over us? bring the men, that we may put them to death." Saul, however, rather than taking this kind of vengeance said, "There shall not a man be put to death this day: for today the LORD hath wrought salvation in Israel" (I Sam. 11:12, 13). Saul might easily have reacted differently, but he did not. He is to be commended.

4) ***An emotional man.*** People vary in respect to emotional stability; some are able to keep their emotions well in control, while others are either at a high peak of joy or a low trough of despair much of the time. Saul clearly was of the latter group. It was no doubt for this reason that in his latter days, an "evil spirit"[3] could bring him into fear and depression, so that the young musician, David, had to be called to play soothing music (I Sam. 16:17-23). Later, Saul would fly into a rage at the young player, and try to kill him—on two different occasions (I Sam. 18:10, 11; 19:9, 10). Later still, in an angry state, he came to Ramah to apprehend David and then, rather than doing so, suddenly fell into a fit of despair and hopelessness when he realized that the young man was apparently approved by the honored Samuel (I Sam. 19:20-24).[4]

5) ***An impatient man.*** Being emotional is not necessarily bad, though it proved to be a detriment for Saul, but being impatient is clearly a negative characteristic. And Saul was given to impatience. Saul's impatience may have become more pronounced as his years of rule passed. Psalm 73:18 says that God puts men in "slippery places" and Saul as king was in such a place. He did not react to the responsibility well, but slipped and fell. Impatience was his undoing at the time of his first rejection (I Sam. 13:8-10). He and Samuel had agreed on a time of sacrifice before engaging in battle with the Philistines—Saul was to wait seven days until Samuel could come. Saul did wait until the seventh day, but when the battle seemed urgent he went ahead and performed the sacrifice himself. Samuel then came, yet on the

[3]A demon, no doubt; see discussion, pp. 149-150.
[4]See p. 158 for discussion.

seventh day, and brought God's severe rebuke to Saul. Saul had simply been impatient, and let this weakness lead him into serious sin.

Another instance of impatience is apparent in a later occasion involving this same battle with the Philistines (I Sam. 14:17-20). At a crucial point in the struggle, Saul directed the high priest Ahiah (Ahimelech), who was present with the ephod,[5] to consult the Urim and Thummim regarding God's will as to procedure. Before the high priest could do so, however, Saul stopped him—with the words, "Withdraw thine hand"—because it seemed to him that conditions did not warrant waiting for God's word. That is to say, Saul ran out of patience, though to wait for the word of God would not have taken long.

6) ***An impulsive man.*** Again on the negative side is the fact that Saul was impulsive. He could act quickly and rashly, even in respect to serious matters, without due thought or consideration. Saul's actions in trying to take the life of David have already been mentioned. Later, he gave the outrageous order to have eighty-five priests of Nob killed, simply because the high priest, Ahimelech, had given some aid to David (I Sam. 22:14-19). Later still he went to see the medium at Endor, whose trade he had earlier outlawed, that he might talk again with Samuel (I Sam. 28:7-25). All these were rash acts, done out of an impulsive spirit, without adequate forethought.

7) ***A man given to acts of injustice.*** The rash acts just mentioned were all unjust, but one can see them more as actions of impulsiveness. On one occasion, however, Saul acted in a way that must be classified as basically unjust. This concerned the Gibeonites. Perhaps his reasoning involved the earlier trickery that the Gibeonites had played on Israel (in Joshua's day—Josh. 9:3-15), but whatever the reason, he took advantage of these people. The fact came to light only much later in the day of David, when a famine was experienced in the country (II Sam. 21:1-9). David inquired of God the reason for the famine and was informed that it was "for Saul, and for his bloody house, because he slew the Gibeonites."

The result was that, at the request of the Gibeonites, David had seven of Saul's descendants hanged in Saul's home city of Gibeah. The Gibeonites' own words as to what Saul had done to them were that he had "consumed" them and worked to the end that they "should be destroyed from remaining" in Israel. Since God sent a famine as punishment, it is evident that Saul's action was highly reprehensible. It may be that he had killed many of this group and then confiscated their land, giving it to his descendants, seven of whom had to give their lives as a result.

[5]Not ark as in Hebrew, for the ark was yet at Kirjath-jearim (I Sam. 7:1); see p. 119, n. 21, for discussion.

B. SAUL'S GOVERNMENT

Saul's reign divides itself into two distinct parts: the period when he ruled with some success, and the period that followed when his effectiveness gravely declined. The two, significantly, are commensurate with the periods when Saul continued to be empowered by God's Spirit and when the Spirit left him and an "evil spirit" took His place (I Sam. 11:6; 16:14). The characterization of Saul's kingdom now to be set forth has in view the earlier and stronger period.

1. GENERAL CHARACTERIZATION

The rule Saul established is commonly characterized as simple, crude, and rustic. R. K. Harrison calls Saul a "rustic chieftain."[6] George Fohrer says his rule was "merely a transitional stage between the tribal or city-state form of government of the so-called period of the judges and the establishment of a true state."[7] Martin Noth says similarly that Saul's rule reminds one of "those charismatic leaders of tribes and groups of tribes which, summoned in the name of God or constrained by the spirit of God, had fought for the rights of the Israelites in the land and had prevailed."[8] In other words, Saul was hardly a true king, but rather a half-judge and half-king, a transition stage.

It is important that we give attention to factors which prompt scholars to come to these conclusions. Was Saul a true king? Or was he only a semiking?

One reason for this semijudge, semiking characterization is that Saul came to his position of leadership in a manner somewhat parallel to that of the judges. He was a handsome man, and this attracted people to him; also his winning a major battle at Jabesh-gilead (I Sam. 11:5-11) led to the actual establishment of his rule, much in the pattern of an Othniel, Gideon, or Jephthah.

The conclusion drawn from this fact, however, does not necessarily follow. It is true that the Jabesh-gilead victory was used of God to bring Saul to the public attention necessary for his coronation, but this was because of the nature of the situation. Saul was called upon to begin a new form of rule, which the people had not known before; nor had they known him. Israel's leaders had come to know Saul at Mizpeh (I Sam. 10:17-24), but this group had not included the ordinary people; and a person does not rule until he has subjects willing to be ruled. An occasion such as the Jabesh-gilead battle was necessary to give him the popular acclaim he needed to begin the actual kingdom. Note also that his own personal

[6]*Old Testament Times,* p. 184.
[7]*History of Israelite Religion,* p. 124.
[8]*The History of Israel,* p. 168.

appearance certainly was a help in prompting this acclaim, but that this fact really set him off from the judges, for none of them are said to have been striking in appearance.

A second reason for the characterization of Saul as a semiking is that the term first used for Saul in the sacred record is *nagid* ("leader") and only later *melek* ("king"). Because of this, Noth doubts that Saul was even thought of as a king-to-be when first designated,[9] and William F. Albright sees the use of the term as a "device by which Samuel persuaded the people to elect a popular leader for life instead of a king who might found a dynasty."[10] It is believed that the term had a military connotation.[11] Thus Saul was first presented only as a leader in military conflict against enemies like the Philistines and Ammonites.

It is true that *nagid* is used for Saul as many as three times—twice before *melek* is used (I Sam. 9:16; 10:1) and once after (I Sam. 13:14), with the reference even there being to Saul's initial appointment. However, there are four matters that argue against the conclusion which has been made. One is that Saul's appointment was obviously in response to the request of the people, and they had asked for a "king" (*melek*) (e.g., I Sam. 8:5, 6, 9, 11). Secondly, when Saul was designated as the coming ruler before the elders at Mizpeh, the people cried out, "God save the king [*melek*]," and this was well before the actual coronation. Thirdly, at the coronation at Gilgal, it is said that the people there "made Saul king [*melek*] before the LORD" (I Sam. 11:15). And, fourthly, David, who surely was anticipated as full king of Israel—after one rule in this capacity had already elapsed—is also called *nagid* no less than four times (I Sam. 25:30; II Sam. 5:2; 6:21; 7:8). If the term did not carry the connotation of semiking for David, then one need not think it did for Saul either. The term seems merely to have been useful for reference to one who was to be a king and had not yet been crowned. In no way did it connote one who would be less than a true king when that time came.

A third reason for the characterization of Saul as a semiking is found in the kind of palace Saul used. Albright, who excavated its ruins, says that what he found illustrates the "rustic simplicity" of Saul's court.[12] Because of its architecture, Albright suggests the building was originally put up by the Philistines as a fortress and then taken over and appropriated by Saul as his palace. It was of good size, but it was not built like an ordinary palace. It was rectangular, 169 feet by 114 feet, with double casemate walls, some

[9] *The History of Israel,* p. 169.

[10] "The Biblical Period," *The Jews: Their History, Culture, and Religion,* ed. L. Finkelstein, p. 48.

[11] The term was often used in military contexts both in the Old Testament and also in some extrabiblical eighth-century texts; see Eugene Maly, *The World of David and Solomon,* p. 23.

[12] "The Biblical Period," p. 50.

parts of which constituted small rooms, while other parts were filled with rubble and stone, making a total wall over thirteen feet thick. Besides this, the fortress had a massive tower on each of its four corners.[13] Its contents were as simple as its design. No abundance of gold, silver, or ivory objects was found in its rubble, as was true of palaces of later kings, but only practical tools, such as used by ordinary people, including pottery, grinding stones, and arrowheads.

This manner of evidence one cannot dispute. It is clear that Saul's rule was simple in its plan and execution. He did not establish a lavish court or manner of leadership. There was good reason for this, however, as will be seen shortly. And that he did put this manner of rule into effect does not show him to have been less than a true king. His manner of rule may have been simple, in comparison with others, but it was still a true kingship and not merely a semijudgeship.

2. A SIMPLE RULE

It is well to continue with this thought of simplicity. That Saul's rule should have been simple is easy to understand. It must be remembered that Saul was Israel's first king. Before his rule, the people had enjoyed complete freedom from human government, only voluntarily following a judge who might arise but had no central governing body.

In this light, two factors kept Saul from an elaborate government. The first is that elaborate government was impossible. He had no tax revenue to spend, so he did not even have a capital or palace at the beginning. He had to start with nothing at a time when his subjects were not of a mind to be regimented quickly or to have harsh, freedom-yielding laws imposed. The other factor is that it would not have been wise to set up an elaborate government, even if it had been possible. The people needed to be educated to new ways of thinking gradually, if rebellion was to be avoided. That Saul began simply, therefore, was to his credit. His people would have been glad that he could live in a simple manner and still fight their battles for them.

3. SAUL'S COURT

Saul's court was as unpretentious as his palace. The name of only one officer is recorded, Abner, the commander of Saul's army (I Sam. 14:50). Monthly meetings, probably to decide issues and plan procedures, seem to have been held. The time was at the new moon, and the place was doubtless the fortress-palace of Saul. In time, David came to attend the meetings, as is indicated by his planned absence during the period when he was being pursued by Saul (I Sam. 20:24-27). It is indicated that at that time Saul's son

[13]Lawrence Sinclair, "An Archaeological Study of Gibeah (Tell el-Ful)," *The Biblical Archaeologist* 27 (May 1964), pp. 54-55.

Jonathan was also a member of the group. It is possible that all four of Saul's sons were. Recall that at least three of them died with him at the final battle with the Philistines at Mount Gilboa (I Sam. 31:2-6). Since Abner was a cousin of Saul (son of his uncle Ner—I Sam. 14:50), and David married the daughter of Saul, Michal (I Sam. 18:27), it is possible that Saul's court was made up only of his own family and close relatives. Perhaps this is indicative of an inner fear of losing control of the government to outsiders.

The make-up of Saul's family was noted earlier: his wife Ahinoam, his four sons (Jonathan, Malchishua, Abinadab, and Eshbaal) and two daughters (Merab and Michal), all by Ahinoam, and his concubine Rizpah, who bore him two sons (Armoni and Mephibosheth). Once again, modesty is manifested by Saul. Royal families were normally large. Even some of the judges had large families. Gideon had seventy sons, born of many wives (Judg. 8:30). Jair had thirty sons (Judg. 10:4), Ibzan had thirty sons and thirty daughters (Judg. 12:9), and Abdon had forty sons (Judg. 12:14). Later, David, while yet ruling only in Hebron, had six wives (II Sam. 3:2-5), and in Jerusalem he took more wives and concubines (II Sam. 5:13). Later still, Solomon had no less than 700 wives and 300 concubines (I Kings 11:3).

4. SAUL'S ECONOMIC SITUATION

Not much is stated regarding Saul's economic program, but a few hints are supplied now and again. Samuel had warned the people that the king would impose hardship by various types of demands (I Sam. 8:11-18). This may have prepared the way for Saul to lay down some tax requirements, but it also may have caused many people to build up an automatic resistance to such demands. It is quite clear, at least, that Saul took a cautious approach in making demands, and probably did not set them very high at any time.

Saul did, however, at some time begin a taxation program. This is indicated by the fact that he did have a government, and any government needs money, little though it may be. A taxation program is also implied by his promise, at the time of Goliath's defiance of Israel's army, that any soldier who would be willing to fight Goliath would, in addition to other considerations, have "his father's house free in Israel" (I Sam. 17:25). Taxes, therefore, were high enough to make this form of incentive attractive to a soldier.

Then there is indication that Saul acquired a rather extensive amount of land in one way or another. One of the royal demands that Samuel had foretold was that the king would seize the people's fields, vineyards, and oliveyards (I Sam. 8:14), and apparently Saul did. It is implied in I Samuel 22:7 that he was able to give fields and vineyards to his officers, and there is a direct indication in II Samuel 9:9, 10 that he owned considerable land. David granted to Mephibosheth, son of Jonathan, all the land left by his grandfather Saul, and assigned a servant, Ziba, to care for it with the help of his sons. It is noteworthy, too, that apparently this land had come under David's control when he succeeded Saul to the throne. The passage shows that he was able to bestow it on Mephibosheth. Later he withdrew it from Mephibosheth (II Sam. 16:4), and later still divided it between Mephibosheth and Ziba (II Sam. 19:29, 30).

It was common in the ancient East for kings to be large landowners. They administered such lands directly or granted them to people as fiefs in return for rent or service rendered. In Egypt, there were periods when the majority of the land belonged either to the king or the priests (cf. Gen. 47:20-26). In Israel, all land belonged to God (Josh. 22:19), and God granted individual parcels of it to Israel's families, with the stipulation that those parcels always remain in the same family (Lev. 25:23). If a man should die childless, his land was to go to his nearest kinsman (Num. 27:8-11). The brother of a deceased husband was obliged by levirate law to marry the widow, that children might be raised up for the deceased and the inheritance passed along and kept in the family (Ruth 4:1-10). A year of jubilee was to be declared every fifty years, when all land that had for some reason been transferred should return to the original owners, that the patrimonies might be continued as instituted at the beginning by God (Lev. 25:8-17, 23-55).

It was on the basis of this patrimony system that Naboth refused to sell his vineyard to Ahab (I Kings 21:3). Not everyone was this careful, however, a fact revealed by prophetic denunciations of those who accumulated large holdings (e.g., Isa. 5:8; Mic. 2:2). This must have been true already in the day of Saul, since he had been able to assume control of much land. Such land was obtained in various ways. Omri of Israel purchased the hill of Samaria (I Kings 16:24); Solomon received the city of Gezer from the Egyptian Pharaoh as a present (I Kings 9:16); apparently land left by people who moved to foreign soil automatically came under the domain of the king, as illustrated in the story of the Shunammite (II Kings 8:1-6); and land might simply be seized, if necessary by nefarious methods, as was the case with Naboth's vineyard (I Kings 21:1-16). Which of these or other methods Saul employed is not indicated.

5. SAUL'S ARMY

George Fohrer refers to Saul as primarily a "military king, called on in time of need."[14] Martin Noth, speaking of Saul at the time of his coronation, states, "The new king was no doubt intended to act primarily as leader of the levies of Israel."[15] There is good reason for these observations, for certainly a prime motivation in Israel's desire for a king was protection against outside enemies, especially the Philistines and Ammonites. Also

[14]*History of Israelite Religion,* p. 124.
[15]*The History of Israel,* p. 171.

Map 2. Saul's Kingdom

much of Saul's interest came to be occupied with military conflict. In view of the information given in the sacred record, Saul's time was spent primarily in military matters, and little with the civil leadership of the country. This may have contributed to the weakness of his kingdom at his death, for a rule based on the military is strong only so long as the army is victorious.

Though much is stated concerning Saul's battles, little is said that characterizes his army or his methods of recruitment. According to I Samuel 14:52, one method of recruitment was by seizing any "strong man or any valiant man" that came to Saul's attention. Logic says that, for the most part, Saul simply made request of the people to provide men, and they complied. After all, if the people had sought a king to lead in battle, they must have realized that they would have to give of their men to be fighters. Some type of conscription may have been laid down, perhaps some manner of proportionate provision by tribes. Whatever the means, an army was raised and Saul was able to use it with a measure of effectiveness.

6. SAUL'S ADMINISTRATION

A clue as to Saul's administration of his kingdom may exist in II Samuel 2:8, 9. The passage describes the kingdom granted to Ish-bosheth by Abner, following Saul's death. The divisions here described could logically be expected to have existed under Saul. The passage reads:

> But Abner the son of Ner, captain of Saul's host, took Ish-bosheth the son of Saul, and brought him over to Mahanaim; and made him king over Gilead, and over the Ashurites, and over Jezreel, and over Ephraim, and over Benjamin, and over all Israel.

From this passage, Yohanan Aharoni identifies the districts of Saul's kingdom as follows: first, Gilead, meaning Transjordan, which no doubt included all the territory controlled by the two-and-a-half tribes there; second, Galilee, represented by the term *Ashurites* for "Asherites"; third, the Jezreel Valley, here represented by a main city within it, Jezreel; fourth, the central portion of the country represented by the important tribe of Ephraim; fifth, the southern region of Israel, where Saul's capital was located, represented by Benjamin; and sixth, the area of Judah, still further south, which is not mentioned here for it did not come under Ish-bosheth's rule.[16] Saul held it, however, and it should be included as part of his kingdom. It may well be that Saul appointed officers to supervise all these districts for the purpose of enforcing regulations and collecting taxes.

7. SAUL'S JUDICIAL SYSTEM

Nothing concrete is stated relative to the judicial system of Saul's day, and one may conclude that courts were allowed to continue as they had been

[16] *The Land of the Bible,* pp. 255-257.

instituted by God in His law. There is no way to know how effectively justice was carried out, but no society can exist without some form of judicial program.

One judicial officer designated in the law was the local elder. Israel had known elders since the days of their Egyptian bondage (Exod. 3:16-18; 19:7; Num. 11:16, 17). They were to serve as judges when someone had been killed by another (Deut. 19:12); they were to conduct inquests (Deut. 21:1, 2), hear family problems (Deut. 21:18f.), settle matrimonial disputes (Deut. 22:13-15; 25:7), and decide cases of controversy in the gate of the city (Ruth 4:2).

Regular courts also existed, many local and one supreme. Each community had "judges and officers" for its local court. They sat in the gate of the city (Deut. 16:18), apparently sharing cases with the elders.[17] When cases were too complicated for the local court, they could be sent to the supreme court (Deut. 17:8f.). This court sat at the central sanctuary, which was at Shiloh for most of the period of the judges, but where it may have been in Saul's time is unknown.[18] It was composed of priests and lay judges. The latter conducted investigations (Deut. 19:18) and the former served as legal counsels. Decisions required at least two witnesses (Deut. 19:15), and if a witness proved false he received the punishment that the accused would have suffered had he been found guilty (Deut. 19:16-19). Punishment was executed without delay (Num. 15:36; Deut. 22:18) and was sometimes carried out in the presence of the judges (Deut. 25:2f.), even at times by the officials themselves (Deut. 22:18). If the sentence was stoning, many people assisted (Num. 15:36; Deut. 22:21), and the witnesses had to throw the first stone (Deut. 13:9).

8. SAUL'S RELATION TO THE PRIESTS AND LEVITES

It has been seen that Saul was a God-fearing man, especially at the time of his inauguration. This would lead one to think that his religious relationships were commendable. This was not the case, however, and various factors show this. In considering them, it is logical to begin with a review of the situation involving the ark, tabernacle, and priesthood at the time of Saul's rule.

a. Situation of the ark, tabernacle, and priesthood

When Saul became Israel's first king, Shiloh no longer was the center of religious life, as it had been during most of the period of the judges. In fact,

[17]The Lachish ostraca were discovered in the gate of Lachish, for they were part of the evidence in a trial in progress at the time of the city's destruction. Cf. Deut. 21:19; Prov. 22:22; Amos 5:15. For the ostraca, cf. Harry Torczyner, *The Lachish Letters,* 1935; or *Documents from Old Testament Times,* ed. D. Winton Thomas, pp. 212-217.

[18]The ark had been away from Shiloh since the battle of Aphek, and the tabernacle was now at Nob (I Sam. 21:1).

it had not been the center since the disastrous battle of Aphek, when the ark had been seized by the Philistines (I Sam. 4:1-11). This had occurred perhaps twenty-five years before.[19] The ark was now at Kirjath-jearim, where it had been since shortly after the battle of Aphek (I Sam. 7:1, 2). The tabernacle was at Nob (I Sam. 21:1). It probably had been taken there —perhaps by Samuel—soon after the battle of Aphek to save it from the Philistines. The high priest of the day was Ahimelech (I Sam. 21:1), and he served at Nob along with eighty-four ordinary priests (I Sam. 22:18). Presumably they conducted sacrifices there, probably attempting to follow the ceremonial law as closely as they could; but, of course, so long as the ark was absent, the atmosphere must have been greatly different. The ark, after all, was the representation of God's presence, and its absence made the tabernacle only a sort of semiofficial place of worship. It is noteworthy that Samuel is never depicted as going there, but instead as offering sacrifice himself at a high place (I Sam. 9:12-19).[20]

The matter to notice, in respect to Saul, is that he did nothing about improving the situation. God had intended from the first that the ark remain in the tabernacle. It should never have been taken out and transported to the battle scene at Aphek; and it no doubt would not have been so transported had the priests in charge at the time been other than the wicked Hophni and Phinehas. When Saul came to office, he had the authority to order the ark returned to the tabernacle, but he did not do so. Though no indication is given regarding his attitude toward the tabernacle and the ark, one is left with the impression that he remained quite uninterested, being occupied instead with military concerns and, in the latter part of his reign, with pursuing David.

b. Relation to priestly activity

Three early occasions are noted when Saul became involved with priestly activity, and two are definitely not favorable to him. The first concerns his initial time of rejection as Israel's king (I Sam. 13:8-14). Because this occasion is discussed elsewhere, it need be said only that at this time (just before the battle of Michmash) Saul actually intruded into the priest's office, as he offered sacrifice himself. Only the priests were to sacrifice, and Saul was not even a Levite (being of the tribe of Benjamin). He was terribly wrong in this action.

[19]Twenty years (I Sam. 7:2) had elapsed between the battle of Aphek and that of Mizpeh (I Sam. 7:7-13), and only a few years—probably not more than five—had elapsed since that time until Saul's inauguration.

[20]High places later came to be denounced in every reference to them (see I Kings 14:22, 23; 15:14), but every mention of them from the loss of the ark at Shiloh until Solomon's building of the temple is in a favorable context (see I Sam. 9:19; 10:5, 13; I Kings 3:2-4; I Chron. 16:39; II Chron. 1:3, 13).

The second occasion is first favorable to Saul and then unfavorable. It also occurred in connection with the battle of Michmash. According to I Samuel 14:18, Saul asked the high priest while the battle was in progress to inquire of God by means of the ephod.[21] This in itself was good, for the Urim and Thummim, contained in the ephod, constituted God's designated method by which to communicate His will to the people (Exod. 28:30; Num. 27:21). A change for the worse came, however, when Saul, suddenly hearing the sound of the battle increase, told the high priest to withdraw his hand. This meant that he should cease making the inquiry. Saul apparently felt it was more important to get back to the struggle than to hear a word from God. In this, he was very mistaken and showed disrespect both for the high priest and especially God.

The third occasion is difficult to assess, but is probably best evaluated as favorable to Saul. In I Samuel 14:35, where the scene concerns a victory in the very battle just noted, Saul is said to have "built an altar unto the LORD." The context does not imply any displeasure on God's part with his action. This suggests that the altar was built as an expression of thanksgiving rather than as a place of sacrifice.[22] If so, this was not a case of intrusion into the priestly office but an indication that Saul desired to do something to show his gratitude to God for the victory just won.

c. An outrageous slaughter of priests

Many years after these early occasions, Saul committed his worst offense in respect to the priesthood. He actually ordered the slaughter of eighty-five priests that lived at Nob, along with their families and livestock (I Sam. 22:18, 19). This occasion has been mentioned earlier and will be at length later. Now it need be said only that Saul here reached the very lowest depths in his relationship with God's priestly representatives. He could hardly have done anything more displeasing to God.

Another action that may have followed this, and would have been related to it, was the appointment of Zadok as the new high priest. It is never said that Saul made this appointment, but at any rate Zadok held the office, along with Abiathar, when David began to reign, and it is not likely that David would have appointed him when he already had a high priest in Abiathar.

[21]Though the Masoretic text uses the word *ark* here, rather than *ephod,* it is better to read "ephod" for the following reasons: 1) Inquiry by the Urim and Thummim is never associated with the ark but with the ephod; 2) the ark at this time was at Kirjath-jearim and it is not likely that it would have been brought to this battle and then returned to Kirjath-jearim; 3) the ark was not an object to be "brought hither" and then treated lightly as here implied, but this expression was not uncommon regarding the ephod (see I Sam. 23:9; 30:7); 4) the Septuagint employs the word *ephod.*

[22]After the conquest of Canaan years before, the two-and-a-half tribes in returning home had made an altar at the Jordan for a nonsacrificial reason (Josh. 22:11-29).

The situation was this. Abiathar, son of Ahimelech, was able to escape the slaughter at Nob and run to David (I Sam. 22:20-23). Since he survived the former high priest, he automatically became the new high priest, and David recognized him as such by soon asking him to consult the ephod for him (I Sam. 23:9-12). With Abiathar gone from Saul's domain, however, the country was left without a high priest. It would have been logical, therefore, for Saul to appoint a new one such as Zadok. In so doing, the selection was made from the line of Eleazar (I Chron. 6:4-8) rather than from the line of Ithamar. Ahimelech and therefore Abiathar were of the line of Ithamar (I Chron. 24:3). Zadok's selection returned the high priesthood to the lineage of Eleazar, the older of these two sons of Aaron, where it had been at the first. The change had occurred sometime prior to Eli.

If Saul did make this appointment, it shows that he continued to respect the office enough to keep it in existence. God had intended only one high priest to serve at a time and Saul would have brought two into existence by such an appointment. This in itself was wrong, but Saul may not have known that Abiathar yet lived. It would seem that he is to be commended, if he did make the appointment.

8

Saul's Rule

The sacred record does not tell about Saul's setting up his kingdom. It proceeds directly from the account of his inauguration as king (I Sam. 11:14—12:5) to describe his first military engagement, which saw the Philistines as the enemy. On the basis of what has been seen in Chapter 7, however, one may imagine him, soon after that important coronation day, putting forth efforts to get things started. Gibeah, his home town, was selected as his capital—perhaps for the reason that, since there was need for land, he could use some of his own for want of funds to procure other. He evidently declared his own family as his official family, and probably formed an army as his first public act. At least he had an army of 3,000 by the time of his first battle, which is the initial matter from his reign to be described (I Sam. 13).

A. THE MICHMASH BATTLE

The criterion God observed in making selection of what material to include in the Bible was clearly the religious significance of an event or action. Since Saul's encounter with the Philistines at Michmash is described at length, one may be sure that God saw it as involving considerable religious significance. The account would be treated improperly if this factor were overlooked.

1. THE DATE

A first matter to consider is the date of the occasion. This is not easily determined because I Samuel 13:1, which gives the date, presents problems in its reading. Literally, it says, "A son of a year was Saul when he began to reign, and two years he reigned over Israel." The phrase "son of a year" is the regular Hebrew idiom for indicating a person's age, and the Targums (Aramaic translations) accordingly paraphrase the verse to read, "Saul was as innocent as a one-year-old child when he began to reign." But obviously Saul was more than one year old at his inauguration, both in view of the story overall and the fact that he already had a son Jonathan who was able to lead a troop of soldiers (I Sam. 13:2). A number which gave Saul's age must at some time have been omitted by the copyist. Since Saul ruled a total of forty years (Acts 13:21) he could hardly have been more than forty here, making then a total of eighty years for his life. He could not have been much less than forty either, to account for Jonathan's age at this time.

Many expositors believe that there is also an omission in the second part of the verse ("and two years he reigned over Israel"), but the evidence is not so conclusive.[1] Their thinking is based mainly on the fact that the total verse carries the pattern of later passages which first give the age of an incoming king and then the total length of his rule (see, e.g., II Sam. 2:10; 5:4; I Kings 14:21; 22:42). It is obvious that Saul ruled more than two years.

In response, however, several matters are noteworthy. First, Saul was Israel's first king, and this manner of formula may not have been employed this early. Second, if a number was omitted before "two," the total number would have had to end in a "two," such as "twenty-two" or "thirty-two," but this is out of keeping with Acts 13:21. And, third, the number here given, "two years," fits in well with an implication found in verse 2, which ends with the words, "and the rest of the people he sent every man to his tent." These words suggest that the particular time in mind at the close of verse 2 was the occasion of Saul's inauguration at Gilgal (which, on this basis, would have been just two years earlier). He had just defeated the Ammonites at Jabesh-gilead and so had the army then employed still with him. From this army he could have chosen the 3,000 mentioned earlier in the verse and then sent the others home. That the battle now described happened soon in Saul's rule follows also from the Philistines' natural desire to make their presence known early to this new king. Two years is about as long as they would have wanted to wait.

In view of these considerations, it seems best to understand the verse in the following manner: "And Saul was ____ years old when he began to rule,

[1]C. F. Keil and F. Delitzsch, *Biblical Commentary on the Books of Samuel,* pp. 122-124; Samuel R. Driver, *Notes on the Hebrew Text of the Books of Samuel,* pp. 96-97.

and when he had ruled two years over Israel [the following story transpired]." If this is the correct solution, the date of the battle was at the close of Saul's second year.

2. THE PLACE

The place of the battle is identified much more certainly. It was in the area of Michmash,[2] approximately four miles northeast of Saul's capital, Gibeah. Various aspects of the battle transpired in different places, but all in this general vicinity where the main Philistine forces gathered (I Sam. 13:5, 16, 23).

3. AN INITIAL VICTORY BY JONATHAN

a. The story (I Sam. 13:1-7)

Saul had kept 3,000 of his troops with him after his inauguration, holding 2,000 for himself and 1,000 for Jonathan.[3] Why Abner did not figure in the struggle is not revealed. It may be that his appointment as military commander (I Sam. 14:50) did not come until later—another argument for the earliness of the battle. Saul kept his men in two places, Michmash and Bethel, and Jonathan kept his in the capital city, Gibeah.

The major battle was precipitated by an early skirmish on the part of Jonathan. Perhaps more bold than his father, he took his 1,000 men and made a raid on a Philistine garrison that was quartered in Geba, about two-thirds of the way from Gibeah to Michmash. He defeated the soldiers there, and news soon came to the Philistines back in their home territory. They quickly set out to bring reprisal, and their number is given as 30,000 chariots, 6,000 horsemen, and a multitude of people (13:5).[4] They came to Michmash, apparently near to where Saul had quartered part of his troops.

Three events transpired for Israel as a result of Jonathan's victory. Saul himself "blew the trumpet throughout all the land," no doubt to let the people know the good news of the triumph (13:3). On hearing the glad sound, the people understood that the Philistines were angry and were coming in strength against them. Consequently, many sought refuge in caves, thickets, rocks, high places, and pits (13:6). And Saul then called for an assembly in Gilgal, down in the Jordan Valley where he had been crowned, about ten miles east of Michmash (though the exact location of Gilgal remains unknown).

[2]Present-day Mukhmas, on the northern ridge of Wadi Suweinit, east of Bethel on the way to Jericho.

[3]Keeping these troops intact, after the battle of Jabesh-gilead, solved the problem of raising an army again.

[4]Some expositors believe the number 30,000 to be the result of a copyist's error, since so many chariots in the hill country of Michmash is hard to imagine; see John Davis, *The Birth of a Kingdom,* p. 55.

b. Points to notice

1) ***The existence of Philistine garrisons.*** One matter concerns the Philistine garrisons, which are shown to have been existent at this time within Israel. According to I Samuel 7:7-13, the Philistines had been thoroughly routed in the earlier battle of Mizpeh, and one might think that they would not have been able to keep garrisons (for the purpose of maintaining control) in Israel following that occasion. Verse 3 of I Samuel 13 (and I Sam. 10:5 and I Chron. 11:16), however, shows that they had been able to do this. Jonathan here attacked and defeated one of these garrisons. No doubt the number of such garrisons and the degree to which they could exercise control were much less following the battle of Mizpeh, but they did continue in some measure. That they had been greatly reduced, indeed, is evidenced by Saul's ability earlier to assemble his large army to fight the Ammonites at Jabesh-gilead—apparently without Philistine interference.[5] Also, during the two years of his rule that had now elapsed, Saul had been able to station his own army at Michmash and Bethel—thus in the very area of the Philistine garrison of Geba—and not be molested by them.

2) ***God's provision for Saul's army.*** It is evident that God used the battle at Jabesh-gilead also for a purpose other than merely to bring Saul to the attention of the people, important as that was in itself. It provided Saul with the basis for a continuing army. He needed such an army; the people had requested a king especially to lead against foreign enemies. But if such an occasion as the encounter at Jabesh-gilead had not come to pass, Saul may have had a problem in raising an army. To do so would have meant some kind of recruitment program, and people might well have been slow to respond. Jabesh-gilead, however, provided just the type of situation to appeal to men waiting for action and to solicit their willingness to enlist. Then, with the battle won, and the new king crowned, it was appropriate to retain many of these men to make the standing army. Saul now had the authority to command this, and the thinking of the men themselves, having won an important battle already, could have been quite amenable to continuing as members in the army.

That Saul chose only 3,000 out of the total that had fought was probably due to two factors: first, they had to be few enough in number for him to be able to feed, clothe, and house; and, second, he probably did not contemplate fighting the Philistines so soon after his inauguration. When Jonathan precipitated matters just two years later, Saul may have wished that he had retained more.

[5]Martin Noth recognizes this unusual situation, and attempts in various ways to account for it, apart from recognizing the significance of the Mizpeh victory (*History of Israel*, pp. 169-170).

3) ***Jonathan's courage and ability.*** Though Jonathan may have acted somewhat hastily in his attack on the Philistine garrison—and probably to his father's consternation at first—he did show remarkable ability and courage in making it. He evidently saw the Philistine garrison as a "cancerous sore" in Israel, and apparently on his own part decided to eliminate it. That he did not consult his father beforehand can be inferred from the fact that Saul did not help. Jonathan may not have wanted to consult him for fear that his father would forbid the action. Jonathan himself was ready for it and thus displayed courage; that he then won the battle showed ability.

4) ***A continuing fear of the Philistines.*** The story shows also that a deep-seated fear of the Philistines still remained among the Israelites. As soon as news of Jonathan's action came to them, along with information that they were now held in "abomination"[6] by the Philistines as a result (13:4), many of them went into hiding and some even left their homes to flee across the Jordan (13:6, 7). They had shown the same fear at the time of the battle of Mizpeh (I Sam. 7:7, 8), and that victory clearly had not removed the fear entirely. Evidently the earlier Philistine oppression had been very severe and had made a lasting impression. The people should have realized, however, that they needed to fear this enemy only so long as they were themselves outside of God's blessing. When they were under His blessing, God could and would protect them, as He had at Mizpeh.

4. SAUL'S SIN AND FIRST REJECTION

a. The story (I Sam. 13:8-14)

Saul's call for an assembly at Gilgal was in itself good, though it resulted in his first rejection as king. Saul arranged with Samuel to meet together for the purpose of offering sacrifice. Saul apparently recognized that a major battle with the Philistines was inevitable, and he wanted God's blessing when it joined. The agreement with Samuel had specified seven days as the time Saul would wait for the great prophet to come to officiate. Saul did wait *until* the seventh day, but then grew impatient and proceeded to make the sacrifice himself. Then, just as he had finished doing so, Samuel came—apparently yet within the seven-day period designated. When he saw what Saul had done, he rebuked the king severely. Saul had acted foolishly, for he had not kept God's commandment (in respect to who should offer sacrifice). Because he had not, Saul's family would not continue to rule, for God would now select another to replace Saul, one who would be after God's own heart. With this severe rebuke and information given, Samuel turned and left, going up to the capital, Gibeah.

[6]Literally, "were odious to"; the same word is used here as for spoiled manna in Exod. 16:20-24.

b. Points to notice

1) ***Saul's choice of Gilgal.*** The place on which Saul and Samuel agreed for the sacrifice was Gilgal, down in the Jordan Valley. Some expositors have suggested that this was because the Philistines so controlled the hill country that Gilgal was the only place that was safe. There may be some truth to the thought, but this degree of control could have existed only after the Philistines had arrived for the battle at Michmash. Before this, when there was merely a Philistine garrison at Geba, the enemy had not been that strong. Another reason—and perhaps more significant—was that Gilgal was the place where the people had crowned Saul just two years before, and it carried a pleasant and triumphant memory for them because of the victory at Jabesh-gilead. Gilgal was also sufficiently removed from the center of the Philistine forces so that people would be willing to come there in adequate numbers for the occasion.

2) ***Reason for the gathering.*** The full reason for calling the gathering was probably threefold: first, it provided a way of rallying the people and giving them confidence, when they were so fearful of the dreaded Philistines. No doubt Saul used his seven days of waiting for Samuel to good advantage in attempting to bolster their courage. Second, the gathering may have served as a way of recruiting more soldiers. Saul now needed more than the 3,000 he had kept with him after the earlier events at Gilgal. This could provide a way of getting them. Saul may have seen the occasion as parallel to the gathering he had called at Bezek (I Sam. 11:8), previous to the Jabesh-gilead battle, when 330,000 had come. Certainly there was nothing like this response now at Gilgal, however. And, third, it was mainly a time to seek God's favor in the forthcoming battle by offering sacrifice. Saul shows that he knew he should not offer this himself by arranging for Samuel (who was a Levite) to come for the purpose and by waiting for him more than six days. All this means that the idea was a good one, and Saul is to be commended for it.

3) ***Propriety of such an altar.*** Some liberal scholars still contend that Israelites could, and did, make altars as they wished, until the time of Josiah. They believe that Saul's altar here (as well as those of Gideon—Judg. 6:24; Manoah—Judg. 13:19, 20; Elijah, I Kings 18:31, 32, and others) gives evidence of this. Accordingly, they argue that Deuteronomy must have been written late for it prohibits such altars (Deut. 7:5-7; 16:5, 6). This view must be rejected, for Deuteronomy was written by Moses (Deut. 1:1; 31:24-26). Israel's one and only place of regular and ordinary worship in sacrifice was at the tabernacle in Shiloh, so long as the ark was there, and later in Jerusalem after the ark had been brought there. Saul's making an

altar (as well as the construction of all similar altars that can be mentioned) was a special instance in view of an unusual situation. Nothing in the story suggests that an altar either had been here before or remained after. There was no continuous altar at Gilgal.

Indeed, that altars could not be made at will is shown by the incident recorded in Joshua 22:9-29. At the time described, the soldiers of Reuben, Gad, and half of Manasseh, who were returning home after helping in the conquest of Palestine proper, had built an altar at the Jordan River. As a result, the western tribes were so disturbed that they were ready to punish the eastern tribes by war. This was alleviated only when a committee was sent to ask the reason for the altar and was informed that it was built only as a memorial and not a place of sacrifice.

4) ***Saul's impatience.*** Patience is a virtue that not many people have. Saul became impatient in waiting for Samuel and went ahead to offer the sacrifice himself. He thought he had good reason (I Sam. 13:11): first, because at least some of the people who had come (of whom there may not have been a great number in the first place) were leaving, probably in fear that the Philistines might come and attack; second, because Samuel delayed in coming; and, third, because the Philistines were gathering at Michmash, thus making Saul anxious to get on with the actual battle.[7] These reasons, though they may have seemed formidable to Saul at the time, were not sufficient to warrant his sinning as he did. He should have trusted God to take care of such matters and kept his promise with Samuel.

5) ***Reason for Samuel's being late.*** That Samuel did not come until the last day may well have been at God's direction. It was probably a way of testing the new king. Would he demonstrate the kind of faith in God that would keep him from becoming impatient, or would he not? Saul demonstrated that he did not have such faith and thereby showed that he was unworthy of continuing as Israel's king.

6) ***Saul's real sin.*** The question has often been asked: what was Saul's great sin that prompted God's rejection at this time? The answer has just been seen in part: Saul failed to demonstrate adequate faith in God to wait for Samuel. The main sin, however, is indicated in I Samuel 13:12—the sin of offering a sacrifice when he had no authority to do so. Thus, he entered upon the priest's office, when he was not even a Levite.

The fact that others who were not of Levitic descent did offer sacrifices without being denounced cannot be cited as an argument justifying Saul's

[7]It need not be thought that the Philistines had already reached Michmash in strength. It would have taken them a little time to group and come there after Jonathan's defeat of the garrison, during which time Saul could have gathered the assembly at Gilgal.

action. The situation was different here. Samuel, a Levite, was available and arrangements for him to do the work had already been made. All Saul had to do was wait for him. In the case of Gideon, Manoah, Elijah, and others, there were no Levites immediately available; moreover, those occasions were of a nature that called for the individuals involved to offer the sacrifice themselves. It is sometimes asserted that Solomon sacrificed (I Kings 3:4, 15), and surely there were priests and Levites available to him. It is true that Solomon is said to have sacrificed, but it is also true that he did so by means of those very priests and Levites. No less than one thousand sacrifices were offered at the time (I Kings 3:4), and Solomon could not have offered them all himself.

7) ***No continuing break between Samuel and Saul.*** William F. Albright believes that with this word of rejection from Samuel, a break in good relations came between Samuel and Saul, and that the break widened with the passing of time.[8] This view is not in keeping with the scriptural presentation, however. There is no word of animosity indicated on this occasion by either Samuel or Saul, nor was there any later at the time of the second rejection. At that time, indeed, Saul even held on to Samuel physically, following the announcement of rejection, in an effort to persuade the prophet to aid him in giving worship to God (I Sam. 15:27-31). Following this, though Samuel did not see Saul again, he so "mourned for Saul" that God asked him, "How long wilt thou mourn for Saul?" (I Sam. 15:35—16:1). And later, Saul missed Samuel so much that, though the prophet had died, he went to a medium to have her bring his former advisor back from the dead in order to ask him regarding a battle with the Philistines (I Sam. 28:7-25). The reason for Samuel's severe words to Saul on the two occasions were not animosity on his part but only an act of obedience to God who had instructed him to speak in this way. The rejections probably hurt Samuel nearly as much as Saul.

8) ***A problem involving a continuing dynasty for Saul.*** In Samuel's rebuke of Saul, he included the words, "For now would the LORD have established thy kingdom upon Israel forever" (13:13). A question logically arises when one considers these words in the light of God's intention to give a continuing dynasty to David, something promised long before, as, for instance, in Genesis 49:10, "The sceptre shall not depart from Judah, nor a lawgiver from between his feet, until Shiloh come." How could the divine intention regarding David's line from Judah have been carried out if Saul's line had been established forever as indicated by Samuel?

[8] "The Biblical Period," *The Jews: Their History, Culture, and Religion,* ed. L. Finkelstein, p. 49.

The answer lies in the eternal decrees and knowledge of God. What Samuel said was certainly true, namely, that had Saul obeyed God, his family would have continued ruling forever; God's interest in and promise to Saul were fully meant. At the same time, it was divinely certain and known from all eternity that Saul would sin, and therefore there would be the need for a change of ruling family from Saul to another. This other was to be David of the tribe of Judah. It should be understood, however, that, even though David's line was eternally chosen, God's promise regarding Saul's line was still fully meant. Something of a parallel can be seen in the fully-meant offer of salvation to the sinner who persists in rejecting Christ as Savior. Just because he does so persist and finally dies in his sin in no way detracts from the validity of God's promise to save him if he would have believed. The offer to him was fully meant whether he took advantage of it or not.

5. THE PREBATTLE SITUATION

a. The story (I Sam. 13:15-23)

The remaining verses of I Samuel 13 give a significant setting for the battle proper. It consists of two parts: the relative strength of the two sides in troop size, and the major advantage the Philistines had in a monopoly on iron.

As to troop strength, the two sides were in no way comparable. Saul had only 600 men still remaining with him (13:15); the rest of his 3,000 had fearfully left him. These 600 were to fight against an enemy described as "the sand which is on the sea shore in multitude" (13:5). Saul had his few troops in Geba (not Gibeah, as in KJV), where Jonathan had earlier won his victory over the Philistine garrison. The Philistines were encamped in Michmash, where Saul's forces had been before. From there the Philistines are described as making forays in three directions: north toward Ophrah (about six miles from Michmash), west toward Beth-horon (about ten miles from Michmash), and toward the valley of Zeboim (unknown, though probably to the east), possibly meaning the Jordan Valley. These raids were likely to pillage and effect terror among the people and possibly to draw Saul out to do battle on Philistine terms.

The Philistine monopoly on iron is set forth by the words, "there was no smith" in Israel. There was no smith because there was no iron, and verse 19 tells the reason: "The Philistines said, Lest the Hebrews make them swords or spears." The Philistines had likely learned the secret of iron technology when they, as part of the Sea Peoples, had moved through Hittite territory in Asia Minor. They had a great advantage in this over the Israelites, for an iron sword could sever one made of copper, to which the Israelites apparently were now limited. And it is quite cleár that Saul's troops had few even of these, for verse 22 says that the soldiers themselves had "neither sword nor spear." Only Saul and Jonathan, the leaders, had these weapons. All this is to say that the advantage held by the Philistines, in both manpower and weapons, was very great.

The final verse of the chapter provides a transition to the following chapter. One group of Philistines went to the passage of Michmash, apparently to warn the main force of any movement by Saul's forces, for the passage lay directly between Geba and Michmash. It was this force that Jonathan was to defeat so remarkably in the early part of the following chapter.

b. Points to notice

1) ***A major test.*** The inequality of strength between the two sides made this portending battle a real test of courage for Saul and Jonathan. Certainly they would have known of this disproportion. Reports would have come to them regarding the Philistines, and they were all too aware of the decrease in their own forces and of their lack of weapons (due no doubt to disarming tactics employed by the Philistines in days gone by). Saul may have failed terribly at Gilgal, in not waiting for Samuel, but at least he did not break and run here. Especially is Jonathan to be commended for the action that will come before us in the next part of the story.

2) ***Meaning of "pim."*** The aid of archaeological research for translation is illustrated in this passage. The meaning of the Hebrew word *pim* was unknown when the King James translation was made, and the conjectured translation, "yet they had a file," was employed (13:21). Excavation has now revealed small weights, found at Lachish, Jerusalem, Gezer, and Tell en-Nasbeh. The weights are about two-thirds of a shekel, or one-quarter of an ounce. The correct translation, then, is "the charge was a *pim*" (a *pim* weight of silver) for having any of the listed items sharpened. Since the Israelites did not have iron, they had to go to a Philistine smith who had the proper iron tool to care for their bronze implements.

3) ***God does not depend on numbers.*** Here is another example that shows God is not dependent on numbers of people or weapons to win His battles. Every natural indicator said that Saul and Jonathan had no chance against the superior force of the Philistines. Yet it was Saul and Jonathan that won, with the Philistines suffering a complete rout.

6. JONATHAN'S OUTSTANDING ACHIEVEMENT

a. The story (I Sam. 14:1-16)

Jonathan has already been seen in a display of courage and ability in defeating a standing garrison of Philistines (I Sam. 13:3). This did not match the occasion now described, however. Between Geba, where Saul and Jonathan were located with their 600, and Michmash, where the thousands of Philistines were quartered, lay the rugged Suweinit Gorge. It runs from the area of Bethel eastward and finally empties into the Jordan Valley. Its sides are sharp and steep in many places. It was to this gorge that a Philistine garrison had come, according to 13:23, no doubt for the purpose of warning the main force of any movement by the Israelite troops.

Jonathan knew of the strategic importance of the garrison and so, without telling his father, went with only his own armorbearer to attack it, depending on surprise and of course God's help to win a victory. His word to his companion, "For there is no restraint to the LORD to save by many or by few" (14:6), is a classic statement of faith in God. Jonathan's plan was for the party of two to traverse the precipitous gorge, thus catching the Philistines by surprise. The two made the crossing, and when they appeared coming up over the cliff, the Philistines said, disdainfully, "The Hebrews come forth out of the holes." They did not reckon with the courage and ability of Jonathan, however, for he immediately charged the group, with his helper right behind, and killed no less than twenty of the enemy before they could turn and run. The Philistines may well have imagined other Israelites coming soon behind the two and concluded that if all fought as these they wanted no part of them.

The result of this initial victory is given in verse 15. When the main Philistine host at Michmash (probably not far from this outpost) either heard of, or actually saw in the distance, this rout of the garrison, they became fearful; in fact they became so fearful that the earth shook with their shouting and confusion. The last phrase of verse 15, "a very great trembling," is literally, "a trembling of God"; the significance is that this confused state was the result of God's supernatural intervention to make Jonathan's victory have the maximum effect on the enemy. Saul's lookout in Geba now saw the Philistine host begin to melt away, as the soldiers fled in panic, even beating on one another as they did so.

b. Points to notice

1) ***Jonathan's courage, faith, and ability.*** Once again Jonathan displayed outstanding courage and ability, with the element of faith made prominent this time. How Saul may have proceeded against such Philistine odds, apart from this remarkable action of his son, one can only guess. That two men alone should have made this manner of attack took the very greatest of courage and faith. The element of faith is made plain by the classic statement mentioned earlier. Apparently Jonathan simply believed God would give him victory, in spite of the impossible odds.

Then he displayed ability. Jonathan—who must have had quite an armorbearer as well—moved ahead against an entire garrison, killing no less than twenty men. This testifies to remarkable strength, agility, and sheer skill. No doubt this element of skill had much to do with the deep friendship that later developed between Jonathan and David, for David possessed the same characteristics. Men naturally make friends among those with whom they find common ground.

2) ***Jonathan's lack of confidence in Saul.*** This is the second time that Jonathan took an action without consulting his father Saul. This is unusual and suggests a basic cause. It can hardly have been an underlying spirit of rebellion on the son's part—in view of Jonathan's character—it suggests rather that he simply lacked confidence in his father. The story which follows gives reason for this lack of confidence; Saul did not possess the same kind of faith and ability as his son. A similar lack of confidence is seen later when Jonathan planned with David how they might test Saul in respect to his attitude toward David (I Sam. 20).

3) ***The use of "signs."*** A common question asked by Christians concerns the propriety of using "signs" for determining the will of God. Jonathan used a sign here. He said to his assistant, if the enemy troops "say thus unto us, Tarry until we come to you; then we will stand still in our place. . . . But if they say thus, Come up unto us; then we will go up." He added that he and his armorbearer would know by this sign that the Lord had delivered the enemy into their hand (14:9, 10). God quite clearly honored this procedure, for He granted a remarkable victory.

Signs seem to be approved of God whenever they concern the enhancement of the project involved. This sign did. If the Philistines did not tell Jonathan and his man to stop when they first saw them, it would mean that they were not in a frame of mind to fight against them seriously, and so could be taken by surprise. The type of sign employed earlier by Gideon, when he asked that God make a fleece of wool first wet and then dry, was quite different. It had nothing to do with fighting the Midianites (his enemy) but was only a trick Gideon wanted God to perform. God performed it, but not because Gideon was right in asking for it, for God had previously told Gideon His will (Judg. 6:14; cf. v. 37).

4) ***God's supernatural intervention.*** The rout of the total Philistine force was partly the result of Jonathan's courageous action, but it was even more the result of God's supernatural intervention. The single triumph of Jonathan would not of itself have caused the panic in the large Philistine camp. After all, the Philistines numbered so many more than the Israelites, and they certainly were aware of this. There is presented here an illustration of what is sometimes called "the divine cooperative." When man has faith to move ahead, though the odds seem impossible, God is ready to step in

and finish the task. History is filled with such occasions, and the work of God would have stopped time and again if this were not true.

It is also noteworthy that God gave this remarkable blessing to the Israelite forces in spite of the recent sin and rejection of Saul. One might have thought that all blessing would have immediately been withdrawn. It was not, however; God continued to bless in spite of the failure. As will be seen when we consider Saul's second rejection, this first occasion was probably a sort of probationary indication, rather than a final rejection, and under this condition God could continue to bless.

7. A MAJOR PHILISTINE DEFEAT

a. The story (I Sam. 14:20-23, 31, 46)

On learning the unexpected good news that the Philistines were in apparent confusion, Saul quickly moved with his 600 troops to the camp of the Philistines at Michmash. On coming there, he found matters as the lookout

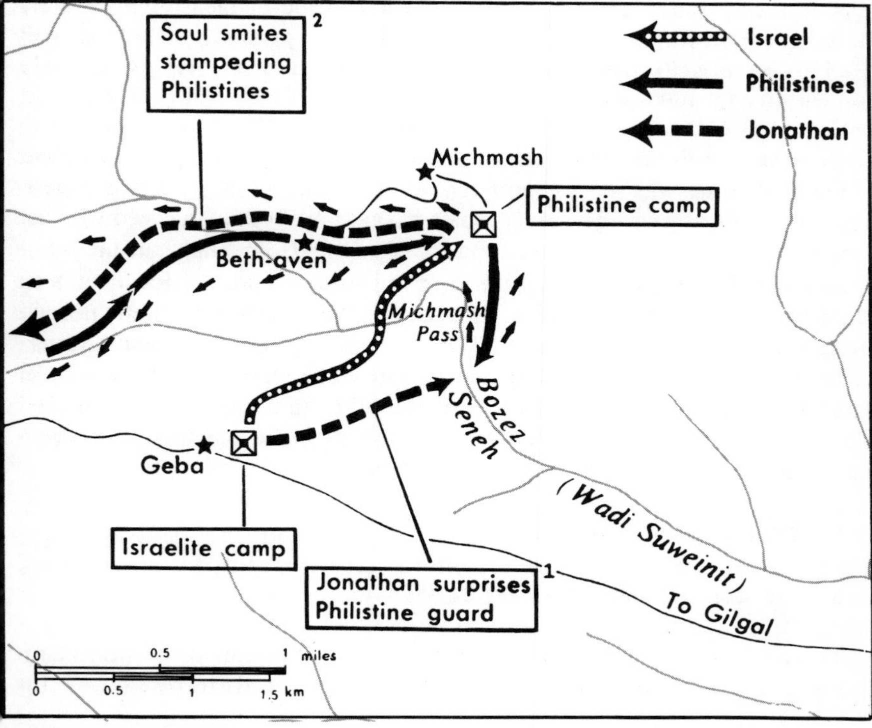

Map 3. The Michmash Battle

had described: "Every man's sword was against his fellow, and there was a very great discomfiture" (14:20). Also, when he arrived he received the pleasant surprise that Hebrews who had been fighting along with the Philistine troops—possibly as hired mercenaries—were now deserting to his side, and that other Israelites, who had earlier hidden from the Philistines, were leaving their hiding places and joining in the fray. This added further both to Philistine confusion and to the strength of Saul's forces, so that now the Philistines retreated rapidly. According to verse 23, the fighting soon had moved westward as far as Beth-aven, about a mile from Michmash, and then all became a rout with the chase continuing as far as Aijalon (14:31), about eighteen miles distant. Thus, Israel came to be rid of the Philistine army that had seemed ready to take over the whole land. And no doubt Saul came to be highly admired by his subjects, though the greatest credit belonged to Jonathan.

b. Points to notice

1) ***God's blessing.*** The blessing of God thus was now bestowed on Saul's action as it had been on Jonathan's. This was not only in spite of the recent rejection, but also in spite of two very unwise, God-displeasing actions by the king, which will be considered next. One can say only that God was still gracious to Israel's new king at this time, apparently giving him every opportunity to make good.

2) ***A lasting Philistine defeat.*** There is reason to believe that this defeat of the Philistines was severe enough so that no further conflict was experienced for several years. Evidence exists in that Saul fought succeeding wars against Moab, Ammon, Edom, and Zobah (14:47). If Saul had had continuing problems with the neighboring Philistines, he would not have been able to fight these other enemies. Though the Philistines are also mentioned along with these other nations (14:47), no major conflict is implied. Apparently none occurred until the much later time when David had come to calm Saul in his times of attack by the "evil spirit" (I Sam. 16-17).[9] God indeed gave Saul a good start in respect to this Philistine menace, which had been a main concern of the people in desiring a king.

8. TWO UNWISE ACTIONS OF SAUL

a. The story (I Sam. 14:17-19, 24-45)

1) ***The Urim and Thummim.*** Saul's first unwise action at this point concerned the Urim and Thummim (14:17-19). Little needs to be said of this

[9]Probably about twenty-five years later—see p. 138.

matter here because it was discussed in Chapter 7. Yet, passing notice should be given, for now the occasion can be seen in its setting.

On learning of the unexpected good news that the Philistines were apparently going into retreat, Saul first asked the high priest, who was present with the ephod,[10] to make inquiry of God as to procedure, and then, before the inquiry could be completed, he told the man to cease. Instead he moved ahead with his own ideas. Thus, Saul first and properly thought of consulting God on procedure, but changed his mind, considering haste more important than hearing from God. This is never right.

2) ***A foolish order.*** Saul's second unwise action concerned a very unwise order to his men. It was probably given already before the first move by the army against the Philistines. It forbade the troops to eat any food until evening, so that Saul might be avenged on his enemies. The order was foolish because the men needed the strength that food would give in order to make pursuit of the enemy. Saul's thinking in making the foolish command is not indicated. He related it to winning the war; this suggests he thought thereby to gain God's favor. Perhaps he thus was trying to offset the mistake he had made at Gilgal. Or perhaps it was an attempt to show the people that though Jonathan had just won a significant battle, he, Saul, was the one with authority to give commands.

One result of this order was that it caused the troops to sin in God's sight. When they captured the spoil of the enemy in the pursuit, they flew upon it in their hunger and ate the meat of the sheep, oxen, and calves raw, with the blood yet in it (14:32). This was in direct violation of the law, which forbade eating blood (Lev. 19:26). On learning of this, Saul commanded a large stone to be set up so that the animals might be killed on it, and the blood might run off (I Sam. 14:33, 34). Then Saul built an altar, apparently in a further attempt to appease God (14:35).

Another result was that the order nearly resulted in the death of Jonathan, the true hero of the battle. Jonathan, not being with the main group, had not learned of Saul's rash order, and so ate some honey he found in the woods as he passed through in pursuit of the enemy (14:27-30). He was told of the order when it was too late, and he appropriately pointed out to the informer that the order had been unwise, since he had personally received strength from the honey. Jonathan's action came to Saul's attention when he attempted again to hear from God by means of the Urim and Thummim (14:37-42).[11] Saul wanted to know whether he should further attack the Philistines; however, no answer from God was forthcoming. Saul then asked that a lot be cast between the two leaders (Saul and Jonathan)

[10]See p. 119, n. 21.

[11]Though the Urim and Thummim are not here mentioned by name, in view of the earlier mention of the ephod, it is all but certain that they were employed.

and the people and, when he and Jonathan were taken, between himself and Jonathan, to determine whose sin was the root cause of God's refusal to answer. The casting of the lot indicated that Jonathan was the guilty party. Then Saul called his son, determined that he should die. After Jonathan told him about eating the honey, the troops intervened to make Saul change his mind about taking the young man's life (14:43-45).

b. Points to notice

1) ***God's revelation to be taken seriously.*** In Saul's first unwise action, he had refused to wait for God's answer to a revelation he had requested. This was an insult to God. It is no wonder that when Saul inquired again (v. 37) God refused to reply.[12] God's word is never to be taken lightly. When God speaks, men are to listen and listen well.

2) ***Hearing from God is more important than haste.*** The reason why Saul had refused to wait for God's answer was that he felt the situation called for haste. It did, but not so much that he could not wait to hear God's directions. By moving ahead at the time, he was saying that his own plans were adequate and that he had no reason to wait for God. He was extremely wrong in this thinking.

3) ***Necessity of responsible decisions.*** Saul did not act responsibly in ordering his men not to eat. Whatever reason he had in mind, it was inadequate. Common sense, which is always so important, said that the troops needed strength if they were to pursue the enemy effectively. Sometimes eating may be more pleasing to God than fasting, if strength is needed to accomplish a work God has given a person to do. One might argue that to fast would be so pleasing to God that He would miraculously give the strength necessary. He did not in the case here, and it would be most unusual for Him to do so at any time.

4) ***Wisdom of listening to people.*** Leaders should always have an ear for what their people are saying. Grave mistakes have been made in the name of authority, mistakes which could have been avoided had the leader listened to his people. In this case, Saul would have made the tragic mistake of killing the best commander he had, Jonathan, if he had not listened to his troops. He might have turned a deaf ear, thinking that his authority had been violated. But if he had, the loss sustained would have been irreparable.

[12]That Jonathan had unknowingly disobeyed Saul's order was certainly only a secondary reason for God's refusal to reply to Saul.

B. SAUL'S PERIOD OF SUCCESS

1. THE STORY (I SAM. 14:47)

In remarkable brevity, one verse only is devoted to telling of a period when Saul enjoyed true success as Israel's king. It says first that he "took the kingdom over Israel." The thought is that Saul now, in view of this most significant victory over the feared Philistines, was able to assume a position of authority not available to him before. People were willing to listen and obey and accept regulations. The first victory over the Ammonites had led to his crowning; this one led to a higher level of authority in his position as king. It is quite possible, as a result, that it was at this time that he imposed a stronger taxation program and perhaps made divisions within his country, as implied in II Samuel 2:9.[13]

The verse sets forth next a list of countries over which Saul in this new position of strength was able to gain victory. They included the formidable powers of Moab and Ammon (both in Transjordan), Edom (to the south), and Zobah (to the far north).[14] The Philistines are also listed, perhaps because they remained a perennial threat, though quiet for a time, or perhaps because some minor battles were fought with them occasionally to keep them in check. But as we have seen, the first major battle with the Philistines after the Michmash defeat was much later. The battle with the Amalekites mentioned in verse 48 is no doubt the occasion described at length in I Samuel 15, to be discussed presently.

2. POINTS TO NOTICE

a. Saul's achievement

Though the indication is brief, Saul's achievement must not be minimized. He did establish himself as a true and commendable ruler during the years in view. He had won decisive victories over the two main enemies that Israel had so feared, the Ammonites and Philistines, and this gave him solid favor with the people. His kingdom became well established at home. And with this firm base in hand, he was able to contend successfully with other outside powers.

Moab, Ammon, and Edom, all close neighbors, were perennial foes of Israel, and apparently Saul was able to keep them in check. Somehow a quarrel developed even with faraway Zobah, and he evidently was successful against this country as well. It should be recognized, however, that he

[13]See pp. 113-114.

[14]This last enemy is especially noteworthy, since it was so far away, even north of Damascus. One has to wonder how Saul became involved with a country this far away, but the identification is unmistakable.

was not successful to the degree David was, for these countries were not brought under the control of Israel at this time. Apparently, they simply were held off from making inroads or taking advantage of Israel, as so many enemy groups had done in the days of the judges. This much, however, would have enhanced Israel's reputation greatly in the world of the day. It also would have added to Saul's popularity at home.

b. Duration of this period

A question of interest concerns the length of Saul's successful years. He ruled a total of forty years (Acts 13:21); how much of this time did Saul's successes cover? The approximate duration can be figured on the basis of David's anointing. David was anointed (I Sam. 16:13) almost immediately after the second rejection of Saul (I Sam. 15). It was this rejection that brought the successful period to a close. So at what point in Saul's reign was David anointed?

The answer is probably about Saul's twenty-fifth year of rule. According to II Samuel 5:4, David was thirty years old when he began to rule in Hebron. This means he was born after Saul had ruled ten years. David's age at his anointing is not given, but he was old enough to care for the family sheep by himself (I Sam. 16:11), a fact which suggests at least the middle teen years. If he was fifteen, this would be added to the ten years noted, making the total twenty-five. It would appear, then, that Saul's successes covered about twenty-five years, leaving fifteen years for his time of downgrade.

c. Criterion of scriptural reporting

The conclusion that Saul ruled well for twenty-five years brings out a noteworthy factor in respect to the recording of history in the sacred text. One verse (I Sam. 14:47) is all that is devoted to the successful years of Saul, whereas the two occasions of rejection—which occupied only a few days each—are both given detailed descriptions (I Sam. 13 and 15). One is reminded that the biblical criterion of what material to include was not merely history as such; it was history that was religiously significant. The two occasions of rejection revealed Saul's attitude toward God and also the reason why God saw the need for a change in Israelite rule. The events of the intervening years, though important to Saul, in terms of a religious relationship to God were apparently not of sufficient importance to merit recording.

C. THE AMALEKITE BATTLE

Saul's battle with the Amalekites involved his second rejection by God. It occurred, as noted, after Saul had reigned twenty-five years, or twenty-three years after the battle of Michmash and the first rejection.

1. THE DIVINE COMMAND

a. The story (I Sam. 15:1-3)

The occasion of this Amalekite battle was a command from God through Samuel: Saul should make an offensive attack against this southern tribal neighbor. The order was: "Go and smite Amalek, and utterly destroy all that they have, and spare them not; but slay both man and woman, infant and suckling, ox and sheep, camel and ass" (15:3). The reason for the severe command was that the "LORD of hosts" remembered "that which Amalek did to Israel, how he laid wait for him in the way, when he came up from Egypt" (15:2).

The occasion in mind is recorded in Exodus 17:8-14. The Amalekites, who lived by raid and pillage, had made Israel their target as the people moved south from the Red Sea and headed toward Mount Sinai. According to Deuteronomy 25:17, 18, the Amalekites met them already at the time of crossing the sea and then kept striking against the stragglers of the host, the weak and feeble who had trouble keeping up with the others. Finally, at Rephidim, which was in the vicinity of Mount Sinai, Moses directed Joshua to select and lead an army against the raiders. He did so, and, with help supplied by God when Moses raised his hands in dependent entreaty (Exod. 17:11, 12), won a decisive victory. At the time, God said that this action by the Amalekites would be remembered against them and that they would in time be utterly destroyed (Exod. 17:14; cf. Deut. 25:19). That time had now come, since Israel was here in a position of sufficient strength to carry the action through.

b. Points to notice

1) ***Samuel and Saul.*** Though this is the first mention of contact between Samuel and Saul in twenty-three years, one need not conclude there had not been others. The contacts described show that Saul held Samuel in high esteem, though the prophet was the one who brought the two messages of rejection. It is reasonable to believe that the two had seen each other quite often during Saul's successful years.

2) ***A severe order.*** God's commanding an Israelite king to destroy an enemy utterly has often been cause for wonderment regarding God's justice. How could a just God give this severe type of command? The answer must be that while God sees all sin as equally serious, the sin of Amalek in continually attacking Israel in her weakness was considered particularly blameworthy. God spoke concerning this enemy in a way that was more condemnatory than were His pronouncements concerning any other enemy. Their great sin evidently was in attacking Israel as they did:

repeatedly taking advantage of the weak and helpless. It is quite clear that God considers this type of sin to be major.

3) ***God remembers.*** It is noteworthy that God had not forgotten the word He had spoken concerning this tribal group, even though more than four centuries had passed.[15] God never forgets sin until its penalty has been met. This is why every person whose sin remains unforgiven at the time of his death, will have to experience the torment of hell through all eternity.

4) ***Israel's strength at this time.*** This order of God shows further that Israel was enjoying a position of strength at this time. If God waited until now to carry out His word of four centuries earlier, there must have been a reason. The one most likely is that at no time during the period of the judges were the people sufficiently strong to carry out the order. That God finally issued it here, then, says that Israel's strength was the highest it had been since the time of Joshua. Saul, therefore, was still enjoying his successful years at this point.

2. THE INCOMPLETE OBEDIENCE

a. The story (I Sam. 15:4-9)

Saul assembled his troops in Telaim (unknown), probably located in the south of Judah. The troops numbered 200,000 (apparently from the eleven tribes) and 10,000 from Judah—in contrast to the mere 3,000 at Michmash. This again shows how much stronger Saul had become in the intervening years. He then moved on south to the area of the Amalekites (who roved about in the desert area south of Palestine), where he encountered some Kenites, who apparently were living among, or at least near, the Amalekites. Because Kenites, in contrast to the troublesome Amalekites, had helped Israel in the wilderness, Saul told them to separate themselves from the Amalekites, and they did.[16] Then Saul attacked the Amalekites and defeated them, apparently pursuing them from Havilah (unknown) eastward to the area of Shur (eastern section of the northern Sinai Peninsula). He was thus able to carry out his assignment, except that he saved the king, Agag, alive and also the best of the sheep and oxen.[17] In doing so he disobeyed the full command.

[15]The Amalekite battle had occurred during Israel's first year out of Egypt—hence about 1446 B.C. on the "early date" of the exodus—and the date here was about 1025 B.C. (fifteen years before David began to rule, which was in 1010 B.C.).

[16]Moses' father-in-law, Jethro, was a Kenite, as well as a Midianite (Judg. 1:16) and reference here may be especially to him (see Exod. 18:1-27).

[17]It may be said that Saul did not kill all the people either, because the Amalekites were strong enough to attack David's people at Ziklag (I Sam. 30:1-5) not more than fifteen years later.

b. Points to notice

1) ***God remembers good deeds too.*** Not only did God remember Amalek's sin for four hundred years, but also the good deed of the Kenites. Certainly Saul was guided by God in his counsel to the Kenites that they remove themselves before he struck against the Amalekites. Their actions deserved commendation, not punishment.

2) ***God wants total obedience.*** Saul obeyed God in major part. He went to the Amalekite area and inflicted almost total destruction on the enemy. He did not destroy all, however, and this degree of obedience was not enough. Final rejection from ruling was now given. God does not want merely "almost" obedience; He wants total obedience.

3. THE SECOND REJECTION

a. The story (I Sam. 15:10-35)

God appeared to Samuel to inform him of the incomplete obedience, even before Saul returned. In essence, the divine word was that Saul was now rejected as head of a royal dynasty for the reason that he had "turned back from following" God (15:11). Samuel was deeply grieved, and "cried unto the LORD all night," no doubt because this indicated the failure of the very first king in Israel's new monarchy. Saul had outwardly been doing well, and this had pleased the aging Samuel, but now he knew that inwardly Saul's heart had been growing more and more rebellious in attitude toward God. This spelled disaster for Saul personally and it meant hardship for the whole country in days ahead.

Samuel now went to meet Saul, who for some reason had returned to Gilgal down in the Jordan Valley, rather than coming back to his capital, Gibeah (15:12). There Samuel first rebuked Saul for sparing the king and the livestock; Saul protested that he had really obeyed, and that the livestock had been saved by the people for sacrifice—thus laying the blame on the people. Samuel responded with the well-known statement, "Behold, to obey is better than sacrifice, and to hearken than the fat of rams" (15:22). At this, Saul did confess that he had sinned and asked that Samuel pray for his forgiveness, but Samuel said he would not, for God had rejected Saul "from being king over Israel" (15:24-26). When Samuel turned to leave, Saul grabbed his garment, ripping it, and Samuel then spoke again of the rejection, likening it to the rip Saul had thus made.

Saul now asked Samuel to remain with him long enough to render worship to the Lord before the elders of the people, and thus give a show of solidarity between the two in spite of the harsh words. Samuel consented, Saul did worship, and then Samuel commanded that Agag, the Amalekite king, be brought, and Samuel killed him himself. At this, Samuel left and went to his home in Ramah and Saul returned to Gibeah, never to see each other again while they lived (15:35).

b. Points to notice

1) ***Saul's basic sin—disobedience.*** The reason why God rejected Saul for the second time was his disobedience (actually the same basic reason as the first time). Saul did not do all that God commanded. God wants His children to obey Him. This was the thrust of Samuel's words when he said that God delights in obedience more than in sacrifice. It was not that God did not want sacrifices made; indeed, sacrifices had been commanded in the law. But sacrifices without obedience were meaningless. A proper attitude of heart had to be in back of the sacrifices if they were to be acceptable.

2) ***So-called sacrifice insults God.*** Actually the sheep and oxen that Saul had spared for the purpose of sacrifice, as he said, were not suitable for this purpose, even if they had now been offered. The reason was that in the order for their destruction, the word used for destruction (15:3) was *haram,* meaning "to devote to God through destruction." God had already claimed these animals, then, and Saul was only to make this claim good by actually killing them. It was completely paradoxical, therefore, for him to think in terms of giving them to God in sacrifice. One cannot give to God what God has already made His. Saul's action was an insult to God and a repudiation of the command given to him.

3) ***Meaning of the rejection.*** This rejection of Saul did not mean that he had to cease in the kingship immediately. History shows that he continued, though in a constantly deteriorating state, for about fifteen more years. The rejection meant that his family would not rule after him. He was rejected as heading a continuing dynasty, something that every king regards as a high privilege. For this reason, though one of his sons, Ish-bosheth, did succeed him for a brief period of two years (II Sam. 2:10), David was made king to head a new ruling family.

4) ***Relation to first rejection.*** The logical question rises as to the meaning of the first rejection when this second one now followed. Why was a second needed? The answer seems to be that the first was basically probationary in nature. God brought that rejection early in Saul's reign, so that he might have opportunity to change. Thus, God could still bless Saul, and his finest years followed that time. God apparently saw fit to give him even twenty-three years in which to change, if he would, but Saul did not do so. The command regarding the Amalekites was clearly intended as a final test, and

when Saul failed in this, his probationary time expired and this final rejection was issued. As a result, Saul lost the special empowerment of the Holy Spirit soon after (I Sam. 16:14).

5) ***Blaming others.*** Saul only added to his sin by seeking to lay the blame for saving the animals on the people. He told Samuel, "I have obeyed . . . but the people took of the spoil" (15:20, 21). Possibly the people had suggested the idea, but even so, because of God's command Saul had the authority and responsibility to say no. He, like people of any day, sought to excuse himself in this manner. But he could not fool God; he could only add to his guilt by such a tactic.

9

Saul's Decline

Following the second and final rejection, Saul's position in Israel declined steadily. His rule was marked by interplay with the young man David, whom God designated as his successor. The sacred account of this second portion of Saul's reign begins with the selection of this young man by God, working still through the prophet Samuel.

A. INTRODUCTION AND ANOINTING OF DAVID

1. ANOINTED BY SAMUEL

a. The story (I Sam. 16:1-13)

It was soon after the day of Saul's rejection—for Samuel was still mourning for Saul (16:1)—that God told Samuel to go to Bethlehem and anoint a son of Jesse as Israel's next king. He also told him to take a young cow for a sacrifice, so that Saul would not become suspicious.[1] Samuel did

[1]The implication is that Samuel often performed sacrifices when visiting communities. It should be remembered that this was an unusual period: after the removal of the ark the tabernacle was no longer an official place of worship (I Kings 3:2).

this, and on arriving in Bethlehem called the men of the city to the place of sacrifice, including Jesse and his sons. Samuel first had to assure the people that his coming was for peaceful purposes, for they were fearful at the presence of so important a man. It may be that Samuel had visited before in the interest of bringing reproof for sin.

After Samuel had offered the sacrifice, he proceeded with the matter of the anointing. He first considered that Eliab, the oldest son, was the one to be anointed; Eliab had a striking appearance, but God told Samuel not to look on the outward appearance, for Eliab was not God's choice. Then Jesse had the oldest come before Samuel, but God said he was not the chosen one either, and this continued for all seven of Jesse's sons who were present. When none of these was chosen by God, Samuel asked if there was not yet another, and Jesse said there was one, but that he had been left to tend the family's sheep. Samuel had him called. When he arrived Samuel saw that he was "ruddy and withal of a beautiful countenance." God now said, "Arise, anoint him: for this is he" (16:12). Then Samuel poured anointing oil over David's head, as all the other brothers looked on. Also, and most significantly, at that moment the "Spirit of the LORD came upon David from that day forward."

b. Points to notice

1) ***A problem in truth-telling.*** The Scriptures are clear that truth-telling is very important in the sight of God (Exod. 20:16; 23:1, 7; Eph. 4:25; Col. 3:9). A problem therefore arises in respect to the pretext God told Samuel to give to Saul for his going to Bethlehem. Samuel had indicated to God that should he tell Saul that he went there to anoint David, Saul would kill him. God then instructed Samuel, "Take an heifer with thee, and say, I am come to sacrifice to the LORD" (16:2). Thus Samuel was to tell Saul part of the truth but not all of the truth. The problem is made more pointed by the fact that it was God Himself who told Samuel to offer this as the reason for his going. The following remarks are in order.

First, that which God told Samuel to say was indeed true. He was not told to say anything untrue. He was to take an animal with him and offer a sacrifice in Bethlehem, and he did. Second, that which Samuel was not to tell Saul makes clear that there are certain situations that call for a concealment of truth. Saul had no right to know the full truth because he would have used it wrongly, possibly even to taking Samuel's life as Samuel himself indicated. Today professional people, such as doctors, lawyers, and ministers have the right—indeed the necessity—of concealment of truth as a protection for people who confide in them. They are professionally obligated to keep information confidential, for if people in general would learn of it they might use it wrongly, to the detriment of those concerned.

It should be recognized that this right of concealment of truth carries with it a high responsibility for the person employing it. There must be good and adequate reason. It cannot be used by just any person, as a way, for instance, of extricating himself from a difficult situation. It is also important to recognize that this right of concealment gives no reason to anyone for speaking an untruth. To tell an untruth is quite different from telling part of a truth. This incident does show the propriety of a partial truth in well-prescribed situations but it gives no basis for telling an untruth.[2]

2) ***David's age.*** It was observed earlier that David probably was in his middle teen years at this time of anointing. He had to be old enough to be entrusted alone with the sheep, and still not so old as to be unwilling to be left behind to do so. Keil[3] suggests the age of twenty, but it is hard to understand why David would have been left behind at that age, for surely the family had servants to care for sheep, and the time required for him to attend the sacrifice would not have been long anyhow.

3) ***David's natural timidity.*** It was observed that Saul was naturally timid at the time of his anointing, and David may have been also. It would have been unusual even for a son of fifteen to be left at home at such a time, unless he was somewhat retiring in nature. Surely, if David had been an aggressive teen-ager, he would have wanted to be on hand. It may even have been his suggestion that he stay with the sheep, while the older brothers accompanied their father. The very fact that he was the youngest could have enhanced such a sense of timidity.

4) ***The first of three anointings.*** This anointing of David was only anticipatory of a day when he would become Israel's actual king. He did not now become king. God let Saul continue for another fifteen years. In fact, there would be two other times of anointing for David: the first as king over Judah (II Sam. 2:4), and the second over all the tribes (II Sam. 5:3).

5) ***Keeping the matter secret.*** There was need that this anointing of David be kept secret from Saul. The history of the following few years would have been quite different had Saul learned of it, for after he came only to surmise that David was to be his successor he began a diligent effort to take his life. Both God and Samuel recognized this in making the occasion at Bethlehem first a time of sacrifice, as a means of camouflaging the greater importance of the anointing. David needed to be protected. Probably Samuel warned Jesse and David's brothers not to say anything, and apparently they didn't. Of course, this would not have been hard for the

[2]For similar discussion see John Murray, *Principles of Conduct,* pp. 139-141.
[3]C. F. Keil and F. Delitzsch, *Biblical Commentary on the Books of Samuel,* p. 163.

brothers, for the matter would have been humiliating to them. They no doubt wanted to forget it. Also, it is quite possible that this anointing was performed when only Jesse and the sons were present; Samuel may well have dismissed the people of the community beforehand.

6) ***Thoughts of the other brothers.*** The older brothers must have been taken aback that their youngest brother was chosen in this way over them. If David had been willing to remain to tend the sheep, one may believe that the older brothers had been quite willing to have him do so. It is evident that they considered him inferior to themselves; this thinking is reflected in an incident which occurred some time later. David visited the three oldest when they were serving in Saul's army against the Philistines and Goliath. When he came to bring them food, Eliab greeted him with unkind words (I Sam. 17:28). After Samuel left the site of David's anointing, therefore, one may believe that the brothers set about giving the young man a difficult time, to remind him of his proper place in the home circle and to keep him from getting any ideas of superiority.

2. BROUGHT TO SAUL'S COURT

a. The story (I Sam. 16:14-23)

It is noteworthy that after David is said to have had the Spirit of the Lord come upon him (16:13), immediately Saul is said to have had the Spirit of the Lord depart from him (16:14). This is not an indication, however, that only one person could be empowered by the Spirit of God at one time. Years earlier, in fact, God had taken of the Spirit that was on Moses and shared Him with seventy elders at the same time (Num. 11:17, 25). Rather, the point of I Samuel 16:13, 14 is that the person of God's special interest for empowerment as king had now changed. God's blessing henceforth would be on David, not Saul. Then not only did Saul lose the presence of the Holy Spirit to aid him, but he gained instead the presence of an "evil spirit" to trouble him. That these two facts are juxtaposed (16:14) suggests that, so long as the Holy Spirit was with Saul, the evil spirit could not come. He did come only when the Holy Spirit had been taken away.

The result of this coming of the evil spirit was that Saul suffered periods of fearful depression; consequently, Saul's servants suggested that a musician be brought to play an instrument and help quiet Saul in these times. Saul approved and David was brought. God obviously directed in this selection as a way of introducing David to court life. Moreover, David was not in danger of being harmed by Saul, for the king did not know that he had been anointed as his successor. Saul accepted David warmly, and David remained at the palace to play the "harp" (*kinnor,* possibly "zither") to soothe the king.

b. Points to notice

1) ***No loss of salvation.*** The departure of God's Spirit from Saul should not be understood as loss of salvation, any more than the coming on David should be regarded as an occasion of gaining salvation. The Scripture is clear that spiritual salvation is not subject to being lost (John 10:28, 29), and certainly David was a child of God before Samuel anointed him, or else God would not have selected him. This coming and departing of the Spirit—as with every such instance in the Old Testament (e.g., Exod. 31:3; Num. 11:25; Judg. 3:10; 6:34)—had to do with empowerment for a task. Saul had been so empowered, evidently, since the time of the battle of Jabesh-gilead (I Sam. 11:6), and this was the special reason for the measure of success he had enjoyed since that occasion; but now this empowerment was transferred to the one who would take his place.

2) ***The "evil spirit."*** The "evil spirit" that now came to influence Saul must have been a demon, sent by Satan. This is evident from the description "evil." The demon came from the Lord in the sense that God permitted the coming. Satan, no doubt, had been desirous of having this emissary do his work on Saul all the while, but the Holy Spirit had kept him away. Now, with the empowerment of the Holy Spirit withdrawn, the evil spirit could make his play. It is not necessary to believe that this demon was able to work from within Saul's personality, having the vantage point enjoyed by the Holy Spirit, because different verbs and prepositions (from those used regarding the Holy Spirit) are used in reference to his relationship to Saul.[4] He seems rather to have influenced him by working from the outside, much as Satan with Eve in the Garden of Eden (Gen. 3:1-6).

3) ***Periods of fearful depression.*** The times of trouble the evil spirit brought on Saul were evidently periods of fearful depression, meaning periods of depression characterized especially by fear. The word translated in the King James as "troubled" (*ba'ath*) is used sixteen times in the Old Testament, and every time it involves the idea of fear (e.g., II Sam. 22:5; Job 7:14; Ps. 18:4). It no doubt involves fear here also. Saul's fear was quite clearly in respect to losing his kingdom, having just been informed by Samuel that this would happen (I Sam. 15:28). As a result, he gradually became suspicious of others, especially of the young David, and finally came to the point of actually trying to kill him (I Sam. 18:10-12).

4) ***God's remarkable ways.*** This story illustrates once more that God accomplishes His will in most unusual and unexpected ways. Saul's times of

[4]See my discussion, *The Holy Spirit in the Old Testament,* pp. 126-144.

fearful depression—caused by fear of someone's displacing him as king—were used to bring into the court and eventually into the public eye the very one who would displace him. Little did Saul know that the one brought to help him was the one God had just anointed to succeed him.

5) ***The power of music.*** The story also provides an illustration of the power of music in shaping a person's moods. Soothing music, from David's stringed instrument, could calm a disturbed Saul; harsh music, with a rhythmic beat, can do much to disturb a calm person.

B. A SECOND MAJOR PHILISTINE BATTLE

About twenty-three years had elapsed between the first Philistine battle (at Michmash), when Saul was first rejected by God, and the events now being considered. Among these events was another major encounter with the Philistines. There may have been minor contacts during the intervening years (I Sam. 14:47), but now another important one occurred.

1. THE STORY (I SAM. 17:1-58)

The place was the western end of the valley of Elah where this valley runs from the level land of the Philistines northeastward toward Bethlehem.[5] Evidently the Philistines wanted to march up this valley into Judah's territory, and Saul met them in an attempt to stop them. The two armies faced each other across the valley, and one day a champion of the Philistines walked across to challenge any Israelite to fight him. He proposed that the outcome of the war be decided by this individual combat.[6] It may well be that, employing this tactic, the Philistines were remembering Israel's champion, Samson, of some years before. Now they had a powerful man of their own, and they were willing to let their fortunes rest on his shoulders. The man was Goliath,[7] nine feet six inches tall, covered with armor from head to foot, with a man bearing a protective shield going before him.

The sight of this powerful man made all Israel's soldiers tremble. Forty days passed, while the giant defied Israel's armies (17:16). Finally young David came to Saul's camp, sent by his father to bring provisions for the three older brothers, who were members of the army, and he saw the humiliating situation. Immediately he volunteered to fight the great man, with Saul at first hesitating but then agreeing to the idea. Without question, Saul

[5]The place can be fixed rather closely because both Azekah and Shochoh (17:1) are well identified.

[6]Other examples of this type of conflict are known from ancient history; see David Erdmann, *The Books of Samuel,* in Lange's *Commentary,* vol. V, p. 228.

[7]Maybe a descendant of the Anakim (see Josh. 11:22).

did not believe the young man could possibly defeat Goliath, and so his amazement was great when that is exactly what happened. With only a sling for a weapon, David shot one stone and struck the giant in the forehead, causing the great one to fall. David ran to cut off his head with Goliath's own sword. At this, the Philistines fled, according to the agreement, and the Israelites won the crucial battle. They chased the enemy as far as two of their five main cities, Gath and Ekron (17:52).[8]

2. POINTS TO NOTICE

a. Saul's courage in spite of rejection

That Saul now came to meet the Philistines, even at the west end of the Elah Valley—and so before the enemy could penetrate Israelite country very far—shows that he had not given up in his rule just because he had been rejected. As far as he was concerned, apparently, he was still king and he was going to carry on as though nothing had changed. There is no indication given of the size of the army, but if he had led 210,000 when he fought the Amalekites (I Sam. 15:4), he probably had a sizable number of troops here. He had come to fight an ordinary type of battle and win it, if he could. He showed courage and strength in this and is to be commended.

b. Saul's reluctance to use David

Saul's hesitation in letting Israel's future hang on the abilities of David is understandable. Sometimes Saul has been criticized for not having gone out to meet Goliath himself, since he probably was the tallest in his army. He was no physical match for Goliath, however, and so is not to be criticized in this way. Saul just did not have anyone who could come close to meeting Goliath on physical terms. It is no wonder, then, that he hesitated in sending David, who was known to him only as his musician. He did finally let David go, but only because of the confidence David showed in his God—a source of strength other than physical—and, besides this, Saul had no one else as an alternative.

c. Saul's inquiry regarding David

After David had won the encounter with Goliath, Saul inquired of Abner, his military commander, "Whose son is this youth?" (17:55). This sounds strange in view of the fact that David had been with Saul as his personal musician previous to the Philistine battle. Liberal scholars see this as a basis for denying that David was Saul's musician and armorbearer prior to

[8]For greater detail concerning David's part in this battle, see pp. 194-199.

this time.[9] A possible answer is suggested by Keil.[10] Saul knew who David was, so far as having had contact with him as an individual and as a musician, but he did not know him in his military role. Moreover, Saul had promised that the parents of Goliath's conqueror would live tax-free, and this made him wonder who David's parents were. Saul had made a brief contact with Jesse when he first asked for David to come to him (I Sam. 16:19), but this had not given him much information regarding the family. He apparently wanted to know more now, in the light of the remarkable achievement of the young man.[11]

d. A major victory for Saul

It should be realized that this victory over the Philistines was of major importance to Saul and Israel. The Philistines had not made a major attempt at invading Israel since their defeat at Michmash. Now they were turned back again, and once more in decisive fashion. Both Saul and Israel were enormously indebted to David that day.

e. The emergence of Saul's rival

While the victory was important to Saul, it also made for the emergence of David as his potential rival. He was an actual rival, of course, in view of the earlier anointing, but neither Saul nor the people knew this. It was only now that David came to the people's attention and, therefore, became an object of fear and jealousy for Saul. He who had earlier been given to fits of fear that a rival might emerge now had one.

C. ATTEMPTS TO KILL DAVID

Saul's jealousy soon grew to the point that he made actual attempts on David's life. The history implies that he came to give so much effort to this endeavor that he neglected the normal duties of a king.

1. AN ADDITIONAL REASON FOR JEALOUSY

a. The story (I Sam. 18:1-9)

At first, following the Philistine victory, Saul did not see David as this sort of rival. He seems to have been properly impressed for a time with the

[9]See Eugene Maly, *The World of David and Solomon,* p. 37.

[10]Keil and Delitzsch, *Samuel,* p. 186.

[11]Another explanation is given by Ethelbert W. Bullinger, *Figures of Speech Used in the Bible,* pp. 706-707. He believes that the history involved in I Samuel 16 and 17 is transposed in the interest of logical order. He believes the real course of events becomes apparent when one reads 16:1-13 followed by 17:1—18:9, and then 16:14-23 followed by 18:10-30. This would make Saul's inquiry to Abner regarding David fall before the time when David came to Saul to play as his musician. This explanation is possible but perhaps not as likely as the one given above.

significance of what David had done. Then there was also another person who was impressed: this was Jonathan, who recognized ability when he saw it. David was a young man after his own heart. Jonathan must have been at least twenty-five or thirty years older than David,[12] but still he took to the younger man, and "loved him as his own soul" (18:3). He also gave David his own royal robes, sword, bow, and girdle, signifying that he recognized David would be king in his place.

As for Saul, he made David captain of the army, setting "him over the men of war" (18:5). In this capacity, David continued to harass the Philistines, always winning, with the result that the saying rose among the people, "Saul hath slain his thousands, and David his ten thousands" (18:7). As a result, Saul in jealousy turned against David.

b. Points to notice

1) ***Jonathan's magnanimity.*** At the same time that we must be critical of Saul, we must commend his oldest son Jonathan. Jonathan had shown great courage and ability at Michmash years before, and now he saw the same qualities in another who was at this time about the same age he had been then. Even Jonathan had not been willing to make an attempt against Goliath, but he had seen this young man do so and win. A magnanimous heart is ready to recognize ability whenever it is displayed. And Jonathan recognized David's ability even though it meant the giving up of any aspirations of ruling himself. It may be assumed that he had learned of the rejection Samuel had declared to his father, and apparently he was more willing to accept the divine word than was Saul. That he here gave his own royal accouterments to David took great understanding and humility on his part. His love for David was based on more than emotion; it knew deep respect for and recognition of genuine ability.

2) ***Abner's position.*** Abner was supposed to be Saul's army commander, but he does not appear to have been very active. He must have been an office-type commander, who was better at suggestions and "paperwork" than in leading in battle. It is true that he may have been active in the wars with Moab, Ammon, Edom, and Zobah—though he is not mentioned in connection with them—but at any rate he did nothing in the two major Philistine encounters, and now David was given the position of field commander. In all this account, Abner is mentioned only once—when Saul asked him to find out about David.

3) ***The harm of jealousy.*** At first Saul reacted to David properly, making him the leader of the Israelite troops. But then, due to David's suc-

[12]See p. 199.

cesses, he became jealous of the young military genius. This drove him eventually to remove David from being military leader; and David's removal, in turn, led to continuous defeats before the Philistines. Saul's jealousy thus led him into a grave mistake. Certainly the people must have been outraged.

2. THE FIRST TWO ATTEMPTS ON DAVID'S LIFE

a. The story (I Sam. 18:10-30)

The day following one of David's successful forays against the enemy, he was playing his instrument before Saul, who was suffering one of his attacks; and suddenly, instead of being calmed as before, Saul became more agitated and thrust at David twice with his spear in an attempt to kill him. It is probable that he only thrust at him (rather than throwing the spear), for it is said that David twice eluded him and no mention is made of the spear sticking into the wall as in a later instance (I Sam. 19:10).[13] David evidently was agile enough to elude both thrusts. Saul now became afraid of David, seeing him more and more as a formidable rival; and so he sent him away from the palace, this time in command of a thousand, which was probably a lesser number than David had commanded before. Still David behaved himself wisely, with the double result that Saul became more fearful of him and the people more in favor of him.

Saul now tried another way of ridding himself of David. He first offered his older daughter Merab to him as wife—really in fulfillment of a promise given before David's victory over Goliath (I Sam. 17:25)—but then gave her to another and offered David his younger daughter, Michal, instead. David at first protested that he was not worthy to be a son-in-law to the king, but finally he did marry Michal, who had fallen in love with him (18:20). As a dowry for Michal, Saul asked "a hundred foreskins of the Philistines," thinking that David would be killed in trying to get them (18:17, 21), but instead David was able to deliver two hundred (18:27). David apparently did not realize that Saul had plotted against him in this, and, when David was not harmed, Saul came to fear him still more, recognizing God's blessing upon him. Other engagements with the Philistines followed, with David regularly winning and gaining still greater favor in the sight of the people.

b. Points to notice

1) ***David's dual role.*** It is quite clear that for a time David played a dual role in Saul's kingdom: as Saul's musician and as the new army com-

[13]The word "cast" (*tol*) is used, true enough, and it often does mean to "throw at from a distance," but it can also have the sense of "thrusting out at."

mander. The two roles differed greatly, and people must have marveled that one who could play so beautifully one day could lead an army so effectively the next. This shows the versatility of the young David and, even more, the blessing of God as the Holy Spirit remained continually upon him for empowerment.

2) ***The evil spirit and David.*** A change in the evil spirit's reaction to David and his playing is noteworthy here. Earlier, the evil spirit had withdrawn when David played, quite clearly not liking the soothing music (I Sam. 16:23). Now, he tried to be rid of the hated music by inducing Saul to kill the player (18:10, 11). The reason for the change can hardly be found in David or his playing; it must have had something to do with Saul. Remember that Saul had now grown to fear David and to be jealous of him. This factor could be used by the evil spirit. He would not have to run away now; he could rather persuade Saul to take the young man's life, and then he would be rid of the music for good. Paul admonishes, "Neither give place to the devil" (Eph. 4:27). Saul had failed in this respect: he had allowed to grow in his life a weakness that Satan could use to his advantage.

3) ***Saul's problem.*** Saul had a problem in respect to fulfilling his promises to the one who defeated Goliath. It concerned in particular the matter of marriage to his daughter. He had promised the marriage, but now he did not want to fulfill his pledge. Marriage to Saul's daughter would give David a legitimate claim to the throne. Quite clearly, Saul held off from fulfilling his promise for a while, but finally conceived the idea that he could turn this situation to his favor by requiring David to kill a large number of Philistines as a dowry payment: David might well be killed in the attempt. Saul first offered Merab, his older, but then for some reason changed his mind—possibly because Merab did not love David—and instead offered Michal, when he learned of her love for the young warrior.

3. THREE OTHER ATTEMPTS

a. The story (I Sam. 19:1-24)

There were three other times when Saul tried to take David's life. Before these occurred, however, a brief period of respite was arranged through the efforts of Jonathan. He learned of orders from Saul that David was to be killed by any of Saul's servants, warned David to be careful, and then went to Saul to speak in David's behalf. As a result, Saul desisted in his jealous endeavor for a time, promising, "As the LORD liveth, he shall not be slain" (19:6). At this, Jonathan, who thought much of both David and his father, brought the two together and David came to be in Saul's "presence, as in times past" (19:7). At this point yet, David apparently regarded Saul's attempts on his life as temporary attacks of madness reflecting the king's depression, and so was quite willing to have a good relationship with the king restored.

Soon, however, David distinguished himself again in a battle against the Philistines, with the result that, as he played before Saul, the king once again tried to kill him with his spear. This time, clearly, he threw the weapon at the agile young man, for it is said to have stuck in the wall. David once more was able to get away unharmed. Saul then sent messengers to David's house, instructing them to prevent David from escaping during the night and to kill him the following morning. Michal now came to her husband's aid, telling him of the men waiting in ambush. She let him down through a window, where those lying in wait could not see him. She also put a figure representing David in his bed, so that the next day Saul's men, being told by her that he was sick, refrained for some time from examining the figure more closely.[14] Finally, Saul insisted that David be taken, and then the trick was discovered. Saul was angry at his daughter. She saved herself by saying that David had forced her into the ruse. Meanwhile David escaped to Ramah, about four miles north of Gibeah, where Samuel lived.

News of David's whereabouts soon reached Saul and he sent messengers to apprehend him. They came to David and Samuel, who were with a company of prophets engaged in the act of prophesying, and when the Spirit of God came upon the messengers, they suddenly found themselves prophesying as well. Saul now sent a second group of messengers, and the same thing happened. He sent still a third group, with the same result. Finally he went himself, in complete disgust, no doubt, at the inefficiency of the three groups of messengers. On the way, however, the Spirit of God came also on him, and he began to prophesy even before arriving where the others were. On reaching the place, he partially disrobed, as the others had done,[15] continued to prophesy, and then, unlike the others, lay down in an apparent stupor the rest of the day and all the following night. David thus was not apprehended at all. Because of Saul's unusual action, people said concerning him—much as at an earlier time (I Sam. 10:12)—"Is Saul also among the prophets?" (19:24).

b. Points to notice

1) ***Jonathan's attempt to make peace.*** Once more Jonathan appears in a commendable light. He tried to make peace between two people he loved,

[14]The figure was made up of teraphim (normally small images; see Gen. 31:19, 34) and a "pillow of goats' hair."

[15]They evidently removed their outer robes to give greater ease of movement; cf. Isa. 20:2; Mic. 1:8. See also Samuel R. Driver, *Notes on the Hebrew Text of the Books of Samuel,* p. 160.

Saul and David, and succeeded for a time. His efforts provide a fine illustration of what Jesus meant in the seventh beatitude: "Blessed are the peacemakers" (Matt. 5:9).

2) ***Widening of Saul's efforts against David.*** The last two attempts of Saul on David's life show him willing to involve many people. At first, he may have wanted to keep his animosity quite secret. Now, however, he forgot about secrecy and commanded servants to aid him in his endeavor, even sending three groups of messengers in the last instance. He apparently did not care any longer who knew of his desire to take the young man's life, though certainly all could see that the only reason was jealousy on Saul's part.

3) ***The woman, Michal.*** Michal, whom David married, had both commendable and noncommendable traits. She could love David and save his life; she could also tell her father a lie afterwards. Later, when David had been forced to flee, she could change her affection and marry another, Phalti (I Sam. 25:44). When David assumed power, she could leave Phalti and return to David (II Sam. 3:13-16—though, in fairness, it must be said that David was mainly responsible for this); and when David danced before the ark, on bringing it into Jerusalem, she could criticize him for lowering himself to the level of the common people. She had felt personally humiliated by David's dancing. Consequently, God made her childless unto the day of her death (II Sam. 6:20-23). It is quite clear that Michal was opportunistic. She sought popularity and accordingly took steps in the direction which she thought would contribute most to that end. Her original "love" for David may have been somewhat feigned—on the basis of his rising popularity of the time, she may have believed her star might well rise along with his.

4) ***The Spirit of God and Saul.*** The Spirit of God had left Saul at the time of his second rejection (I Sam. 16:14). Now it is said that He came on Saul again, though apparently only for this passing occasion. If the Spirit had been on Saul earlier to enable him for the kingship, what was the purpose now? Liberal expositors see the meaning to be that Saul here became an ecstatic, but this explanation does not fit, for one must be a sympathetic participant to experience an ecstatic state. And Saul was anything but sympathetic to the group of prophets who were here prophesying.

An explanation more in keeping with the story is that the Spirit came on Saul—quite as He had on the three earlier groups of messengers—for the purpose of protecting David. Had Saul's emotional state not been changed, from being intensely angry to actually prophesying along with Samuel's prophets, he would have had David killed probably right there at the time.

Not long after this, he did not hesitate to have eighty-five priests and their families killed (I Sam. 22:18, 19). Something had to be done, therefore, to protect David. The act of prophesying, being carried on by Samuel's prophets, the three groups of messengers, and finally Saul, was very likely an act of rendering praise to God.[16] The prophets were rendering praise, probably in song; the three groups of messengers then joined them in turn; and finally Saul did the same. When one is brought into such a frame of mind as to render praise, all evil intents (e.g., the desire to take someone's life) are removed. The Spirit of God, then, effected such a change in the thinking of Saul that he started to praise God and no longer wanted to kill David. It is significant that David was not harmed in any way as a result.

5) ***Saul's apparent stupor.*** It is alleged that the apparent stupor which came on Saul shows further that he became an ecstatic at this time. Again, however, there is a better explanation. Saul alone experienced the stupor, though the others also removed part of their clothing. Lying behind Saul's stupor was a fit of despair. He had tried so hard to take David, even enlisting the help of others, who did not cooperate with him very well. He himself had now come to apprehend David and had ended up doing nothing at all, because of the change in thinking that had come over him. Moreover, he had just seen David in the approving company of the great Samuel, whom Saul still highly respected. This made the king keenly aware of the truth of Samuel's earlier rejection of him. It was clear that he had lost to the young man, and this truth made him lie down motionless the rest of that day and all the following night in remorse and despair. Saul clearly was a man of extreme emotional moods, and here he suddenly fell from a mood of intense anger to one of complete despair.

D. DAVID BECOMES A FUGITIVE

1. THE FINAL TEST OF SAUL'S INTENTIONS

a. The story (I Sam. 20:1-42)

David now returned to Gibeah to find Jonathan. Matters had deteriorated so far in the strained relation with Saul that he realized a major change might well be necessary. No longer could Saul's attempts on his life be explained as outbursts of mental depression. Therefore, Jonathan, the peacemaker, entered into a plan with David by which to judge the true intentions of Saul. The regular monthly meeting at the time of the new moon was at hand, at which David as well as Jonathan would be expected to be present. It was decided that David should absent himself. Jonathan

[16]The validity of this meaning is established by I Chron. 25:1-3.

would report Saul's reaction to David's absence, and David would then know whether or not it was safe to return to the palace.

The meeting normally lasted two days. On the second day, Saul displayed anger that David was absent; and when Jonathan sought to speak in his behalf, Saul threw a spear even at him (20:33). This made Saul's attitude only too clear, and Jonathan went to warn David. The two friends had arranged a signal which involved shooting arrows either beyond a certain point or in front of it, so that, if secrecy should be needed, David would know Saul's reaction without an actual conversation. Jonathan did shoot the arrows, but apparently it was possible for him to talk with David as well. They embraced each other in the emotion of the moment, and then parted, Jonathan bidding the younger man God's blessing.

b. Points to notice

1) ***The life of a fugitive.*** One reason, no doubt, why David did not flee sooner was the unpleasant nature of the fugitive's life. He could not just go back home to Bethlehem where Saul would quickly find him. He would have to keep running from the king. This would mean deprivation, hunger all too often, and especially the knowledge that he was a hunted man. In recent years, he had been the honored David, winner of battles with the Philistines; if he ran, he would become the hunted David, with few being willing even to befriend him for fear of reprisal. Still more, it would have been difficult for a fugitive to believe that he would become Israel's king. It had been easy to believe this when he had been the champion of the people, but it would be different if he became a fugitive.

2) ***Saul's strange expectation.*** It seems strange that Saul really expected David to come to the monthly gathering, in view of his attempts to take David's life. Yet he did expect him to be present, for he asked Jonathan, "Wherefore cometh not the son of Jesse to meat?" (20:27). Perhaps he thought, since David had not been apprehended at Ramah, David would believe that all danger was past. No doubt, Saul himself felt charitable after that time, but basically the same jealousy was still present, as revealed by his anger when David did not appear. Had David come, Saul may not have tried for his life that day, but he would have again as soon as David distinguished himself in battle. His reaction to David's absence was all too significant.

3) ***The "Bethlehem excuse."*** David and Jonathan have been criticized for "prevaricating" to Saul in saying that David had gone to Bethlehem to sacrifice (20:6, 29). David suggested that Jonathan tell Saul that this was his reason for being absent from the meeting, and Jonathan did so. However,

David may well have actually gone to Bethlehem. The feast at the palace was to last two days. So then, Jonathan would have the answer on the third day (20:12, 19) after David's speaking with him. The distance from Gibeah to Bethlehem is only about ten miles, which David could have walked in a few hours. Therefore, he could easily have gone to his home city for such an occasion and then returned.[17] Though sacrifice would not have been the main reason for David's going to Bethlehem, no lie would then have been involved, much in the pattern of Samuel's having earlier told Saul that he was going to Bethlehem to sacrifice, when the main reason was the anointing of David (I Sam. 16:2).

4) ***The wisdom of David and Jonathan.*** Both David and Jonathan showed wisdom in their procedure. David might have fled from the country posthaste, after the Ramah episode, thinking he was doing well just to escape with his life. He did not, however, but sought counsel from a trusted friend and then saw fit to make absolutely sure that flight was the only alternative. He did not act precipitously, but wisely. At the same time, Jonathan saw the wisdom in David's procedure and was willing to aid in it. He did not press his father the first day at all, but replied only on the following day when his father himself brought up the subject of David. In addition, Jonathan made his decision regarding David's best courage only when Saul's true intentions became all too evident. Wise, careful action is always in order. Hasty actions, not well thought out, lead to mistakes and regret.

2. DAVID, AHIMELECH, AND SAUL

a. The story (I Sam. 21:1-9; 22:6-23)

David's flight took him first to Nob, about two miles southeast of Gibeah. Here was where the tabernacle had been transferred from Shiloh, likely following Israel's defeat at Aphek (I Sam. 4:1-11), and here served the high priest of the day, Ahimelech (I Sam. 21:1), son of Ahitub and great-grandson of Eli (I Sam. 14:3; Ahiah is identical with Ahimelech). Ahimelech was fearful of helping David at first, no doubt knowing the political conflict, and David believed wrongly that the situation warranted his telling a lie. He told the high priest that he was on a secret errand for the king. Then he urged that he be given food, and finally Ahimelech gave him some of the sacred bread from the table of showbread. David also asked for a weapon, and Ahimelech gave him Goliath's sword, that apparently had been brought there following David's victory over the giant. Viewing the whole scene was an Edomite named Doeg, there present because of having

[17] At this time when the ark was removed from the tabernacle, festivals (such as the feast of new moon), normally held at the central sanctuary, were probably held in local communities.

been "detained before the LORD."[18] He was a head shepherd for Saul and loyal to him.

A few days later, when David had made good his escape, and news of him had reached Saul, the king made accusations in the presence of several of his attendants to the effect that no one was on his side in his quarrel with David. Doeg, the Edomite, who had now returned from Nob, then spoke up concerning what he had seen at Nob, quite clearly as a way of enhancing his position before Saul. Immediately Saul sent for Ahimelech to demand an explanation, and the brave high priest told him what had happened, making clear that he considered David a faithful servant of Saul and that he had been completely ignorant of David's reason for coming to him. Saul was not satisfied with the reply, however, and ordered nearby footmen[19] to "slay the priests of the LORD," giving as a reason that they had helped David and not reported the matter of his flight to Saul. The footmen, normally given to obedience, refused this outrageous order. Saul then turned to Doeg to order him to do it. He killed eighty-five priests, including Ahimelech, along with their families, and their livestock.

One priest, however, escaped. This was Ahimelech's son, Abiathar. He was able to get away to David, apparently knowing where David was at the time. When Abiathar told David what had happend, David took the full blame upon himself, no doubt remembering the lie he had told Ahimelech (22:22). Then he bade Abiathar remain with him.

b. Points to notice

1) ***David's lie.*** One cannot explain away nor defend David in his prevarication to Ahimelech. He apparently thought that the end justified the means and, in his need for food, told the lie to satisfy Ahimelech. The dire consequences of the untruth are all too clear in the complete destruction of the priests that resulted. David's remorse was great when he learned of the harm he had done, but it was then too late to mend the wrong. How often this same story has been repeated in the lives of God's children!

2) ***The tabernacle of this time.*** Not much is known regarding the condition of the tabernacle at this time. Being at Nob, it clearly had been moved from Shiloh, and, as suggested, this no doubt had occurred following the Philistine victory at Aphek. Later, in the time of Solomon, it was located at Gibeon, about eight miles northwest of Nob (II Chron. 1:3), probably having been moved there after this devastation by Saul at Nob. That the high priest and eighty-four other priests served there, shows that ceremonial

[18]Perhaps for purification purposes or possibly as a way of gaining acceptance into the Israelite community, he being from Edom.

[19]Literally "runners" (*ratsim*); these may have been officers like those Samuel had predicted in I Sam. 8:11, when he spoke of men who would run before the king's chariot.

activity was being carried on, though the extent is questionable, inasmuch as one reads of Samuel's making sacrifices in other cities (I Sam. 9:12, 13; 16:2-5). The great brazen altar apparently was being used, for it was to this altar that Solomon came to offer a large number of sacrifices (II Chron. 1:5, 6).

3) ***Ahimelech's difficult position.*** Ahimelech was in a difficult position the day David asked for his assistance. How much he knew of the full story involving Saul and David is not clear, but surely he had no way of knowing that David was now fleeing from Saul. He tried to be careful, but when David lied to him, he thought he was acting properly in giving him help. His later testimony before Saul certainly was innocent and sincere, but still Saul punished him severely. Ahimelech must have asked why God would permit such a wrong to be done to His high priest—as many others have had occasions to wonder regarding God's ways since.

4) ***Doeg, a tool of Satan.*** Doeg was on hand to observe what Ahimelech did in respect to David and then tell Saul all about it. In this he was a tool of Satan. He did much to further the evil that Satan wanted Saul to commit. Often Satan uses people as his tools; sometimes they are quite innocent and ignorant that they are being so used.

5) ***Saul's outrageous action.*** Saul's act in having the eighty-five priestly families destroyed was outrageous in the extreme. It would have been serious enough to order the slaughter of eighty-five ordinary families; but these were priestly families, those whom God had set aside as religious leaders. It is no wonder that Saul's footmen would not obey in slaying them. And, further, the priests had done nothing wrong. Even the high priest, Ahimelech, who alone had been involved, had acted in complete innocence. There had been no way for him to know that David was fleeing from Saul; and, even if there had been, it could easily be argued that he had a perfect right to aid the fleeing young man, who had done nothing wrong. Saul was the one at fault, both in respect to David and now in respect to Ahimelech and his priestly companions. God certainly held the matter against Saul most severely.

E. SAUL'S PURSUIT OF DAVID AND SAUL'S DEATH

1. PURSUIT OF DAVID

a. The story (I Sam. 23:14-28; 24:1-22; 26:1-25)

Saul was not satisfied merely that David had fled; he wanted the life of the young man. According to I Samuel 23:14, he "sought him every day," meaning that he made inquiries that often and, when information came, gave actual pursuit. Before Saul received his first information as to where David was, Jonathan made contact with the fugitive. Jonathan found David in "Ziph in a wood"[20] (I Sam. 23:15); the meeting was simply a time of renewing their covenant, and Jonathan indicated again that he knew David would be king and that he, Jonathan, would serve under him. The occasion no doubt encouraged David, in his time of emotional and physical stress.

The people of Ziph, who apparently were loyal to Saul, now reported to Saul that David was in their area, and Saul came with his troops to apprehend him. By the time he arrived, David had moved six miles south to the area of Maon, but Saul followed him and surrounded him there. Then God intervened by bringing news of a Philistine invasion so that Saul had to withdraw to counter this attack (I Sam. 23:27, 28).

When he had finished with this Philistine encounter—no indication is given as to the result—Saul learned that David was at En-gedi, on the Dead Sea shore, about sixteen miles east of Ziph.[21] Saul now took three thousand troops and gave pursuit again. On coming to an area of numerous caves, Saul entered one to "cover his feet" (i.e., to answer a call of nature; cf. Judg. 3:24). David and his men were in that very cave. They saw him enter and, apparently, leave his robe to one side. The men urged David to take the king's life then and there. David refused but did cut off a piece of the royal robe, evidently without attracting Saul's attention. When Saul left the cave, David, feeling guilty that he had done even this to God's anointed, went after the king and told him what he had done. He also spoke of himself as merely a dead dog and a flea in comparison with Saul in importance. When Saul recognized David's mercy toward him, he was repentant, confessed that he knew David would be the next king, and asked him to be merciful to his posterity. David promised that he would, and Saul took his army home.

After some months elapsed, a similar occurrence transpired back in the country of the Ziphites, who again reported David's presence to Saul. Saul came once more with 3,000 men, and David, learning of this, had his own spies out to watch the king's movements. On an opportune night, David, accompanied by Abishai,[22] approached Saul's camp and identified the sleeping Saul by his spear stuck in the ground at his head. Quietly, the two moved to where Saul lay, took the spear and a water container, and then withdrew without hurting the king or being detected. Though Abishai had

[20]See p. 207, n. 8.

[21]For a description of the area of En-gedi, see Elmer B. Smick, *Archaeology of the Jordan Valley,* pp. 85-86.

[22]Abishai was a brother of Joab, and became David's general. They were sons of David's half sister, Zeruiah. This is the first mention of either and both may have first associated themselves with David at this time.

urged David to end Saul's life, he had refused to do so, even as at En-gedi, for Saul was God's anointed. When he was a safe distance away, David called out as before. This time he first mocked Abner for not having guarded his master better, and then he conversed again with Saul. What was said was quite similar to the earlier occasion, with David again likening himself to a flea and saying that Saul's pursuit of him was like hunting a partridge in the mountains.[23] He also stated that the king should bid a soldier come and reclaim the king's spear, which was Saul's symbol of authority. At such words, Saul again was deeply moved and admitted that God had great things in store for the young David. Once more he went home empty-handed.

No more pursuits by Saul are recorded; one reason is that David soon moved to the country of the Philistines, out of Saul's territory.

b. Points to notice

1) ***Saul's persistence in seeking David.*** Saul's persistence in his pursuit of David is further cause for wonderment. One would think that he would have been satisfied that he was rid of the young man, since David was no longer in the public eye and therefore not a threat as he had been. But Saul was not satisfied; for some reason he felt he had to take the young man's life, even if it cost him a great deal of time and effort. Certainly it was not pleasant running after David, over the difficult terrain of southern Judah, and it was expensive besides, having to use an army of 3,000 in this way. Saul showed determination in this, but even more he showed foolishness, as David himself pointed out both times they had contact.

2) ***Suffering of both the country and Saul's reputation.*** With Saul occupied so extensively in this one interest, the country certainly suffered; Saul was needed to operate a government, not run after one man. Then, people would have known of the foolish action and come to think ill of the king for it. And Saul's atrocious act against the priests at Nob would have added to this negative attitude. No doubt, in these years of chasing David[24] Saul lost out greatly with his people. What reputation he had gained in his successful years very likely all but dissipated.

3) ***God's protection of David.*** That David had fled from Saul did not mean that God's Spirit had abandoned watching over the young man. For

[23]Partridges were hunted in lowland areas, where they could be found in number, and not in the difficult mountain terrain, where they would be very few. In other words, Saul was using his time most unwisely in pursuing here in the mountain one of so little importance as David.

[24]Probably four or five in number.

this reason, Saul actually had no chance of apprehending him. At one time Saul's efforts were interrupted by a raid by the Philistines, and at two other times God saw to it that David actually was able to bring severe humiliation on the king. God protects those who live within His will.

2. SAUL'S DEATH

a. The story (I Sam. 28:5-25; 31:1-13)

Saul's death finally came at Mount Gilboa in a pitched battle with the perennial enemy, the Philistines. The Philistines had marched north to the Esdraelon Plain, and then eastward through the plain as far as Shunem (28:4). When Saul recognized the purpose of this encircling move—to cut him off from his northern tribes—he knew he would have to attack and was fearful of the outcome. His army evidently was few in number, people having lost confidence in his leadership, and he did not have a capable commander like David. As a result he sought counsel of God, but God would not answer him either by dream, Urim, or prophet (28:6); this no doubt

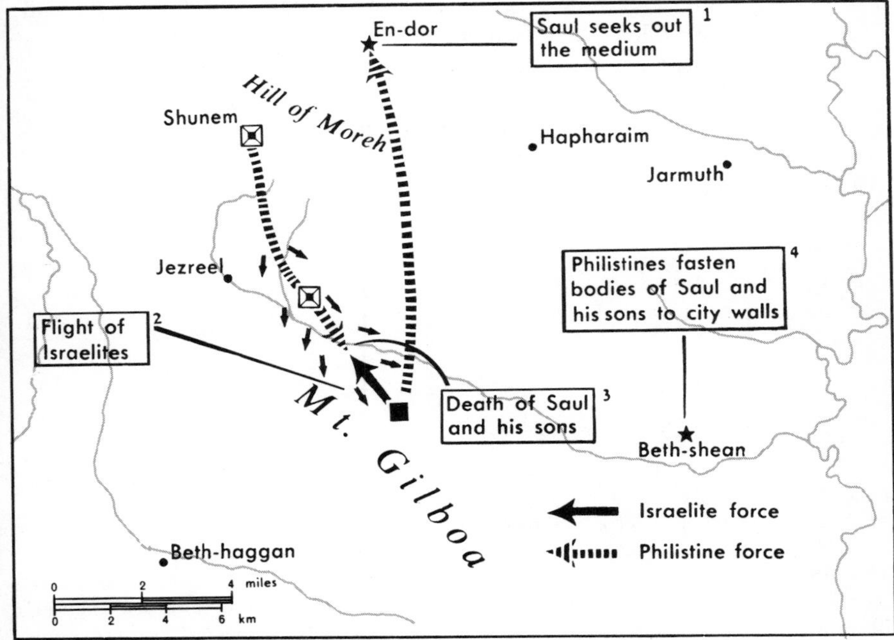

Map 4. The Battle of Gilboa

reflected the fact that in view of his deficient conduct the Spirit had been taken from him.[25]

As a result, Saul fell to another low in his life: he went to consult a woman who was a medium, living at Endor.[26] Earlier he had outlawed such people throughout his country but now he sought a person of this kind himself. He wanted her to make possible a consultation with Samuel, who had died a few months before (I Sam. 25:1). He disguised himself so that the woman would not recognize him. When the woman attempted to make the contact, she was amazed and frightened that, not only was contact made, but the very form of Samuel appeared before her. Her fright shows that she did not expect such a result and indicates that it was God who brought about the supernatural appearance.

Samuel spoke a message to Saul, and his words were those of God. He told Saul again that he had been rejected from ruling for the reason that he had been disobedient, and he stated that on the morrow Saul would suffer complete defeat before the Philistines, with both himself and his sons being killed. On hearing this shocking news, Saul fell to the ground in despair, refused food when offered by the woman, and ate only when urged both by the woman and subordinates he had brought with him. Then he returned to his troops to await the foreboding morrow.

When the battle joined the next day, all that Samuel had foretold came true. Israel's forces were defeated; Saul's sons, Jonathan, Abinadab, and Malchishua, were killed; and Saul was overcome by fear.[27] In desperation he asked his armorbearer to take his life that he might avoid abuse at the hands of the Philistines, and, when the man refused, Saul fell on his own sword. On hearing of this development, people of the surrounding area fled, so that the Philistines occupied their towns. Then the enemy cut off Saul's head and took his armor back to Philistia for propaganda purposes. They fastened his body and those of his sons to the wall of Bethshan, about eight miles east of the probable site of the battle. The next day, however, men of Jabesh-gilead, who remembered the deliverance Saul had effected for them, came and took the bodies back to their city for cremation and burial.

[25]Though I Chron. 10:14 says that Saul did not inquire of the Lord, no contradiction exists. Saul did not seek God truly, since he was out of fellowship with God, but used the means indicated only in a forced, perfunctory manner.

[26]This person is sometimes called a "witch" but this is improper. A witch deals in magic. This woman was a medium.

[27]The Hebrew of I Sam. 31:3 is best taken to mean that the "archers" overtook Saul with the result that "he was greatly alarmed at them," not that he was "wounded" by them (as in KJV); cf. Keil and Delitzsch, *Samuel,* p. 279.

b. Points to notice

1) ***Philistines and Canaanites.*** For the Philistines to have pushed as far north as the Esdraelon Plain and then east to Shunem means that they had been campaigning against the Canaanites as well as the Israelites. Canaanite land, lying along the Mediterranean, was attractive to them for it was level. They had conquered up to the Esdraelon Plain and then moved eastward through the fine plain to Shunem. If they had continued all the way to the Jordan Valley, they would indeed have cut off Saul's northern tribes; and if then they had occupied much of the Jordan, they would have cut off the northern Transjordanian people as well.

2) ***Geographical positions.*** The relative geographical positions of the Philistines, Saul, and the woman of Endor must be recognized to understand how Saul could go to see this woman and not be in danger from the Philistines. The three locations formed a triangle. Shunem was the western point, Mount Gilboa lay about four miles to the southeast, and Endor was roughly six miles north of Mount Gilboa (and Endor and Shunem were on opposite sides of the hill of Moreh).

3) ***A new "Urim."*** It is said that Saul had tried to consult God, unsuccessfully, by dreams, Urim, and prophets. This reference to the Urim is of particular interest because Abiathar had some time before left the country and taken the ephod (with the Urim and Thummim) with him (I Sam. 22:20; 23:6-12). It seems likely, then, that Saul had ordered the making of a new Urim and Thummim, which would fit in with the idea suggested earlier that he had also appointed Zadok as a new high priest. If this was not the original Urim and Thummim, we have another reason why God did not answer him.

4) ***The actual appearance of Samuel.*** Various explanations have been attempted to show that Samuel did not really appear when Saul consulted the woman of Endor. None have been satisfactory, however, for the indication is clear that he did appear. For one thing, the woman was taken with evident surprise at what transpired, showing that something happened she in no way expected; and for another, a conversation took place between Samuel and Saul such as the woman never would have contrived of herself. It was the kind of message that God alone would have wanted Saul to hear.

5) ***Samuel's appearance effected by God.*** The occasion has sometimes been used as evidence supporting present-day spiritism. It cannot be used in this way, however, for Samuel's appearance was not due to manipulations of the woman; it was due rather to God's supernatural intervention as the

following matters show: First, the woman herself was made fearful by the development, so that Saul had to counsel her, "Be not afraid" (I Sam. 28:13). Second, she was brought to a recognition that the one who had requested Samuel's appearance was Saul himself. If Samuel's appearance had been something she had effected according to plan, there would have been no reason to think her client was anyone unusual. Third, the nature of the message shows that God was the prime mover in the event. As just observed, the content was not at all what either the woman or Saul would have wanted spoken. The words were those of God alone! And fourth, after Samuel had again disappeared, the woman did not act like a professional medium who had just successfully produced a desired result. She showed sympathy for Saul, in view of the character of the message, and offered him something to eat. One would have expected her to set a large fee for so important a person. Her kindness cannot be laid to any favor she hoped Saul would grant her, either, for the message had said that Saul would die on the very next day.

6) ***The form of Samuel.*** The form in which Samuel appeared is not made clear. It may have been corporeal in nature, or it may have been more like an apparition. The woman was able to see the form, but apparently Saul was not, for the woman had to describe Samuel to Saul (28:14). It is possible that the woman and Samuel were in one room, Saul in another; or it may be that God gave only the woman the ability to see Samuel. The presence, however, was real, whether in corporeal form or as an apparition. Saul was able to converse with Samuel. If Samuel was in another room, the conversation must have been through a door or passageway.

7) ***The possibility that an Amalekite killed Saul.*** Though the implication of I Samuel 31 is that Saul died from a wound he inflicted on himself by falling on his sword (31:4, 5), it does not preclude the possibility of what an Amalekite later told David. The man claimed to have been the actual executioner of the king (II Sam. 1:8-10). He may have spoken an untruth in this, thinking thereby (wrongly) to gain favor with David, or it may be that Saul did not wound himself fatally and so asked this Amalekite standing nearby to strike a final blow. There is no way to be sure regarding this matter.

8) ***Israel's situation at Saul's death.*** The political and military situation when Saul died on Mount Gilboa could hardly have been worse. The benefit Saul had brought to the land in the form of unification and strength had largely dissipated during his final poor years of rule. The army now was small in number and here in this battle was devastated. Matters had already been bad enough in respect to the Philistines, in that they had been able to move as far north as the Esdraelon Plain, but now, with this victory won,

almost all of the land lay open to their control quite as they wished. This fact is made clear by Ish-bosheth's action in making his capital in Transjordan (II Sam. 2:8, 9), apparently not daring to rule from Gibeah or anywhere west of the Jordan. It is made clear also by the degree of panic that was experienced in Gibeah when news of the defeat came: it was at this time that Mephibosheth was dropped by his nurse as she fled in terror. The result was lameness in both his legs (II Sam. 4:4).

9) ***Saul's remorse.*** As Saul fell on his sword that day, the remorse he felt in view of all that had happened must have been very great. He had experienced a wonderful opportunity when young, and here he was dying with nothing to show for it. Forty years had passed, and the people were actually worse off than when he had started. Instead of his defeating the Philistines, they had now defeated him and could take over the land. He could not have avoided remembering Samuel's two messages of rejection, as well as the words of doom uttered on the previous day. All that Samuel had declared each of these times had come true. And now another man would sit on Israel's throne, the man, indeed, he had wasted recent years in pursuing. He had lost and David had won. It was an awful way to die.

10

David's Kingdom

Our interest now turns to Israel's second king, David. The Bible speaks of him as Israel's greatest king and accordingly devotes more space to him than to either Saul or Solomon. It is appropriate and necessary that we also give more attention to him. As in the case of Saul, it is well to look generally at the kingdom he instituted before considering the details of the history as presented in the sacred record.

A. DAVID THE MAN

1. HIS FAMILY

David was of the tribe of Judah, the son of Jesse and great-grandson of Boaz and Ruth (Ruth 4:21, 22; I Chron. 2:12-15). He had seven older brothers, Eliab, Abinadab, Shammah, Nethaneel, Raddai, Ozem, and one unnamed who may have died shortly after David's anointing (I Sam. 16:5-10; I Chron. 2:13-15). He also had two half sisters, Zeruiah and Abigail, who were born to David's mother while she was the wife of Nahash, before she married Jesse. Zeruiah had three sons, Abishai, Joab, and Asahel, and Abigail had one, Amasa (II Sam. 17:25; I Chron. 2:13-17), all of whom came to be close associates of David. The possibility exists that Nahash was the king of Ammon, the man whom Saul had defeated at Jabesh-gilead (I Sam. 11:1f.). At least the name is the same; for some reason this Nahash, in contrast to his bitter relationship with Saul, was friendly toward David (II Sam. 10:2) as was also his son Shobi (II Sam. 17:27-29). It may be remembered that Ruth, Jesse's grandmother, had come from Moab, which was historically related to Ammon. This tie makes it seem more likely that David's mother may once have been married to the king of Ammon. Also it was back to Moab that David sent his parents for safety during the days of his flight from Saul (I Sam. 23:3, 4), showing a continuance of the same close tie.

While still young, David was considered the least in his father's household, for he was assigned the family flocks to tend, recognized in the day as a humble task. He was not even taken along by the rest of the family to the community time of sacrifice, when Samuel had come to Bethlehem (I Sam. 16:11). Also, when later he brought food to his three older brothers in Saul's army, the oldest, Eliab, spoke most scornfully to him (I Sam. 17:28), and this happened well after the time when David had been anointed. David, however, did not return evil for evil, for after he became king he actually appointed Eliab to be head of the tribe of Judah (I Chron. 27:18; Elihu equals Eliab). The third brother, Shammah, is also mentioned during the time of David's reign: his son Jonadab was the one who gave wicked advice to Amnon (II Sam. 13:3-5, 32, 33), and another son, Jonathan, killed a giant in Gath (II Sam. 21:21). Still another relative is mentioned later on, an uncle of David, named Jonathan. David made him a counselor (I Chron. 27:32).

2. THE MAN HIMSELF

a. His birthplace

David was born and raised in the vicinity of Bethlehem of Judah. Here he learned the beauties of nature, as he cared for the family flocks. Here, too, he learned how to care for himself in the rugged hills of Judah, a lesson which was to hold him in good stead in later days of fleeing from Saul. He practiced with the sling, with which he killed the mighty Goliath one day. He also learned the ways of guiding and disciplining sheep. As a result, he developed the wisdom necessary for governing Israel well (cf. Ps. 78:70-72). It may be that he gave a portion of his patrimony in Bethlehem to the son of Barzillai, Chimham, because of Barzillai's friendship at the time of David's flight from Absalom (II Sam. 19:31-40); if so, Chimham's family held it for a long time (cf. Jer. 41:17).

b. His appearance

David was not tall like Saul, but he evidently was of fine appearance. When Samuel first saw him, he is said to have been "ruddy" and of "a beautiful countenance, and goodly to look at" (I Sam. 16:12). Later, Saul's servants described David to the king as "a comely person" (I Sam. 16:18), and later still, Goliath saw David as "ruddy and of a fair countenance" (I Sam. 17:42). These expressions all suggest an appearance that was pleasing and handsome rather than the ruggedness of a warrior type. At the same time, Saul's servants spoke of David as mighty, valiant, and a man of war. Evidently they knew of something David had done to show his ability in combat already as a lad. That he indeed had such ability is demonstrated by his later handling of both a lion and bear with his bare hands, catching, as he says, the lion by his beard as the beast rose up against him. Such a feat called for strength, swiftness of movement, and excellent skill. He showed similar dexterity in escaping from Saul's attacks with the spear (I Sam. 18:10, 11; 19:10). David himself said that God gave him feet like "hinds' feet" (feet of a deer) and "hands to war, so that a bow of steel is broken by mine arms" (Ps. 18:33, 34). These notations show that David was agile, strong, and skilled in combat. Jesse's eighth son was an attractive and capable young man.

c. His character

1) ***A man of God.*** First and foremost David was a man of God. In fact, already before Samuel went to anoint the young man, God referred to him as a man after His own heart (I Sam. 13:14; quoted in Acts 13:22). Following his rule, the degree to which other kings were faithful to God was measured by David's standard (e.g., I Kings 3:14; 9:4; 11:4, 6, 33, 38; 14:8; 15:3). It was because of David's fine rule that his posterity would continually rule (II Sam. 7:12-16; I Chron. 17:11-14), and it was for the same reason that God would defend Jerusalem (Isa. 37:35) and not take the throne entirely away from Solomon's son (I Kings 11:12, 13, 32, 36; 15:4). Much later kings are said to have occupied David's throne (Jer. 22:2, 4, 30; 29:16), and the ruler of the far future is identified as David (Ezek. 37:24, 25; Hos. 3:5). David is used as the measure of strong men in that future day (Zech. 12:8). Of special significance is it that Christ Himself is called the "son of David" many times (e.g., Matt. 1:1; 9:27; 12:23; 15:22), and that it was necessary for Christ to be born in Bethlehem because it was the city of David (John 7:42). David did have his failures, especially in respect to Bathsheba and her husband Uriah (II Sam. 11) and later in calling for a census of the country (II Sam. 24), and the biblical stress is never on David's sin, as with Saul, but on his righteous acts.

The main reason for this exemplary life of David is that he was continuously empowered by the Holy Spirit from the day of his anointing onward. This is the significance of I Samuel 16:13, "And the Spirit of the LORD came upon David from that day forward." During the approximately fifteen years prior to his reigning, then, he was empowered so that he would be protected until that time; and he was empowered during the forty years while he ruled. That he recognized this empowerment and cherished it highly is revealed by his prayer at the time of his sin with Bathsheba and Uriah, "Take not thy holy spirit from me" (Ps. 51:11). He remembered the downfall of Saul when the Spirit was removed from him; he did not want the same thing to happen to him. And that he knew the Spirit was not removed at that time is shown by his words in his last days, "The Spirit of the LORD spake by me, and his word was in my tongue" (II Sam. 23:2).

2) ***A man of ability.*** Saul's servants, who found and described David to Saul as his prospective musician, recognized the young man as unusually able. They said that he was "cunning in playing" and "prudent in matters" (I Sam. 16:18). They of course would not have recommended him at all if he had not been unusually skillful with his stringed instrument. David may have been able to play more than one instrument (II Sam. 6:5) for he is said to have been an inventor of instruments (I Chron. 23:5; II Chron. 7:6; Amos 6:5). Besides playing instruments, David was renowned as a writer of words that could be put to music. For this reason he is called the "sweet psalmist of Israel" (II Sam. 23:1). In Hezekiah's time, the Levites were commanded to "sing praise unto the LORD with the words of David" (II Chron. 29:30). And the titles to the Psalms indicate that David wrote no fewer than seventy-three of them.

Further, David was expert as a leader of men. This follows from his success as a king, and it is demonstrated most dramatically by his success with a conglomerate group of followers during his days as a fugitive. These men are described as those who were "in distress," those "in debt," and those who were "discontented" (I Sam. 22:2). People so described are not normally easy to live with; they have had trouble elsewhere and can be expected to have more in any new situation. David, however, was able to weld them into a unit that stayed with him as a splendid fighting force, not only during his days of fleeing, but also during his time of rule.

Closely allied with David's ability for leadership was his success as a military man. After he was appointed to be Saul's commander, Israel did not lose a battle with the Philistines. For this reason the people described his vanquished foes as ten thousands and Saul's only as thousands (I Sam. 18:7). He did not lose battles after he became king either, though then Joab was the principal commander. It was David himself, however, who defeated the Philistines decisively just after being accepted as king over all Israel (II Sam. 5:18-25).

David's expertise as a marksman with the sling should not be overlooked either. He took five stones when he went to meet Goliath, but he needed only one. No doubt he had practiced long and diligently when in the pasture fields. That his first stone went home to its mark was no accident; he simply was skillful.

Besides this, David was a statesman of high quality. He became Israel's finest king. This was due to God's blessing, but God uses means, and the means here would have been David's ability in statesmanship. As will be seen, David took a kingdom that was in shambles and built it into an empire. Such an accomplishment does not just happen. The man at the top is all-important. David, in fact, was so important that Israel came to be known as David's country rather than David as Israel's king. Then, when Solomon came to power, the king of Egypt permitted his daughter to marry Solomon (I Kings 3:1). Though this was not to Solomon's advantage religiously, it was most significant as to the respect Egypt had for Israel at this time. In times past, Egyptian rulers had been extremely selective in their royal marriages.[1] Though Egypt at this time was not as powerful as earlier, the fact that the marriage was permitted is highly indicative of the height to which David had brought his country.

3) ***A man of humility.*** David, for all his ability, was humble. When chased by Saul through the barren hills of Judah, though he had long before been anointed as Saul's successor, he still spoke of himself as a dead dog, a flea, and a partridge (I Sam. 24:14; 26:20). Never did he speak insultingly to Saul, but always respected him as God's anointed. Most young men, if anointed to be king, would become boastful and proud. David was still willing to tend sheep.

4) ***A likable person.*** One test of greatness is whether a person is liked by others or not. People whom others admire are liked; those not admired are shunned. David was liked by other people. Jonathan, the logical heir to Saul's throne, came to love David as his own soul. This was in spite of a marked age difference between them[2] and David's replacing him as the heir apparent. Hiram, king of Tyre, is said to have been ever "a lover of David" (I Kings 5:1). The two had many business relationships, and clearly Hiram had taken to David as a person to be trusted and liked. But perhaps the most striking example is what David's band of refugee soldiers thought of him. One day when David wished for a drink from his old favorite spring at

[1]See pp. 305-306.
[2]See p. 153.

Bethlehem, three of the leaders broke through the enemy lines of the Philistines to get it for him (II Sam. 23:15-17; I Chron. 11:17-19). This was devotion of the highest kind.

5) ***A patient person.*** David displayed patience, which is perhaps one of the rarest virtues. One almost has to wonder why he did not flee or take some drastic measure of retaliation against Saul much sooner than he did. Saul had tried to kill him five different times before David was convinced that he would have to leave. Even then, he wanted Jonathan to test Saul once again to see if there were any possibility of reconciliation (I Sam. 20).

6) ***A nonvindictive person.*** Small people hold grudges; magnanimous people overlook them. David might have held a grudge against his older brother Eliab for belittling him all during his younger days, especially at the scene of the Philistine battle (I Sam. 17:28). He did not however, but, as noted, even appointed the man as head of the tribe of Judah. He might also have been vindictive toward Saul, but he was not. He had opportunity twice to take Saul's life, but both times, contrary to the urging of his men, refused to do so (I Sam. 24:3-7; 26:5-11).

7) ***A person not above passion and scheming.*** Two matters may be noted to David's detriment. The first is that he was not above passion and scheming to his own advantage. He schemed while a fugitive, when he became a mercenary soldier for the Philistines, serving Achish, the king of Gath (I Sam. 27). He was with Achish for sixteen months (27:7), and during this time convinced the man that he was truly serving him, though he was really building a base of friendship with the people of Judah. He would raid southern cities and then distribute the booty to Judah's people; later, when he returned to his Philistine base at Ziklag, he convinced Achish that he had served only Philistine interests. Then the well-known instance of David's adultery with Bathsheba shows that he was a man of passion (II Sam. 11); and his dealing with Uriah, her husband, in having him sent to the front lines of battle to be killed, shows again his weakness for scheming.

8) ***A poor disciplinarian.*** The second weakness is that David was not a good disciplinarian of his children. It is said of his fourth son, Adonijah, that his father had "not displeased him at any time" by bringing reprimand (I Kings 1:6). It was no doubt in large part for this reason that David had problems with his family. Absalom killed the oldest son of David, Amnon (II Sam. 13:28, 29), and later revolted against his father. Even then, David's love for his son caused him to urge Joab not to kill the young man in a battle that was soon to occur (II Sam. 18:5). He loved his family dearly, a noble quality, but he let this stand in the way of proper discipline.

B. DAVID'S GOVERNMENT

1. GENERAL CHARACTERIZATION

David ruled first over Judah only, making his capital at Hebron. Next to nothing is known of the organization he established for this period. After seven-and-a-half years, however, he was asked by the other tribes to rule them as well, and then he made his capital at Jerusalem. It is the organization he established at that time that is the object of our interest here. It was an efficient organization, expanded considerably over that established by Saul, but still less pretentious than what was instituted later by Solomon. It was adequate for the task of ruling, while not extravagant.

2. THE COURT

a. David's family

David's family was larger than that of Saul. From various lists given (II Sam. 3:2-5; 5:13-16; I Chron. 3:1-8; 14:4-7; II Chron. 11:18), one finds included no fewer than eight wives and twenty-one children. The wives were: first, Michal, married to him while at Saul's court, from whom no children were born; second, Ahinoam, who bore Amnon; third, Abigail, who had been the wife of Nabal and who bore Daniel (also called Chileab); fourth, Maacah, who bore Absalom; fifth, Haggith, who bore Adonijah; sixth, Abital, who bore Shephatiah; seventh, Eglah, who bore Ithream; and eighth, Bathsheba, with whom David sinned when she was yet the wife of Uriah and who bore Solomon. The first seven had become David's wives before he became ruler in Jerusalem. Bathsheba was married to him after that time. And besides Bathsheba, there were other unnamed wives taken at Jerusalem, II Samuel 5:13 stating, "And David took him more concubines[3] and wives out of Jerusalem, after he was come from Hebron." Though the total number of these additional concubines and wives is not given, at the time of David's flight from Jerusalem before Absalom, at least ten concubines were left to keep the palace (II Sam. 15:16). It was customary in that day for powerful kings to keep large harems, and David apparently followed the practice.

To Bathsheba, in addition to Solomon, were born Shammuah (or Shimea), Shobab, and Nathan (II Sam. 5:14; I Chron. 3:5; Bathshua equals Bathsheba), besides her first child that died (II Sam. 12:19). Other sons born to unnamed wives were Ibhar, Elishua (or Elishama), Nepheg, Japhia, Elishama, Eliada, Eliphalet, Nogah, and Jerimoth. One daughter is known, Tamar, sister of Absalom (II Sam. 13:1; I Chron. 3:9). According to I Chronicles 3:9 there were also sons of the concubines, who are unnamed.

[3]These were wives of a second-class status.

b. David's officers

Two similar lists of leading officers under David are given, one from the beginning of his rule (II Sam. 8:15-18; cf. I Chron. 18:15-17), and one from its close (II Sam. 20:23-26). Serving in a military capacity were Joab, commander of the army, and Benaiah, commander of two foreign divisions that appear to have served as David's personal bodyguard, the Cherethites and Pelethites. Superintending civic duties were Jehoshaphat, the *mazkir,* and Seraiah, the *sopher.*[4] The *mazkir* ("one who reminds") was probably a person who kept records and reminded the king of appointments and responsibilities. He may also have served as official herald for assemblies. The *sopher* ("scribe") was the official secretary. Named in the second list is Adoram as superintendent over the *mas* ("tribute labor").[5] Since he is included only in the second list, it is probable that he was not needed until late in David's reign, when apparently this type of unpopular, conscript labor came to be used. Leading in religious matters were Zadok and Abiathar, the two high priests. These David inherited, due to the atrocious deed of Saul, as discussed earlier.

Another list of officers, though evidently of secondary status, is given in I Chronicles 27:25-34. Here two officers seem to have been more important: Azmaveth, in charge of the king's treasuries, and Jehonathan, in charge of field products, city materials, and provisions stored in towers (strongholds). Under the latter the following seemed to have served: Ezri, over workers of the fields; Shimei, over the vineyards; Zabdi, over the wine from the vineyards; Baal-hanan, over the olive and sycamore trees; Joash, over the olive oil; Shitrai, over livestock in the Sharon Plain; Shaphat, over livestock in the valleys (probably valleys that cut into the inner hill country); and, under these last two, Obil took care of camels, Jehdeiah asses, and Jaziz goats and sheep. Besides these, in other categories, Jonathan (an uncle of David), Ahithophel, and Hushai served as counselors, and Jehiel acted as governor of the king's children. When Ahithophel died (II Sam. 17:23), Jehoiada and Abiathar took his place as counselors.

How many of these officers sat at the king's table is not indicated. Probably at least the more important did. Along with David's family, the total number would have been sizable. And besides these were Mephibosheth, to whom David showed kindness for the sake of Jonathan (II Sam. 9:1-13), and probably Chimham, whose father Barzillai had befriended David in his flight from Absalom (II Sam. 19:37, 38).

[4]These two officers find parallels in known Egyptian court personnel. See William F. Albright, *Archaeology and the Religion of Israel,* p. 120.

[5]Probably the same as Adoniram of Solomon's day (I Kings 4:6; 5:14), whose task was essentially the same.

3. THE ECONOMIC SITUATION

The economic situation of David's kingdom was much stronger than that of Saul. No longer did the monarch have to be modest in his program. David was not extravagant in spending, as was Solomon later, but it is clear that his possessions as king became very extensive. Though he operated a strong government and maintained a large army that fought many battles, he apparently was able to avoid financial difficulty. Even the wealthy Solomon, who spent far more lavishly than David, at one time had to borrow as much as 120 talents of gold from Hiram of Tyre (I Kings 9:14).[6] Note also that David was able to leave an incredible amount of silver and gold for Solomon to build the temple (I Chron. 22:14). His sources of revenue included the following:

a. A taxation program

Though no details are given as to how David organized a taxation program or how much was assessed, it is clear that the people were taxed, and possibly quite heavily, as Samuel had predicted (I Sam. 8:14, 15, 17).[7] One indication is the list of officers just noted. David had general superintendents over the palace treasuries, over products that came in from the fields and cities, and over what was stored in stronghold towers. He had subofficers over various divisions of field workers, vineyards, olive trees, and livestock. These people were no doubt responsible for income from these sources, probably in accord with prescribed assessments. Another indication is that Solomon later had a taxation program so oppressive that people asked for relief following his death (I Kings 12:4); it is not likely that he began this without having learned the basic principles from his father. Moreover, David had an excellent opportunity for beginning such a program. He had signed an agreement with the tribal leaders at the beginning of his reign over all Israel (II Sam. 5:3), and one may be sure that a part of that agreement involved taxation. David had seen the weakness of Saul's rule because of lack of money and power, a problem he would have wanted to avoid.

b. Tribute money from vassal states

David took over control of one foreign country after another, and each was required to pay annual tribute according to the custom of the day. Even the king of Hamath, far to the north, whom David never encountered in

[6]A talent weighed over 66 pounds. At the present rate of over $200 per ounce, each talent was worth about $200,000.

[7]Ugaritic references show that high taxation was common for the day; see Roland deVaux, *Ancient Israel: Its Life and Institutions,* p. 140.

battle, sent him "vessels of silver, and vessels of gold, and vessels of brass" (II Sam. 8:10). This followed David's defeat of Hamath's southern neighbor, Zobah; the ruler of Hamath apparently did not want the same thing to happen to him. No doubt David received an immense sum in gold and silver annually from this source.

c. Gifts from visitors to David's royal court

It was customary for state visitors to bring gifts. No specific gifts are recorded from David's time, but in a later day the queen of Sheba brought no less than 120 talents of gold, besides other valuables, when she came to see Solomon. Still later, the king of Syria sent "ten talents of silver, six thousand pieces of gold, and ten changes of raiment" (II Kings 5:5) when his army general, Naaman, came to see King Jehoram of Israel. David, having brought a great empire under his control, would have had many such gift-bearing visitors.

d. Revenue from caravan travel

It was customary that caravans, traveling with their merchandise from one country to another, pay a tax to countries they passed through on the way. In Saul's day yet, much of the caravan travel between Egypt and northern countries would have by-passed Israel, staying on the *via maris* that lay near the Mediterranean. But David's control reached all the way to the Mediterranean and so he would have been able to impose the tax. Since caravan travel was extensive, this too would have been a fruitful source of income.

Besides monetary income, two other matters of an economic nature call for mention. The one concerns forced labor, the corvée, that was generally so hated by people. Solomon came to use this source of unpaid labor extensively and there is reason to believe that David did in his later days, at least, with non-Israelites of his kingdom. It was noted earlier that the second list of David's officers, which comes from the last part of his reign, contains an Adoram who "was over the tribute [*mas*]" (II Sam. 20:24), meaning that he was superintendent of tribute labor. Forced labor, though not a source of income in silver or gold, was a distinct asset; building operations could be carried on without expense to the public treasury.

The other additional matter concerns land ownership. Though no figures are given regarding the amount of land controlled by David, he must have owned a great deal. When Mephibosheth was brought to the palace, David had no problem in giving to the young man all the land that Saul had controlled (II Sam. 9:9, 10). David apparently had plenty of his own. All income from such land would have gone directly to the government.

4. THE ARMY

a. The men

Several indications are given relative to David's army, which, in view of the remarkable success achieved, must have been formidable and well trained. It appears to have consisted of three parts.

The first was the core group, which David had recruited during his days as a fugitive. At first 400 men had constituted this group (I Sam. 22:2) and later 600 (I Sam. 25:13; 27:2). This original complement had been made up of men "in distress," "in debt," and "discontented" (I Sam. 22:2). Some at least were from foreign countries, such as Zobah, Ammon, and Hatti (II Sam. 23:36-39). Uriah, the husband of Bathsheba, for instance, was a Hittite (II Sam. 11:6f.). It was this group that David hired out to Achish as mercenaries stationed at Ziklag (I Sam. 27:1-12), and that became very successful there in defeating southern tribal peoples, such as the Geshurites, Gezrites, and Amalekites (I Sam. 27:8).

After David became king of all Israel, it was this core that twice defeated the Philistines decisively in the valley of Rephaim (II Sam. 5:18-25). The Philistine force was much larger, but David's troops were well drilled and mobile, and took the larger group both times by surprise. It was probably this group that is referred to as "Gittites" in II Samuel 15:18 and "mighty men" (*gibborim*) in several other passages.[8] This term *gibborim* is used, for instance, when a group is mentioned as being with David in his flight from Absalom (II Sam. 16:6); also when David's supporters are listed in the account of the revolt of Sheba (II Sam. 20:7); later when supporters of Solomon are named in the account of the attempted rebellion of Adonijah (I Kings 1:8, 10); and still later when attendants are listed on the occasion of David's closing admonitions as king (I Chron. 28:1). It was probably from this group that the special "mighty men" were selected, named in II Samuel 23:8-39 and I Chronicles 11:10-47, all of them probably commanders in the main group. The recorded list of thirty may have named leaders over divisions of twenty each, and a special group of five may have served over them.[9] The high caliber of this group is indicated by the remarkable exploits of its members (II Sam. 23:8-21; I Chron. 11:11-25). Note also the conduct

[8]The term *gibborim* is used for armies other than David's but almost always with an added term, such as *hayil,* "of valor." This is never true for David's group. Also, when used of David's army, the term, especially in I Kings 1:8, 10 and I Chron. 28:1, seems to carry a particular reference.

[9]The elite five are listed in two classes: first, Jashobeam, Eleazar, and Shammah; second, Abishai (brother of Joab, with Joab himself not named) and Benaiah, each listed with corresponding exploits. The "thirty" (actually thirty-two are named, probably indicating later additions) are listed without exploits. I Chron. 11:41-47 adds sixteen additional names, suggesting further additions.

of one, Uriah the Hittite, who, when called back from battle by David, would not even go to his own home, since this comfort would be out of keeping with his duty as a soldier (II Sam. 11:11).

The second part of David's army was much larger, but probably not used as often. This was a group of 24,000 that David kept in service as a standing army, changing the personnel every month (I Chron. 27:1-15). This means that he had a total of 288,000 men on which to draw, who probably were expected to be prepared at all times for immediate action if needed. These may have been recruited on the basis of a thousand per clan. This at least seems to have been a system used in earlier days. That is the reason why the phrase "captain of a thousand" (*sar 'eleph*) is used so often (e.g., I Sam. 17:18; 18:13), and even "captain of a hundred" (I Sam. 22:7), and "captain of fifty" (I Sam. 8:12). The units of a thousand evidently were broken down into units of a hundred and of fifty. It was likely this group that turned against David when Absalom called on them, and their number is then described as "the sand that is by the sea" (II Sam. 17:11).

The third part of David's army was made up of foreign mercenaries. At least one group of these appears to have served as David's private bodyguard, made up of Cherethites and Pelethites (II Sam. 8:18; 15:18; 20:7; I Kings 1:38, 44). Not much is known about this group, but on the basis of the names it is believed the members were of Cretan and Philistine background. They remained loyal to David in the rebellion of Absalom (II Sam. 15:18; cf. 20:7) and were present and last heard from at Solomon's anointing to kingship (I Kings 1:38, 44). They may not have gone to war frequently but stayed with the king for his personal protection. There is no indication how David obtained their services.

b. The weapons

The principal weapon was the sword or dagger (*hereb*). The weapon of Ehud, one of the judges, is called a *hereb* and is described as double-edged and only a cubit long (Judg. 3:16).[10] Probably most swords were similarly short for easy handling. Goliath, however, had a *hereb* which he carried in a sheath and was probably much longer, in keeping with his size (I Sam. 17:51).

Another weapon was the spear or javelin. Two words are so rendered in the Old Testament. One is *romah,* which may originally have referred only to a pointed stave, but in time came to signify a staff with a metal head fastened by a pin or socket. It was this weapon that Phinehas used to kill the Israelite man and Midianite woman at Baal-peor (Num. 25:7, 8). It is mentioned frequently (e.g., II Chron. 11:12; 14:8; 25:5; 26:14). The other is *hanith.* It is thought to have been a shorter spear which could be thrown.

[10]The word translated "cubit" is *gomed,* which is used only here and so the exact length is not known. It had to be short, however, to fit on Ehud's thigh and be hidden.

This is the weapon which Saul threw at David and imbedded itself in the wall (I Sam. 19:9). It was also the weapon which Saul stuck in the ground to mark his place among his troops and which revealed his identity to David (I Sam. 26:7). It too is mentioned frequently (e.g., I Sam. 20:33; 22:6; 26:7; II Sam. 1:6). Specimens believed to be the *hanith* have been found in excavations.

A third main weapon was the bow (*qesheth*). By the middle of the second millennium, it had already become a sophisticated weapon, made of a combination of wood and horn, which gave it a long range. It may not have been used extensively by Israel in earlier days, though Jonathan had one (I Sam. 20:20), and at least one group that came to David in his days as a fugitive were armed with bows and slings (I Chron. 12:2). Probably others had them also. Arrowheads have been found dating back to 1300 B.C., in both Phoenicia and Palestine.

A fourth weapon was the sling. It was a primitive weapon but continued to be used in warfare for some time (II Kings 3:25; II Chron. 26:14). It was used effectively by the men of Benjamin, who did not miss with it by a hairbreadth (Judg. 20:16). Its most famous use, of course, was by David against Goliath.

5. THE ADMINISTRATION

Little is revealed regarding the actual administration of David's kingdom. Since it was a strong administration, one would think that more would have been said, but the absence of information only points up further that God's criterion of what to include in the sacred text concerned what was religiously significant, not just general facts.

That the administration was well organized follows from the capacity of the kingdom to expand as it did. An empire is not built without a strong home base. It follows also from the agreement that David made with the Israelite leaders at Hebron, as noted in respect to taxes. Saul had not established a strong rule, and David would have wanted to avoid such weakness. One may be sure that David had provisions written into the agreement that would give him power for organizing and unifying the tribes.

There are two lists of people who quite clearly were appointed as officials in this organization. One is in I Chronicles 26:29-32; it pertains to Levites who served in the "outward business" (*mela'kah hitsonah*), which is defined in verse 32 as "every matter pertaining to God and affairs of the king." These men appear to have been appointed over administrative tasks both religious and civil in kind. On the west of the Jordan, some 1,700 were given appointments, apparently under the headship of one named Hashabiah, and on the east (Transjordan) no fewer than 2,700. No reason is given why more were needed for the two-and-a-half tribes on the east than for the nine-and-a-half on the west.

The other list is in I Chronicles 27:16-22, where heads of tribes are named. It would seem that David appointed a head for each tribe, no doubt to oversee its affairs, like a governor over a state. This man probably had people working under him. What his relation may have been to the Levites just noticed is not indicated. David appointed his older brother Elihu (Eliab) as head of Judah, as noted earlier (27:18). For some reason which is not revealed the tribe of Levi is included in the list and also both halves of Manasseh as separate entities, while Gad and Asher are omitted.

6. THE COURTS

Nothing specific is revealed in respect to courts as operated under David. It may be presumed that the court system established by the Mosaic law was continued. Since the reign of David was more law-abiding than was the period of the judges or the reign of Saul, it may be that the system was carried out more carefully than at any time since the days of Joshua. Levitical cities continued,[11] and therefore, no doubt, the cities of refuge, to which one who had killed another might flee. He would be judged by the elders of the city of refuge to determine his degree of guilt. If he was innocent of intent to kill, he was allowed to live, though only in that city, where he would be protected from the blood-avenger of the one slain. If he was guilty, he was killed.

7. THE EMPIRE

With the home country firmly established and controlled, and with an effective army organized and available, David was in a position to wage war on foreign soil as need arose. Many such wars were fought, with the result that David built what may truly be called an empire. One cannot call his kingdom a military government, as with Saul, though he made far more conquests than Saul. Fighting was not an end with him, nor did the strength of his rule depend on fighting and winning battles. He was a statesman, as well as a skilled military tactician, and his government was well organized and staffed. When the occasion arose, however, he did not back down from war but was able to meet any enemy that came. His army, whether led by himself or Joab, was seldom if ever defeated. The result was that his borders continually enlarged, and an empire was formed. His main conquests include the following:

[11]Albright (*Archaeology and the Religion of Israel* p. 121) believes that it was David who first designated these cities. The Scriptures show them, however, as already established under Joshua (Josh. 21:1-41).

Map 5. The Empire of David and Solomon

a. Moab and Edom

The first major conflict was with Moab, on the east side of the Dead Sea (II Sam. 8:2; I Chron. 18:2).[12] This was the country with which David had been remarkably friendly in earlier days. He had found refuge there while a fugitive and had taken his parents there for safekeeping during the same period. Now, however, for some unknown reason, a battle ensued and David inflicted a complete defeat. Afterward he used very harsh measures against Moab; this suggests that the provocation for the battle had been serious. The result was that Moab now became a vassal state, apparently being allowed to keep her own king but having to pay tribute.

Some time later, David fought and defeated Edom, located south of the Dead Sea (II Sam. 8:13, 14; I Chron. 18:12, 13). Little description is given regarding this battle. It occurred in the Arabah Valley (''valley of salt''; cf. II Kings 14:7),[13] and a severe slaughter was inflicted. According to I Kings 11:15-18, Joab killed ''every male in Edom'' (likely meaning every man of the army), remaining in the land for six months to accomplish the gruesome goal. The royal household was slain as well, with only Hadad and a few servants being able to escape to Egypt. Garrisons of Israelite soldiers were left, indicating that the state became a vassal to Israel. These two victories gave David sovereignty on the east and south of the Dead Sea, including an avenue to the Gulf of Aqaba, an important waterway for trade.

b. Damascus, Zobah, Hamath

In the north, David achieved victory over strong Zobah from whose king he seized 1,000 chariots, 700 horsemen, and 20,000 foot soldiers (II Sam. 8:3-12; I Chron. 18:3-11).[14] David spared from slaughter only enough horses for a hundred chariots. It is clear that, though the Philistines had used chariots for years (Judg. 1:19) as had the Canaanites (Judg. 4:3), still David did not do so. This was probably because much of his fighting was done in mountainous terrain where the chariot is only a hindrance.

When the Aramaeans of Damascus came to assist Zobah, arriving after the defeat had been inflicted, David won a further victory over them. He demanded tribute as a result and received it. It was at this time that Toi, king of Hamath, sent his son to bring tribute to David. This brought all the northern region under David's control. David placed garrisons in Damascus, as he had in Edom, indicating the imposition of vassal status. How far

[12]Both II Sam. 8:1 and I Chron. 18:1 list a preceding engagement with the Philistines. This was a minor battle, however, for only a few towns were taken.

[13]The term *valley of salt* is also available to Wadi el-Milh near Beersheba, but it is not likely that an offensive war with Edom (which this seems to have been) would have been waged so far into Israelite territory.

[14]Albright (*Archaeology and the Religion of Israel,* pp. 130-131), in opposition to Winckler and others, points out that this Zobah was truly north of Damascus.

north the power of Damascus reached at this time is not clear. It did not reach as far as Hamath on the Orontes River, for this area merely acknowledged David's sovereignty by their tribute.[15] The resulting status of Zobah, between the two areas, is not made clear.

Regarding the coastal region to the north, along the Mediterranean, David had early made a treaty with Hiram, king of Tyre, respecting material and labor for building David's palace (II Sam. 5:11). This resulted in peaceful conditions—never is warfare indicated between David and Phoenicia.

c. Ammon and Zobah

An important war with Ammon, again to the east, is described in greater detail (II Sam. 10; I Chron. 19). Chronologically, this engagement may well have preceded the northern struggle just noticed,[16] though the record of it follows in the biblical account. David's kindness toward Hanun, a new king of Ammon, had been misunderstood, and messengers sent by David had been insulted. Ammon, fearing reprisal from David, immediately prepared for war. Hanun hired mercenary soldiers from the Aramaean states, Beth-rehob, Zobah, and Maacah.[17] David sent Joab with Israel's army to meet this combined force, and Joab displayed marked ability in deploying his troops so that a decisive victory was won.

Joab then returned to Jerusalem, but Hadadezer, king of Zobah, wanting to save face for his defeated forces, came again with fresh troops for a return battle. David's army moved across the Jordan to meet him at Helam[18] and once more won a complete victory. The opposing force, now sorely depleted in numbers, retired from the scene, acknowledging Israelite supremacy.[19]

Joab then laid siege to Rabbah, identified with present-day Amman, capital of Jordan, twenty-two miles east of the Jordan River. Rabbah was then the capital of the state of Ammon, and this move by Joab seems to have been a continuation of the struggle begun earlier by Ammon (II Sam.

[15]Abraham Malamat, "Aspects of the Foreign Policies of David and Solomon," *Journal of Near Eastern Studies* 22 (Jan. 1963), pp. 6-7, notes that Toi seems to have changed his son's name from Hadoram (I Chron. 18:10), typically West Semitic, to Joram (II Sam. 8:10), typically Hebrew, thus showing a strong Hebrew influence. Hamath evidently became quite dependent on Israel.

[16]Because Zobah was involved at this time, too, and actively engaged against Israel, whereas in the northern struggle she was fully subdued and so no longer in a position to assist should Ammon or any other have called.

[17]For location of all three, see pp. 40-41.

[18]See p. 239, n. 5.

[19]Cf. Malamat's presentation of the chronological order of David's contacts with Hadadezer and his allies: "The Aramaeans," *Peoples of Old Testament Times,* ed. D. J. Wiseman, p. 142.

12:26-31; I Chron. 20:1-3). It was during this time of siege that David sinned with Bathsheba and had her husband, Uriah, placed at the point of heaviest fighting so that he would be killed (II Sam. 11:1-27). Rabbah was finally taken and David assumed the crown of Ammon, thus annexing this country, making it a part of his own kingdom.

This was the extent of David's conquests. Taken together, the victories made the breadth of his authority most impressive. The kingdom proper included both all land originally allotted to the twelve tribes (except for a part of Philistia along the southern Mediterranean) and the kingdom of Ammon. Vassal states, which were permitted to keep their own kings, included Moab and Edom, east and south of the Dead Sea, and the Damascus area to the northeast. Zobah was probably also included, though this is uncertain. And an area which at least acknowledged Israelite sovereignty was Hamath, still farther north. Since the boundary of Hamath reached northeast to the Euphrates River, David's authority was recognized, in some measure, all the way from the Gulf of Aqaba and the River of Egypt[20] in the south to the Euphrates in the north. This was the area which God had promised to Abraham for his posterity centuries before (Gen. 15:18). It did not rival the vast territories of Egypt, Assyria, Babylonia, Medo-Persia, or Greece in their empire days, but David was no doubt the strongest ruler of his time.

8. THE RELIGIOUS PERSONNEL AND SANCTUARY

a. The prophets

Among David's religious personnel, two prophets, Nathan and Gad, were of special significance. Gad had been with David even in his days as a fugitive (I Sam. 22:5) and more than once offered helpful advice. In the last part of David's reign, he was still active—he was the one who offered David the choice of three punishments from God for the sin of taking a census (II Sam. 24:10-15). It was Nathan who told David that God would not permit him to build the temple (II Sam. 7:2-17), and later he had the hard task of reprimanding the king for his sin with Bathsheba (II Sam. 12:1-15). He also played a prominent role in Solomon's acclamation as king (I Kings 1:11-45). David always showed the highest respect for both men, even when they brought words of reprimand. This speaks well for the prophets, who

[20]River of Egypt (*nahal misrayim;* Num. 34:5) is best understood as designating the Wadi-el-'Arish, reaching the Mediterranean 45 miles southwest of Gaza and 80 miles east of the Pelusiac mouth of the Nile. For discussion, cf. Kenneth Kitchen, "Egypt, River of," *New Bible Dictionary,* pp. 353-354.

evidently conducted themselves in a manner to warrant respect, and it speaks well for David who, though he was king, recognized them as proper spokesmen for God.

b. The priests

Notice has already been made that David had two high priests, Abiathar and Zadok, a situation contrary to the law, which called for only one. Abiathar had escaped to David when Saul had killed the priests at Nob, and he had remained with him since. On coming to power, David found that Zadok was recognized in Israel as high priest, quite possibly having been appointed by Saul after the Nob massacre. Both were descendants of Aaron, and so both had rights to the position. Contrary to what one would expect, Zadok came to be favored by David; he put Zadok in charge of the ark during Absalom's revolt (II Sam. 15:24-29). Later, Zadok helped in the anointing of Solomon as king while Abiathar supported Adonijah (I Kings 1:7f.). As a result Zadok and his family continued in the office of high priest, and Abiathar was expelled by Solomon to his home city, Anathoth (I Kings 2:26, 27).

Under these two high priests, David organized the priests and Levites into specific courses.[21] The priests were divided into twenty-four courses, with each course designated to serve at the central sanctuary for a week in turn. Thus each course usually had two weeks total service during a year (I Chron. 24:1-19). He may also have similarly divided the Levites, previously sectionalized into "singers," "gatekeepers," "officers and judges," and general priestly assistants.[22] At least the "singers" were so divided (I Chron. 25:1-31) and, if these, probably the other sections as well.[23] It is clear that David was properly concerned with the religious life of the people and believed that efficient service by the priests and Levites, as enhanced by this manner of organization, would help in making it the finest possible.

[21]The main reason was that the priests and Levites were too numerous to serve at one time. Since this condition would have existed also in the period of the judges, David may have had precedent for what he did. When the ark was away from the tabernacle, this system could have fallen into disuse, with David now reviving and strengthening it.

[22]When these distinctive Levitic groups came into existence is not indicated. I Chron. 9:17-26 shows that at least the "gatekeepers" were distinct from the time of Moses. The "singers" were the religious musicians; the "gatekeepers" the guardians of the sanctuary (with specific gates assigned—I Chron. 26:13-19); and the "officers and judges" (*shoterim, shophetim*) seemingly the special recorders and court judges assigned to various tribes (I Chron. 26:29-32). Most Levites conducted the more normal Levitic duties, as described in I Chron. 23:28-32.

[23]The large number of Levites would have been the reason, for David's census revealed 38,000 Levites of service age, of whom 4,000 were "singers," 4,000 "gatekeepers," 6,000 "officers and judges," and the remaining 24,000 general assistants (I Chron. 23:3-5).

In further contrast to Saul, who had such a poor relation with priestly personnel, David had the ark brought to Jerusalem. It had been at Kirjath-jearim since the battle of Aphek (I Sam. 7:1), which had been fought more than seventy years earlier.[24] Saul had left it there, but David now brought it to the city he had recently established as Israel's new capital. He placed it in a special tent he had prepared (II Sam. 6:17). David wanted to make a grand temple for it, but God forbade this, so David contented himself with the tent. He made there an altar, however, probably after the fashion of the altar at the tabernacle, and it was to this altar that both Adonijah and Joab fled for safety following the coronation of Solomon (I Kings 1:50; 2:28). Certain Levites were assigned to conduct ceremonies at this tent (I Chron. 16:4-6), while Zadok and others were assigned to the original tabernacle which was then at Gibeon, about six miles northeast (I Chron. 16:39).

[24]Intervening had been the twenty years between the battle of Aphek and that of Mizpeh (I Sam. 7:2), a few years between that battle and Saul's anointing, the forty years of Saul's reign (Acts 13:21), and then David's seven years at Hebron.

11

David's First Thirty Years

David was made king in Hebron when he was thirty years old (II Sam. 5:4). Some of his experiences up to that time have been noted from Saul's viewpoint, but not from David's, and many have been by-passed altogether because they did not pertain to Saul's history as much as to David's. These events, now from the viewpoint of David, call for attention in this chapter.

A. ANOINTED BY SAMUEL

1. THE STORY (I SAM. 16:1-13)

David is introduced into the sacred record at the time Samuel anointed him as Israel's future king. We can only conjecture regarding his life before that occasion. Since he was left with the sheep on that day, it is certain that shepherding was one of his tasks, and probably had been since he had been old enough to assume it. The story of David's anointing suggests that his father, Jesse, was a recognized member of his community, being called along with others to the sacrifice. Jesse probably was at least moderately affluent, and no doubt was proud of his eight sons. That David had seven older brothers, who clearly tried to dominate him (I Sam. 17:28; 20:29), could have made life difficult for the boy and given him something of an inferiority complex. As suggested earlier, if he had really wanted to come to the sacrifice, it would seem that he could have; for surely there were servants who could have cared for the sheep for a few hours. He may have been quite willing to stay at home, preferring the quietness of the open field to the bustle of a sacrificial gathering.

David had been doing more than caring for sheep, however; he had also been developing various skills. One concerned music. He must have become proficient, too, for he was selected one day to play before the king. Another skill was writing. In that he wrote at least seventy-three of the recorded psalms, he must have had a gift for writing and used that gift from these early days. He may well have written verses while tending the sheep. Still another was expertise with the sling. One part of a shepherd's job was protecting sheep from predators. The sling, when used accurately, was a helpful weapon for this purpose. Since David, in using one against Goliath, struck the giant precisely on the forehead—his one vulnerable spot—it may be concluded that he had practiced long and well. He probably could have qualified among the Benjamites who could hit a mark with hairbreadth accuracy (Judg. 20:16).

The day when David was anointed must have been an extraordinary experience for him. So far as he knew, the occasion was to be merely a sacrifice at Bethlehem. It was true that the honored Samuel would be present, but this had not stirred his young blood enough to want to be present. When his father came to call him from the field, then, he could only have been most surprised. And when his father informed him of the reason—that Samuel wanted to anoint him as Israel's future king, since all seven of the older brothers had not been chosen—he must have been astonished. Upon arrival at the scene, he would have become the center of interest. The honored Samuel himself would have greeted him, and then the anointing ceremony would have taken place. What an experience this must have been! He, David, was thus honored, while the older brothers could only look on. Probably the occasion seemed quite like a dream to him at the time. The oil was poured on his head, he heard Samuel's words that God had chosen him as Israel's future king, and then it was over. Apparently, a meal was eaten (16:11), at which David would have had the honored seat.

It is interesting to speculate what David's life was like following this occasion. For one thing, he must have relived those moments before Samuel again and again. He had actually been anointed king. As to his daily activities, however, they probably changed little from what they had been. It is clear that caring for sheep continued to be his job (I Sam. 17:15). Then, as to the difference David experienced because of having been empowered by the Spirit, one can only guess. It may be that he became more God-conscious than ever before. He may have seen nature around him in a more

God-centered light. The greatest significance, however, would have come when he met situations that challenged his own powers. At these times there would have been the extra ability granted by the Spirit—such occasions, for instance, as when he met and killed a lion and a bear (I Sam. 17:34, 35).

2. POINTS TO NOTICE

a. God's use of natural abilities

It is true that God uses the "weak things of the world to confound" the mighty—for the reason that weaker people are usually more humble people—but it is also true that God looks for able people and uses their ability when it is properly dedicated to Him. David may have been the youngest in his family and given the most humble task, but he was also the most able member. The others may not have wanted to admit it, but even before the day of the anointing they must have recognized that he had unusual talents. He could play music, write verses, and throw a stone with a sling better than any of the older brothers. They did not know, of course, that one day God would use these natural abilities in avenues of the most important service. God knew, however. First in priority for one so to be used is the dedicated heart, but when that is present, then the more ability that can be given to God, the more the person can be used and the more effectively.

b. God's way of preparation

God sometimes prepares His servants in unusual ways. The normal place for a future king to be trained is in a palace, where he can learn the ways of courts and administration. David, however, was prepared in a field, tending sheep. Though David could not have learned the ways of courts and administration there, he could have learned much in terms of oversight and protection. God knew that these would be prime requisites when he ascended the throne, for people, after all, are much like sheep. They need a shepherd, who gives oversight and protection. Patience is one of the choicest virtues of every true shepherd, for sheep go astray and act stupidly; David would need great patience when he became king. God knew where Israel's greatest king could best get the finest training.

c. God's judging by the heart

Samuel thought, when he saw the oldest of Jesse's sons, Eliab, that he must be the chosen one, for he was tall and handsome. God refused Eliab, however, and reminded Samuel: "Man looketh on the outward appearance, but the LORD looketh on the heart" (16:7). The character of Eliab's heart was made all too clear by the way he treated David later when David came to him in the army camp (I Sam. 17:28). He showed on that occasion that he would not have made a suitable king for Israel.

d. God's empowerment by the Spirit

God not only had David anointed, but He immediately gave him special empowerment for tasks and challenges he would face until the day his actual rule would begin. And there would be tasks and challenges! He would go to the palace to play for the king; he would encounter the giant Goliath; he would lead Israel's armies against the Philistines; he would have to keep a cool head while his life was sought by the king; while a fugitive he would lead a band of discontented men in difficult circumstances. David was eminently successful in all, and the main reason certainly was this special empowerment.

e. The interval between anointing and actual rule

The question has well been asked why God saw fit to have David anointed so many years before he would actually reign. The reason may well have included the following matters: First, the interval gave David time for further preparation for the kingship. He was given opportunity to experience palace life and learn about courts and administration. Second, the interval provided a challenging test for David's faith—would God really bring fruition to his anointing? (That the last of these years were spent as a fugitive made the test especially challenging.) Third, the interval gave opportunity for him to become known, prior to his time of rule, so that he could more easily be accepted as ruler by the people. The great victory over Goliath would have been publicized far and wide, and also his later conquests over the Philistines as the brilliant young leader of Saul's armies. Saul had found it necessary to wait until he could display his ability at Jabesh-gilead before he could become actual ruler, but such was not the case for the already famous David.

B. THE DEFEAT OF GOLIATH

1. THE STORY (I SAM. 16:14—17:58)

One of David's earliest and greatest challenges came when he met the giant Goliath. God intended this occasion to prepare David for the kingship, and brought the encounter about in His own remarkable way.

The first step was an invitation to the young man to come to the palace as court musician. There was need for such a musician because of the spells that came on Saul following his second and final rejection as king. There is no way to know how long David was at the palace before the Philistine threat arose. It was probably a few months at least, and during this time David was called on to play in the king's presence whenever a spell came on him. What else David did during this time is not indicated, though it is said that he was made an armorbearer of the king. He evidently was not the chief armorbearer, however, for he was not taken along to battle when the Philistine encounter occurred. He at least proved satisfactory in his task of playing music, and this gave him a unique opportunity to learn the ways of court life.

When Saul's troops marched out to meet the Philistines, David, for some reason, was sent home. He suddenly found himself back with the sheep (17:15), instead of out with the army, where he probably wanted to be. It may have been during this time at home that the episodes involving the lion and bear transpired, of which he spoke to Saul later (17:34). If so, these episodes would have been nicely timed in preparing David for the still greater challenge of the giant.

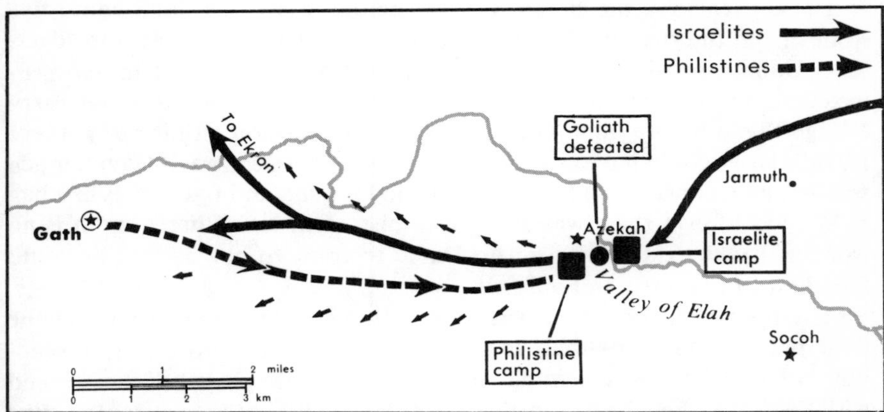

Map 6. The David and Goliath Battle

A second step in bringing about the encounter with Goliath occurred when David's father, Jesse, asked David to go and see how three older brothers, who were in Saul's army, were faring. He sent along bread, corn, and cheese for them, which the young man probably carried in a donkey-drawn wagon. It would have been about a fifteen-mile trip to the battlefield, which David likely made early in the morning, taking perhaps four or five hours for the journey.

On arrival, David left the wagon and moved quickly to the Israelite army and found his brothers (17:22). About the time he located them, the boastful Goliath made his daily appearance. David was shocked at the defiance he bellowed forth, but even more astonished at the lack of response by anyone in Israel's army to do anything about it. It was at this point that his brother Eliab reprimanded David, perhaps because he felt a personal sting at David's reaction. Soon Saul learned that David was in the camp and called for him. To the king the young musician said, "Let no man's heart fail because of him [as indeed had been happening for the last forty days]; thy servant will go and fight with this Philistine (17:32).

These words no doubt sounded foolhardy to the king—coming from one whom he knew only as a player of beautiful music—but they came from a heart full of remarkable faith. To convince the king that the words were not empty, David told Saul of his conquests of the lion and bear (17:34, 35). Finally convinced, probably in part because he had no real alternative, Saul agreed and had David try on his own armor with which to meet the giant. It did not fit, however, and David put it off. David further indicated that he really did not want it since "he had not proved it," meaning that he was not skilled in its usage.

David then took the simple weapon he did know, his sling, chose five stones from the stream of Elah nearby, and went forth to meet the adversary. Goliath saw him coming and disdained him. The big man had protected himself with armor from head to foot; in addition he had a man carry a large shield before him. There was just one place on all his body where David's stone could have any effect: his forehead. In contrast, David, much smaller, had no armor and only the sling in his hand and five stones in a bag at his side. If ever there was a physical mismatch, it was here; and it is no wonder that the giant cried out to David to come to him so that he could feed him to the birds and animals.

The mismatch, however, was purely physical. David retorted that the huge man of nine-and-a-half feet was coming merely with material weapons, while David was coming in the name of the Lord of hosts; and with the Lord's help he would give not only Goliath but the entire Philistine army to the birds and animals (17:46). The Philistine then started for David, no doubt angered by these outrageous words, and David took aim. He waited until the protecting shield was down, and then let fly. The stone went home to its mark, the small moving target of a few square inches of forehead, and the great man fell to the ground. Apparently the shield-bearer did not try to interfere as David ran to the fallen man and cut off his head, giving himself and the whole army of Israel a great and significant victory.

2. POINTS TO NOTICE

a. David's opportunity for training

It was pointed out earlier that David had experienced valuable training for being king while a shepherd of wayward sheep. He needed to know about court life, too, however. God now brought this about. Certainly his job of playing for Saul did not require a great amount of time, and one can imagine that a diligent person like David would have used this time well to learn all he could. He would have had access to conversation with almost everyone in the palace, and simply to observe would have been valuable for future days.

b. Man's disappointment and God's appointment

One may assume that David was disappointed when he was not allowed to go to battle against the Philistines. He probably heard the plans being made at the palace for countering the invasion, but when the time came to effect them he was sent home to tend the same sheep he had left a few months earlier. If it was during this time that the incidents with the lion and bear occurred, as suggested, this disappointment was really God's way of getting David ready for the bigger encounter with Goliath. His confidence would have been bolstered greatly by his success in killing these two powerful animals. How often are man's disappointments really God's appointments!

c. Evidence of David's faith

The shock David experienced on seeing the giant and hearing his defiance was mainly due to his own remarkable faith in God. Others in the army were concerned, all right, but principally out of fright; no one had the courage to do anything in retaliation. David was completely taken aback at this. His attitude was: how can an Israelite, who believes in the true God, possibly let this manner of defiance go on without answer? David simply had a greater and more genuine faith in God than did anyone else in the camp and therefore was ready to go against the huge man, if no one else would.

d. Disappointment in Eliab

Older brothers are supposed to be examples to younger brothers. They are supposed to lead the way and give help. Eliab, David's older brother, not only did not do this but was a tool of Satan to hinder David at the crucial moment. He tried to quiet the boy in his inquiries regarding Goliath and even charged him with insolence in coming to the camp at all. David might have responded in anger, for he had not come insolently, but only at his father's request and in the interest of the brothers. He must have been extremely disappointed in Eliab, though probably this was not the first time the man had acted in this way.

e. David's wise choice

Saul wanted David to use the normal protection of armor and the customary weapon of a sword, but David wisely refused. He had not learned to wear armor or use a sword as he watched over the sheep, but he had learned to use a sling. Also, quickness of movement had always been a strong point in his favor (as demonstrated in the incidents with the lion and bear, and later in avoiding Saul's spear), and the armor would only slow him down. He knew his own abilities and he chose to use them. Sometimes Christians try to do things for which they are not qualified, just because they have seen others do them; the result is normally disaster.

f. A great demonstration of faith

The faith in God that David displayed, as he moved out against Goliath, should thrill everyone who reads the account. Goliath presented a terrifying sight. When he told David that he would feed him to the birds and animals, he was saying only what seemed completely possible and likely. Every natural measure of the coming encounter said that David had no chance. But in spite of this, David replied to the giant that he would feed not only him to the birds and animals, but the whole army of the Philistines. And, having said this, he measured the man, stood his ground, let fly the stone at the right moment, and felled the great one as a giant oak. It must have been a tremendous thrill to see the mighty opponent downed by merely a sling!

g. The value of previous practice

David's accuracy that day was not a stroke of luck, or even the result solely of God's supernatural guidance of the stone. David had chosen to use the sling because he knew the weapon, and he knew what he could do with it. God blessed him in using it, so that the stone did find its mark, but God clearly used the means of David's own expertise. And this had been gained certainly through hours of practice. David had used his time in the field to good advantage. The practice may have seemed tedious at times, but now it paid off. One never knows when skills that have been developed through long hours of effort will be of prime importance in the work of God.

h. The potential of just one man of faith

Sometimes it is easy to think that one man alone can do very little that is effective for the Lord. Many people are needed if important developments are to be seen. David, however, was only one man and he made the big difference in this time of battle. The whole army of Israel had been held in fear until he arrived in camp. He was no larger than anyone else, and he had certainly experienced less combat in war than most others there. From a human standpoint, his presence could have made little difference. But he had something the others did not have; he had great faith in God. And with this, he alone made the difference. Israel won over the Philistines in the crucial battle because of the one man David.

C. DAVID, JONATHAN, AND SAUL

An unusual triangular relationship now developed between David, Saul's son Jonathan, and Saul. David came to love Jonathan, but only to respect and fear Saul. Jonathan respected his father, but came to love David. He attempted to effect a good relation between his father and David. Saul loved his son Jonathan, but came to hate David and desire his life.

1. DAVID AND JONATHAN

a. The story (I Sam. 18:1-4; 20:1-42)

The story of David and Jonathan, in their love for each other, is most unusual. For one thing, as has been pointed out, they were of different ages. Jonathan was already old enough to command an army in his father's second year of rule (I Sam. 13:1, 2); David, on the other hand, was not born until eight years after this, because he was only thirty when he began to rule, following Saul's forty-year reign. Jonathan, then, was probably between twenty-five and thirty years older than David, really old enough to be his father. Another remarkable feature is that Jonathan was the heir apparent to Saul's throne, being the oldest son. One would expect that if anyone were to be jealous of David, it would have been Jonathan. He was not, however.

Instead it is said that Jonathan came to love David as his own soul, following the victory over Goliath. In token of this close friendship, he gave David his robe, garments, sword, bow, and girdle (18:3, 4). These gifts were his indication to the younger man that he knew David would reign in his place. Whether David revealed to Jonathan that Samuel had actually anointed him to the kingship is not indicated, but somehow Jonathan recognized the destiny of the young man. No doubt a part of this recognition lay in the knowledge he had of his own father's rejection. Saul had not been willing to accept the rejection as final, but quite clearly Jonathan had. Jonathan was evidently a man of greater faith than his father, as demonstrated already in his battle at Michmash (I Sam. 14). Besides this, Jonathan, being highly capable himself, was quick to recognize ability in another. David was his kind of man.

It was because of this deep friendship that David came to Jonathan for counsel before fleeing from Saul. David raised the question of why Saul persisted in seeking his life. Jonathan replied that his father always confided in him regarding his plans, and since he had never said anything regarding a desire to take David's life, these prior attempts must have been passing outbursts of anger and not planned occasions. David then observed that probably the reason Jonathan did not know of such plans was that Saul knew Jonathan loved David. When David insisted that death could come at any time, Jonathan asked what David wanted of him. David formed a plan to absent himself from Saul's regular monthly meeting and to wait for Jonathan to report to him Saul's reaction to his absence.

Jonathan agreed to the plan, urging David always to be kind to himself and family, in the event this should be their last opportunity to see each other. Then, after making arrangements for signaling to David what the results might be, he went to the meeting. The first day, Saul said nothing about David's absence, but the second day he did, asking Jonathan the reason. When Jonathan spoke up in David's favor Saul became angry, charged Jonathan with befriending David, and even cast a javelin at his own son.

At this, Jonathan became convinced of his father's evil intentions toward David. The next morning he told David what had happened and then left him to pursue his life as a fugitive from the king. The parting must have been very sad, for the two did not know if they would ever have opportunity to see each other again.

b. Points to notice

1) ***The value of friendship.*** Any normal person needs friends and the encouragement they can offer. In David's trying days, while he was being hunted by Saul, it is without question that this close friendship with Jonathan was a comforting and sustaining force. Their friendship made it natural for David to seek out Jonathan for counsel in the crucial hour before making the final decision to leave the palace.

2) ***The importance of accepting God's will.*** In that Jonathan was willing to give David his tokens of heirship to the throne shows that he had accepted God's revealed will regarding the next king; Jonathan accepted the fact that he was not to ascend the throne. This would not have been easy. And Jonathan probably would have made a fine king, in view of his excellent qualities. He might have reasoned that, because he had these qualities, God was not being fair in denying the throne to him, and so refused to acquiesce to the revealed will. Jonathan did not do this, but, unlike his father, accepted the fact.

3) ***Age difference and friendship.*** Normally, close friendships develop between people of the same age. This is because their interests are similar. Age does not have to be a barrier, however, to close friendship. It was not in the case of David and Jonathan. Their mutual respect and their need for the strength they could give each other were reasons enough to bind them together. Years earlier, Naomi and Ruth had shown a similar love, though Naomi was a generation older than Ruth. Age does not have to prevent close friendships.

4) ***The importance of counsel.*** It is almost always wise to seek counsel from a trusted friend before making an important decision. David might have argued that he had reason enough to flee from Saul, without conferring with Jonathan that day. There had been several outright attempts made on his life by Saul, and they could not all be laid to outbursts of uncontrolled anger. The decision to leave, however, was a crucial one. David would no longer be the commander of Israel's army. He would no longer have the comforts of palace life. He would have to leave his new wife Michal. He would have to part from his close friend Jonathan. In place of this pleasant life of his, he would have the unpleasant prospect of having always to run for his life and find ways of procuring food without ever trusting himself too much to someone who might give him away. The decision, then, was a vital one, and David wisely sought counsel before making it. The man is wise who follows a similar procedure.

5) ***Secrets even among "confidants."*** Jonathan thought he knew the innermost plans and desires of his father. He told David that Saul did not keep anything great or small from him (20:2). Such relationships are fine, but sometimes secrets are kept even from those who are closest. Probably Saul and Jonathan were as close as a father and son could be. They planned strategies and battles together, as at Michmash. But because of Saul's bitterness toward David, in contrast to Jonathan's love, he did not reveal to him his plans or intentions toward the son of Jesse. Jonathan was surprised when he learned the truth. This provides a lesson that one must not trust confidants too far, especially if they have special prejudices.

6) ***Accepting demonstrated truth.*** When shown what Saul really thought concerning David, however, Jonathan was willing to accept the truth. He did not persist in his prior opinion in some false show of maintaining face. He had been wrong in his statement to David and he was quite willing to admit it. The truth was apparent: Saul did want to take David's life. Jonathan recognized the fact and acted accordingly.

2. DAVID AND SAUL

a. The story (I Sam. 18:5—19:24)

David must have felt very exhilarated at winning over Goliath. He had come to the palace, had been sent home prior to the battle, and now had become the honored champion of the battle after all. Also, the close friendship with Jonathan that developed must have been very gratifying, and finally there was the captaincy given him over Israel's troops; and he probably was still not more than twenty years of age. Capping this would have been his continuing victories as commander and then the plaudits of the people as they proclaimed, "Saul hath slain his thousands and David his ten thousands."

All this was brought to a rude halt when Saul suddenly showed the jealousy that had been building within him and attempted to kill David with his javelin. David must have felt both surprise and disappointment. He had been serving the king well, and now he was being repaid in this manner. The story implies that he believed the attack was due only to a sudden outbreak of anger on Saul's part, however, and so he did not try to get away or take any steps to change his life pattern.

For this reason he did not suspect an ulterior motive on Saul's part when he now offered Merab to him in marriage. He thought of Saul as merely paying off the promise he had made before the victory over Goliath. He did not suspect anything even when the plans were changed and Michal was substituted for Merab, nor when Saul asked for a dowry of the lives of one hundred Philistines. In fact, David apparently felt relieved at this demand for he had stated that he had nothing adequate to give the king, since he did not come from a family of sufficient standing and affluence. He, therefore, set out to bring Saul the dowry, actually doubled it, and then married Michal.

Though Saul's plan for David's death at the hand of the Philistines thus did not work out, he was now temporarily assuaged in his attitude toward David due to a timely intercession by Jonathan (19:1-6). As a result, David was permitted to lead the Israelite troops when war with the Philistines broke out once more. He won again, and this once more prompted jealousy on Saul's part and also a new series of attempts on David's life. First Saul tried again to kill him with a javelin. Then he ordered soldiers to seize and kill David when he left his house one morning. Finally there was the occasion when three groups of messengers were sent to apprehend the young man. Saul himself eventually went, and instead of seizing David, joined with assembled prophets and the three groups of messengers in rendering praise to God.[1]

[1]See discussion of these occasions, p. 156.

It was after these three attempts on his life that David went to consult Jonathan. Though he had explained away Saul's earlier behavior in terms of angry outbursts, these attempts on his life could not be so explained. Saul's intentions were very clear.

b. Points to notice

1) ***Suffering of the innocent.*** It is common to think that any conflict involves wrong on the part of both parties. This is very often true, but not always. Sometimes the wrong is entirely on the part of one. This was the case with David and Saul. No hint is given that David was anything but circumspect in his behavior, and yet Saul persisted in wanting to kill him. One might guess that surely David had done something to provoke the king. But the story indicates that David did only what the king had told him to do, and did it very well. He led the army and continually won, and having done so, was still willing to continue his role as musician to the king. For this, the king tried to take his life these several times.

2) ***Honor not guaranteed by good performance.*** It is common to think that a good performance of duty leads to honor. Again, this is generally true. Sometimes this does not happen, however. David performed well. But in fact, this contributed to his trouble. Because he won all his battles, the people acclaimed him, and Saul became jealous. It may be that David also played too well to suit Saul, and this could have added to the king's jealousy. It may have seemed there was nothing the young man could not do. David, for whom excellence seems to have been a driving force, must have been taken aback when he realized the reason for Saul's anger. The king was actually angry because David did his job too well. Similar situations can occur today, when people become jealous of those who do things with excellence.

3) ***Benefit of the doubt.*** For as long as possible, David gave Saul the benefit of the doubt in respect to attempts on his life. Not many would have still played for the king after a direct attack with a javelin. But David did. He evidently reasoned that it was because of the spell Saul was having, and that he therefore should not think ill of the man. How many people of any day are quick to judge another person to his disadvantage, even when there is insufficient cause! How much better it is to be charitable and give the other person the benefit of the doubt. There comes a time, of course, when no doubt remains—as it did finally with David—but all doubt should be removed before making a judgment. If one is to make a mistake, it is better to make the mistake on the side of overcredulity than overcriticism.

4) ***Humility in spite of prominence.*** David still remained humble, though Israelites were singing of the ten thousands he had killed. He might have become proud and assumed an attitude of "look-who-I-am," for indeed no one else had defeated Philistines on such a scale, and apparently few others could play an instrument as he could. Given this newly attained popularity, he might easily have refused to continue the more menial task of playing music for the king every time he had a spell. This, however, David did not do. Instead, when offered the king's daughter—whom he as victor over Goliath had a right to marry (I Sam. 17:25)—he spoke only of his unworthiness to be son-in-law to the king (18:18). Humility is pleasing to God. It is always in order no matter what accomplishments a man may have achieved.

5) ***David's military ability.*** Deserving of special notice is David's evident military ability. No one else could win over the Philistines, but David did. How or where he had learned military strategy is not revealed. He had learned personal combat when a lad in the field, demonstrated in his encounters with the lion and bear. But personal combat is one thing and troop combat another. He may have learned much from Jonathan, who had been victorious earlier at Michmash. In any case, he was capable also in this art.

6) ***God's protection.*** The thought must not be missed that God was with David at all times and saw to it that Saul was never successful in taking David's life. David was to be Israel's next king and therefore must not die. Natural means seem to have been used to provide the necessary protection until the last attempt on his life, when, as noted in Chapter 9, God intervened directly. The Holy Spirit was sent upon the three groups of messengers and then on Saul in such a way that none of them so much as touched David. He was spared from any harm, while Saul lay all the following night in a fit of despair. Saul had great power as Israel's king, but so long as God's protection was over David there was no chance for Saul to take his life. This should be a comforting thought to every child of God who faces perilous conditions.

D. LIFE AS A FUGITIVE

When David fled from Saul the change in his relation to the king presented new difficulties for him. One problem was that he had to face a new kind of life, requiring a psychological adjustment not easy to make. Previously he had been a favorite of the people and applauded on every hand; now he would be a fugitive, legally an outlaw, hunted by the king. Another problem concerned his relation to the people as their future king. How would this new life affect the people's opinion of him? And still a third problem concerned his personal protection from Saul. The king would pursue him, and how could he avoid being caught?

Two possible alternatives confronted him. One was to move outside the land, where Saul could not follow; but this would involve risk, for he had been the leader of Israel's army and could easily be recognized by the enemy. The other was to remain in the land, gather a substantial protective band of men, and remain in sparsely populated areas where pursuit would be difficult. This, however, involved the necessity of obtaining food and shelter for many men. Further, he could not really hope to gather a force sufficiently large to withstand Saul's army. The events now to be traced show him trying both alternatives.

1. DAVID'S COURSE OF ACTION

a. The story (I Sam. 21–26)

After leaving Jonathan and procuring assistance from Ahimelech at Nob,[2] David first tried the foreign alternative. He went to the Philistine city of Gath.[3] He was soon recognized there, however, by the servants of Achish,[4] the local king, and he quickly feigned madness that he might escape harm.

David now tried the second alternative. He returned to his homeland and took up residence in a cave near Adullam,[5] where he began gathering a protective force of men. Since he was within ten miles of his home at Bethlehem, he was near enough for his father and brothers to visit him. Somehow David was able to make known—possibly by the help of his family—that he wanted men to join him. A total of 400 came—men described as in distress, in debt, or discontented (I Sam. 22:1, 2; I Chron. 12:8-15). Many like David may have been political fugitives, having fled from the capricious Saul.

Surprisingly, when the band had been assembled, David again tried the foreign alternative, this time going east to Moab.[6] He took his parents with

[2]See pp. 160-162.

[3]Often identified with Tell el-Areini, but better with Tell es-Safi, about twenty-three miles southwest of Gibeah; cf. A. F. Rainey, "Gath of the Philistines," *Christian News from Israel* 17 (Sept. 1966), pp. 31-38.

[4]In the title to Psalm 34, this man is called Abimelech. "Abimelech" may have been a Philistine title of long standing (cf. Gen. 20:2f. and 26:1f.).

[5]Identified with modern Tell esh-Sheikh Madhkur, Adullam was about nine miles east of Gath, halfway between Gath and Bethlehem.

[6]He may have crossed the Dead Sea at the Lisan (see Yohanan Aharoni and Michael Avi-Yonah, *The Macmillan Bible Atlas,* map 92) or he may have moved around the southern end of the Dead Sea. David's great-grandmother, Ruth, had come from Moab.

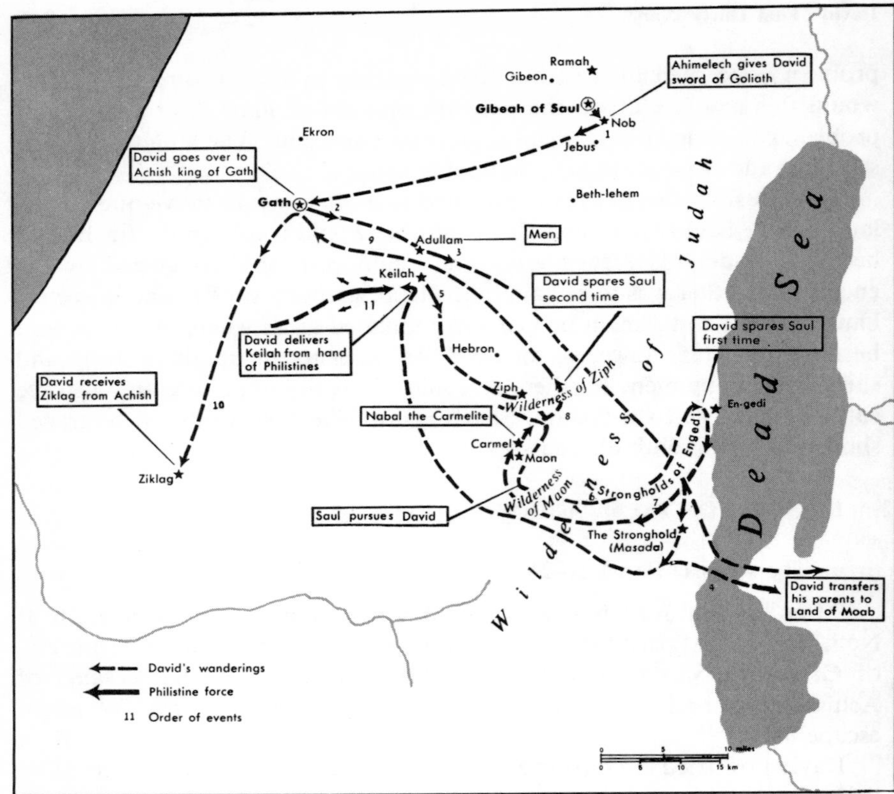

Map 7. David's Wanderings

him this time, no doubt fearing reprisals against them by Saul. For some reason, however, Gad, a prophet who had joined David's band, soon counseled him to leave Moab, and David moved once more back to Judah, locating now in an area called "the forest of Hareth," which is unknown.

Here Abiathar, son of Ahimelech, fleeing from Saul, came to David (22:20-23). The time was soon after Saul's terrible slaughter of the priests of Nob, from which Abiathar had escaped. He was high priest now, since his father had been killed. Accordingly, he brought the ephod with him, apparently including the Urim and Thummim for divine inquiry. We can imagine David's grief at news of the atrocity, but also joy that Abiathar had been able to reach him, especially since he brought the ephod.

It was not long before David had opportunity to put this divine means of inquiry to use. He learned that the Philistines were preying on the inhabitants of Keilah[7] and he sought God's will whether or not he should give

[7]Identified as Khirbet Qila, six miles east of modern Beit Guvrin, eighteen miles southwest of Jerusalem, and three miles south of Adullam.

them assistance (23:1-13). David had an interest in making friends wherever possible and he had a long-standing desire to defeat Philistines at any time. God gave a positive answer through the Urim and Thummim, and David did go to the relief of Keilah. Though he thus helped these people, further inquiry of the Urim and Thummim revealed that they would betray him to Saul if he remained with them, and so he left.

David now moved southward to the region of Ziph and Maon, below Hebron.[8] Here David had a pleasant visit from Jonathan (23:16-18), which must have encouraged him. Soon after, however, Saul made an attempt to seize David, since the Ziphites had informed Saul of David's presence among them. The king was unsuccessful for he had to return unexpectedly to fight Philistines (23:14-28). David then moved eastward to En-gedi[9] on the shore of the Dead Sea, where Saul again pursued him after the Philistine encounter (24:1-22). It was here that David spared Saul's life for the first time, when Saul entered the very cave where David was hiding and David only cut off a part of his clothing without taking his life. After this, David moved back to the region of Maon. At this time he sought food for his men from a wealthy landholder, named Nabal, who lived near his camp (25:2-42).[10] David believed that he had a right to ask for Nabal's assistance, since his men had been giving protection to the man's flocks from Bedouin robbers (25:7, 14-17). But Nabal, a surly person, was of no mind to accede, and David prepared to punish him. He would have, too, had not Nabal's more understanding wife, Abigail, intervened to supply the food needed. Nabal died ten days after she did this, perhaps partly due to the shock of learning from his wife how near to disaster he had come at David's hands. David then took Abigail as his own wife.

Not long after this, the Ziphites tried to gain favor with Saul once more by telling him of David's presence (26:1-25). Saul came and for the second time David spared his life when he could have killed him.

b. Points to notice

1) ***Problems that David faced.*** Sometimes David is criticized for seemingly vacillating between alternatives of policy and for moving about so often while a fugitive, as though uncertain and undecided. One must realize, however, that he faced enormous problems. A lesser person could easily have wilted beneath them. There was the problem of maintaining safety

[8]Ziph, identified with modern Tell Zif, is four miles southeast of Hebron and fourteen miles southeast of Keilah. Maon, identified with Khirbet Ma'in, is six miles south of Ziph.

[9]En-gedi is still called by the same name, after a fresh-flowing spring. It is sixteen miles straight east of Ziph.

[10]The procurement of sufficient food for 400 men would have been a constant concern for David.

for himself and his men, when he knew that Saul was constantly looking for them. Also, there was the problem both of persuading a sufficient number to join him and of controlling them when they did. Further, it was necessary to feed and provide for this group. This in itself must have been a tremendous challenge. After all, he was a fugitive and could not trust just anyone; and, moreover, the band lived continually in desert areas where food and water were at a premium. Still further, he had the problem of keeping friends among the general populace. If he was going to keep their favor, so that they would not report his location to Saul, he could not simply seize food wherever he might find it. He had to acquire it by proper means and in a manner which would keep people sympathetic to him.

2) ***David's remarkable success.*** On all these counts, David clearly did very well. He did continually escape Saul's efforts. He was able to gather a band of men and control them. In fact, he was able to weld them into a unity that has seldom been matched. And as for keeping friends with the populace, few people revealed his location to Saul, except the Ziphites, who did so twice. And when the time came for him to rule, it was the people of Judah—certainly including the people among whom he moved during these days—that were the first to crown him (II Sam. 2:4).

3) ***Leadership ability.*** This fact is so important that it deserves mention again: David showed remarkable ability in leading his band of men. Men of the kind that gathered to him are the very hardest to lead. That they were willing to come to David at all is noteworthy. Probably most knew of his military ability from days when he led Saul's armies, and this would have helped. But once he had assembled the group, the task of keeping them together and maintaining their loyalty was most challenging. Men of this kind respond to a leader only if he is able to do difficult tasks himself. He must have been both fair and firm when disputes arose. His judgment in procedures must have been sound, so that they recognized they could trust his direction. Seldom has history seen a leader as capable as David.

4) ***Respect for Saul as king.*** David always showed the highest respect for Saul, since Saul was God's anointed king. This is seen especially in the two times he spared Saul's life, and it is seen also in David's general attitude. Not once is he found speaking ill of Saul, in spite of Saul's unfair treatment of him. There must have been plenty of opportunity, too, when he had in his band so many others who were in distress like himself. Even when the Ziphites twice reported his position to Saul, David did not retaliate against them. Nor is it recorded that he ever spoke derogatory words about them. David's attitude in all this is remarkable and commendable.

5) ***David and Nabal.*** Sometimes David has been criticized for having had harsh intentions toward Nabal, planning to punish the man severely for not providing food for his men. One must understand the situation, however. For one thing, David was in constant need of food, and here was a man that had plenty he could share. Nabal might well have even volunteered to help David, who had been unjustly forced to flee from the king. Besides this, David clearly had been doing important service for Nabal, protecting his livestock from marauders. He not only had not seized the livestock himself, but he had served to keep it from harm at the hands of others. Therefore, Nabal owed him something in return. David probably thought he asked for very little, in view of the situation. Since he was flatly turned down, one can understand his belligerence.

2. DAVID AT ZIKLAG

a. The story (I Sam. 27:1—28:3; 29–30; II Sam. 1)

Following the second instance of sparing Saul's life, David went again to the foreign area of the Philistines; he apparently believed he could not expect always to escape from Saul as he had until that time (27:1). Then there was probably another reason for this move; it is suggested by David's request for food from Nabal. David's troops now numbered 600 (27:2), and though this was reassuring as a protective measure, it meant a major increase in food supplies. The Philistines, as others of the day, employed mercenary troops, and, if they would accept David's group, the food problem would be solved and there would be remuneration besides. Saul would not follow him there either.

The difficulty with the idea was that the Philistines might not accept David and his band, though with this protective group around him David did not have to fear for his life as at the first time he visited. David made the move and Achish did accept him. Probably the fact that David had now been a fugitive so long, as well as an apparent need Achish had for such troops, helped in the decision. At David's request (27:5), Achish assigned David to the city of Ziklag,[11] well south of Gath though still in Philistine territory, as a base of operations.

David played a dual role at Ziklag (27:5-12). Pretending to serve Achish as a mercenary, he attacked southern foreign tribes, which had been perennial enemies of Israel, particularly the Geshurites, Gezrites, and Amale-

[11]Tentative identification has been made with Tell al-Khuwailfa, twenty-three miles almost due south of Gath and twelve miles north-northeast of Beersheba. Ziklag had been one of the cities allotted to Simeon (Josh. 19:5), but apparently had been taken by the Philistines, though far from the center of Philistine activity.

kites.[12] He let Achish believe that he was distressing southern Judah, thus maintaining standing with him; all the while, however, he was distributing booty among the cities of southern Judah (30:26-31), thus keeping their favor against the day when he would be their king. This was a precarious path to tread, but David apparently did it without raising suspicion on the part of Achish.

After sixteen months of this activity (27:7), the final Philistine battle with Saul drew near, and David found himself in difficulty. He apparently had committed himself to Achish to a degree where he could not remain uninvolved without endangering his own position. Consequently he purported to go along with the Philistine plan. It is unthinkable that he really wished to participate in the battle against his own people,[13] even though he did accompany Achish on the way to battle as far as Aphek, the place of general assembly. Accordingly, he must have felt greatly relieved when the other Philistines objected to his presence and insisted that he be sent home to Ziklag.[14]

Catastrophe met David on his return to Ziklag. The Amalekites, apparently in retaliation for David's earlier raids against them, had ravaged the town and taken David's wives and the wives of all his men, besides booty. As a result, David's men, otherwise so loyal to him, came near mutiny. It may be that they had earlier disagreed with David on his whole Philistine policy, and so were ready to blame him for this major loss. David, however, was quick to act and immediately set out after the captors. Learning the location of the Amalekites from a captured Egyptian, left behind because of illness, David stormed the Amalekite camp and recovered both wives and booty. This healed the wounded feelings of the men and peace was restored. The booty taken exceeded that which had been lost, and there was enough even to distribute some to cities of southern Judah.

Three days after returning from this pursuit David learned of Israel's tragic defeat at Mount Gilboa and the death of Saul and his sons. The news was brought by an Amalekite who thought he might obtain favor from Israel's next king by claiming to have killed the prior one. He told the story that Saul, realizing that the battle was lost and that the enemy was pressing hard upon him, had called to the young man to kill him. The Amalekite

[12]The Geshurites were of Geshuri, south of Philistine land (Josh. 13:2), not of Geshur in Syria (II Sam. 15:8). Gezrites are unknown, but were not of Gezer to the north. Amalekites are well known as inhabitants of the northern Negeb.

[13]David's words to Achish never directly indicate that he wanted to go, but are carefully phrased to have made Achish think so. Had David really found it necessary to go he may have defected to aid Saul, even as the Philistine captains suspected. Certainly he would not have fought against Saul, whom he recognized as God's anointed.

[14]It is about forty-eight miles straight south from Aphek to Ziklag, a distance which took David into the third day to cover (I Sam. 30:1).

indicated that he had done so. He carried Saul's crown and bracelet as evidence to support his story.

This was convincing to David, who had no reason to doubt the man's testimony, and he responded by weeping and fasting until the evening of that day.[15] Then he returned to the young man again, though not to honor him as the man had hoped; instead he ordered the man's death for having dared to put his hand on the anointed of God. This gesture was in keeping with David's own earlier refusal to touch the king's life.

David now spoke a lamentation for Saul and Jonathan that is one of the most beautiful and touching odes of Scripture. David wanted the lamentation taught in Judah[16] and recorded in the book of Jasher.[17] The lamentation is composed of two parts, each beginning with the words, "How are the mighty fallen" (II Sam. 1:19-24, 25-27). The first consists of a description of Saul and Jonathan as fallen heroes, a deep mourning for their death, praise for their courage, and a presentation of the virtues of Saul as king; the second is a memorial to the deep friendship of David and Jonathan. No one could possibly accuse David of hypocrisy in this lamentation; its message and tone are sincere. David cared deeply for Jonathan, and he also had respect for Saul as the one God had chosen to be Israel's first king.

b. Points to notice

1) ***A spiritual trough for David.*** David's sixteen months at Ziklag probably marked a low point in his spiritual walk with God. He displayed a lack of faith in going there, as though God could not protect him in his own land; he was not honest with Achish after he arrived there; and it was only because of God's intervening grace that he was spared from having to fight his own people. Significantly, too, it was during this time that his men nearly mutinied against him, not being sure that he was leading them aright. He had been doing so well until this time, but here he definitely slipped.

2) ***The evil of duplicity.*** It was during this time that David displayed duplicity. He tried to make Achish think he was working faithfully in his behalf, while in reality he was working in his own, distributing favors to southern Israelite cities. This is always a precarious game to play, and it is displeasing to God. It is a form of deceit and dishonesty.

[15]The crown and bracelet were evidence that the man had been on hand at least shortly after Saul's death. He may have procured them, however, after Saul had died and so they were not absolute proof that he had killed the king.

[16]The translation "bow" (*gesheth*) in KJV is better thought of as the title of this ode, which was military in tone.

[17]Or, perhaps better, "book of the righteous"; "jasher" (*yashar*) means "righteous."

3) ***David's problem and God's deliverance.*** Achish apparently never came to realize David's dishonesty with him, but God brought David into a very difficult and embarrassing situation. He was nearly made to fight his own people. God apparently wanted David to see the real harm of his decision to come among the enemy. God let him come to the brink of having to fight Israel for the Philistines, the very enemy he had sought to defeat for Israel so many times in the past. It was only at the last moment that God worked matters out so that David did not actually have to do this, but God let him come close enough to teach him the lessons he needed.

4) ***Use of the word* satan.** When the other Philistine leaders, who objected to David's presence, made their point to Achish, they employed the word *satan* in a way that significantly shows its basic meaning. They said that if David should go with them he might well be "an adversary" (*satan*) in their midst. This is the Hebrew name for the devil, "Satan." The Philistine princes believed that David, while outwardly working for them, could well be actually working against them and in behalf of Israel. Satan is thus shown to be one who purports to work in a person's behalf but who really works against him.

5) ***Reprimand from God.*** God further permitted punishment for David through the raid of the Amalekites. It was a terrible blow to David when he returned from Aphek to find his wives and the wives of all his men captured, along with extensive possessions. Then in addition, his men came near to rebellion (30:6), and this must have hurt nearly as much, when they had manifested such loyalty before. Humanly speaking, the raid was doubtless in retaliation for David's earlier raids on the Amalekites; but from God's point of view it was a reprimand for David's duplicity with Achish as he made those raids. God allowed him to recapture the wives and possessions, but only after great anxiety and effort. God has His own effective and appropriate ways of bringing discipline.

6) ***Another purpose for the raid.*** This attack of the Amalekites may well have been permitted by God for another purpose; namely, to soften David's heart and prepare him to receive the news of Saul's death. One might well wonder whether the great lamentation for Saul and Jonathan would have flowed from David's pen had this raid not occurred. It made him tender again and made him realize his dependence on God. It brought him to the place of according due honor to one whom God had chosen to be king of Israel, even though that one had brought great hardship into his life. God has His own way of preparing His children for occasions He knows they will face.

7) ***The nonvindictiveness of David.*** Thus prepared, David showed his true nature in composing the lamentation and speaking only of the fine points of both Saul and Jonathan. He might have been vindictive. He might have said that this defeat on Mount Gilboa was just what Saul deserved. He might have honored the Amalekite who said he had taken Saul's life. He might have expressed relief that now he finally could make definite plans for becoming king. However, he voiced only regret and sorrow that Saul and Jonathan had both fallen in death. Again he sets a fine example.

12

David—Twice Crowned

Though Saul's death was a cause for sincere lament on David's part, it was also a signal for steps to be taken toward his own installment as Israel's king. God had promised him that position in the anointing performed by Samuel, and David had never forgotten that significant occasion. It had no doubt been a cause for encouragement through the difficult days of being a fugitive. Now the time for action had come, and it is to the manner and results of that action that we now address ourselves. David became king first of Judah, ruling at Hebron for seven-and-a-half years, and later over all Israel, ruling at Jerusalem for thirty-three years (II Sam. 5:5). He thus was crowned twice.

A. DAVID'S RULE AT HEBRON

1. THE CROWNING OF DAVID AND ISH-BOSHETH

a. The story (II Sam. 2:1-4, 8-10)

David did not move ahead on his own in seeking the kingship but first sought the mind of God, probably through the Urim and Thummim. The answer was that he should proceed, but only in the southern area, making his center at Hebron. David therefore did move with his family and all his 600 men to Hebron, with the result that the people did anoint him king over the house of Judah (2:4).

The reason for the confinement of David's kingdom to Judah at this time is not difficult to see. David was much better known in the south than in the north. He was from Bethlehem of Judah, and most of his activity had been south of Saul's capital, Gibeah. This had been true even during his years with Saul, and it was all the more true while he had been a fugitive. He had been the champion of these people, renowned for his military exploits for many years; and during his days at Ziklag his gifts and favors had been distributed among Judah's cities. No doubt a large majority were glad for the opportunity to make him king, giving them at last one in whom they could place their confidence.

The situation was different with the other tribes, because they did not know David as well. Stories would have circulated among them regarding his prowess while he was still Saul's army commander, but after he fled he probably dropped from their attention. One must remember that communications were not then as today. Consequently, on learning of Saul's death, logic led them to think first of Saul's surviving son, Ish-bosheth.[1] Three sons had died with Saul, but this one remained, along with the two daughters, Merab and Michal. Abner, who somehow had survived the slaughter on Mount Gilboa,[2] took the lead in establishing Ish-bosheth as king, significantly changing the location of the new capital to Mahanaim[3] on the east side of the Jordan. This change from Gibeah was caused by the Philistine domination of Israel on the west since the Gilboa rout. The forty-year-old new ruler was proclaimed king on both sides of the Jordan, though the extent to which people on the west either benefited or felt responsible to him is questionable. Their main concern was with the threatening presence of the Philistines.

One may ask regarding the thinking of the Philistines toward both kings, Did they consider them dangerous enemies, helpful vassals, or were they unconcerned? Regarding Ish-bosheth, they probably were quite unconcerned. His influence at most would be minimal, ruling east of the Jordan. David they may have thought of as a vassal. He had been among and served them for the prior sixteen months, and might even cooperate with them if the oc-

[1]Cf. pp. 106-107.

[2]Again Abner appears in a poor light. If he had been in the thick of the battle, as were Saul and his sons, why was he not killed as well?

[3]Identified by Aharoni with Tell edh-Dhahab el-Gharbi, on the Bithron gorge (II Sam. 2:29), thirty-two miles north of the Dead Sea and eight miles east of the Jordan River. It is mentioned by Shishak (Sheshonq I) in his victory inscription as *mhnn* (see *Ancient Near Eastern Texts,* ed. J. B. Pritchard, pp. 242-243), thus indicating its importance in the day.

casion required. Certainly they were pleased that Israel was now divided and they probably thought in terms of soon taking actual possession of the entire country.

b. Points to notice

1) ***Seeking God's will.*** David properly sought God's will before moving to seek the kingship. Since he had been anointed for the task long before, he might have reasoned that of course he should now assume this position, and then proceeded to do so without seeking further divine guidance. He sought out God's will, however. Abiathar was no doubt still with him, making the ephod and the Urim and Thummim readily available, as they had been back at Keilah (I Sam. 23:9-12). It would appear that God's discipline of David, especially in the raid of the Amalekites, had reminded David of his complete dependence on God. The commendable lament for Saul and Jonathan and now this inquiry of God both closely followed that raid. It would seem that David's spiritual trough had passed and he was restored to a place of close fellowship with God.

2) ***Gratifying acceptance at Hebron.*** Though it was only the people of Judah, and not all Israel, that crowned David at Hebron, still the experience must have been gratifying. When David had fled as a fugitive, it must have seemed that human prospects for becoming king were dim—though he knew that God had anointed him, which meant that somehow it still had to work out. The fact that it now had would have been pleasing. The thrill of the crowning would have stayed with him as a memorable occasion.

3) ***Hebron as capital.*** Hebron is located about twenty miles south of Jerusalem and nearly thirty miles northeast of Ziklag. It is in the center of Judah's territory and high in the hill country, making it easier to defend. The people of the area knew David well from his fugitive days, since his travels had taken him near the region numerous times.

4) ***Ish-bosheth not crowned immediately.*** Whereas David was crowned very soon after Saul's death, it is not likely that Ish-bosheth was. David ruled a total of seven-and-a-half years at Hebron, while Ish-bosheth reigned only two years at Mahanaim (II Sam. 2:10). He ceased ruling before the close of David's time at Hebron, but hardly five-and-a-half years earlier. He must, then, have been crowned later, and this is understandable. At first, after the Mount Gilboa catastrophe, the situation in the north was likely complete confusion. How soon and completely would the Philistines

take control, as it seemed inevitable now that they would? Could Israel survive at all under these circumstances? Ish-bosheth himself may have hesitated in wanting to rule, for fear of his life at the hands of the Philistines. Then there was the question of where to put the capital, since Gibeah did not seem safe any longer. Mahanaim was chosen, but this would not have been done quickly. Likely, then, Abner's move to crown Ish-bosheth came only after some answers to these questions emerged. David may have ruled two years or more before this move in the north.

5) ***Division of the land.*** The division of land between Judah in the south and Israel in the north, established when David became king only of Judah, was to reemerge in David's later reign at the rebellion of Sheba (see II Sam. 19:41—20:22) and climax with a complete division in the time of Rehoboam, Solomon's son (I Kings 12:1-16). It actually had already begun before the time of David. For instance, it is evidenced in the account of the numbers that responded to Saul's call before the battle of Jabesh-gilead: 300,000 from Israel and 30,000 from Judah (I Sam. 11:8). And it is implied in the description of Saul's army at the time of Goliath's defeat, when it is said that the men of Israel and of Judah took up the pursuit of the fleeing enemy (I Sam. 17:52).

The background of this division probably lay in the early indication by Jacob that the scepter would "not depart from Judah . . . until Shiloh come" (Gen. 49:10) and in the fact that Judah was the largest tribe (Num. 26:22) and was allotted much more territory than the others (Josh. 15:1-12). The other tribes apparently developed a jealousy towards the favored southern neighbor.

2. THE REIGNS OF DAVID AND ISH-BOSHETH

a. The story (II Sam. 2:5-7; 2:12—4:12)

One of David's first acts was to commend the people of Jabesh-gilead for their thoughtful deed in rescuing the bodies of Saul and his sons from further Philistine humiliation at Bethshan (2:5-7; cf. I Sam. 31:10-13). He learned of this through an informant and immediately sent messengers to the city. There was probably some political motivation in the gesture, for it could be helpful in the future if the Saul-favoring populace of Jabesh-gilead thought well of him, but there was also sincerity in the act. One may confidently assert this in view of David's earlier demonstration of benevolence toward Saul during his days as a fugitive.

A conflict between Judah and Israel was almost inevitable as soon as Ish-bosheth had been made king. It broke out first in a relatively minor skirmish at Gibeon,[4] about six miles northwest of Jerusalem (2:12-32). There Abner met David's chief, Joab,[5] by the pool of Gibeon.[6] At first only twelve men of each side fought, but the conflict widened and a small war ensued. Finally David's force emerged victorious. Because of the battle, the place came to be called Helkath-hazzurim ("field of the sword's edges"). Following the battle, Joab chased Abner's forces, but Abner was able to escape and get back across the Jordan to Mahanaim safely. On the way, he was chased by Asahel, the fleet younger brother of Joab, and Abner turned and killed him, a deed Joab was not to forget. Besides Asahel, nineteen men of David died, while from Israel's side, no fewer than 360 (2:30, 31).

As months passed, a state of tension continued between Judah and Israel (the meaning of 3:1) and all the while David became stronger in his rule and Ish-bosheth weaker. Finally a quarrel issued in a rupture between Ish-bosheth and Abner. Ish-bosheth charged his military head with having relations with Rizpah, the concubine of Saul (which, if true, was a manner of claim to the throne), and Abner became angry. As a result he offered his services to David (3:7-16). In this, Abner showed his recognition of where his best prospects lay. He had gained respect for David's ability long before, when both he and David had been active in Saul's inner circle Now that David was becoming stronger than Ish-bosheth, he wanted to change sides.

Sending a message to David, he agreed to deliver all Israel into David's control in return for his own safety and, no doubt, an honored position. David agreed, but insisted that Abner first arrange for Michal, David's former wife, to be returned to him. He probably still held a love for her, but perhaps an even stronger motivation lay in the help Michal could be to David politically. This marriage tied him with the house of Saul and could help make him more acceptable to those still loyal to Saul's family. Abner assented and brought about the return of Michal to David, much to the sorrow of her husband of the time, Phaltiel (called Phalti in I Sam. 25:44).

Abner also communicated with the elders of the northern tribes, urging that they now turn their allegiance from Ish-bosheth to David. Before he could effect an actual change, however, he was killed by Joab (3:17-27). This wanton act by David's leader was committed mainly in retaliation for the death of Asahel (3:27), though his fear of a rival for military leadership may also have played a part. David, desiring to court favor with the north-

[4]Identified with el-Jib, excavated in 1956, 1957 and 1959; see J. B. Pritchard, *Gibeon, Where the Sun Stood Still.*

[5]Abishai, brother of Joab, was mentioned earlier (I Sam. 26:6-9), but this is the first mention of Joab himself. Asahel was the youngest of the three.

[6]A pit identified with this pool has been excavated. It was dug to a depth of thirty-five feet in the rock and had a descending stairway. Further steps were found to lead another forty feet down a tunnel to a water chamber. The pit may have been used at one time as a large granary.

ern tribes, now did all he could to disassociate himself from the deed, showing true sorrow that it had happened (3:28, 29).[7]

With Abner gone, Ish-bosheth's position became still weaker and finally two of his lesser officers assassinated him. Then they carried his head to David in Hebron, thinking they would be rewarded (4:1-12). But, as with the messenger of Saul's death, David reacted in an unexpected manner and ordered that both be killed. Probably two matters motivated him in this: first, David's respect for one who had been duly appointed king of Israel, especially since he was a son of Saul, and, second, David's desire once more to disassociate himself from a deed which could bring disfavor with the northern tribes.

b. Points to notice

1) ***Words of appreciation.*** Words of appreciation to others are always in order. Too often they are not spoken. As soon as David heard of what the people of Jabesh-gilead had done for Saul and his sons, he sent words of appreciation to them. No doubt, as suggested, there was an element of political motivation involved, but David's past attitude toward Saul and his house indicates that the words were also sincere and well meant. The people of Jabesh-gilead had no reason to expect these words—in fact, they were probably surprised when the messengers came bringing them—but still David made the effort to give them. It was a demonstration of commendable thoughtfulness.

2) ***Political motivation not necessarily wrong.*** One cannot charge David with a wrong attitude even in respect to the political motivation involved, to whatever degree it existed. Political motivation is wrong when the action that results is wrong. But certainly the message of appreciation to Jabesh-gilead was not wrong, and David cannot be criticized for wanting to cultivate the friendship of these people. He cannot be criticized either for taking steps that would pave the way for him to be installed as Israel's king, so long as these steps were right in themselves. God had anointed him to be king of all the tribes, not merely of Judah, and therefore it was in the interest of having God's will accomplished that he took such steps.

3) ***The evil of vengeance.*** Because Abner killed Asahel, the younger brother of Joab, Joab harbored a spirit of vengeance afterwards that finally led him to kill Abner. He was wrong both in harboring the attitude and in

[7]David clearly believed Joab's deed was unjustified, for (1) Abner had earlier killed Asahel in self-defense, and (2) Joab killed Abner in Hebron, a city of refuge, in which it was illegal for an avenger of blood ever to kill another (Num. 35:22-25).

the murder that resulted. Abner's killing of Asahel was not outright murder. He warned Asahel beforehand, and there was even an aspect of self-defense involved—though it is possible Abner might have handled the matter without actually taking the young man's life. Joab, however, murdered Abner by plan and treachery, even doing it in Hebron, a city of refuge. It is no wonder that David fully disassociated himself from the act. Any person must be careful about harboring grudges that may lead him to drastic actions of retaliation. God said, "Vengeance is mine; I will repay" (Rom. 12:19).

4) ***The man Abner.*** It is well now to assess the man Abner, killed here by Joab. What kind of man was he? He was a cousin of Saul (I Sam. 14:50, 51). Having been chosen by Saul as military commander early in Saul's reign, he met with Saul's official administrators at their monthly meetings (I Sam. 20:25). When one looks for accomplishments by Abner in this capacity, however, he looks quite in vain. In fact, at no time is the man seen in a favorable context.

Abner is not mentioned at all in connection with the victory at Michmash. He may have been active in Saul's wars with Moab, Ammon, and Zobah, which are not described, but he is not mentioned in connection with the victory over the Amalekites, which is presented in detail. All that is said of him in connection with the time of Goliath's death is that he made inquiry for Saul regarding the background of the young David (I Sam. 17:55-57); he did nothing to fight Goliath himself. He is mentioned in connection with the occasion when David took Saul's spear and water-jug (I Sam. 26:5, 7, 14, 15), but then he appears in the poor light of one who did not protect his king. Whether he had any part at all in the final battle when Saul and his sons died is not indicated, but, if he did, he remarkably survived for he was the one who finally anointed Ish-bosheth (II Sam. 2:8, 9). Then, under Ish-bosheth, he lost the battle at the pool of Gibeon (II Sam. 2:12-17). He closed his life by defecting to David and then being murdered before he could fulfill his promise of bringing the northern tribes to accept David as king. One must say that Saul had not been very wise in choosing this man as his commander, and surely David did not lose greatly when he did not procure his services because of his murder.

5) ***David and Michal.*** The question has often been posed regarding the propriety of David's insisting that Michal be returned to him as his wife. Was he right in this? A quick, easy answer is not appropriate or possible. Michal had been David's wife at one time, and a wrong had been done to him when she was given to Phaltiel (I Sam. 25:44). Wrong as it was, however, she did become this man's wife; and the wrong of taking her from David did not make right the insistence that she come back to David again.

On the other hand, one does have to give David credit for moving through proper channels to get her back, having Ish-bosheth, the king and brother of Michal, give the order (II Sam. 3:14). It may well be, also, that Michal was not opposed to the idea. As was pointed out earlier, she was ready to be with David so long as his star was rising, but when it wasn't she was ready to marry someone else. That Phaltiel wept at this time does not necessarily mean that she did. In summary, one cannot say that David was right, but one can also see extenuating circumstances that at least make the action understandable.

B. KING OF ALL ISRAEL

1. CROWNED KING OF ALL THE TRIBES

a. The story (II Sam. 5:1-5; I Chron. 11:1-3; 12:23-40)

Though Abner had not been able to effect the union of all the tribes under David, he did lay the groundwork (II Sam. 3:17-19). It may be, however, that it was not necessary for him to do even this in order to persuade the northern tribes to come to David, for when they did, they came with a united heart and with urgency.

Exactly what may have prompted the movement is not revealed, but something did and in a big way. According to I Chronicles 12:23-40, which gives the number of people that came from each of the tribes (including Levi, for a total of thirteen), the total was in excess of 300,000. They came in this large group probably for two reasons: to demonstrate the degree of interest and sincerity that the tribes had in asking for David's leadership, and to present themselves as a military people, "armed to the war" (I Chron. 12:23), ready to do battle under David if he would accede to their request. The sight for David must have been most gratifying, after having hoped for such a day for many years. The fact that the people came "with one heart to make David king" shows full unity in the movement.

This immense group remained with David at Hebron for "three days, eating and drinking" (I Chron. 12:39). They came prepared, for they brought bread, meat, meal, figs, raisins, wine, oil, oxen, and sheep from as far away even as Issachar and Zebulun and Naphtali. The indication that "there was joy in Israel" shows that it was a happy time, as the people fellowshiped together. Such a large number can be imagined as having been spread out over a considerable part of the countryside around Hebron.

All this means that David no longer was in the undesirable position of merely wanting to be the people's king; the people were urging him to be their ruler. In fact, they cited three reasons: first, they were of like heritage with him, being the same bone and flesh; second, under Saul David had proven his ability to lead an army; and third, David, had been divinely appointed to be king over all Israel (II Sam. 5:1, 2; I Chron. 11:1, 2). Just how they knew this last reason is not clear, but somehow they did. In stating it, they spoke of David both ruling over Israel and feeding the people.

Another matter of note is that, when David expressed his willingness to accede to the request, he did so by making a league or covenant with the people. This was almost certainly an agreement between himself and the Israelites regarding his powers if and when he became their king. That he would have wanted such an agreement is understandable. The kingdom was still relatively new. One king had ruled, and he had not ruled very well. He had faced the enormous task of unifying a people fractionalized into twelve separate and quite independent units. He had made a start, but only a start. David knew that, if the kingdom ever was to be a true kingdom, it had to be built on well-understood kingly powers. His life at Saul's palace had taught him this.

It may be assumed, also, that David knew the time to acquire these powers was at the beginning of his rule. The people wanted him as king, and this put him in a favorable bargaining position. The people had come with a show of strength to persuade him to be king and this very show gave him a distinct advantage for acquiring what he needed. It would be interesting to know just how the document that finally resulted read, but, in view of the strength David manifested, when once he had taken over as ruler, one may be sure it included a broad base of authority for himself.

It is noteworthy, further, that not only the northern tribes had representatives present, but also Judah and Simeon.[8] The reason they were present was no doubt to see that their rights were not violated. After all, David was already their king. Now the other tribes were asking that he become theirs as well. Judah and Simeon wanted something to say about such a change, though they were hardly in a position to demand that David turn down the requests of the others, even if they had desired this; David was in too strong a position. But they would have wanted to insure that their rights were maintained. Furthermore they would have had to agree to the additional powers that David was now insisting on. He probably had laid down some requirements when he became king in Hebron, but he would have demanded more now, having had the experience of actually serving as king for over seven years.

One should not think critically of David for making demands in this way. That Israel should have a strong king was, after all, in the people's interest. They had been slow in giving up tribal prerogatives to Saul, and the country had been weaker because of this slowness. David knew this better

[8]Simeon, it should be remembered, had cities within Judah, and David had really been their king, as well as Judah's, for these past years.

than anyone else, for he had been in Saul's palace to see the weakness firsthand. What he was doing, then, was for the people's good, even if some were not able to see this at the time. Probably all three days were needed for the leaders to work out the details of the agreement.

b. Points to notice

1) ***God's will accomplished.*** If David was fifteen years old when first anointed, it took over twenty-two years for this third and final time of anointing to take place. But it came, just as God had intended all those intervening years. Saul had done his best to interfere, and David certainly had wondered at times how God could possibly bring His promise about, but now it happened. David was crowned king of all Israel.

2) ***Extent of the people's desire.*** For so many people to come at one time to request that David become king shows that the desire for this was very deep-seated. People generally were convinced that David was the one they needed. Even with such an attitude commonly shared, however, there would still have been much that needed to be done to assemble a gathering of this size. With every tribe represented, and in such large numbers, a great amount of organization for communication and inspiration would have been called for. Weeks would have had to be spent in making plans and getting agreement on a time and procedures. Then the provisions for so many would have been immense. Days of preparation would have been necessary to get these ready. And a day for the actual gathering would have had to be set well in advance so that the entire group—some coming from a much farther distance than others—could arrive at the same time. It would have been necessary that all tribes be represented before negotiations on a matter so important could start.

3) ***David's efforts unneeded.*** All this says that the efforts David had made to bring this movement about had really been unnecessary. He had sent the commendation to Jabesh-gilead and had taken Saul's daughter, Michal, back as his wife. He had also made an agreement with Abner to effect this manner of gathering. But in view of the desire now expressed for him to be king, all this had been without need. The desire had been building of itself within the people, as God wanted it to. They needed relief from the Philistine domination, and Ish-bosheth, trying to rule across the Jordan at Mahanaim, had not been the one to do the job. The person they needed was the leader who had been so successful against the Philistines under Saul.

This is not to say that David's efforts had been necessarily wrong. God might have been pleased to use them, and maybe He did in some measure. It is quite possible, for instance, that it had been Abner's work that had been the spark to start matters under way. It is to say, however, that whatever anxiety David may have had, which may have prompted some of these efforts, had been out of place and unnecessary. If God had said he would rule, then he would, no matter what obstacles lay in the way. When God's time finally came, the remarkable manner in which God fulfilled His promise must have been quite overwhelming to David.

4) ***The appropriateness of honest negotiation.*** One should not think of David in a poor light for entering into negotiation with the tribal leaders. This was a matter of business that was necessary. Without question the tribal leaders' thinking on what powers the king should have differed from David's thinking. They saw the matter from their point of view, and David saw it from the perspective of what he had learned at Saul's court and also since ruling at Hebron. Besides this, there were the rights of Judah and Simeon to be protected. These matters needed to be discussed and careful decisions made. Then it was appropriate that an agreement be signed, so that everyone would know exactly what to expect and plan on for the future. It is much better to have agreements worked over carefully at the beginning of a venture than to have problems arise later because they were not made.

2. THE PHILISTINE PROBLEM SOLVED

a. The story (II Sam. 5:17-25; 23:13-17; I Chron. 11:15-19; 14:8-17)

It is clear that the biggest factor in motivating the northern tribes to come to ask David to be their king was their fear of the Philistines. This nation of warriors had been the plague of the tribes for nearly a century, with the recent years following Saul's defeat at Mount Gilboa being the worst. The people were very desirous of getting relief. If they had known how easily David would solve this problem, however, they might have negotiated differently before signing the agreement at Hebron, for he did solve it both quickly and without great difficulty.

Actually David was in an unusual position in respect to the Philistines. At one time he had been their vigorous enemy, leading Saul's troops against them, and then he had become their outward ally, actually fighting for Achish, one of the Philistine lords. Now he was the enemy again. Probably the Philistines were puzzled over him. Was he on their side or not?[9] So long as David was king only of southern Judah, thus making Israel a divided country of two ineffective parts, they did nothing to test David. Now that an agreement had been signed making David king of all the land, however,

[9]For discussion of Philistine thinking regarding David, see F. F. Bruce, *Israel and the Nations,* p. 28.

it was quite obvious that he was again a formidable enemy and needed to be treated as such. The result was that a battle soon shaped up between the two sides.

If David had wondered just how he would initiate a solution to the Philistine problem, he did not have to wonder long; the Philistines did the initiating for him. They soon moved up into the Rephaim Valley, just south of Jerusalem, to challenge him. Their strategy in this is apparent. They

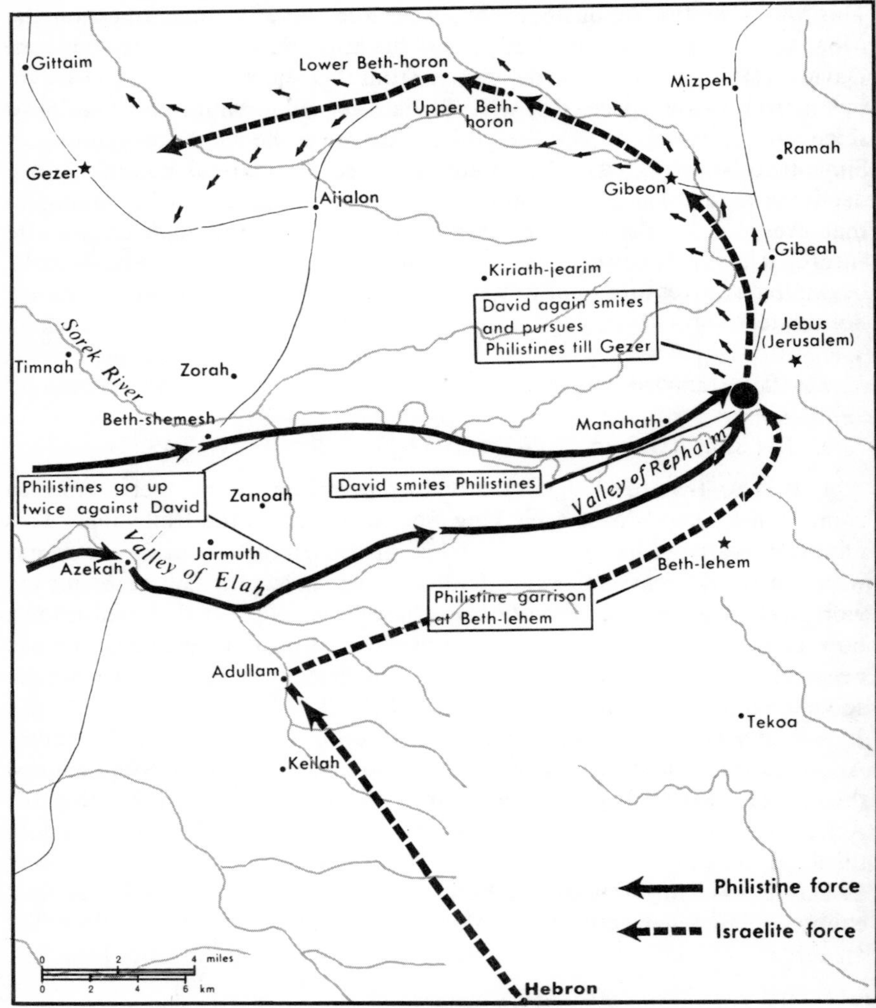

Map 8. David's Wars with the Philistines

already had a garrison of soldiers in Bethlehem (II Sam. 23:14; I Chron. 11:16), no doubt established after the victory at Mount Gilboa, and they wanted to supplement that group. This would serve the purpose of keeping David from carrying out the agreement just signed, for the country would then be divided by the Philistine force, whether David wanted it so or not.

David countered by assembling his troops at a spot he knew well: the cave of Adullam[10] (II Sam. 23:13, 14; I Chron. 11:15), where the initial 400 had been first assembled. God assured David of victory, and David attacked at Baal-perazim (location unknown), quite clearly taking the enemy by surprise. The Philistines were thoroughly defeated, so that they actually left images of their gods behind in their headlong flight. David found and burned the images.[11]

The Philistines were not through, however. They regrouped, probably with a still larger force, and came again into the same valley, attempting a similar divisive tactic. This time God instructed David to change the direction of his attack and come at them from the rear at an opportune moment, which God would signify by a sound in nearby balsam trees. This strategy made use of the mobility of David's men to effect surprise once more. The result was that the ensuing attack brought decisive victory again, and David this time drove the Philistines as far as Gezer.[12] This major triumph ended the domination of the Philistines over Israel.[13] What further contacts there were in later years occurred on Philistine soil and were of relatively minor significance (II Sam. 21:15-22; I Chron. 18:1; 20:4-8).

b. Points to notice

1) ***An auspicious beginning.*** David's beginning as king was thus made most auspicious. In two brief encounters, he solved the problem of the Philistines. The impression on the northern tribes, which had been so long oppressed by this enemy, must have been very great. Saul had never defeated them so thoroughly as this, and had finally fallen in death before their onslaught. What he had not been able to do in forty years, David had done in a matter of weeks. The tribes had been willing to concede David extensive powers if he would solve this problem, and here he had done so already. One need not think anyone was displeased, however. This twofold

[10]See p. 205, n. 5.

[11]David's burning these images is the direct opposite of the action of the Philistines when years earlier they had captured the ark at Aphek (I Sam. 4:11). They had taken the ark in parade as symbolic of victory, but David burned these images in disdain.

[12]Gezer, at the northeast boundary of Philistine territory, was about twenty miles from the point of this battle. The city is identified with Tell Jezer.

[13]That David had lived and fought with the Philistines helped him to know their ways and plan his own strategy. This certainly helped also to break their monopoly on iron.

victory would only have confirmed the people in their decision. The people probably were now all the more willing to cooperate with David in whatever he desired. David's reputation would have been at a high level already at this early point in his rule.

2) ***Reason for the headquarters at Adullam.*** Some have wondered at David's reason for choosing the cave of Adullam as his marshaling headquarters. It was about eleven miles northwest of Hebron (David's old capital) and fifteen miles southwest of the Rephaim Valley. The following factors probably were involved: first, there was the historic factor, for Adullam would have brought significant memories to the troops; second, from here David could send out spies to witness the movement of the Philistines on their way to the Rephaim Valley, for their likely routes were not far away; third, though the place was somewhat out of the way, it was also about equidistant from both Hebron and the Rephaim Valley; fourth, from here David could strike quite by surprise, for the Philistines were not likely to suspect Adullam to be his quartering point; and fifth, by going to Adullam he avoided the Philistine garrison in Bethlehem.

3) ***Advantage of a small army.*** Normally a large army is better than a small one, but one advantage of a smaller force is mobility. David's well-trained troops had mobility. They had lived, worked, and fought together for several years now. They had great respect for their leader. They could move quickly and quietly and be expected to obey orders to the letter. It is quite apparent that David used this advantage to its full potential in winning both of these battles.

4) ***Israel's true problem.*** The fact that David was able to defeat the Philistines so quickly shows that Israel's true problem in past years had not been the power of the enemy, but the sin of the people. Because David followed God, he was able to win a victory very quickly. God reassured him before the first encounter (II Sam. 5:19; I Chron. 14:10), and He gave him specific instructions and a supernatural signal in carrying them out during the second (II Sam. 5:23, 24; I Chron. 14:14, 15). David did what God told him to do and God blessed him in granting the triumph.

5) ***The time sequence.*** Because the sacred record tells of David's capturing Jerusalem as his new capital (II Sam. 5:6-12) before describing these Philistine encounters, some expositors believe that the capture of Jerusalem chronologically preceded the Philistine encounters. Several reasons, however, suggest that the opposite was true:

First, II Samuel 5:17 (I Chron. 14:8) implies that the Philistines attacked soon after David's anointing and therefore before he had enough time to establish a capital at Jerusalem. Second, chronological sequence is not always the criterion for the order of reporting in the Scriptures. For instance, the record of these events in I Chronicles places the occasion when David returned the ark to Jerusalem ahead of this Philistine attack (I Chron. 13:1-14), while II Samuel places it after (II Sam. 6:1-23). Third, the episode recorded in II Samuel 23:13-17 (regarding David's men getting him water to drink) almost certainly transpired at this same time—since the Philistines are described as attacking in the valley of Rephaim and also it is the "mighty men" of David who are mainly involved. This reflects an early encounter rather than later. In addition, David at this time had his headquarters at the cave of Adullam (the story so indicating), and this would not make sense if David had already captured Jerusalem. Fourth, the Philistines had a garrison at Bethlehem and enough troops in the area so that David's three mighty men went only at great risk of their lives to get water for him, and this would not make sense either, if David had already progressed from Hebron to take Jerusalem. Surely he would not have left any Philistine garrison between the two cities. Fifth, if David were already in Jerusalem, the attempt of the Philistines to cut the country in two, to keep David from uniting it, would not make sense. Their procedure, then, would have been to capture Jerusalem from David. Further proof once again is the presence of the Philistine garrison in Bethlehem and David's making his stronghold in Adullam.

3. ESTABLISHMENT OF JERUSALEM AS CAPITAL

a. The story

1) ***As the national capital*** (II Sam. 5:6-12; I Chron. 11:4-9). With the Philistine menace removed, David could think about an appropriate capital for the enlarged kingdom. Hebron was central for Judah but too far south to serve all the country. A city like Shechem was central for the northern tribes, but too far north for Judah. Gibeah, Saul's former capital, was not a particularly good location, for its water supply quite clearly was only by cistern, since no spring runs nearby.[14]

As a result, David's choice fell on a city in between, in fact right at the border of northern Judah. It was a city, further, that had no prior Israelite history and therefore was completely free from any complaint of favoritism on the part of other cities; the reason for this was that it still belonged to the Jebusites. And still further, the city needed to be captured anyhow, for it had long been a foreign island in territory otherwise controlled by Israelites

[14]See G. Ernest Wright, *Biblical Archaeology*, pp. 122-124; P. Lapp, "Tel el Fûl," *The Biblical Archaeologist* 28 (1965), pp. 2-10.

(cf. Josh. 15:63; II Sam. 5:6). The city, of course, was Jerusalem,[15] which held a strong position for natural defense and also boasted a fine water supply in the copious spring of Gihon.[16]

David evidently sought to take over the city by peaceful means at first, for the Jebusites told him, "Except thou take away the blind and the lame, thou shalt not come in hither" (II Sam. 5:6), meaning that even if the city were protected by only blind and lame people David would not be able to capture it. The reason for their confidence was no doubt that the city had not been taken from them by Israelites before (except temporarily—Judg. 1:21; cf. 19:11, 12), and also it had a strong position in being protected on three sides by sharply rising slopes.

The Jebusites did not know David well or the capability of his men, however, for they did not hold the city long after David set his mind to take it. David promised his men, "Whosoever smiteth the Jebusites first shall be chief and captain" (I Chron. 11:6), and Joab, who already was David's commander (II Sam. 2:13), went up first. Just what he did, however, is not made clear.[17] In the phrase used by David, "Whosoever getteth up to the gutter" (II Sam. 5:8), the word for "gutter" is *tsinnor,* which is used only one other time in the Old Testament, Psalm 42:7, where it is translated "water spout." Most authorities believe it refers here to a Jebusite water tunnel that is known to have led from the spring of Gihon through the rock and under the city wall, to make the water accessible without having to go outside of the wall.[18] This view makes sense, for if Joab could have made his way through this tunnel (which would have involved scaling a forty-foot vertical ascent), he would have had ready access into the city, apart from storming the strong gates of the city.[19] Whatever the method, Jerusalem was taken and David had his new capital.

With Jerusalem in hand, David set about strengthening it. He "built round about from Millo and inward" (II Sam. 5:9). The identity of this "Millo"—its designation usually appearing with the article—is not clear. It probably was some type of fortification, for David seems clearly to have been involved here with making his new capital as strong for defense as possible, and a later usage of the term, from the time of Hezekiah, is found in a fortification context (II Chron. 32:5). Further, it is parallel in type to a

[15]For a helpful survey of the advantageous site of Jerusalem, see Hershel Shanks, *The City of David,* pp. 15-22.

[16]Located in the Kidron Valley, to which the Jebusites had an ingenious tunnel access; see Kathleen Kenyon, *Royal Cities of the Old Testament,* pp. 23-27. Hezekiah later dug a much longer tunnel to it; see II Kings 20:20; II Chron. 32:30.

[17]See Shanks, *City of David,* pp. 31-37.

[18]See n. 16.

[19]Another view is that the word means "hook" and that Joab used a scaling hook to climb over the wall. William F. Albright so suggests; see his "The Old Testament and Archaeology," *Old Testament Commentary,* ed. by H. C. Alleman and E. E. Flack, p. 149.

tower in the time of Abimelech (Judg. 9:6, 20), when the word *house* is used in connection with it, as also in the time of Joash (II Kings 12:20). Kathleen Kenyon, who has done much archaeological work around Jerusalem, believes it means the rock-filling by which terraces were formed in the capital city.[20] She bases her view on the meaning of the word *Millo* ("filling") and on the fact that such stone supports were found in considerable number in her excavations. Her argument is impressive, but the contexts of the word in the Old Testament argue quite convincingly for the idea of fortification.

David is said to have "dwelt in the fort" (II Sam. 5:9), which probably means a type of citadel that the Jebusites had constructed earlier. David undoubtedly took it over as his temporary palace. So situated, and with the building operations in the city completed, David called the city after his name, and God blessed him so that he became great, in the eyes of his own people, and in the eyes of foreigners (II Sam. 5:10). Hiram, for instance, the wealthy king of Tyre, sent messengers with greetings and also builders to aid in constructing a fine palace for David to replace the citadel. Thus David grew in power and his reputation spread.

2) ***As the religious capital*** (II Sam. 6:1-23; I Chron. 13:1-14; 15:1-29). David desired to make Jerusalem also the religious capital. It was not long, therefore, before he sought to bring the ark, which was basic to all true worship of God, to the city. The ark was at Kirjath-jearim, about ten miles west of Jerusalem, where it had apparently been since the days following the battle of Aphek (I Sam. 7:1) some seventy years before.[21] David made grand preparations, assembling as many as 30,000 people for the occasion (II Sam. 6:1), and then went to the house of Abinadab in Kirjath-jearim[22] to get the ark. The method used for transporting it, however, was wrong: an open cart pulled by oxen was employed instead of poles placed through the rings of the ark, as prescribed in the law.

All went well, in spite of this impropriety, until the group reached the threshing floor of Nachon. No indication is given as to how much of the ten miles had been covered by that time. As the cart came to this point, it was jostled as the oxen stumbled, probably due to the rough terrain,[23] and Uzzah, the son of Abinadab, put out his hand to steady the ark. Immediately "the anger of the LORD was kindled against Uzzah; and God smote him there for his error" (II Sam. 6:7). David was displeased, called the

[20]*Royal Cities,* pp. 33-35.

[21]See p. 94, n. 11.

[22]The phrase "in Gibeah" (II Sam. 6:3) means literally, "on a hill," and is better so taken here. Abinadab's house was on a hill, and the idea fits the topography of the region well.

[23]The way from Kirjath-jearim to Jerusalem leads constantly upward as the mountains become higher, making for steep and rough ascents.

place Perez-uzzah ("rent of Uzzah"), and took the ark into the nearby house of Obed-edom. After this, David and the people returned to Jerusalem, and the house of Obed-edom came to be blessed of God because of the presence of the ark.

Three months passed before David returned to finish the task of bringing the ark to his capital. This time, however, he profited from his former mistake and had Levites carry the ark in the proper manner (I Chron. 15:2). Besides having Levites transport the ark, he also had others offer sacrifices along the way—in fact, as often as every six paces (II Sam. 6:13)—and play instruments in making music of praise to God. David himself wore a garment of fine linen and danced before the Lord, apparently all the way into the city. Thus, David spared no effort to bring the ark into the city this time in a manner that would please God. The effort led to the successful completion of the task, and David housed the ark in a special tent he had previously erected for it (I Chron. 15:1).

The people rejoiced at what had been accomplished, but Michal, who had seen her husband dancing before the ark, was displeased. When David returned home, she reproved him, believing that his action and dress had been too humiliating for a king in the presence of his people. She thus showed her lack of understanding of David's true intent—and appreciation of the importance of the ark—and David accordingly reproved her in turn. That God was pleased with David and displeased with Michal is indicated by the fact that Michal now "had no child unto the day of her death" (II Sam. 6:20-23).

b. Points to notice

1) ***David's good judgment.*** In addition to the numerous other virtues of David, he had a sense of good judgment. This actually is one of the finest qualities a person can have. When David chose a capital for his kingdom, he did so with great care. It may be assumed that he was fully aware of the factors in the selection noted earlier. If he showed good judgment in this matter, it follows that he also did in others.

2) ***Joab, an able leader.*** In contrast to Saul's military leader Abner, David's commander Joab was highly capable. He has already been seen defeating Abner's troops at the pool of Gibeon (II Sam. 2:12-17), and now he is witnessed capturing the strategic city of Jerusalem. Whatever way he accomplished this feat, whether by the water tunnel or some other, it had to be in a clever and unexpected manner, for the city clearly was taken with ease, when the Jebusites had been so confident of security shortly before. Evidently, Joab was the type of person that rose the highest when the challenge was the greatest. He had his faults, as he demonstrated in killing

Abner in cold blood, but he also could do his job. This probably was the main reason David kept him as his commander, even though he disapproved of several cruel deeds he committed.

3) ***The matter of Joab's being made chief.*** David promised that whoever was first in capturing Jerusalem would be "chief and captain"; and I Chronicles 11:6 says that Joab, being first, was made chief. The question arises how he could be made chief at this time when he already was David's military leader, as shown in his battle with Abner (II Sam. 2:12-17; cf. 2:23-26). The answer probably is that he was now elevated to a higher position than he had held earlier. Significantly, he is not called by either the term *captain* or *chief* on earlier occasions. He was clearly a leader, but perhaps without an official title, or at least not as high a title. He was officially made chief now.

4) ***The object of David's anger.*** At the time that God smote Uzzah in death, for reaching out his hand to steady the ark, it is stated that "David was displeased" (II Sam. 6:8; I Chron. 13:11). One might understand that David was displeased at God, but, in view of David's immediate fear of God (II Sam. 6:9; I Chron. 13:12), this is not likely. His displeasure was probably directed at the failure this meant for the whole undertaking. He had made grand plans and assembled many people. The bringing of the ark to Jerusalem meant much to him. Now the endeavor had to be postponed. Whether his thinking went still further, that is, whether he realized that the failure really was his own in not bringing the ark in a proper manner, is hard to say. Later, he realized this, for when three months had passed, he returned to finish the task in the proper way.

5) ***The severity of Uzzah's punishment.*** It is easy to think that God's punishment of Uzzah was too severe. After all, the young man was only trying to steady the ark, and so was quite innocent of wrongdoing. One can know, however, that the penalty was not excessive, for God deals with man in perfect justice. It may be that Uzzah had been the one who had first suggested taking the ark in this way, possibly because his cart was used and he wanted the honor of having his cart transport such an important object. God knows the heart of man and brings judgment accordingly. Another reason for the severity was that God wanted to impress the people with the importance of the ark and of handling it in the proper way.

6) ***Obed-edom, a Levite.*** The oxen stumbled by the threshing floor of Nachon, but David took the ark into the house of Obed-edom, which evidently was also nearby. One has to ask why he did not take it to the house of

Nachon.[24] The answer may well be that Obed-edom was a Levite and therefore a proper person with whom to leave it. At least an Obed-edom is mentioned in I Chronicles 15:18, 24 as one of the porters of the Levites used when the ark was brought to Jerusalem three months later. It is said that he was a Gittite (II Sam. 6:11) but this means only that he was from the city of Gath, probably Gath-rimmon, one of the Levitic cities (Josh. 21:24) in the tribe of Dan (Josh. 19:45). He could not have been living in Gath-rimmon at this time, however, for that city was not between Kirjath-jearim and Jerusalem. He must have moved.

7) ***David's humility.*** Once again the humble attitude of David, especially before God, is noteworthy. Though he was the great king of Israel, he did not consider it too demeaning to dress in simple linen and dance with great exertion before the ark. Somehow he felt that this would help insure God's pleasure, and, whether it did or not, it did show his willingness to do anything that he felt would help to this end, and this attitude was pleasing to God.

8) ***The tabernacle left at Gibeon.*** One is tempted to ask why David did not bring the tabernacle, which was just six miles away at Gibeon, into Jerusalem so that the ark could have been placed in it again. He did not, but made a new tent for it. Perhaps the reason was that David at the time was hoping to build a grand temple for the ark shortly, and saw this tent as only temporary. Then, later when God told him that he should not build such a temple, it may have seemed too late to bring the tabernacle, since the special tent had been used for some time already and people were accustomed to it. Also, God at the same time told David that his son would be allowed to build the permanent temple, and he could have reasoned that it would be less awkward to take the ark out of the temporary tent than out of the historic tabernacle. It is also possible that the tabernacle was not in very good condition by this time. It had been made more than four hundred years earlier and could have suffered considerable deterioration.

[24]C. F. Keil and F. Delitzsch, *Biblical Commentary on the Books of Samuel,* p. 332, suggest that since *goren nachon* means "the threshing floor of the stroke," the name *Nachon* may not have been of a person but simply of this particular threshing floor. This is possible, but perhaps not likely.

13

David the King

With Jerusalem having been established as capital and the Philistines fully defeated, David was ready to begin his rule over all Israel. He was in a position of strength to do so. He had adequate power, designated by the agreement at Hebron; he had the invaluable experience of seven-and-a-half years of rule over Judah; and, most important, he had God's blessing on his life as the Holy Spirit continually empowered him for his God-given task. His actions as king, in this position of strength, are the center of attention in this chapter.

A. CONSOLIDATION OF THE TRIBES

1. THE STORY (II SAM. 8:15; I CHRON. 18:14)

The sacred text says little about David's consolidation of the Israelite tribes into a centralized government; much more is given regarding his foreign wars. These foreign encounters, however, would have been possible only if a strong home base had been established. Moreover, David would have seen consolidation as his first order of business. Since Saul's rule had never been strongly established, David would have wanted to achieve consolidation all the more. That he accomplished it is the clear intimation of II Samuel 8:15 (cf. I Chron. 18:14): "And David reigned over all Israel; and David executed judgment and justice unto all his people."

Several factors would have contributed to making this consolidation possible, when Saul had failed. For one thing, David had made the initial agreement on regulations with the people. For another, David earned the good will of the people early by his remarkable victory over the Philistines. Further, he had the capacity to work with people and bring them to agree with his thinking. This he had clearly demonstrated while a fugitive in welding his hard-core troops into an effective fighting unit. And, still further, he was a man of convictions and confidence, two qualities that regularly inspire others to follow. People are ready to fall in step if they believe in the one who leads the way.

This consolidation would have involved the acquisition of land originally allotted to the tribes but never occupied by them. Until this time, the Israelites had been confined mainly to hill country, with the Philistines and Canaanites holding the better lowlands. This situation now changed. When David later had a census of the country taken (II Sam. 24:5-8), the census-takers quite clearly were able to move along a continuous route in doing so. They went north on the east side of the Jordan, crossed over in the north to the area of Sidon, and then returned south on the west side of the Jordan. Also, the description of the land which David in time passed along to Solomon (I Kings 4:7-19) implies an overall, blanket control, including both lowlands and hills. And further, excavation has shown that lowland towns now came under Israelite supervision—towns like Gezer, Taanach, Ibleam, Rehob in Asher, Jokneam, Nahalal, Eltekeh, and Gibbethon.[1] Strata dating before David's time show either a Philistine or Canaanite type of habitation, but from David's time on they evidence Israelite.

One may think of David's territory, then, as extending from north of the Sea of Galilee to Beersheba in the south, and on both sides of the Jordan River. The only area in this expanse of land not under his control was the confined space still held by the Philistines to the southwest, along the Mediterranean. David let this neighboring people remain in their land, though their territory was measurably reduced from what it had been in the time of Saul. All this means that, when David had completed this work of consolidation and occupation, the Israelites could know for the first time that they existed as a true nation. The tribes had become fully united, they controlled almost all the land that had been originally allotted to them, and they had a fine king of whom they could be proud.

[1]See William F. Albright's discussion, *Archaeology and the Religion of Israel,* pp. 121-122.

2. POINTS TO NOTICE

a. David's satisfaction

All of this would have been most satisfying to David. Hopes and dreams he had visualized since the day of his anointing at Bethlehem had finally come true. And all was quite as he had planned. Years earlier he had no doubt vowed that, when he eventually ruled, things would be different from what they had been under Saul's weak rule. He would make sure his own rule was strong and the tribes consolidated. Now this had become a reality: he was king, the tribes had been welded together, and things were indeed different. His satisfaction must have been very pronounced.

b. The people's satisfaction

Though the people were now under a much more rigorous hand than Saul's, one may be sure that they experienced real satisfaction also. They now had what they had hoped for at the time they first approached Samuel to ask for a king. This had not been realized under Saul, but now it was. They indeed had a king like all the nations—in fact, finer than any of the nations. He had quickly solved the terrible Philistine problem; he had at last given the Israelites fertile lowlands to farm; and he had occupied the fine lowland cities, which were very desirable as places of residence. Further, the people now had a sense of unity as a nation, ready to assume their place in the community of nations of the world. This would have given a sense of confidence and pride that is so important for morale among any people.

c. God's blessing

All this of course was due to the blessing of God. David was very capable, but none of this could have happened had not he enjoyed the blessing of God on his life. With this blessing, centered especially in the empowerment of the Spirit, his dream had been made possible and did come to reality.

B. FOREIGN CONQUEST

1. THE STORY (II SAM. 8:1-14; 10:1-19; 12:26-31; 21:15-22; I CHRON. 18:1-13; 19:1—20:8)

With the home country firmly established, and with an effective army available,[2] David was in a position to wage war on foreign soil as need arose. The need did arise, and the result was an empire. The principal bat-

[2]See pp. 181-183.

tles involved in this formation of an empire were set forth in Chapter 10. It remains here to fill in some of the story given only in general survey at that time.

a. The Ammonite battle

Though all David's battles were important in the expansion of Israel's power, the sacred record tells the story of his battle with Ammon at much greater length than the others. When Ammon's king, Nahash, died, who had earlier showed kindness in some undisclosed way to David, David sought to return the favor by sending messengers to express sympathy to his son and successor, Hanun.[3] Hanun's advisors wrongly interpreted this as a trick of foreign intelligence, and urged the young king to answer in kind. Accordingly, he had the messengers' beards half shaven and their clothes cut off at the buttocks, and sent them back to David. On hearing of this, David told the men to stop at Jericho until their beards were grown, and immediately he prepared for war. Hanun, realizing his mistake, did the same, not only mobilizing his own troops but hiring mercenaries from the northern Aramaean countries of Beth-rehob, Zobah, and Maacah.[4]

The battle was joined at Medeba (I Chron. 19:7), about eighteen miles southwest of the capital of Ammon, Rabbah (Rabbath-Ammon). Hanun's troops took a position just outside the gate of the city, and the northern Aramaeans remained a short distance away from the city. Joab, sizing up the situation, divided his troops into two groups. He took the best of them (probably including the core of 600) to make an attack on the Aramaeans, whom he evidently considered the more formidable, and left the others in charge of his brother, Abishai, to face and withstand the Ammonites. Quite clearly he hoped the Ammonites would refrain from attacking until they saw how the battle with the Aramaeans developed. This apparently happened, for when Joab was able to defeat the northern group, the Ammonites quickly retreated inside the gate of the city for safety, and the battle was suddenly over. Joab then took his troops back to Jerusalem, not pressing on to set up a siege of Ammon's capital, Rabbah, since the time of year was apparently too late for this (cf. II Sam. 11:1).

The Aramaeans, feeling extremely humiliated at this defeat, were not through. Hadadezer, their leader as king of Zobah, summoned more troops

[3]This incident occurred early in David's thirty-three-year reign in Jerusalem. It had to precede his sin with Bathsheba, for Rabbah, Ammon's capital, was taken as a climax to the whole affair with Ammon (II Sam. 12:26-31) and it was during the siege that Uriah, husband of Bathsheba, was killed (II Sam. 11:1, 14-17). It was after this time that Solomon was born (II Sam. 12:24); he must have been at least twenty years old at David's death, because Rehoboam had been born to him prior to that time (I Kings 14:21).

[4]That he was willing to pay a thousand talents of silver (this means 66,000 pounds of silver) shows the extent of his desire to defeat David.

from beyond the river Euphrates, thus from the far north, and took a stand at Helam.[5] David responded by taking personal charge of Israel's troops, crossed the Jordan, and made an attack. The result was the same as when Joab led the army: the Aramaeans were routed and their commander was killed. The Aramaeans now had enough and made peace with David, thus becoming a tributary region.

Joab now was given charge of the army again, as he returned to Ammon's capital, Rabbah, to finish the task he had postponed earlier due to the time of year. Rains fall during the winter season; the "time when kings go forth to battle" (II Sam. 11:1) was the springtime, when the rains had ended. Joab laid siege to the city. He made commendable progress and then called for David to come personally, so that he could have the honor of achieving the actual capitulation. David did so, took the city, appropriated the heavy crown of the Ammonite king,[6] and made the people serve with saws, harrows, and axes.

b. Philistine encounters

Some comment is yet called for relative to continued conflicts between David and the Philistines. This enemy had been decisively defeated at Rephaim, but there were a few minor engagements that still occurred. One is mentioned in II Samuel 8:1 and four others in II Samuel 21:15-22 (cf. I Chron. 18:1; 20:4-8). These probably happened at different times during David's reign but are grouped here in the record because they all involved this same southwestern enemy.

The result of the first skirmish was that David captured Metheg-ammah, meaning "bridle of the mother city," which, acording to I Chronicles 18:1, is a reference to Gath, possibly the leading city of the Philistines at this time (see I Sam. 27:2 and 29:2f.). That David took control of all Philistia as a result, however (as some have suggested), does not follow. These other skirmishes show clearly that he did not.

The other four contacts concern the death of four giants in Philistia. All four occasions are described in II Samuel 21:15-22 and the last three in the parallel passage, I Chronicles 20:4-8. In the first, David himself was nearly killed by one of the giants, Ishbi-benob; Abishai, brother of Joab, killed the big man just in time. In the second, Sibbecai the Hushathite, one of David's mighty men (I Chron. 11:29) and leader of the eighth division of the army (I Chron. 27:11), killed the giant, Saph, at the city of Gob (unknown). In the third, Elhanan, son of Jaare-oregim killed Lahmi, the brother of

[5]Identification uncertain. Yohanan Aharoni suggests 'Alma, about thirty miles east of the Sea of Galilee and on a latitudinal parallel with its southern end.

[6]It was made of a talent (66 pounds) of gold and was studded with precious stones.

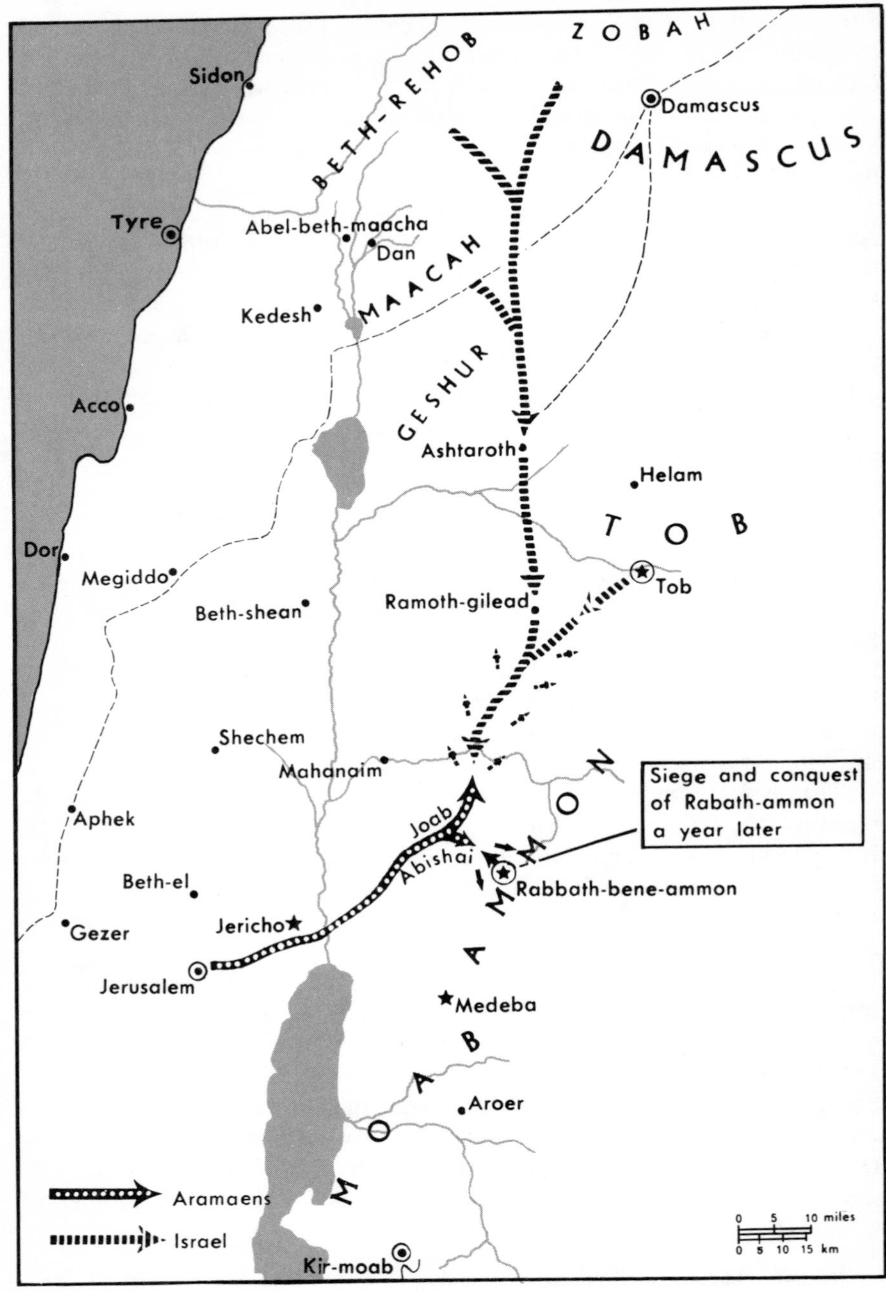

Map 9. War with Ammon

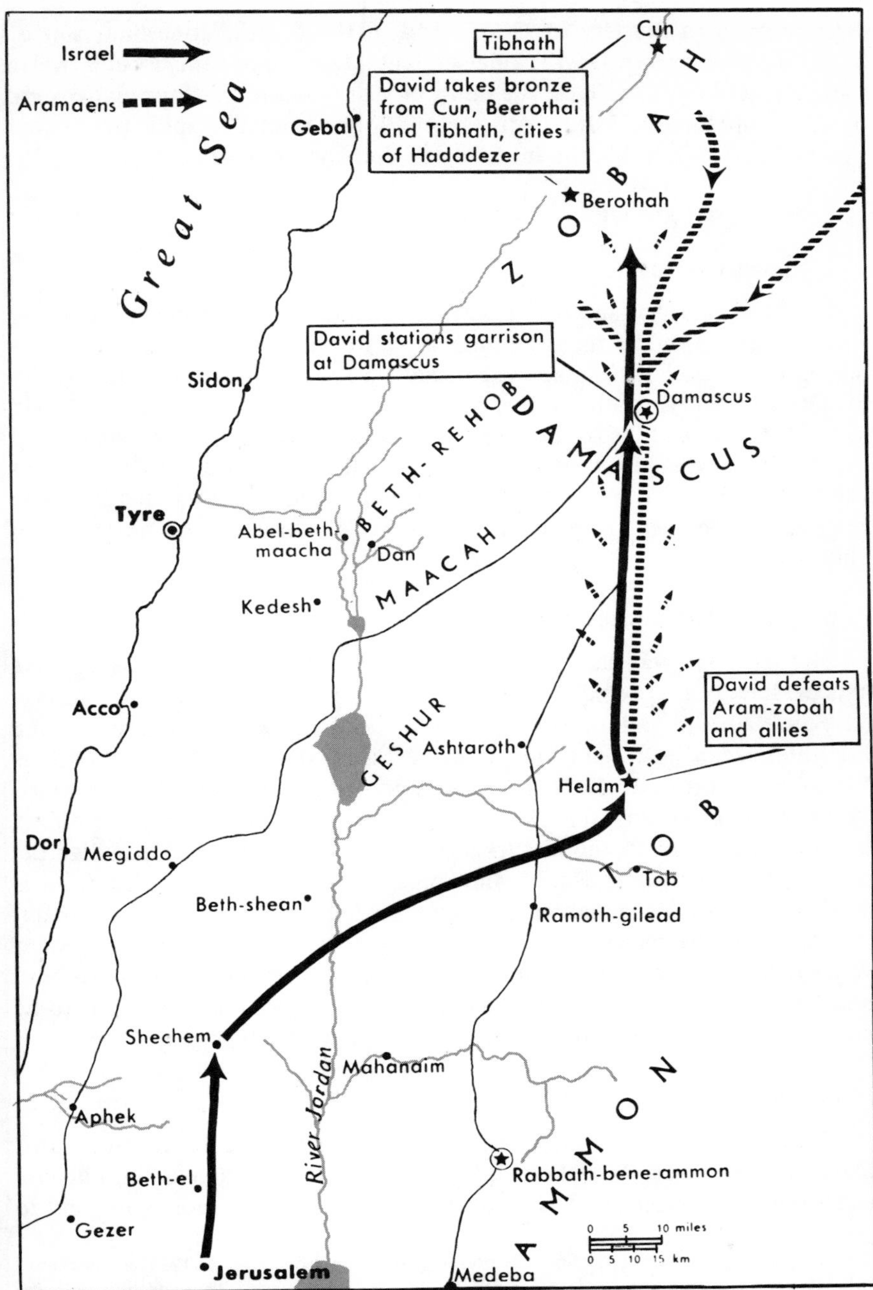

Map 10. War with Zobah

Goliath, also in the city of Gob.[7] And in the fourth, Jonathan, son of Shimeah, a nephew of David, killed a giant having twelve fingers and twelve toes. This occurred at Gath, the home city of Goliath. All four giants were of the same family from Gath, born to one named Rapha (translated "giant" in KJV), a descendant likely of the Anakim (see Josh. 11:22).

2. POINTS TO NOTICE

a. Quality of David's army

David's record of success in battle is outstanding. Whenever an enemy was engaged, David's troops emerged victorious. This was due to God's blessing, but God again made use of natural means, in this case the ability of David's army, both in troops and leadership. Occasionally, David himself would lead, as in the second engagement with the Aramaeans, but usually Joab was entrusted with the task. He clearly was capable, as was David, and his men were well trained. David evidently demanded the same level of competency from those who served under him that he did from himself.

b. Joab's harsh measures in Edom

Though Joab was capable, he also could be harsh in his measures. He had personally murdered Abner, and later was to do the same to Amasa (II Sam. 20:10); and he seems to have been unnecessarily cruel to the Edomites when he fought and defeated them (II Sam. 8:13, 14; I Kings 11:15-18; I Chron. 18:12, 13). As pointed out in Chapter 10, Joab killed "every male in Edom" (likely meaning every man of the army), remaining in the foreign land six months to accomplish this result. He also killed the royal family, with only Hadad and some servants escaping to Egypt. It is doubtful that such a slaughter was necessary in order to subjugate the country; much of the reason for it must be found in Joab's distorted idea of vengeance. The Edomites probably had done something to provoke him, and he took out his vengeance on them in this severe manner. He is to be criticized for this, and surely God was not pleased.

c. Hanun's serious mistake

Hanun the Ammonite king made a serious mistake the day he humiliated David's messengers. They had come in peace, yet he believed the purpose was disguised espionage. The result was that he lost the money he paid to

[7]The reading of I Chron. 20:5 is to be preferred over that of II Sam. 21:19. The latter omits "the brother of," making Goliath himself the victom of Elhanan. This conflicts with the earlier account of David's having slain Goliath. No doubt a copyist's error occurred in II Samuel.

the mercenary soldiers, the lives of many of his own men, and finally the kingdom itself when his capital was captured. Too often, people look for ulterior motivations which do not exist.

d. Chronological order of these battles

A question in chronology concerns the time when David fought his battle with the Aramaeans at Helam in respect to the time of Joab's siege on Rabbah. If it was before, as the record seems to imply, then either it was fought during the rainy season or else Joab began his siege of Rabbah sometime following the coming of the spring season. It was observed that Joab had not taken up the siege the prior fall, because of the coming onset of the rains. The two battles could not have been fought at the same time, either, for the size of David's army would not have permitted this; and, moreover, it was while Joab was at Rabbah that David sinned with Bathsheba back in Jerusalem. Perhaps the answer is that David met the Aramaeans very early the following spring and then Joab went to Rabbah as soon as David had returned. It may be that David led in the one campaign in order to give Joab a chance to rest and plan for the siege of Rabbah.

e. Joab's deference to David

Joab had his poor qualities, as just seen, but he also had good ones. One of his virtues was evident during his siege of Rabbah. Having brought the struggle to a point where victory was assured, he called for David to come so that David might have the honor of taking the city. This was remarkable and commendable on Joab's part. Not many leaders would have done this, being desirous of achieving victory for themselves and enhancing their own reputations. Joab apparently had a high respect for David, as David for Joab. This no doubt was one reason why David kept him as his military commander, even though Joab committed some outrageous deeds.

f. The harsh measures imposed on Rabbah

Two views exist as to David's treatment of the Ammonites after the fall of Rabbah. The views arise from an alleged conflict between II Samuel 12:31 and I Chronicles 20:3. The former (as translated in KJV) says that David "put [the Ammonites] under saws. . . ," meaning that he made them serve by laboring with saws, harrows, axes, and the brick-kiln; and the latter says he "cut them with saws. . . ," meaning that he put them to death in this manner. Keil believes the text of Samuel should be amended to conform to the text of Chronicles.[8] A better answer, however, seems to be to translate the text of Chronicles differently. The Hebrew word rendered "cut" is

[8]C. F. Keil and F. Delitzsch, *Biblical Commentary on the Books of Samuel,* p. 395.

sur, which normally means "rule" (e.g., Judg. 9:22). This meaning leads to the translation that David "ruled with saws. . . ," meaning that he dominated the Ammonites by forcing them to labor with the instruments listed. This makes the two renditions agree in meaning.

g. Rationale for reporting the Philistine encounters

One might well ask why the Scriptures take time to report David's encounters with the Philistine giants, when each was obviously of minor significance. The answer lies in a common stress made in all four: a giant from the same family was killed each time. And the likely reason why this was seen to be significant is that God saw fit to follow up on this family after David's first triumph over one of its members, Goliath. Probably Goliath was the largest, for he was chosen as the Philistine champion, but these others were huge also. Goliath had breathed out his defiance of Israel's God and army, with probably all of the brothers looking on, and now God was saying that not only did He see to it that Goliath himself was killed, but also all other members of this same family. That only one is specifically called "the brother of Goliath," when evidently all were (since all had the same father), may reflect their having different mothers. The other three may have been only half brothers of the two.

C. DISAPPROVED DEEDS

1. SIN WITH BATHSHEBA

a. The story (II Sam. 11:1—12:25)

One of the remarkable characteristics of Scripture is that it reports the failings of outstanding people as well as their fine deeds. Two such occasions are reported from David's life. The better known concerns the time of Joab's attack on Rabbah. David, walking on the roof of his palace one evening, saw the woman Bathsheba washing herself at her home, which apparently was open to view from David's vantage point. David made inquiry as to who this person was and learned that she was the wife of Uriah the Hittite, one of David's fine soldiers. This did not deter his desire for the woman, and he sent to bring her to the palace, where he had relations with her. Bathsheba later sent word to David that she was pregnant by him, whereupon David sent for her husband Uriah to return to Jerusalem from the battle at Rabbah.

David's intention was to make it appear that the child had been born to Uriah, but Uriah did not go to his home as David instructed him. When David asked the reason, Uriah replied that this would be unfair to the other soldiers who were yet at the battle lines. David then went one step further by attempting to make Uriah drunk, but still the honorable man would not go to his wife. Finally David, in desperation, sent him back to the battle with instructions to Joab to put him in the front line where he would surely "be smitten and die" (11:15). This Joab did and Uriah was killed. Joab sent a messenger to inform David, who then took Bathsheba as his wife.

God knew and highly disapproved of the entire action and sometime later sent His prophet, Nathan, to bring rebuke to the king. Nathan told David an allegory about a rich man who, on desiring to feed a friend, seized the one ewe lamb owned by a poor neighbor instead of one of his own many animals. David was indignant that such a thing should happen. Then Nathan told him that he was really this rich man, for he had taken the wife of one of his subjects. He told David further that, as punishment, the sword would never depart from his house from that time on.

Though David was extremely blameworthy for his action, he is to be commended for readily accepting Nathan's reprimand and then confessing his sin before God. When he did, Nathan told him that God would not take his life—as the law prescribed for such cases (Lev. 20:10)—but that the child born of the sin would die. This prediction soon came true, following a period of illness for the little one. Not long after, however, God extended grace to David in the birth of another son by Bathsheba, and this was Solomon, who was to be Israel's next king.

b. Points to notice

1) ***Remarkableness of the report.*** The fact that this sin of David is reported is one of the clear evidences that the Bible is truly God's supernatural word. A report that was merely human would not have included it. This is true, not only in that negative matters regarding kings were not often recorded, but it was quite acceptable for kings of that day to take whom they pleased as wives, no matter the sorrow it might make for grieving husbands. The Bible reports this episode, however, in the strongest condemnatory terms.

2) ***The proper use of one's eyes.*** God has given man wonderful powers, and the power of sight is one of the finest. It can be used wrongly, however, and when it is it can lead to gross wickedness. David first saw this woman, then he desired her, and then he took her. When he had chanced to see her, as he walked on his palace roof, he should have immediately turned away and put his mind on other matters. Instead, he let himself dwell on what he had seen. David's eyes were used improperly and he fell into terrible sin.

3) ***Bathsheba the woman.*** The question has often been raised whether or not Bathsheba was guilty of some part in this sin herself. Why was she

bathing herself where she could be seen from the palace roof? And there is no indication that she resisted in any way when summoned by the king. It may also be asked why she did not later seek out her husband Uriah, who she must have learned had been summoned back from the battle lines. If he did not come to her, why did she not go looking for him? These questions are real and are of a kind to cause one to lay at least part of the blame on her. The text says that she did mourn for her husband when she learned of his death, and she is to be commended for this. One should not be too hard on her either, since God honored her with the birth of Israel's next king. At the same time, one finds it difficult to exonerate her from all blame. This is not to relieve David of any of his guilt, for the fact of his guilt is clear enough.

4) ***Uriah the husband.*** In contrast, Uriah stands out as a man of the highest integrity. Summoned home from the army, he refused to go to his own house where he would have comforts as well as the companionship of his wife. The only reason he gave was that he could not enjoy such things when his fellow soldiers were still in the field. There may also have been another reason. He may have learned, on getting to the city, of his wife's infidelity. David's servants knew of it, and news of this kind travels fast. If he did know, the fact could explain further his unwillingness to go home, but this should not lower our estimate of him as an outstanding individual.

5) ***David's wrong conduct.*** David's guilt in taking Bathsheba was compounded by his reprehensible conduct with Uriah. This was planned treachery, to cover up another sin. The very excellent behavior of Uriah in contrast should itself have been a rebuke to David, but he found it only infuriating. Finally he sent the man to the hottest part of the battle so that he would surely be killed. This was conduct like that of Saul years before. David was here stooping to do what he had found so objectionable in his predecessor. What fools men can become in moments of weakness.

6) ***Nathan's rebuke.*** David deserved rebuke and God brought it through the prophet Nathan. God had told Israel before entering the land that He would communicate with them by prophets (cf. Deut. 18:15-19), and He regularly did so, as here. It should be realized that the rebuke was given nearly one year after the sin with Bathsheba, for the child apparently had already been born (see II Sam. 12:14, 15). God seemingly waited until the punishment of the child's death could be brought immediately after. It should be recognized also that this rebuke by Nathan would have taken courage on his part. David was the king, and one does not bring this manner of rebuke to kings easily. Nathan did as God directed, however, and David received the word as from God.

7) ***A warning to all God's servants.*** The fact that a man of the spiritual stature of David could fall into sin such as this provides a warning to all God's servants. No one is immune; all are targets of Satan. It is only as one trusts in God daily for the strength he needs to resist Satan's temptations that he is enabled to do so.

8) ***David's confession.*** The one bright spot in the overall story is David's willingness to confess his sin to God. Apparently he had not confessed it of himself, during the several months that elapsed before Nathan was sent to him. But at least he did so after Nathan's rebuke. The words of his confession are found in Psalm 51, where he cries out, "Against thee, thee only, have I sinned, and done this evil in thy sight" (51:4), and also beseeches God, "Take not thy holy spirit from me" (51:11). David knew that he had been specially empowered by the Holy Spirit since the day of first anointing for his ministry as Israel's leader, and he did not want to lose that all-important provision as Saul had.

2. SIN IN CENSUS-TAKING

a. The story (II Sam. 24:1-25; I Chron. 21)

The second disapproved deed of David occurred a few years after the first one;[9] it was the taking of a census of the people. David told Joab to oversee the task of numbering the people from Dan to Beersheba. Joab, normally a man of harsh measures, sought to dissuade David from this project, but David held firm and insisted that it be carried out. Joab then took captains of the host and started counting on the east of the Jordan. He moved north and later crossed westward to the region of Tyre and Sidon, from where he came south as far as Beersheba. Nine months and twenty days elapsed during the work. Joab delivered the total number to David: it was 800,000 men that drew the sword in Israel and 500,000 in Judah.

With the task completed, David repented of his sin and asked for forgiveness. God now sent the prophet Gad to David to offer him three choices of punishments for his sin: either seven years of famine in the land, three months of defeat before Israel's enemies, or three days of pestilence. He chose the last, and 70,000 of David's recently counted people died. The

[9]However, not at the very close of David's rule as one might think from the story's being recorded at the end of II Samuel. The sacred writer sometimes groups his subject matter more in terms of content than chronological order. Such a census as here conducted would have had a goal in view such as a king would set in his years of strength. Perhaps the place of reporting it in I Chronicles (chap. 21) is significant, between the battle against Ammon and David's organization of the priests and Levites.

pestilence was stopped by God just outside Jerusalem at the threshing floor of Araunah the Jebusite, the place where Solomon was later to build the temple. At Gad's further direction, David went to the location and purchased both the threshing floor as a place to build an altar and oxen to sacrifice, paying fifty shekels total. The altar was built, the sacrifice was offered, and God's anger was appeased.

b. Points to notice

1) ***Responsibility for sin.*** The question has often been raised as to who was responsible for this sin of David. According to II Samuel 24:1, it was the Lord that moved David to order the census, due to His anger at Israel for some offense. But, according to I Chronicles 21:1, it was Satan that "stood up against Israel and provoked David to number Israel." And, of course, it was David that had to confess to doing wrong and had to choose among the three punishments. How can these facts be harmonized?

Actually, the answer is not difficult, for the same situation occurs commonly when God's people sin. In the last analysis, it is the person himself who is to blame, for every man makes up his own mind whether he will sin or not. David did here; he wanted to take this census and gave the order. At the same time, Satan, is often behind the scenes, presenting attractions to persuade one to choose wrongly. Satan did this already in the Garden of Eden, persuading Eve to eat of the tree. She was the one who made up her mind to do it, however, not Satan. Satan evidently presented attractions to David here to order the census. And then, before Satan can ever bring temptation to man, he must be permitted to do so by God. Satan could not tempt Job until God removed the hedge of protection (Job 1:10) that God had placed around him. Satan could not tempt David in this instance until God gave permission. The permission was granted as a result of provocation brought by Israel. In a very real sense, Israel herself was to blame, and it may be noticed that actually it was mainly Israel that was punished; 70,000 of the people died in the pestilence.

2) ***Nature of David's sin.*** Another important question concerns the real nature of David's sin. What was so wrong about taking a census? This is done regularly in modern countries, and no one suffers. This question is not so easily answered. The sin was serious, for God did send severe punishment, and, before the census was even taken, Joab, normally hardhearted, urged the king to refrain from the action. One part, no doubt, was David's pride. He gave as a motive for the census that he might "know the number of the people" (II Sam. 24:2). Pride is always wrong in God's sight. Then another part of David's sin may be that the census was for the purpose

of imposing high taxes and possibly even conscription of Israelite labor.[10] In keeping with this possibility, as noted in Chapter 10, is the listing among David's officers (II Sam. 20:24) of Adoram as supervisor of "tribute labor." This term normally refers only to foreign labor, but David may have now thought to add levies from his own people, such as Solomon did later on (I Kings 5:13, 14), much to the discontent of the people (I Kings 12:4). However, if David did levy Israelites as conscript laborers, he probably did not carry through on it, in the light of his own repentance for the sin and God's reprimand through Gad.

3) ***The number of people.*** Joab counted 800,000 of Israel and 500,000 of Judah. These, however, were only men of military age, those "that drew the sword." The two figures lead to a total of approximately 4,000,000 people, which is about double the number that entered the land at the time of Joshua's conquest (see Num. 26:1-65). It should be noticed also that the census listed Judah and Israel separately, thus observing the continuing division between the north and south, which was to come to full fruition in the separation of the kingdom after Solomon. That the number from Judah was more than half that from the northern tribes shows that Simeon's number was likely included in it and perhaps some of Dan's, since not all of Dan had migrated north. Danites who remained in the south may well have amalgamated with the people of Judah. It should be noted further that the total number did not include the people of either Levi or Benjamin, for Joab did not complete the count since the whole matter was so offensive to him (I Chron. 21:6).

4) ***David's willingness to make confession.*** It is most significant that though David sinned, as all men do, he was willing to make confession afterward. He did after his sin with Bathsheba and Uriah, and he did again in this instance. This willingness is probably a main reason why he continued to hold his high place in God's estimation of Israel's kings.

5) ***God's severe punishments.*** It should be noticed that, though David maintained his high position in God's sight and though he was willing to make confession of his sin, still God brought severe punishment upon him. Following his sin with Bathsheba and Uriah, Bathsheba's child died and after this David suffered continued difficulty in his family, just as Nathan had foretold (II Sam. 12:10). On this occasion of taking a census, 70,000

[10]The view that the sin lay in a mustering of Israel's troops finds several difficulties: One is that David's army of three main parts (see pp. 181-182) had likely been formed prior to the time of this census. Another is that Joab's repugnance at the sin would be difficult to understand, since he was a military man. And further, God's displeasure would be hard to explain since He otherwise blessed David in the use of his army against many enemies.

people died. David had wanted to know how many people were under his rule, and God quickly removed 70,000 from that number. God's way of chastisement is not easy.

D. APPROVED DEEDS

1. KINDNESS TO MEPHIBOSHETH

a. The story (II Sam. 9)

The sacred text gives also two commendable deeds of David. Surely he was responsible for many more than two, but apparently the Spirit of God saw these two as particularly noteworthy. It is almost as though He saw fit to offset in the record the two bad deeds by two good ones.

The first is David's gracious gesture toward Jonathan's lone surviving son, Mephibosheth. Because of the nature of the action, it likely happened quite early in David's rule, soon after he had come to Jerusalem. David made inquiry if anyone of Saul's house still lived, that he might show him kindness for the sake of Jonathan. A servant of Saul named Ziba was found, and he came and told David of Mephibosheth, indicating that he was lame on his feet. This lameness had been caused when Mephibosheth, who was only five years old at the time, was dropped by a nurse as she ran in panic at news of Saul's disaster on Mount Gilboa (II Sam. 4:4). Ziba said that the young man[11] was living with Machir in Lo-debar[12] and David immediately summoned him from there to Jerusalem. He came in great fear, for such a summons to a member of a deposed royal family could mean death. David, however, quickly calmed his fears and then rejoiced his heart by granting him all the land which Saul, his grandfather, had owned, besides giving him a place at the royal table. David further assigned Ziba, the one who had told him of Mephibosheth, to be the overseer of this property for the young man, something Ziba was quite able to do for he had fifteen sons and twenty servants of his own (9:10).

In this action, David showed a great heart. Monarchs of the day normally disposed of members of rival families; it was rare to bestow such an honor. Some benefit accrued to David, however, because he would have thus endeared himself further to any of the northern populace who still felt a loyalty to Saul's departed house.

[11]Probably between fifteen and twenty years old (five plus David's seven-and-a-half at Hebron, plus a few years of rule at Jerusalem). He could not have been too young, however, for he already had a son named Micha (II Sam. 9:12).

[12]Lo-debar was located east of the Jordan, in the general area of Mahanaim, for this Machir came to David later, when David had fled from Absalom to Mahanaim, to offer provisions to David and his troops (II Sam. 17:27). Yohanan Aharoni suggests an identification with Umm ed-Dabar, located just south of the Sea of Galilee and about twenty-six miles north of Mahanaim.

b. Points to notice

1) ***The action for Jonathan's sake.*** It is noteworthy that though David asked if anyone remained "of the house of Saul," his action was prompted "for Jonathan's sake," not for Saul's. The reason for the broader inquiry was probably that David was not sure whether any of the former royal house still lived, much less someone from Jonathan's particular family. That Mephibosheth was from Jonathan's family, therefore, no doubt rejoiced David's heart and prompted him all the more to make gracious gestures toward the young man. Though David had respected Saul as God's appointed king, it is not likely that such a gesture would have been made except for the special place Jonathan held in his memory.

2) ***A promise remembered.*** This leads to the thought that David was hereby remembering his promise to Jonathan that he would never cease in kindness toward Jonathan's house (I Sam. 20:15, 42). People often forget promises, though made in sincerity. It would have been easy for David to forget this one, having now become the great king of Israel and busy with daily schedules. He did not, however, and in this he provides an excellent example. Promises given should always be kept, even though considerable time might elapse.

3) ***David's gift to Mephibosheth.*** If David had given Mephibosheth only the privilege of eating for the rest of his life at the king's table, this would have been a substantial benefit, for it would have meant a life of ease for the young man as long as he lived. In addition, however, he gave him all of Saul's lands, which probably were extensive. Mephibosheth really did not need them, for all his needs would be met by living in the palace. Still David granted them, besides the services of Ziba and his family and servants to work the land.

4) ***The virtue of magnanimity.*** Few people are magnanimous in their attitude towards others. Most desire to look out only for their own interests and let others do the same. Many people live in the small world of self-interest. David, however, was a much greater person than this; he could think of others for their own sake, even if it meant putting himself out for their benefit.

2. JUSTICE TO GIBEONITES

a. The story (II Sam. 21:1-14)

A later commendable deed was David's rectification of a wrong committed by Saul against the Gibeonites. No clues are given as to the point in

David's reign at which this occurred, though the fact that it is reported late in II Samuel suggests that it came comparatively late in the reign. The Gibeonites were the people who had tricked Joshua into making a league with them during the time of conquest of the land (Josh. 9:1-27). Though the pact never should have been made, God still held His people responsible to keep it. Saul had not done so, but had killed many of the Gibeonites and appropriated their possessions for himself and his family. A famine of three years prompted David to inquire of God concerning some possible wrong in the kingdom, and the misdeed of Saul was indicated.

David immediately sought to make amends. He asked the Gibeonites what they would like to have done for them, and they requested that seven descendants of Saul ("men of his sons") be delivered to them for hanging. David agreed and set about assembling the seven. He spared Mephibosheth, for the sake of Jonathan, but took two sons of Rizpah, Saul's concubine, and five sons of Merab.[13] He delivered these seven (two sons and five grandsons of Saul) to the Gibeonites, who hanged them on a hill in Gibeah, Saul's home town. The time of year was the beginning of barley harvest (meaning mid-spring). The reason for the indication of time of year is to point up a tender note regarding Rizpah, the mother of two of the slain. She remained at the spot of the execution from that time until the first rains (mid-fall) to keep both birds and beasts from touching the unburied bodies.

David now added to his commendable deed. The death of these seven prompted him to think again of the bones of Saul and his sons, which were yet at Jabesh-gilead. He brought these bones from there and, together with the bones of the seven, interred all in the burial plot of Kish, Saul's father, at Zelah in Benjamin. When this had been done, "God was intreated for the land," meaning that there was no longer reason for Him to punish the land with famine.

b. Points to notice

1) ***Necessity of keeping agreements.*** An outstanding truth illustrated here is that God wants agreements to be kept by those making them. The agreement with the Gibeonites had been made as a result of trickery on the part of the Gibeonites, but still God wanted it kept. Saul had not done so, apparently on the basis that the Gibeonites were foreigners to Israel and he

[13]According to II Sam. 21:8, five of these were sons of Michal. If so, they must have been born when she was married to Phalti, for she was barren with David as a result of her criticism of him for dancing before God (II Sam. 6:20-23). However, there is textual evidence of a copyist's error in which "Michal" was substituted for "Merab." Also, the husband cited in II Sam. 21:8 is Adriel, whom Merab, Saul's older daughter, married (I Sam. 18:19). It is, of course, possible that Michal raised these children for Adriel (Merab perhaps having died). If so, David's action in taking them from her would have been difficult for David as well as for her; for, though they had quarreled, she likely still lived in the palace.

was interested in Israelite purity (21:2), but God was more interested in keeping the promise. He sent a three-year famine as punishment for Saul's action, and was not satisfied until the demands of the Gibeonites—even though this involved the death of seven of Saul's descendants—were met.

2) ***The principle of capital punishment.*** When the Gibeonites asked for the lives of seven descendants of Saul, they were following the principle of capital punishment set forth in the Old Testament (Num. 35:31; cf. Gen. 9:6). They did not want silver or gold from Saul's house, nor the lives of just anyone in the land. They wanted seven descendants of the man who had wronged them. If Saul had still been alive, they probably would have asked for his life, but this they could not do. In that God was appeased when their request had been carried out, it is clear that what they requested met with His approval.

3) ***The justice involved.*** It might be argued that a penalty was here exacted from seven men who had not been guilty of the crime involved. Saul had brought the wrong on the Gibeonites, and, since he was dead, they should have let the matter drop. If only the hard feelings of the Gibeonites were involved, this argument would have merit, but God Himself sent the three-year famine to show His displeasure. This leads one to believe that these descendants were not without guilt. It may be that they had been much involved, perhaps helping in the slaying of the Gibeonites and appropriating their property. God never acts unjustly, and one may be sure He did not in this case.

4) ***Rizpah's devotion.*** The devotion of Rizpah to her two sons is touching. For at least a half year she remained in the open by the exposed bodies, in their decaying condition, to protect them from predators. It should be observed that Saul's daughter Merab, the mother of five of the slain, did not do the same. It is possible, of course, that she had some good reason. At any rate it was only Rizpah, a lesser wife of Saul with the status only of concubine, who showed this love. Certainly she had no part in the wrong done to the Gibeonites, however guilty her two boys may have been, for her reaction is not compatible with the hardheartedness shown in the slaying of the Gibeonites. One can only feel sorry for this faithful mother, but the fact that the death of her sons was necessary points up further the high price of sin.

5) ***David's burial of Saul and his sons.*** If one should wonder why David had not brought the bones of Saul and his sons back for burial when he had sent his words of commendation to Jabesh-gilead (II Sam. 2:5-7), it should be realized that he did not at that time have control of the burial place in

Benjamin. He ruled then only over Judah, with Benjamin yet remaining under the rule of Ish-bosheth. All he could do at that time was send a message. Now, being king of all the land, he could bring the bones back and put them in the family burial plot. Again he is to be commended for a thoughtful gesture toward the former ruler and his family. Further, by this action he demonstrated that, in his giving of Saul's seven descendants to the Gibeonites, he was not showing vindictiveness toward the whole house of Saul. He went out of his way to give a proper burial to all of the family.

E. DAVID'S DESIRE TO BUILD THE TEMPLE

1. THE STORY (II SAM. 7; I CHRON. 17)

One of the earlier portions of II Samuel tells of David's desire to build a fine temple for God in Jerusalem. The time falls in the early part of David's rule because Solomon was not yet born (I Chron. 22:8-10). It could not have been at the very beginning, however, as three facts show: (1) David's palace had been built by this time (II Sam. 7:2); (2) Hiram of Tyre had helped him build it (II Sam. 5:11), and this was the same Hiram who aided Solomon (II Chron. 2:3) following David's forty-year reign; and (3) by this time David had defeated all his enemies (II Sam. 7:1), meaning that the initial enemies David faced had been turned back so that he now had time to think about a major domestic venture.

One day, following David's defeat of these enemies, the king indicated to the prophet Nathan that he wished to build a temple in which to house the ark.[14] Nathan bade him do so, but that night God appeared to Nathan to inform him that this was not God's will. Nathan was to reply to David in the following vein: God had not dwelt in a temple, but only a tent (the tabernacle) in prior years and had never asked for anything more; God had greatly blessed David in taking him from the life of a shepherd and establishing him as a great ruler in the world of the day; God would set up one of David's children as a great ruler and this child, too, would be blessed; this successor would be permitted to build a house for God's name; and through this successor, David's posterity would rule over Israel as a continuing dynasty.

When David received this message from the prophet, he did not object or become bitter. Rather, he confessed that God indeed had been gracious to him in bringing him to his present high position and now even more in

[14]George Fohrer (*History of Israelite Religion,* p. 126) believes that David's desire to build a temple came from an inclination to be like the Canaanites. This cannot be, however, both because there is nothing in the text to this effect and because David actually was opposed to all Canaanite influence. He conquered land from the Canaanites, he revitalized the work of the priests and Levites in its distinctive Israelite character by a thorough organization of structure, and his name came to be remembered as the greatest king in following the God of Israel.

promising a continuing dynasty. He further praised God's own inherent greatness for redeeming His people from Egypt and for being Israel's God in the land He had given them. Then he spoke again of God's promise concerning the continuation of his own posterity as rulers. In substance, David thus accepted God's refusal of his desire concerning the temple and gave vent to heartfelt praise that God had promised that his posterity would remain on Israel's throne. He did not mention the fact, but no doubt took careful notice that God had also said his son would build the permanent temple.

David's later instructions to Israel's assembled leaders indicate the reason why God had refused him the privilege of building a temple. He told them, "But God said unto me, Thou shalt not build an house for my name, because thou hast been a man of war, and hast shed blood" (I Chron. 28:3).[15] Just when this important information was conveyed to David is not indicated (but see I Chron. 22:8-10). No doubt the refusal was a matter of major disappointment for David, but he at least moved ahead with making preparations for the endeavor: he assembled the incredible amount of "an hundred thousand talents of gold, and a thousand thousand talents of silver" besides an abundance of brass, iron, timber, and stone (I Chron. 22:14). In other words, he did all he could for the project, short of actual construction. He even gave the plan for the building to Solomon, something the Holy Spirit had guided him in making (I Chron. 28:11, 12).

2. POINTS TO NOTICE

a. A good and proper desire

There was nothing wrong with David's desire to build a temple. It was in fact good and proper on his part (I Kings 8:18). As he said, he was himself then living "in an house of cedar" while the ark was located in a mere tent. He wanted to give it a more honored setting. To do so would be to honor God in the sight of pagan nations about, for they measured how much any nation thought of its god(s) by how fine a temple was erected for worship. There would have been some honor for David as well, true enough, for his name would become linked to the building; but still the main interest David had was for God's honor and was therefore altogether proper.

b. David's wars not disapproved

It might be thought that, because God refused David's request for the reason that David was a man of war, God thereby disapproved the wars he

[15]Kathleen Kenyon believes the main reason for David's not building the temple was that he did not have time to do it; see her *Royal Cities of the Old Testament,* p. 37. This view, however, is contrary to Scripture and must be rejected.

fought. This does not follow, however, for God blessed David in these wars and the victories he won were the result of God's approval. The issue was that the extent to which David had made war was not in keeping with building the temple. God is a God of peace and He wanted to be so known both by Israelites and foreigners. For a temple to Him to be built by a person known for war-making activities would have been incompatible with this desire; it would be better to wait until Solomon's time, who would be interested in peaceful pursuits, so that a proper association of ideas would be made.

c. A major disappointment

Though David's words, following Nathan's report to him, do not reflect disappointment, one may be sure that he felt it keenly. This is evidenced by the extent of preparations he made for the building, even though he could not construct it. The gold, silver, and other materials he assembled were of an immense amount. He was very disappointed, and therefore is to be commended for taking God's words so graciously. He gave only praise to God for His goodness; he did not complain of deprivation.

d. Proper reception of a "no" answer

God's answer to the requests of His children is often "no." Too often, Christians are unwilling to accept this answer and feel that, because a "yes" is not forthcoming, God has not heard their prayer. God does not and cannot respond affirmatively to all that is asked of Him. This would not be good for the one asking. The right attitude is to be prepared for a "no" answer as well as a "yes." David evidently was, even though the disappointment was keen.

e. David's house to be built

Instead of David's building a house for God, God's reply indicated that God was going to build a house for David. David's house would not be made of wood and stone, but it would be just as real. He would have a continuing dynasty on Israel's throne. This was the hope of every king, that his name and line might continue. Saul clearly had desired this, and therefore had tried to take David's life many times. David realized the privilege being granted him and gave sincere praise accordingly. It may well be that he considered this—as God really intended—a greater blessing than being permitted to build a temple.

14

David's Last Years

David's closing years as king were not marked with the happiness of the early years. Nathan's warning that the sword would not depart from his house, as a result of his sin with Bathsheba, came true.

One factor that contributed to the unhappy situation concerned the choice of David's successor. As David's reign drew to a close, this problem became increasingly acute. Israel's kingdom had not existed long enough for a pattern to be established for naming a successor, and people quite clearly expected David to make his own selection from his sons. No public announcement was forthcoming, however, though David had actually designated Solomon at the time of his birth.[1] For some reason he had not made this known, perhaps because the time of Solomon's birth had been comparatively early in his rule. David's other sons probably knew of the designation, and at least two sought to circumvent it. First Absalom and then Adonijah made a try for the throne. Before Absalom made his

[1]This designation by David is not recorded directly in the story, which states only that God loved Solomon (II Sam. 12:24). However, when Adonijah attempted much later to seize the throne, Nathan, who knew of the designation, reminded Bathsheba, who also knew of it (I Kings 1:11-13); she in turn reminded the king (I Kings 1:17), and David himself then referred to it (I Kings 1:29, 30).

attempt, however, an episode involving his older half brother Amnon occurred that must be noticed. This episode prepared the way for Absalom's attempt.

A. AMNON AND TAMAR[2]

1. THE STORY (II SAM. 13)

Amnon developed a sensuous love for Absalom's full sister Tamar. A nephew of David named Jonadab wickedly suggested to Amnon that he pretend sickness so that Tamar might be persuaded to come and minister to him, at which time he could force himself upon her. Amnon did this, persuading the king himself to send Tamar to him, and when she came he did force her to sin with him. As soon as Amnon had done the deed, he coldly sent her away, thus making his sin more reprehensible. Absalom learned what Amnon had done, sought to comfort his sister, and planned revenge as soon as an opportunity came.

Absalom waited for two years—probably thinking to put to rest by this delay any suspicion Amnon might have had—and then instituted a plan of action. He called all the sons of the king to a feast he held at the time of sheepshearing. The place was Baal-hazor[3] where apparently he owned property. He instructed his servants to kill Amnon when he had become "merry with wine" (13:28). The servants did so, and then all the other sons quickly fled for home on mules. Before they arrived, news reached the king that Absalom had killed all the sons, but Jonadab, the very man who had wickedly advised Amnon, assured the king that only Amnon was dead.[4] This was shortly confirmed by the arrival of the other sons. Meanwhile Absalom, knowing that David would be highly displeased, fled northward to Geshur[5] where Talmai, his grandfather (mother's father), ruled. There he stayed for three years, not daring to return to Jerusalem.

2. POINTS TO NOTICE

a. Power of sexual attraction

This sad story began as a result of illicit sexual attraction. Amnon's love was not sincere, but only sensual. When he had gotten what he wanted from Tamar he coldly told her to leave. He thus brought grief to her, death to himself in due time, and sad hearts to others. Every person needs to be on his guard against this powerful attraction to sin.

[2]This and the following stories must be placed in David's later years for all participants were adults and all had been born after David became king in Hebron (II Sam. 3:2-5).

[3]Aharoni identifies this with Tell 'Asur, about fourteen miles north of Jerusalem.

[4]He must have guessed this, perhaps on the basis of some knowledge of Absalom's plans which had come to his ears. Evidently this Jonadab was a crafty schemer.

[5]See pp. 40-41.

b. Importance of good counsel

Some people give good counsel and others bad. All too often the latter is followed rather than the former. This was true of Amnon in following the bad advice of Jonadab, who evidently was a nefarious person. Good counsel would have sought to change Amnon's wicked intentions, not further them, and how much better everything would have been if that had been done.

c. Warning against taking vengeance

Because of Amnon's sin against Tamar, Absalom planned vengeance for two full years. This means he was intent on bringing vengeance, and would not permit himself to be dissuaded. Outwardly he seems to have let others believe everything was all right, but inwardly he seethed with bitterness. This is a dangerous frame of mind and can lead only to dire actions, as it did with Absalom. One should not harbor grudges; they only fester and become more intense as time passes.

d. Rumors worse than truth

So often rumors of some catastrophe are worse than actual truth. The news that first reached David was that all his sons had been killed by Absalom. The truth was that only one had lost his life. This was bad enough, but nothing like the rumor. David suffered unnecessary grief for a while because of the false report. It is important that messages be given accurately. Some people, however, seem to take delight in making news as bad as possible.

e. Cost of Absalom's sin

Absalom paid a dear price for the wrong he perpetrated. He succeeded in killing Amnon, but he then found it necessary to flee for his own life and to remain away from Jerusalem for three years. He may not have thought the time would be nearly that long when he left, but before he was able to get back he realized he had paid a dear price. He may have asked himself more than once whether the deed had been worth this much. Sin always demands a heavy price.

B. ABSALOM'S PLOT FOR THE THRONE

1. THE STORY

a. The return to Jerusalem (II Sam. 14)

David's military commander, Joab, now worked in Absalom's behalf, to make possible his return to Jerusalem. Joab saw that the king longed to see

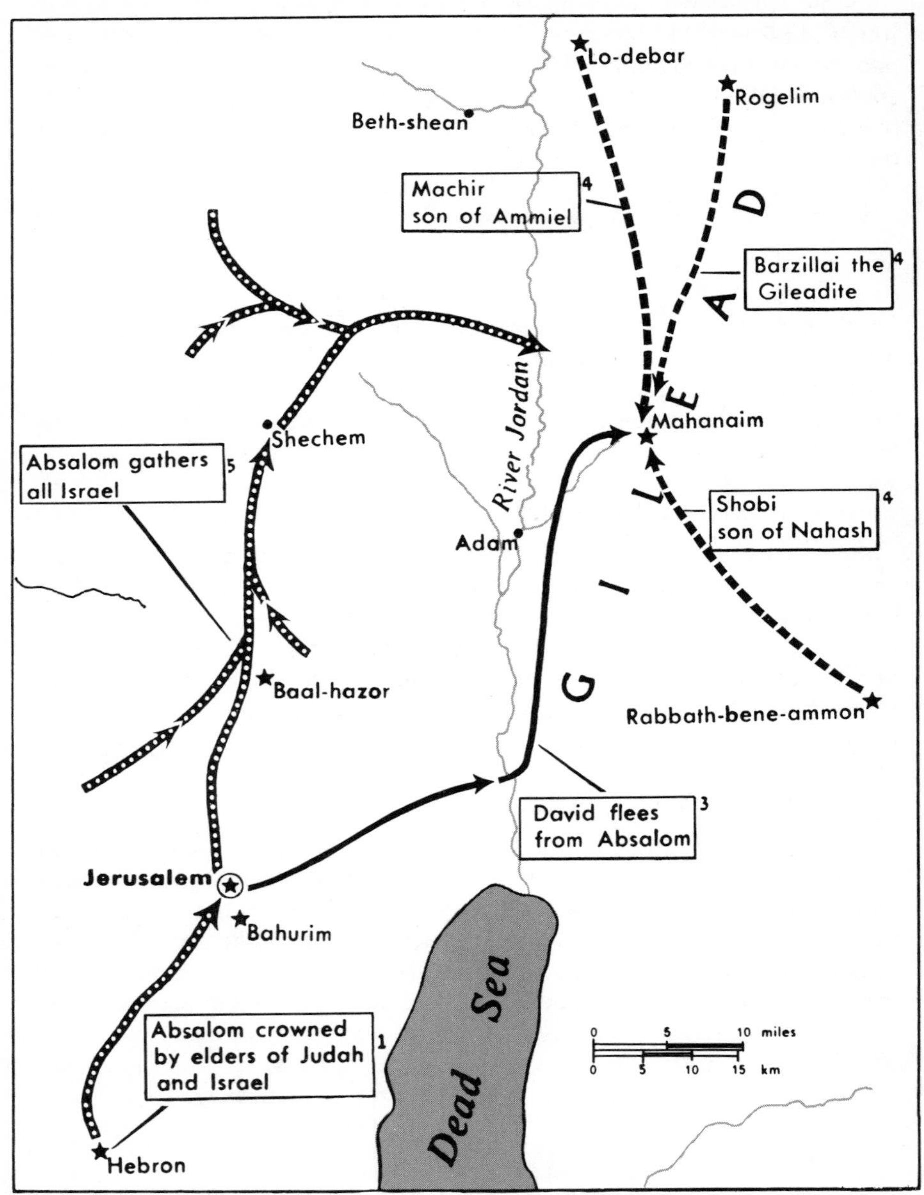

Map 11. Absalom's Rebellion

Absalom, and so plotted with a wise woman from Tekoah[6] to persuade him to grant permission for Absalom to return. The plan worked. David now called Joab and told him to bring Absalom back. Joab went personally to Geshur to fetch Absalom, but when the two arrived back at the capital, David still refused to see Absalom for two more years. Absalom, therefore, sought Joab's help again; when he did not receive it immediately, he even set Joab's grain field on fire to get his attention. Joab thus had some of his own harsh measures turned on himself, but he did do as Absalom wanted and persuaded David to see his son, with the king then kissing the young man as a token of forgiveness.

b. The plot carried out (II Sam. 15:1-12)

It is difficult to tell at what point Absalom actually decided to plot for the throne. The idea probably arose gradually and likely was present at least as early as the time he murdered Amnon. In fact, this may have contributed to his desire to commit the murder. The reason is that with Amnon, David's oldest son, out of the way he, Absalom, would be next in line for the throne—on the basis of the oldest son being the heir apparent. For though Absalom was the third son, the second son, Chileab (II Sam. 3:3—called Daniel in I Chron. 3:1), had evidently died while still young, for he is never mentioned following the time of his birth.

Having been reinstated in the king's favor, Absalom began to put his plan for grabbing the throne into action. His first step was to curry favor with the people. He was a handsome man (II Sam. 14:25, 26), a factor which naturally attracted people. He created an air of importance by moving through the country with a retinue of chariots and fifty attendants. He assumed the posture of one vitally interested in people by intercepting those with problems, before they could get to the king's appointed officers, and telling them how much better matters would be if he were king. He was clever and convincing, so that these efforts did bring many people to favor him. After four years,[7] when Absalom believed that sufficient good will had been generated, he took the second step. He went to Hebron[8] with the king's unsuspecting permission, assembled his followers, and had himself anointed king.[9] With a considerable force of men, he then marched north

[6]Home of the prophet Amos of some years later, located about five miles south of Bethlehem.

[7]The number given in II Sam. 15:7 is "forty," but this is impossible in that David ruled only a total of thirty-three years in Jerusalem. This must be a copyist's error and so is better read with the Syriac, Vulgate, Arabic, and others: "four years."

[8]Perhaps Absalom chose Hebron for this anointing since David had been anointed there twice.

[9]It is not directly stated that he was anointed at Hebron, but this follows from the story taken as a whole.

against his father in Jerusalem, and David, taken unawares, found it necessary to flee.

2. POINTS TO NOTICE

a. The evil of deceit

The episodes in this story involve the repeated use of deceit. Amnon used it to bring Tamar to him, Absalom used it to kill Amnon, Joab used it to persuade David to bring Absalom back to Jerusalem, and finally Absalom used it to work rebellion against David. It led to unhappy results in every instance. This is the regular consequence of deceit.

b. Joab an opportunist

One has to wonder why Joab made the effort in Absalom's behalf to persuade David to bring his son back to Jerusalem. Joab was not the type of person who did things for others without a reason. It is likely that he believed Absalom would one day be king, and he wanted to be on his side when he did. If so, Joab is shown to have been an opportunist, taking the side which he believed would help him the most in the end. It may be that when Absalom burned Joab's field of grain he lost this favor, however, for when David finally fled from Jerusalem before Absalom, Joab remained loyal to him and was actually the one who killed Absalom.

c. Reasoning of Absalom

Absalom clearly was motivated in his attempt for the throne by the fact that he was next in line for it, on the basis of the oldest living son being the heir apparent. The fact, however, that he saw fit to seek the throne by way of rebellion—rather than waiting for the natural death of his father—shows that he did not believe David thought in these terms. It is probable, in fact, that he knew of David's earlier decision in respect to Solomon and here sought to circumvent it.[10]

d. Some dissatisfaction in Israel

The fact that Absalom was able to persuade a sizable number of Israelites to follow him in his rebellion shows that there was a degree of dissatisfaction in the land. Possibly David had raised taxes to a height which made for some unrest. Also, with the development of the empire the king's interests had become wider than his own land, and some people may have thought they were being neglected. Besides this, any regime, no matter how

[10]Adonijah, who next tried for the throne, certainly knew, since it was Solomon alone, of all the brothers, that he did not invite to his coronation feast (I Kings 1:9, 26).

good it is, loses sympathizers and gains enemies with time, and David was now in the latter years of his reign. Absalom had become aware of this dissatisfaction and turned it to his advantage.

e. The ease of deception

History shows that a substantial segment of almost any populace can be easily deceived. Many people are attracted more by outward appearances, pompous displays, and high-sounding promises than by hard facts and careful reasoning. They believe the lies of glib speech more quickly than the truths of common sense. Absalom had the fine appearance, the pompous display of chariots and attendants, and the high-sounding promises of benefits for everyone. The result was that he soon had a large following. David headed the finest government in all the world of the day, but people were ready to turn from it for this fast-talking young man.

f. Ahithophel persuaded

Even one of David's official counselors, Ahithophel, was persuaded to join with Absalom (15:12). There may have been a special reason for this, however. Ahithophel was the father of one of David's mighty men named Eliam (II Sam. 23:34), and Bathsheba was the daughter of a man named Eliam (II Sam. 11:3). Since Bathsheba had married another of David's mighty men, Uriah the Hittite (II Sam. 23:39), it was quite possible that the same Eliam is in view in both instances, making Ahithophel the grandfather of Bathsheba. It may be, then, that Ahithophel held a grudge against David for taking his granddaughter from her husband and here saw a way of gaining revenge. If so, this was another case of an old grudge festering to become an unwise action, which turned out very tragically for the person involved (see II Sam. 17:23), even as with Absalom.

C. DAVID VERSUS ABSALOM

1. THE STORY

a. David's flight (II Sam. 15:13—16:14)

Those who left Jerusalem in flight with David were his personal bodyguard (the Cherethites and Pelethites), the faithful 600 mighty men, numerous servants, and a Philistine military leader named Ittai who had recently come to David. Zadok and Abiathar, the two high priests, also desired to accompany him and bring the ark, but David sent them back. He asked them to send him information regarding Absalom's plans, using their two respective sons, Ahimaaz and Jonathan, as messengers. David also told his lone remaining counselor, Hushai, to return, to seek to counter the advice Ahithophel might give Absalom about pursuing David, and then to tell Zadok and Abiathar what Absalom decided to do. All three did return to do as David had directed.

As David moved away from Jerusalem, he experienced varied reactions from people he met. Just past the crest of the Mount of Olives (16:1; cf. 15:32), Ziba, the servant of Mephibosheth caught up with him, bringing two riding animals and a sizable quantity of food. David asked him where his master was and Ziba answered falsely that Mephibosheth remained in Jerusalem, expecting now to be installed king in place of his grandfather Saul. Though Ziba surely lied, the king did not recognize the falsehood and immediately told Ziba he could have all the lands previously assigned to Mephibosheth, something Ziba had apparently hoped for.

Further along at Ba-hurim,[11] a descendant of Saul named Shimei met the king and, still being loyal to Saul, took the opportunity to shout curses and throw stones at the royal party. Abishai wanted the king's permission to kill the man, but David graciously and remarkably refused to allow this, even though Shimei persisted in his efforts, following the party along the road for some time.

b. Action in Jerusalem (II Sam. 16:15—17:23)

Back in Jerusalem, Absalom entered the city in all his glory and was met by Hushai, as David had instructed. Through clever speech, Hushai gained the favor of Absalom—whose pride made him easy prey to flattering words—and he did counter Ahithophel's counsel. The latter's advice had been for Absalom to pursue David immediately with 12,000 men and catch the king before he could make ready for such an attack. Hushai, however, urged Absalom to wait long enough to gather a much larger army and then attack, because, as he said, this would give a greater chance of success against one as crafty and able as David. Hushai's advice was accepted by Absalom, and the plan was put into effect.

Hushai, glad of his success, let Zadok and Abiathar know, and they sent their two sons with the information to David, who was waiting just beyond Ba-hurim. Though the two boys were seen en route and pursued, they were hidden in a well by a sympathizer at Ba-hurim and saved from capture. Thus spared, the two went on to find David and told him their information. Having heard the good news, David moved on across the Jordan and north to Mahanaim,[12] knowing now that he could do so safely. Meanwhile in Jerusalem, Ahithophel, feeling he had been disgraced, hanged himself (17:23).

[11]Commonly identified with modern Ras et-Tmim on the east side of the Mount of Olives, along the old Roman road to Jericho.

[12]See p. 216, n. 3.

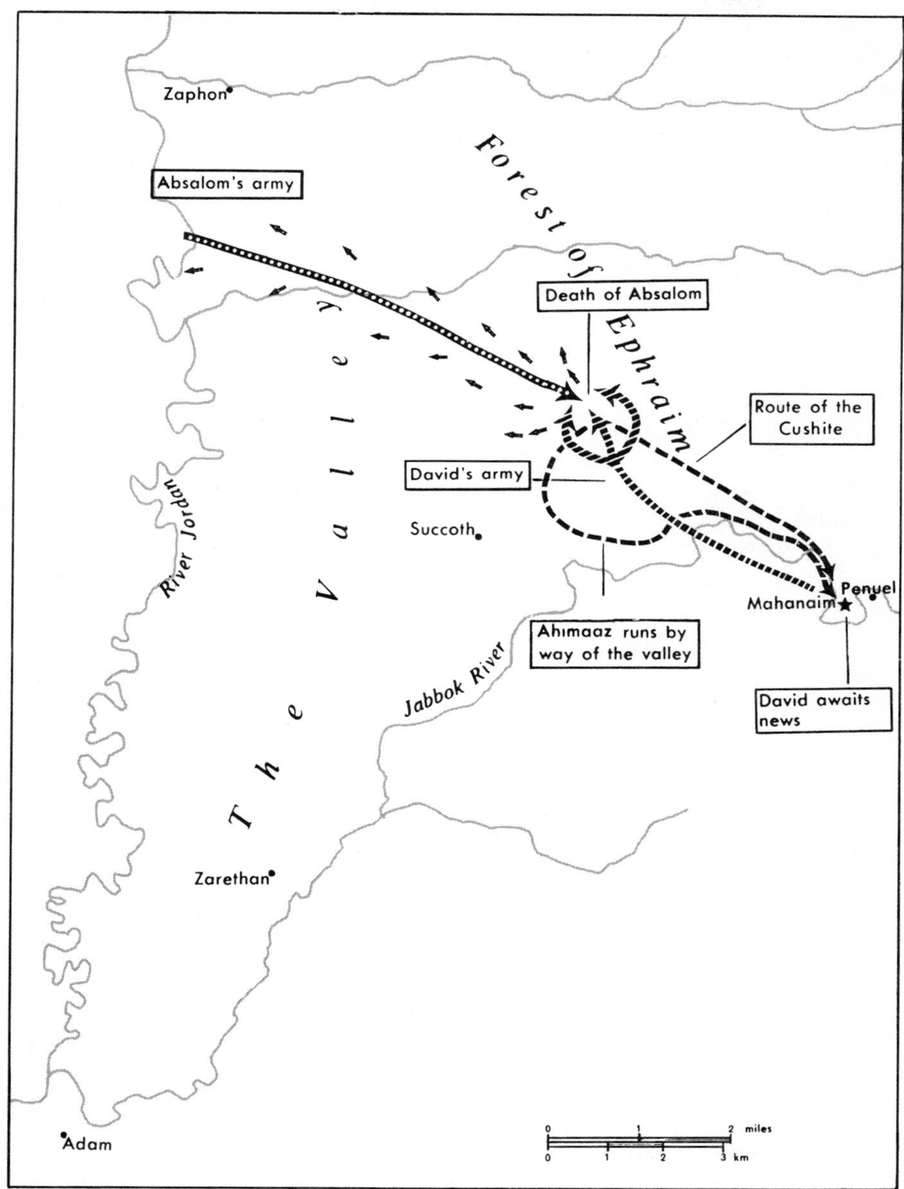

Map 12. The Battle with Absalom's

c. The battle (II Sam. 17:24—19:8)

Having taken enough time to gather a large number of troops,[13] Absalom followed after David, crossing the Jordan also and moving to the area of Mahanaim. He made Amasa, a cousin of Joab (17:25), his commander, for Joab had gone with David, having changed his favor from Absalom by this time.

David, meanwhile in Mahanaim, the former capital of Ish-bosheth, had been given provisions by three prominent people: Machir of Lo-debar, Barzillai of Rogelim, and Shobi, a son of the Ammonite king. These provisions were of immense help to David, both in physical and emotional support. Thus supplied, David made ready for battle. He divided his army into three groups, headed by Joab, Abishai, and the Philistine newcomer, Ittai of Gath. He sent them off with the command that, whatever happened, they were not to kill Absalom, in spite of the rebellion the young man had perpetrated.

The two armies met in what is called the wood of Ephraim.[14] Though the number of David's troops was much smaller than Absalom's, they were his mobile, hard-core soldiers, who knew how to fight. Under the leadership of the three capable captains, they soon demonstrated that Absalom's hastily assembled army was no match, especially in the woods where massed forces were of little value. David and Joab may have purposely planned to strike the oncoming troops of Absalom in this type of country, knowing the advantage it would give them. The result was that David's men won a decisive victory, under the blessing of God, and Absalom's men were put in full retreat, with 20,000 killed.

Absalom, trying to get away, found himself caught in a tree by his flowing hair, which left him hanging in a helpless condition. This fact was reported to Joab, and, in spite of David's earlier order, he came and killed the young man as he hung in his humiliating situation. This done, two runners were dispatched to take word of the victory to the king. Cushi (or a Cushite) was sent first and then Ahimaaz, son of Zadok, who pleaded to be sent also. He was one of the two who had earlier brought important information to David when he first left Jerusalem. Ahimaaz took a different route than did Cushi, going "the way of the plain."[15] and though it was

[13]Probably from David's reserve troops of 288,000 who served in divisions of 24,000 per month; see p. 182.

[14]Though the tribe of Ephraim was on the west of the Jordan, this wood must have been on the east because both David and Absalom crossed the Jordan before the battle. No reason is known for ascribing the name *Ephraim* to it.

[15]The word for "plain" is *kikkar,* which is normally used for the Jordan Valley. Evidently the wood of Ephraim was near the valley, and by going along a part of the valley, Ahimaaz had better terrain for running than did Cushi. For further discussion see Elmer B. Smick, *Archaeology of the Jordan Valley,* p. 87.

probably longer, it was evidently easier and he reached David first. He told David of the victory but did not speak of Absalom's death, feigning ignorance. Cushi, however, let the king know and David then went off by himself to bewail the death of his son.

When Joab returned and learned of the king's grief, in a spirit of virtual reprimand he went to David. Joab told David that he as king was making those who had fought valiantly for him feel as though they had really lost. He also advised him that, if he did not soon appear before the people and speak properly to them, all would forsake him. David then did as Joab advised, and everyone was relieved.

2. POINTS TO NOTICE

a. David caught unawares

One cannot help but wonder how a man as astute as David could have been caught so unawares by Absalom's rebellion. He seems not to have been prepared for it at all, having to flee as quickly as he did. Certainly the activities of Absalom had been known to people around him, for too many persons were involved to keep them secret. Either people feared to warn David, or he did not believe the warnings he heard. In his love for Absalom—as indicated by his deep remorse at the young man's death—he may have simply refused to accept any words that spoke against his son.

b. His only defeat

The result of David's blind credulity was that he was driven from the throne, not by a foreign enemy—whom he could and did defeat in every encounter—but by one of his own house and family. David's love for a son, then, became a weakness and worked his only defeat. David's heart must have been heavy as he left Jerusalem. It was bad enough to be driven from his capital, but that this should be as a result of rebellion by one of his own flesh and blood must have been almost more than he could bear.

c. David's gullibility with Ziba

It probably was the result of David's confusion of mind that Ziba was able to make the king believe his story regarding Mephibosheth. If the king had not been so emotionally torn, it is likely that he would have seen through the man's story. It did not make sense that Mephibosheth thought the people would now instate him on the throne. The rebellion, after all, was led by Absalom, and there was no reason to think there was any connection between Absalom and Mephibosheth. Moreover, that Mephibosheth was crippled made it unlikely the people would want him as king, and surely he had never given David cause to think he had any such aspirations.

Distraught emotions, however, are not conducive to clear thinking, and David simply did not respond with his normal sense of judgment in this instance.

d. Graciousness toward Shimei

This same condition of torn emotions may have contributed to David's gracious gesture toward Shimei, who cursed the king and threw stones. David forbade Abishai to punish the man. If his own son had been permitted by God to do what he had, then why should this Benjamite not be permitted to do what he was doing? The implication is that David believed God was bringing some of the punishment, of which Nathan had earlier warned, through this rebellion of Absalom and now this cursing of Shimei. Therefore, it was not for David to stop the man but to let God's punishment take its course. Perhaps God would in the end "requite [David] good," when enough punishment had been inflicted. David's torn emotions must have brought the humility that led to this manner of thinking.

e. Hushai's wisdom

When Hushai countered the advice of Ahithophel by advising Absalom to wait and gather a huge army, he was using clever strategy. To persuade Absalom to delay would give David time to get to the best area for making a stand—it is clear that the king was not ready to fight immediately where he was. Moreover, in gathering troops from all across the land, Absalom would be gathering men who had always before been loyal to David and would thus not make an effective fighting force. In giving this advice, Hushai was playing on Absalom's vanity. The proud man would think that these troops surely would fight for him now, since he had done such a good job of laying a foundation for his rebellion; and, anyhow, the people should want him as king just because of who he was. Hushai saw the vanity and took advantage of it. His strategy worked quite as he had planned.

f. David's wise choice of location

That David made his way to Mahanaim was likely due to the type of terrain that he knew was in the vicinity. It was a wooded area and it was rough land, filled with holes and pits. In fact, when the battle was over, the wood had "devoured more people that day than the sword" (18:8). David knew that his men, well trained as they were, could handle themselves in such country, and he knew that the kind of troops Absalom would be recruiting would be far less capable. Numbers would not be much of an advantage; but knowledge, skill, and mobility would. David and Joab had much more experience in fighting, whether in easy or bad terrain, than Absalom or any of his people, and this too would be an advantage. No doubt, David and

Joab together planned where the best place to make their stand would be and picked this location accordingly.

g. Absalom's pride and fall

There is little question but that Absalom was a proud man. His every action shows this, as he planned and schemed, first against Amnon and then against his father. At no point does he show any dependence on God. He even used as an excuse for going to Hebron his desire to pay a vow, which was probably only a pretext to gain his father's good will. Of nothing, however, was he more proud than of his handsome appearance and especially his hair. Each year he cut and weighed it. It is highly significant, therefore, that it was this very hair that brought about his downfall. It caught in the branches of a tree and caused him to hang suspended, quite helpless and surely humiliated. He thus became an easy target for anyone to slay him, as Joab did. One can hardly find a clearer example of the object of a person's pride becoming the cause of his own fall.

h. David's display of grief

One has to be touched by David's love and remorse for Absalom, when this son had done so much harm to him. In all fairness, however, one has to judge that Joab acted more wisely than David in this matter. Absalom deserved to die for what he had done. David should have kept his emotion to himself and not let it make those who had fought valiantly for him feel as though they had done something wrong. They had hazarded their lives in his behalf, and he seemed to show no appreciation. He should have thought about them, as well as his son. Joab's counsel to him, after the battle, was appropriate and wise. No doubt David realized this as Joab spoke to him, and therefore he did as his military commander urged. There were other considerations for him to think about besides his remorse.

D. RENEWAL OF THE KINGSHIP

1. THE STORY

a. Return to Jerusalem (II Sam. 19:9-40)

When information concerning David's victory over Absalom reached the western tribes—no doubt first by the return of Absalom's troops that had escaped (19:8)—a united movement arose for bringing David back to the throne. News of the movement reached David, but there was no indication that Judah, his home tribe, was involved. Therefore, he sent word to Zadok and Abiathar to urge Judah's leaders to act. The two did so, and the message David wanted was received from these leaders. Then the king made ready to return to the Jordan.

Before he returned to the Jordan, however, he appointed Amasa to replace Joab as his military commander. This was surely an unwise action. Amasa had just lost the battle for Absalom. The action was in retaliation for Joab's having killed Absalom, an action which was really in the king's best interest. And the appointment was certain to lead to further trouble, because Joab was not one to stand idly by and see himself supplanted in this manner, as David was to learn shortly once again.

On reaching the Jordan, David was met by a large welcoming committee. It included many men of Judah, a thousand Benjamites of whom Shimei (who had earlier cursed David) was one, and Ziba with his fifteen sons and twenty servants. Together they conducted David across the river, having a boat ready to ferry the king, his family, and his possessions.

After crossing, David had three significant contacts. The first was with Shimei, who now approached the king to beg his forgiveness for what he had done. Again Abishai urged that the man be put to death, but the king answered him roughly—apparently thinking of Abishai as exhibiting here the same quality as Joab—and declared that on this happy day no one should be put to death. David thus granted mercy to Shimei—though he clearly did not forgive him, for later, when Solomon came to the throne, David instructed Solomon to take Shimei's life (I Kings 2:8, 9).

The second contact was with Mephibosheth, who now arrived with a large group from Jerusalem.[16] He came to David to make explanations why he had not bidden the king farewell on David's leaving the city. He told David that Ziba had deceived him at the time, having promised to saddle a donkey so that he could come to David, but Ziba had not done so in his endeavor to win the king's favor for himself. The indication that Mephibosheth had not dressed his feet, trimmed his beard, or washed his clothes since the time of David's departure, shows that what he said was true. David evidently saw this also, and now gave orders that the land, which he had previously given entirely to Ziba, be divided equally between Mephibosheth and Ziba. This was hardly fair to Mephibosheth, but David may have tried thus to save a little face for himself in having made an improper judgment earlier. He is not to be commended for this decision.

The third contact was with Barzillai, who had brought provisions to David at Mahanaim, and had now accompanied him all the way to the

[16]The KJV reading of 19:25, "when he was come to Jerusalem to meet the king," should be, "when Jerusalem was come to meet the king."

Jordan. David quite properly urged this eighty-year-old friend to go all the way to Jerusalem where he could spend the rest of his life at the king's expense. Barzillai declined, however, saying he could not appreciate such luxurious living, but his servant Chimham (probably his own son, I Kings 2:7) could go along if the king so pleased, and this was arranged.

b. Revolt of Sheba (II Sam. 19:41—20:22)

At this point, evidently while the king was at Gilgal still near the Jordan, trouble broke out between the representatives of the northern tribes and those from Judah. It seems that most of the Israelite representatives arrived after the actual crossing of the Jordan had taken place, and they were offended that David had not waited so that they could have a part in the occasion. Heated words resulted, and finally a Benjamite named Sheba called for all the northern people to follow him in a revolt against the king. They did so and left the scene, allowing the men of Judah alone to bring David up to Jerusalem.

David now gave Amasa his first order as the new commander. He should assemble the men of Judah (who had comprised Amasa's main troops under Absalom) to pursue Sheba and put down this revolt. Amasa took more than the three days David allowed him, and so David sent Abishai with Joab's hard-core troops, together with the Cherethites and Pelethites, to do the job. At Gibeon, however, just six miles from Jerusalem, Amasa caught up with the group. This was his undoing, for now Joab approached him and cruelly stabbed him with a sword, leaving him to wallow in his blood on the road. Joab and Abishai then went on north. When the men of the army paused to look at Amasa, one of them took him from the road and covered him with a cloth. Then all moved on after the two leaders.

The chase of Sheba led to the far north, even to Abel-beth-maacah, near Dan, where Sheba had taken refuge. Evidently the northern representatives had not followed the man very far, but had left him quite alone after departing from the scene at Gilgal. A siege was set up against Abel-beth-maacah, but a wise woman called out to ask what the purpose was, desiring to avoid destruction of the city. Joab told her that Sheba was there, and she promised that Sheba's head would be thrown over the wall, and it soon was. This done, Joab brought the troops back to Jerusalem, and the revolt was over.

c. David's closing years (II Sam. 21–23; I Kings 1:1-4)

By the time these events had transpired, and David was settled securely on his throne again, probably not more than three to five years of his reign remained.[17] Since David had begun to reign at age thirty, he was approximately sixty-five by now. During these closing years, David's actions probably included the writing of the psalm recorded in II Samuel 22,[18] the delivery of his "last words" (II Sam. 23)—in which are included names of his mighty men (23:8-39)[19]—the accumulation of materials for the temple Solomon was to build, and the maintenance of his political position as head of the empire.

One matter which is definitely from the very last of these years is recorded in I Kings 1:1-4. It concerns David's inability to keep himself warm in bed. He may have become bedridden by this time, or it may be that when he went to bed he did not have enough vitality to generate sufficient heat for himself. Consequently a young lady was found and brought to help give him warmth; her name was Abishag of Shunem. Though she lay with the king in his bed, he did not have relations with her. She evidently was a comfort to the king as well as a source of heat for him. The fact that David needed this kind of help shows that his closing years were characterized by physical weakness. He died at the age of seventy and probably was near that age when Abishag was brought to him.

2. POINTS TO NOTICE

a. Invitation to return to Jerusalem

The action of the northern tribes and then David's request to Judah show that an invitation was appropriate before David could return to Jerusalem. The people in considerable number, after all, cooperated with Absalom's revolt. This meant that they had indirectly rejected David's rule. With Absalom dead, however, they recognized the greater ability of David and were ready to have him back; but he needed to be asked. The northern tribes surprisingly did this first, and Judah did it only when a special request was sent to them. David wanted to be reinstated as king of all the land, not just of the north, and Judah, after all, was his own tribe. He wanted their invitation more than any other.

b. The strange appointment of Amasa

As indicated, David's appointment of Amasa did not make sense. If David wanted to be rid of Joab as leader, a more proper time would have

[17]David ruled a total of forty years (II Sam. 5:4), and Absalom was born to a wife David married after beginning to rule. By the time of Amnon's violation of Tamar, Absalom, having sheep and property of his own, was probably at least twenty. Since that time, approximately eleven years had elapsed (see II Sam. 13:23, 38; 14:28; 15:7, where read "four," not "forty"); add another year for all that happened during the revolt proper and David's return to Jerusalem, and it is evident that about thirty-five years of the reign had elapsed.

[18]Also recorded as Psalm 18.

[19]See pp. 181-182.

been when he had murdered Abner, not when he had just won a brilliant victory for the king. Moreover, Amasa was the losing commander. Joab had shown definite superiority over him. The only way David's action can be understood is in the light of his torn emotions over Absalom. The appointment was made more on an emotional impulse than a rational judgment. It is true that Joab had disobeyed a direct command when he killed Absalom, but the command had not been proper, and David should have realized this. Joab also had later approached the king in a blunt way to give advice, but this too was necessary. Perhaps he could have been a little less direct, but the advice surely was in order.

c. David and Shimei

David would certainly have been justified in letting Abishai inflict punishment on Shimei, either when he first uttered his curses or when he later begged for forgiveness. Shimei, a descendant of Saul, still favored a dynasty from Saul's house, and therefore was a risk to David at any time. His plea for forgiveness was clearly in behalf of his own life, now that David had won over Absalom, something Shimei had not expected. At the same time, David was not entirely without fault in promising him on oath that he would not die; note that David later told Solomon to kill Shimei (I Kings 2:8, 9). Probably torn emotions again, as David linked Abishai's desire to Joab's slaughter of Absalom, were largely responsible for the promise, which David later saw to be unwise.

d. David and Mephibosheth

David was not without fault in respect to his dealings with Mephibosheth either. He acted here quite differently than he had a few years earlier, when he had given the young man all Saul's property. In view of the general situation, it must have been clear to David that Mephibosheth was the one telling the truth, in contrast to Ziba, but still David only divided the possessions between the two. It would seem that he should have restored all to Mephibosheth and, further, brought punishment on Ziba for his deception.

e. David and Barzillai

In contrast, David's action in respect to Barzillai was fully commendable. This eighty-year-old man had helped David at Mahanaim and now accompanied the king all the way to the Jordan. David appreciated this very much and wanted to return the favor. When Barzillai refused the favor for himself, David extended it to his son, Chimham, who would thus represent his father. David was gracious and proper in this. Appreciation should always be shown for favors given.

f. David and the revolt

One must judge that David was not without blame also in respect to the revolt that broke out. When the northern representatives arrived, they objected that David had not waited for them. It would seem they had a valid point in their favor. They, after all, were the ones who had first asked David to return. Yet David had not waited for them but had permitted the people of Judah alone to bring him across the Jordan. This crossing was considered symbolic of an official reception back into the land and therefore should have had all involved parties present. From the words of the people of Judah, as they responded to those of Israel (19:42), it seems clear that David had played favorites in so doing, because Judah was his tribe—or at least the people of Judah had so interpreted the action. Then it would seem that David, after making this initial mistake, should have been strong enough to control the bitter animosity that broke out, so that actual revolt would not have resulted. The implication is, however, that he stood to one side to watch the two groups argue, without inserting his authority to give directions. A little diplomacy could have helped very much, had David used it.

g. Joab and Amasa

When Joab first learned of Amasa's appointment in his place, he no doubt was hurt deeply. Though he had disobeyed the king's orders in killing Absalom, he had done this, as well as win the battle, for the king's benefit. Then, when he came to Jerusalem, and Amasa was given the responsibility to catch Sheba, his disappointment must have increased. And, still further, David's putting Joab's troops into the hands of his brother Abishai would have served as a final crushing blow. All this must be realized as one judges Joab's action in killing Amasa. This is not to say that he was justified in the act—for he surely was not—but it helps one to understand the motivation.

h. Wise action in Abel-beth-maacah

Joab and Abishai were ready to storm and destroy much of the city Abel-beth-maacah in their effort to capture Sheba, had not a wise woman taken matters in hand to stop the unnecessary onslaught. What her thinking was regarding Sheba at the time, or whether she even knew of his presence, is not indicated. Her inquiry as to the reason for the siege, however, shows that she was at least not aware of the seriousness of the situation. When she recognized this, she put forth effort to persuade the other people to save their city rather than Sheba's life. She used common sense in this, and common sense is often extremely important in settling misunderstandings that can grow into major conflicts.

i. David and Abishag

The purpose of recording the story of David and Abishag is twofold: first, to show that David became weak in his last days of rule, a fact which doubtless gave Adonijah encouragement to try for the throne; and second, to introduce this young lady into the record since she was to be involved in Solomon's determination to put Adonijah to death (I Kings 2:13-25). The fact of her being brought to David must be understood in the light of the day when kings commonly had large harems. David already had several wives and concubines, but apparently none of these was judged suitable for the purpose in view.

E. REVOLT OF ADONIJAH

1. THE STORY

a. The revolt proper (I Kings 1:5-9)

Adonijah was David's fourth son and this made him next in line for the throne, following the death of Absalom—on the basis of the oldest living son being the heir apparent. In view of David's poor health, he now made his try. It is stated that his father had never reproved him for any action, which probably gave him courage to make his attempt; he also had a pleasing appearance like Absalom. Further, in the pattern of his older brother, he "prepared him chariots and horsemen, and fifty men to run before him," to give him an air of importance in the sight of the people.

For support in his endeavor, Adonijah was able to persuade Joab and Abiathar to assist him. Joab, opportunist that he was, had at one time supported Absalom, but then turned back to David. Now that David had sought to replace him with Amasa, he was ready to change again to be on Adonijah's team. That Abiathar was persuaded may have been due to his jealousy of Zadok. Zadok seems to have come to be favored as high priest by David, since he is regularly named first in any mention of the two together (II Sam. 17:15; 19:11; 20:25) and also the ark appears to have been placed under his supervision (II Sam. 15:24-29).

Adonijah now invited both Joab and Abiathar, along with some servants and the other sons of David (except Solomon), to a feast to be held at En-rogel, just outside the southeast corner of the city wall in the Kidron Valley. The feast was in preparation for the anointing ceremony, when Adonijah hoped to be crowned king.

b. The counterplot of Nathan and Bathsheba (I Kings 1:10-37)

News of this clandestine gathering, however, soon came to the attention of opposition forces. These were comprised mainly of Nathan the prophet,

Zadok the other high priest, Benaiah the leader of David's bodyguard, and David's elite mighty men. This was a formidable group, a fact which accounts for Adonijah's secrecy. Nathan took the lead in countering Adonijah's move.

He worked through Bathsheba, the mother of Solomon. He urged her to approach the king and remind him of the promise to make Solomon his successor, indicating that he (Nathan) would come in after her and bring the same reminder. Bathsheba complied, speaking also about Adonijah's feast and intention in respect to the throne. Then Nathan came before the king, spoke in the same vein, and added that Adonijah had not invited himself (Nathan), Zadok, Benaiah, or Solomon.[20] David immediately reacted as Nathan and Bathsheba had hoped, and ordered that Solomon be taken on David's own mule[21] down to the spring of Gihon (also in the Kidron Valley but about 2000 feet north of En-rogel) and there be anointed as his successor. This was done as quickly as possible, so that Solomon's coronation could be conducted before that of Adonijah.

c. The anointing of Solomon (I Kings 1:38-53)

When all were assembled at the spring, Zadok the priest took a horn of oil and poured it on Solomon's head.[22] A trumpet was blown and the people cried out, "God save king Solomon." At En-rogel, the feast for Adonijah was just finishing, and the noise came to the ears of those gathered. Very soon word arrived of what had happened. All the guests in fear quickly left the place of the feast. Adonijah himself also left and ran to the altar David had constructed at the sacred tent; he caught hold of its horns and asked that Solomon show him mercy. When Adonijah's action was reported to the new king, he responded that Adonijah had nothing to fear providing he showed himself a worthy man. Adonijah then came before Solomon, and Solomon sent him to his house unharmed.

d. A coregency (I Kings 2:1-11; I Chron. 22:6-19; 28:9—29:22)

With Solomon thus crowned prior to David's death, a coregency existed between David and Solomon. It ended, of course, at David's death, but there is no indication how long before this it began. It probably was not more than a few months, however, in view of David's physical deficiency already when Solomon was crowned.[23]

[20]The fact that only Solomon of all the king's sons had not been invited shows quite clearly that Adonijah knew of David's selection of the young man as his choice.

[21]This was significant for only the king or his successor was to ride on this animal.

[22]For discussion of the occasion and the topographical relationship of Gihon and En-rogel, see Hershel Shanks, *The City of David,* pp. 38-39.

[23]Some believe it was as much as two or three years; cf. Yeivin, *Encyclopedia Biblica,* vol. II, col. 640.

David spent these few months in preparing both the new king and the people for the period of rule before them. He made a public proclamation of Solomon's new position (I Chron. 28:1-8), charged Solomon in turn with the weighty responsibilities that faced him (I Kings 2:1-9; I Chron. 28:9, 10), involving especially the building of God's temple (I Chron. 22:6-19; 28:11-21), and spoke parting encouragement and instruction to the people (I Chron. 29:1-22). The day when he gave this encouragement and instruction ended with sacrifices and celebrating with great joy, even going through the ceremony of crowning Solomon a second time. Solomon's reign was thus given a fine beginning.

These things done, David, Israel's greatest king, "died in a good old age, full of days, riches, and honor" (I Chron. 29:28).

2. POINTS TO NOTICE

a. Adonijah's thinking

The thinking of Adonijah in trying for the throne was quite different from that of Absalom. The latter had rebelled against his father, trying to take the throne from him, while Adonijah, knowing that David's death was near, rebelled primarily against Solomon. He wanted the rule and knew that, if David died before he procured it, Solomon would be crowned. He probably thought that if he could get himself crowned by such important people as Joab and Abiathar, he would be able to gain enough public support to make his crowning generally accepted. That he did not invite Nathan, Zadok, or Benaiah, besides Solomon, shows that he knew he would have potent opposition.

b. Attendance of the other princes

Adonijah invited all of David's sons to attend his coronation except Solomon, and apparently they all came. This shows that Adonijah must have known of David's selection of Solomon, and it suggests also that the other sons favored Adonijah over Solomon. Perhaps the fact that Solomon was not one of the older brothers—in the pattern of David himself in respect to his own brothers—brought about at least a part of this attitude. No indication is made how the other sons had earlier felt about Absalom, but they quite clearly favored Adonijah at this time.

c. The danger of clandestine movements

Adonijah's movement had to remain secret. Neither the king nor others who would oppose it should learn of it. For this reason alone, Joab, Abiathar, and the other princes should have been wary regarding it. Only in the most dire of circumstances are clandestine gatherings proper, so that one can join with a clear conscience. Normally the fact that they have to be of this kind is indication enough that they are wrong. Several of the people who attended this one came to be sorry they did.

d. Rationale of Nathan's plan

One may well ask why Nathan schemed through Bathsheba in respect to Solomon's coronation. Why did he not simply go directly before the king himself and ask that David approve the immediate crowning of Solomon? The probable answer is that, though he might have done this with good results, he wanted to be as sure as possible that the king would be persuaded to act quickly. Certainly Nathan held a high place in the king's evaluation, but perhaps Nathan was not certain that it was high enough to bring the quick action necessary. The king might merely say that he would make inquiry and check. If both Bathsheba—to whom the promise regarding Solomon had been directly given—and then Nathan himself came before the king with the same report, the king would be more likely to act as the need demanded.

e. David caught by surprise

Apart from this movement by Adonijah, and the information about it brought by Bathsheba and Nathan, David probably was thinking in terms of Solomon's assuming the throne only when he had died. At least a few people knew whom he wanted to succeed him, and he probably planned to make the matter public prior to the actual day of his death; this would make Solomon's succession quite automatic. Though Absalom had made a try for the throne by rebellion, David probably did not imagine that Adonijah or any other son would do so. In fact he may have thought this all the more unlikely since Absalom had tried and failed. The fact that David had never displeased Adonijah suggests that this fourth son had been generally obedient and submissive to his father, and therefore unlikely to instigate rebellion.

f. A poor disciplinarian

David had many excellent qualities, but being a proper father in exercising discipline was not one. If David had never displeased Adonijah, it is likely that he had been easy on his other sons as well. That he strongly longed for Absalom, even after the boy had driven his father from the throne, shows that he loved his children dearly. This in itself was good, but love should not hinder a parent from bringing proper discipline. And all children need it in some form, at one time or another. One may be sure that Adonijah did, but David had not given it and here reaped the sad result of rebellion.

g. The need for quickness in action

One might ask why Nathan believed there was need for quickness relative to Solomon's crowning. What if Adonijah was declared king prior to Solomon by a few hours? Would the declaration have been valid in view of the fact that Solomon was the choice of David, and especially in view of the fact that Adonijah would have been crowned in a clandestine manner? To know the answer, one would have to know the strength of Adonijah's following at the time. It may have been quite large, to judge from Nathan's action. And if it was, Adonijah might have been able to gain the additional support needed to make his enthronement acceptable, once he had actually been crowned. At least a serious struggle could have resulted, and Nathan quite clearly believed this could be averted if Solomon was crowned first.

h. Quick breakup of Adonijah's gathering

The same line of thinking indicates why there was such a quick breakup of Adonijah's followers as soon as news of Solomon's crowning reached them. The plan of Adonijah had depended from the first on secrecy. Adonijah had to be crowned before the opposition knew, so that a public announcement could be made and the necessary additional following be gained without delay. That Solomon was now crowned, even before Adonijah, meant, therefore, that all possibility of this happening was gone. And this in turn meant that all those who were associated with Adonijah were in immediate danger of their lives as partners in a rebellion. Of course, then, everyone present left the scene as quickly as possible in an endeavor to save his own life.

i. The horns of the altar

Adonijah's guests fled to their homes, but Adonijah himself fled to the horns of the altar (I Kings 1:50). The idea was common in ancient nations that an altar was a place of refuge for criminals in danger of death. In Israel, this was true only for one who killed unintentionally (Exod. 21:13, 14). The concept was quite like that of a city of refuge. The thought seems to have been that, by grasping the horns of the altar, the person placed himself under the protection of God's grace and mercy. Adonijah so acted here, for he had not killed anyone and no doubt believed that his life would be spared. Solomon did spare him, at least for the time. The altar to which he fled was the one David built at the special tent in Jerusalem, erected for the ark. The original brazen altar of the tabernacle was out at Gibeon, which was six miles away.

j. David's instructions to Solomon

David's instructions to Solomon included not only general matters, but specifically what he should do regarding certain people. Solomon should take Joab's life, because of what Joab had done to David (probably in killing Absalom) and to the two captains of the host of Israel, Abner and Amasa. One had to believe that David had wanted to take Joab's life himself, but for some reason had not acted. Perhaps when Abner was killed, he thought his position was yet too weak to displace a man with Joab's popular appeal; and when Amasa was killed, David was again not in a strong position due to the rebellion of Absalom and later Sheba. Also, Joab had helped David in covering his sin with Bathsheba by putting her husband in the front line, and in so doing had put the king in his debt.

Solomon was to treat the sons of Barzillai kindly, because their father had helped David so much in his time of need at Mahanaim. And Solomon should kill Shimei, who had cursed David on his flight from Jerusalem. David said that he had not done this himself, since on meeting Shimei at the Jordan he had made a promise that he would not, but Solomon should now do it. Both David and Solomon knew that Shimei would be a danger so long as he lived, having a strong loyalty to the house of Saul.

15

Solomon's Kingdom

We come now to consider Solomon, Israel's third king, and the last of the united kingdom. It has been observed that David as king was different from Saul, and it will now become apparent that Solomon was different from either of his predecessors. Each of the three had his respective strengths and weaknesses, with David having the greatest overall strength and Saul the greatest weakness. Solomon lay between the two. Once more it is well to look first at the nature of the kingdom established before moving on to consider the details of the history.

A. SOLOMON THE MAN

1. HIS FAMILY

Solomon's family of course was the family of David, which has been presented in Chapter 10. He was the second son of Bathsheba, being born after the death of David's first son by her (II Sam. 12:24, 25). He had three full brothers who lived, Shammuah (or Shimea), Shobab, and Nathan (II Sam. 5:14; I Chron. 3:5). These must have been born after Solomon, for he is said to have been born directly after the child that died. Josephus (VII.

14. 2) must then be in error in saying that Solomon was the last of David's sons. He had at least six older half brothers, all of whom were born while David ruled in Hebron. Solomon was born in Jerusalem, and only after David had been there for several years. He is named fourth in the list of Bathsheba's sons in II Samuel 5:14, but this cannot be the chronological order, as just seen. David's sons by other mothers listed in the following two verses need not be thought of as following chronologically either. Several of them were almost certainly born before David took Bathsheba as his wife.[1]

2. THE MAN HIMSELF

a. His early home life

Solomon's early home life was entirely different from that of either Saul or David. Whereas they grew up on farms and were men of the field, Solomon knew only the luxuries of a palace. Having been born well after David had established his kingdom, he did not even know the less prosperous days of David's early reign. By the time he was old enough to know the world, the empire was fully established. Foreign nations were thought of only as sources of revenue, not menacing enemies. His home was the palace, and since he had been chosen as the heir apparent, one may be sure he had every advantage in terms of education and privilege.

At the same time that Solomon knew wealth and power, however, he also knew something of palace intrigue. His older half sister Tamar was raped by his older half brother Amnon. Another half brother, Absalom, killed Amnon in turn, and finally rebelled against his father, driving him temporarily from the throne. Solomon, along with his mother and brothers, was no doubt taken along on the flight at that time. The hurry and excitement of the occasion would have made a lasting impression on Solomon, probably then in his teen years. Recently, there had been the attempted coup by his older half brother Adonijah. This, too, was the product of scheme and intrigue. It would have left another lasting impression.

b. His physical appearance

At the time of the hasty coronation, Solomon was probably about twenty years old. David spoke of him at the time as still young and tender (I Chron. 22:5), and Solomon referred to himself as yet "a little child" (*na'ar qaton*—I Kings 3:7). He could hardly have been less than twenty, however, for at the close of his forty-year reign (I Kings 11:42) Rehoboam,

[1]This follows because David was thirty-seven when he became king in Jerusalem, and probably another dozen years had elapsed before this marriage.

his son and successor, was forty-one (I Kings 14:21), meaning he was born a year before Solomon's accession.

Nothing is said of Solomon's appearance, unlike Saul and David. No doubt, when he was arrayed in his royal garments, he made a striking figure, but whether he had the natural assets of physical strength, dexterity, or handsomeness of face is not indicated. The very fact that he was not a man of war suggests that he was not of athletic aptitude like David, but rather of indoor pursuits, such as he displayed in extensive writing.

c. His character

1) ***A man of God.*** Though Solomon is not given the same place as a man of God that David is, still he was truly a follower of the Lord. God designated him by name even before his birth, and said of him, "He shall build an house for my name; and he shall be my son, and I will be his father; and I will establish the throne of his kingdom for ever" (I Chron. 22:10). At his birth he was given the name Jedidiah, meaning "beloved of Jehovah"; Nathan the prophet gave this name according to God's instruction. Early in his reign Solomon went to Gibeon, where the tabernacle was, to offer a thousand burnt offerings, and, while there, he had a glorious experience with God (I Kings 3:4-15). In a dream by night, God asked him what he wished for most, as he anticipated the years of rule before him. Solomon did not ask for wealth or long life, but very commendably for wisdom in his task. Still another indication that he was a man of God comes from Solomon's fine words in his prayer of dedication at the completion of the temple (I Kings 8:12-61; II Chron. 6:1-42). These words show a heart in tune with the will of God. Then at the close of the grand occasion, he offered no fewer than 22,000 oxen and 120,000 sheep in sacrifice to the Lord.

Under the guidance of the godly David, Solomon would have been raised and nurtured in the fear of God and taught the importance of rendering obedience from earliest days. Jewish tradition says that Nathan was his tutor, and that would account for this manner of instruction, for Nathan was easily the outstanding prophet of the day. It would have been like David to put the heir apparent under the care of this godly man.[2]

For some reason, however, Solomon is not said to have been endowed with special enablement by the Spirit of God, as were Saul and David. Saul had the Spirit to empower him for proper kingly administration, and then, due to sin, suffered the loss of the special provision. David received it at the time of his initial anointing and never did lose it. But Solomon, apparently, never was so endowed. The reason is not easy to discern. No king after

[2]No contradiction need be imagined between this thought and the indication of I Chron. 27:32 that Jehiel was "with the king's sons." David could well have made special arrangements for Solomon, who was destined to be the next king.

Solomon, including the godly Hezekiah and Josiah, is said to have been empowered in this way either. Perhaps God saw the first two kings, in that they had to inaugurate the kingship, as being in greater need of special ability than those later. Solomon, after all, was the first of the dynastic kings, those that came to rule by right of inheritance. His kingdom was fully established when he took over and he did not have the challenge of unifying and consolidating as his two predecessors did.

2) ***A man of ability.*** Solomon, like David, was a man of ability, though his talents were somewhat different. He was not, for instance, capable of fighting a lion and bear or of hurling a stone with a sling. He was not a military man who could lead armies to victories again and again. It is not indicated that he played an instrument as did David, and he never organized a group of discontents, welding them into an efficient fighting force.

He did share a talent with David for administration, however. David had organized a strong government, and Solomon did the same. In fact, he went beyond David and, as will be seen, established twelve districts for the land which only in part observed the old tribal boundaries. He apparently made the new system work, demonstrating he did have leadership and administrative ability.

Another shared talent was writing. Here, if anything, Solomon outshone his esteemed father. He is called, in fact, the great patron of Israel's wisdom literature. One contributing factor was that he had more time than David for this sort of pursuit, since he was not involved in war and internal revolution. But one must still have ability for it, and Solomon did. He is said to have spoken "three thousand proverbs; and his songs were a thousand and five" (I Kings 4:32). He was responsible for most of the Book of Proverbs and authored both the Song of Solomon and Ecclesiastes. At least two psalms came from his pen, 72 and 127.

Besides this, Solomon was a man skilled in business. He apparently recognized the strategic position he held in that Israel constituted a bridge between Egypt and Asia, and he employed the fact skillfully and profitably. Various caravan routes passed between Egypt and Asia, and all had to cross Solomon's territory at some place; these provided excellent sources of revenue, He also became the exclusive agent for the trade of chariots and horses between Egypt and the people of Anatolia. His business ability is shown further in his considerable building activities, for which he obtained material and expertise from the Phoenicians. No other Israelite king built to the degree Solomon did, including especially the temple and his own palace. He also established an extensive network of strategically located defense cities.

3) ***A man of wisdom.*** Probably Solomon is best known for his wisdom. This is the first thought that comes to the mind of many people regarding

him, no doubt because God especially promised wisdom to him. Significantly, the record gives an example of his wisdom immediately after the granting of the promise (I Kings 3:16-28). It concerned a quarrel between two women as to which of the two was the true mother of a baby son. Solomon settled the matter by a surprising but effective method. The wisdom Solomon showed in handling this case came to be told throughout Israel (I Kings 3:28). According to I Kings 4:30, "Solomon's wisdom excelled the wisdom of all the children of the east country, and all the wisdom of Egypt."

4) ***A man of humility.*** At least at the time of his beginning as king, Solomon displayed an attitude of humility. Especially significant is his prayer to God that he was only a child and needed wisdom above all else for knowing how to govern such a great people. A proud heart would not have prayed this way. Solomon, in spite of his royal upbringing and cultural advantage, did not consider himself adequate for the task before him, and he properly asked God for the help he needed. This attitude no doubt changed in years that followed, but he must be given credit for it at the start. So often it is the young beginner who is the proudest, being confident that he knows all the answers, but Solomon was not like this.

5) ***A man of peace.*** Even before Solomon was born, God said he would be a man of peace. This was indicated when David had wanted to build a temple and God rejected the idea because David was a man of war. In consolation God added that a temple would later be built by David's son Solomon, through whom God would give "peace and quietness unto Israel" (I Chron. 22:9, 10). In keeping with this, I Kings 4:25 states concerning Solomon's later rule, "And Judah and Israel dwelt safely, every man under his vine and under his fig tree, from Dan even to Beersheba, all the days of Solomon."

6) ***A nonvindictive man.*** David had not been vindictive, and neither was Solomon. For instance, he did not take the life of Adonijah, though this older half brother tried to seize the throne. Solomon might have done so, for this was the common procedure in the world of his day. He did not, however, at least not at that time. He did only later when Adonijah asked for Abishag to be his wife, the significance of which will be noted in the next chapter.

7) ***A man of expensive tastes.*** Solomon's monetary income was enormous, yet he did not live within his means. According to I Kings 9:14, he found it necessary to borrow no less than 120 talents of gold from Hiram, king of Tyre. He used the money for the expensive buildings he erected and

probably for the daily supply of his court. He lived and entertained lavishly by any standard. To supply his table for one day required no less than thirty *kor*[3] of fine flour, sixty *kor* of meal, ten fat cattle, twenty pasture-fed cattle, one hundred sheep, and other animals (I Kings 4:22, 23).

8) ***A man desirous of women.*** It was customary in the day for kings to have large harems, but Solomon went well beyond what was normal. He had 700 wives and 300 concubines (I Kings 11:3). As Keil points out, these may not have all been in his harem at one time.[4] Many of the wives may have been gained from treaty alliances with foreign countries, since it was customary to cement such alliances with a marriage, but one cannot account for all in this way nor for the numerous concubines. Solomon clearly had an excessive desire for women which was not commendable. It was Solomon's wives, in fact, who had much to do with his spiritual downfall in the later days of his reign (I Kings 11:1-4).

B. SOLOMON'S COURT

Solomon's situation for establishing a government was quite different from that of either Saul or David. Both of them had to begin from nothing, and David had to set up a rule first at Hebron and then at Jerusalem. Solomon, however, already had an established kingdom. He merely had to take up where his father left off, with a strong organization already existent.

1. SOLOMON'S FAMILY

Solomon's family was extremely large, but little is known about it. As just mentioned he had several hundred wives and certainly many children. The names of only one son and two daughters, however, are known. The son was Rehoboam, who succeeded Solomon as king (I Kings 11:43) and the two daughters were Taphath and Basmath, both of whom married officers under Solomon (I Kings 4:11, 15).

2. SOLOMON'S OFFICERS (I KINGS 4:1-6)

Solomon's principal officers were similar in position to those of David. Two, however, were additional: one named Azariah, who was "over the officers" (*'al ha-nissabim*), likely meaning over the district officers, and

[3]The *kor* or *homer* (same measure) was the largest capacity measure and was probably equal to 58.1 gallons liquid measure or 6¼ bushels dry; cf. R. B. Y. Scott, "Weights and Measures of the Bible," *The Biblical Archaeologist* 22 (1959), pp. 22-40.

[4]C. F. Keil and F. Delitzsch, *Biblical Commentary on the Books of Kings,* p. 169.

one named Ahishar, who was the overseer of the palace (*'al ha-bayith*).[5] Among the others were Benaiah, who took the place of Joab whom Solomon killed. Benaiah had been the commander of the two foreign divisions that served as David's bodyguard. Superintending civic duties were Elihoreph and Ahiah as secretaries (*sopherim*), Jehoshaphat as recorder (*mazkir*), and Zabud as counselor (*re' eh ha-melek*).[6] The high priests were again Zadok and Abiathar, but this can have been true only at the very beginning of Solomon's reign, for Abiathar was soon deposed and sent to his home town of Anathoth (I Kings 2:26, 27), and Zadok probably died shortly after Solomon began to rule. This would account for his son, Azariah, also being included in the list. Finally, serving over the tribute (*mas*), was Adoniram, probably the same as the Adoram under David.

3. SOLOMON'S TWELVE DISTRICTS (I KINGS 4:7-19)

A major change in administration was Solomon's formation of twelve districts in Israel, each supervised by an appointed official. These were established mainly for the purpose of taxation, with each district supplying provisions for the court one month per year, though there was no doubt other functions the districts served as well. The twelve districts were as follows:

1) The hill country of Ephraim, perhaps including parts of Manasseh to the north, in charge of the son of Hur.[7]

2) A region including the cities of Makaz, Shaalbim, Beth-shemesh, and Elon-beth-hanan, which embraces somewhat more than the general area originally assigned to Dan, in charge of the son of Dekar.

3) A region including the cities of Aruboth, Sochoh, and Hepher, which embraces the central Sharon area, stretching along the Mediterranean, in charge of the son of Hesed.

4) A region including principally Dor, just north of the previous district, and probably extending on north to embrace the tip of Mount Carmel, in charge of the son of Abinadab, who married Taphath, a daughter of Solomon.

5) A region including the cities of Taanach, Megiddo, Bethshan, Abelmeholah, and Jokneam, which embraces the north part of western Manasseh, much of the Esdraelon Plain, and some of the Jordan Valley on the west of the river, in charge of Baana, son of Ahilud.

[5]The same office was held by Obadiah in Ahab's reign (I Kings 18:3) and also by others (see II Kings 15:5; Isa. 22:15).

[6]Literally, "the king's friend" (cf. I Chron. 27:33), which Roland deVaux (*Ancient Israel: Its Life and Institutions,* p. 129) says was "rather an honorary title, probably Egyptian in origin."

[7]Several of the administrators are identified only by their father's name. This apparently was an accepted procedure since parallel administrative lists found at Ugarit do the same.

6) A region including the cities of Ramoth-gilead, the towns of Jair, and the area of Argob, meaning primarily eastern Manasseh, in charge of the son of Geber.

7) A region including principally the city of Mahanaim, the old capital of Ish-bosheth and later a site of refuge for David, meaning probably much of the valley of the Jordan on the east in addition to a large section of Gad, in charge of Ahinadab, son of Iddo.

8) The land area of Naphtali in northern Galilee, in charge of Ahimaaz, who married Basmath, another daughter of Solomon.

9) The land area of Asher, including an unknown region designated Aloth,[8] in charge of Baanah, son of Hushai.

10) The land area of Issachar in the Esdraelon Plain, in charge of Jehoshaphat, son of Paruah.

11) The land area of Benjamin, in charge of Shimei, son of Elah.

12) Another Transjordanian area called Gilead, including territory at one time controlled by both Sihon and Og. The geographical relation of this region to the other Transjordanian regions (6 and 7) is not clear.

All these districts and their supervisors were under the general direction of Azariah, son of Nathan, noted in the earlier and main list of officers (4:5). The overall organization must have been established after Solomon had been ruling for some time, for two of the supervisors had married his daughters (see 4:11, 15).

It appears that Solomon tried to hold at least in part to former tribal boundaries, no doubt to keep from stirring up animosity on the part of those who still favored tribal rights. He could not do this entirely, however, for much of the land he now controlled had never before been under the supervision of the tribes. Then he had to keep in mind the matter of equality of potential for filling the required monthly supply of provisions, so that hardship would not be worked more on some people than on others.

A highly significant matter is that the tribe of Judah was omitted from the districts. The Septuagint translation tried to rectify this omission by adding to 4:19, "and there was one officer in the land of Judah," but this is obviously an addition. DeVaux suggests that the districts of Judah set forth in Joshua 15:21-62 (see summaries in vv. 32, 36, 41, 44, 51, 54, 57, 59, 60) were actually not determined until the time of Solomon.[9] It is clear, however, that these districts were in existence from Joshua's time, though it is possible that the distinctions were still kept in the time of Solomon. At least, one can be sure that Solomon made a distinction between the administration of Israel to the north and Judah to the south. It may be that Israel was required to pay more taxes than Judah, which would have been a

[8]Yohanan Aharoni (*Land of the Bible,* p. 279) believes this is a reference to Zebulun.

[9]*Ancient Israel,* pp. 135-136. DeVaux also includes a list from Benjamin in Josh. 18:21-28.

clear case of favoritism of Solomon for his own tribe. If so, this may well have contributed to the rebellion of the northern tribes in the time of Rehoboam (I Kings 12:1-19). This distinction would have kept alive the old sense of rivalry between north and south, and one has to wonder at the judgment of Solomon in making such an arrangement.

C. LAND AREA AND ECONOMIC CONDITIONS

The land area over which Solomon ruled is described as "all kingdoms from the river unto the land of the Philistines, and unto the border of Egypt" (I Kings 4:21; cf. II Chron. 9:26), and again as "all the region on this side the river, from Tiphsah even to Azzah, over all the kings on this side the river" (I Kings 4:24). The river in reference is the Euphrates. In other words, Solomon controlled the same general area as David; the supervision simply passed from father to son, without, apparently, any of the outer regions rebelling.

The times were prosperous for Israelite people. They had high taxes to pay, but it is quite clear that the average family had the means to pay them. The people were numerous in population, "as the sand which is by the sea in multitude," and they were "eating and drinking, and making merry" (I Kings 4:20). There was also a sense of security, for "Judah and Israel dwelt safely, every man under his vine and under his fig tree, from Dan even to Beersheba" (I Kings 4:25). Neighboring countries, rather than being feared as potential enemies, were considered sources of income in the form of tribute. By the time of Solomon, the people who had lived under the judges, when Israel was oppressed by foreign nations, would have been dead. The new generation knew only the strength of David and now of Solomon. Israel was the leading country of the Middle East, prosperity reigned, and life was good. No doubt Solomon's subjects were proud to be Israelites, in spite of the hardship imposed through the taxation program.

D. BUILDING ACTIVITY

One factor which certainly added to this sense of satisfaction was Solomon's extensive building activity. This activity would have contributed much to the tax burden, but the negative feature in this was probably well offset by the pride the people felt in the splendid buildings that were erected. In this activity, Solomon far outshone his illustrious father. William F. Albright says that no buildings from David's reign have been found in excavations, whereas many from Solomon's have.[10]

[10]*From the Stone Age to Christianity,* p. 224.

1. THE TEMPLE

First and foremost was the grand temple, for which David had made extensive preparations. In Solomon's fourth year of rule (I Kings 6:1), he began to build this splendid edifice.

a. Building the temple

Solomon's first action was to contract with Hiram, king of Tyre, for timber of cedar and timber of fir (I Kings 5:8). This wood was world-famous at the time for its building qualities. Gudea (ca. 2100 B.C.), ruler of Lagash in southern Mesopotamia, had acquired cedar from Lebanon already in his day; and the Egyptian, Wenamon, was commissioned to bring cedar to his country about 1100 B.C.[11] Hiram took responsibility for transporting the logs by sea to a Palestinian port, and Solomon was to take charge of them there. Hiram also supplied stonecutters to help prepare the great quantity of stone needed (I Kings 5:18). In payment, Solomon gave Hiram 20,000 *kor*[12] of wheat, 20,000 *kor* of barley, 20,000 baths[13] of wine, and 20,000 baths of olive oil (II Chron. 2:10).[14]

The plan of the temple proper called for a building similar to the tabernacle, but with doubled dimensions. It contained the same two divisions: the Holy Place and the Holy of Holies, occupying two-thirds and one-third of the total respectively. It was built of stone, but paneled with cedar overlaid with gold. The Holy of Holies was for housing the ark of the covenant with its gold cover and two cherubim. Two additional cherubim were of carved olive wood overlaid with gold and stood fifteen feet high (I Kings 6:23-28; II Chron. 3:10-13).[15] In the Holy Place were to be the altar of incense or "golden altar" (I Kings 7:48; II Chron. 4:19), ten golden lampstands standing five on each side (I Kings 7:49; II Chron. 4:7), and ten tables of showbread (I Kings 7:48; II Chron. 4:8). Unlike the tabernacle, the Holy Place of the temple had a porch thirty feet wide and fifteen feet deep, and on the porch were two bronze pillars named Jachin and Boaz (I Kings 7:15-21).

b. Dedicating the temple

A building of this grandeur and significance called for appropriate dedication ceremonies. Solomon first had the all-important ark of the covenant brought from the tent David had erected and placed it in the Holy of

[11] See G. A. Barton, *Archaeology and the Bible,* pp. 449f., 455.

[12] See note 3.

[13] One bath equals 5.8 gallons.

[14] The difference given here from the payment indicated in I Kings 5:11 is probably due to the fact that Chronicles gives the amount for both wood and workers and Kings for just wood.

[15] Since the two cherubim of the mercy seat were of one piece with it (Exod. 25:18, 19), these two large cherubim were additional.

Holies. Other articles of furniture might be newly made, but not this special one. Since it was the same ark that was constructed earlier at Mount Sinai in the time of Moses, it had represented God's presence in the tabernacle and would continue to do so in the temple. Significantly, when it was placed in its assigned location, the cloud of God's glory filled the building (I Kings 8:1-11; I Chron. 5:1-14), even as it had the tabernacle. Then Solomon preached a brief sermon to those gathered (I Kings 8:12-21; II Chron. 6:1-11), after which he offered an extended prayer of dedication (I Kings 8:22-53; II Chron. 6:12-42). When he finished, miraculous fire fell from heaven to ignite the burnt-offering placed on the brazen altar (II Chron. 7:1-3). Then Solomon continued with other sacrifices until the enormous total of 22,000 oxen and 120,000 sheep had been offered, during seven days of celebration (I Kings 8:62-66; II Chron. 7:4-11).

2. OTHER FINE BUILDINGS (I KINGS 7:1-12)

Solomon erected several other fine buildings as well. He probably located them near the temple in an area on Mount Moriah now added to David's city.[16] One of these was his personal residence, the palace. It must have been an elegant structure, for it took thirteen years to build, six years longer than the temple. Another building was the house of the forest of Lebanon, perhaps so named because it was supported by rows of cedar pillars.[17] It was used at least in part to store arms (I Kings 10:16, 17; Isa. 22:8). A third was the porch of pillars. In the fourth structure, the porch of judgment, where Solomon judged the people, he sat on a six-step throne of ivory overlaid with gold (I Kings 10:18-20). Last was a special house made for Solomon's most honored wife, the daughter of Egypt's Pharaoh. The temple was built first and these other buildings later, over a period of twenty years (I Kings 9:10). Apparently Hiram continued to help with material, workmen, and even gold all this time, bringing Solomon heavily in debt to him.[18]

E. MILITARY MEASURES

Though it is indicated that Solomon was a man of peace and not a military figure like his father, this does not mean that he did nothing of a military nature. He needed to take at least defensive measures, and he did.

[16]For a helpful discussion of the area Solomon added to David's city for his buildings, see Kathleen Kenyon, *Royal Cities of the Old Testament,* pp. 41-46.

[17]It is possible that this was not a second building but the name of the palace. In fact, the other buildings listed may refer to sections of the total palace.

[18]See Kathleen Kenyon, *Royal Cities,* pp. 51-52, for discussion relative to these additional buildings of Solomon.

These consisted principally in the fortification of key cities that bordered Israel's heartland (I Kings 9:15-19; II Chron. 8:4-6). The cities were Hazor to the extreme north, Megiddo at the strategic north-south pass into the Esdraelon Valley, and Gezer, Lower Beth-horon, Upper Beth-horon, and Baalath guarding the western approaches from Philistine territory. Tadmor is also listed, but if it is to be identified with the northern trading center bearing this name, it cannot have been an inner defense center.[19] It may have been an outer command point, however, to give early warning of enemy movement from the northeast. In favor of this is the fact that II Chronicles 8:3 (just before the mention of Tadmor) says that Solomon "went to Hamath-zobah, and prevailed against it." Hamath-zobah refers to the combined areas of Hamath (region around the city Hamath) and Zobah, which lay well north of Damascus and west of Tadmor. Solomon, then, must have made at least this one offensive battle; the theory that he fortified Tadmor at the same general time would fit very well.

Troops quartered in the inner defense cities would have provided a wall of protection from foreign attack and could have moved quickly to put down attempts at revolution from within. In Jerusalem itself, Solomon built a wall and the Millo to give added strength (I Kings 9:15). The wall in reference was probably an extension of David's wall, to enclose the new temple area that Solomon added. It may also refer to a section which closed up a break (*perets*) that somehow remained in David's wall (see I Kings 11:27). The Millo in view was no doubt the same structure that David strengthened in his day; now Solomon strengthened it, perhaps by adding to it.

Another significant defense measure was Solomon's employment of the war chariot, in which he differed from David. David had destroyed enemy chariots rather than keeping them for himself (II Sam. 8:4). His fighting was more in the mountains, however, whereas Solomon's defense cities, where these chariots were mainly located, were in flat areas where chariots could be used to advantage. Of these cities, at least Hazor, Megiddo, Gezer, and Lower Beth-horon had been royal cities of the Canaanites, who had their own chariot force, a fact which may have suggested to Solomon the idea of continuing this method of protection. He assembled as many as 1,400 chariots and 12,000 horsemen and maintained 4,000 stables to house the horses (I Kings 10:26; II Chron. 9:25).[20] Besides the cities mentioned above, both Taanach and Eglon have also revealed to excavators evidence

[19]The Kethibh reading in I Kings 9:18 is "Tamar." This, however, is not the best reading, in view of the reading "Tadmor" in II Chron. 8:4. If the same locality is not intended in both passages, there was a Tamar south of the Dead Sea, which would have been a logical defense post toward the south.

[20]The figure of 40,000 in I Kings 4:26 must be a scribal error in view of the figure of 4,000 in II Chron. 9:25 and the fact that 1,400 chariots suggests 4,000 horses, not 40,000.

of strong defenses and chariot stables from this general time. The stables discovered at Megiddo could house 450 horses, and, though these have now been dated quite surely to Ahab's reign rather than Solomon's, they probably reflect what Solomon himself built there and the type of stables he had in these other cities as well.[21] To staff these cities with adequate military personnel and maintain such chariot forces, Solomon would have had to keep a large standing army, calling for enormous amounts of food and other provisions.

F. REVENUE SOURCES

Fortification of defense cities, support of a standing army, extensive building activities, and provisions for a lavish court called for large revenue. Solomon's sources appear to have been of four types.

1. TAXATION

There was the normal source of direct taxation of the people. This, as has been seen, was done mainly through the twelve districts established by Solomon. Each district was required to furnish provisions for the court one month per year (I Kings 4:7-28). There was need for barley and straw to feed the horses, as well as food for the people. Given the fact that so much had to be provided and the people knew that their taxes were being collected to supply such a lavish court,[22] the cry for relief that was later raised to Rehoboam becomes understandable (I Kings 12:3, 4).

2. LABOR CONSCRIPTION

Solomon maintained a program of labor conscription. The corvée was common in the ancient world, but it was always disliked. David had used foreign labor, even having a minister of cabinet rank in charge toward the close of his reign (II Sam. 20:24). Solomon used foreign labor as well, especially large numbers of Canaanites who still lived in the country (I Kings 9:20-22; II Chron. 8:7-9), but he also employed Israelites (I Kings 5:13). Supervising this form of labor was one of Solomon's chief officers, Adoniram (I Kings 4:6). He, or possibly his son of the same name, still served similarly in Rehoboam's early days and was killed when he tried to collect tribute from the rebelling northern tribes (I Kings 12:18). Men conscripted for labor in this manner simply worked for the government without pay, for the length of time designated. This free labor provided a major source of financial benefit for the country.

[21]Yigael Yadin has challenged the dating of these stables at Megiddo to Solomon, believing the time of Ahab more likely; see "New Light on Solomon's Megiddo," *The Biblical Archaeologist* 23 (1960), pp. 62-68.

[22]See pp. 285-286.

3. FOREIGN TRIBUTE AND GIFTS

A third source of revenue imposed no burden on the Israelites themselves. It consisted of tribute and gifts from foreign countries. Tribute was already being paid in regular amounts in David's time by countries that had been conquered. No doubt many gifts from visiting dignitaries were also received then, but it is likely that these increased in Solomon's time. He enlarged contacts with foreign countries, which led to more visitors; and his reputation for wisdom caused many to come out of curiosity. When they did, "they brought every man his present, vessels of silver, and vessels of gold, and garments, and armor, and spices, horses, and mules" (I Kings 10:24, 25; cf. II Chron. 9:23, 24). One visitor, the queen of Sheba, brought as much as 120 talents of gold[23] besides quantities of spices and precious stones (I Kings 10:1-13).[24]

4. TRADE

One of Solomon's greater abilities lay in the area of merchandising and trade. He saw his geographical advantage for trade: his land was located astride the north-south caravan routes of the day between Egypt and Arabia in the south and the important countries of the north.

One avenue of trade was south through the Red Sea to the Indian Ocean. David's southern conquest had reached the Gulf of Aqaba, making this sea route accessible. With the aid of Phoenician experts, Solomon constructed and provided crews for a fleet of ships leaving Ezion-geber at the tip of the gulf (I Kings 9:26-28; 10:11, 12, 22).[25] The ships went as far as Ophir[26] no doubt, stopping at numerous ports en route, for the trip took three years (I Kings 10:22).[27]

No indication is given as to what type of products Solomon exported, but likely they included wheat, wine, and oil from his own country and perhaps other products that he received from Phoenicia in trade. A major export must have been copper, for Solomon's ships are described as ships of Tarshish (I Kings 10:22). This designation was reserved for vessels that the

[23]For indication of value, see p. 179, n. 6.

[24]For discussion of her visit, see pp. 327-328.

[25]For discussion of Phoenician shipbuilding and trade see D. R. Ap-Thomas, "The Phoenicians," *Peoples of Old Testament Times,* ed. D. J. Wiseman, pp. 274-281.

[26]The identity of Ophir is uncertain. Four sites are suggested—southwest Arabia, southeast Arabia, Somaliland, and Supara in India. In favor of the last are the facts that the journey took so long, that all items imported are from India, and that trade is known to have existed that far away at the time. Albright, however, favors the third suggestion; cf. *Archaeology and the Religion of Israel,* pp. 133-135.

[27]"Three years" means all of a middle year and at least some part of the prior and following years.

Phoenicians employed for transporting copper ingots from their refineries on Sardinia and Cyprus. It was formerly thought that a large installation near Ezion-geber was a copper refinery owned by Solomon, but it has now been shown to have been a stronghold and storehouse.[28] Apart from this, however, it is known that copper mines did exist in the Jordan Valley and in the Arabah south of the Dead Sea; Solomon no doubt took the raw product from these and may have refined it someplace before shipping it out.[29] Goods that were imported included gold, silver, ivory, apes, and peacocks (I Kings 10:22).

Solomon also carried on trade involving horses and chariots. This concerned overland caravan travel. He was probably led into this source of revenue by first filling his own need for horses and chariots. Egypt had been producing the finest chariots since the middle of the second millennium, while Cilicia[30] of Asia Minor was famed for its horses. Having supplied his own need, he apparently saw the possibilities of acting as agent for these two countries in exporting their horses and chariots to other countries. Acting the part of middleman (I Kings 10:28) provided Solomon with substantial income.

G. LITERARY ACTIVITY

The time of David and Solomon is commonly called Israel's golden literary age. David displayed marked ability in the fine arts, including writing, and Solomon inherited this skill. Their interest, in turn, would have encouraged others to develop their talents. It was a day which lent itself to artistic expression: a day of optimism and prosperity, a day of importance for Israel as a world power, a day of sufficient wealth to give time for leisure and reflection, and especially a day when stress was on true worship of God.

1. HISTORICAL WRITING

The age saw works of history produced. Both David and Solomon had official court scribes, and from their formal records histories of the reigns of each king were written. Nathan the prophet wrote a history which covered the rule of both David (I Chron. 29:29) and Solomon (II Chron. 9:29). Solomon's history given in I Kings seems to have come mainly from

[28]See John Bright, *History of Israel,* p. 212, n. 75, 76.

[29]For discussion see Elmer B. Smick, *Archaeology of the Jordan Valley,* pp. 91-93.

[30]The Hebrew word, *miqweh,* of I Kings 10:28 (translated "linen yarn" in KJV) is best taken in reference to the Asia Minor country, Kue, and so translated "from Kue" (Kue equals Cilicia). Egypt had fine chariots for export, introduced apparently by the Hyksos. Kue had excellent horses. For discussion, see Albright, *Archaeology and the Religion of Israel,* pp. 135-136.

the "book of the acts of Solomon," whose author is not identified (I Kings 11:41). The prophets Ahijah and Iddo, both of whom continued to live after Solomon, wrote histories that included accounts of his reign (II Chron. 9:29).

2. MUSIC AND PSALMODY

Music and psalmody were also written. David, in anticipation of the day when the temple would be built, gave instructions regarding music in worship. Some 4,000 Levites were designated as singers, and instruments for accompaniment included lyres, harps, and cymbals (I Chron. 25:1-6). No less than 288 of these singers were to constitute a choir (I Chron. 25:7). Asaph was appointed to be chief of choral worship (I Chron. 16:4, 5), and eventually penned twelve psalms. The sons of Korah quite clearly constituted a special choral group, and ten psalms are ascribed to them, either as authors or performers (see I Chron. 6:31f.). Ethan and Heman, two men whose wisdom was judged inferior to Solomon's (I Kings 4:31), are credited with one psalm each, and Solomon himself is ascribed two (72 and 127).

There is every reason to believe that Solomon put David's instructions into effect when the temple was completed. At the time of its dedication, "the singers, all of them of Asaph, of Heman, of Jeduthun, with their sons and their brethren . . . having cymbals and psalteries and harps, stood at the east end of the altar, and with them an hundred and twenty priests sounding with trumpets" (II Chron. 5:12). Then in II Chronicles 9:11, there is indication that harps and psalteries for singers were made at the king's direction. The fact that Solomon himself composed no fewer than 1,005 songs (I Kings 4:32) shows his own interest in this area.

3. WISDOM AND DRAMATIC LITERATURE

A third type of literature produced was wisdom and dramatic writing.[31] Some of the psalms are to be classed as wisdom literature, but the finest Old Testament examples are the books of Proverbs and Ecclesiastes. Solomon wrote all of the latter and most of the former. The book of Job, too, falls under this classification, but may have been written earlier.[32] Solomon also wrote the Song of Solomon, classed as semidrama. In summary, most of the third division of the Hebrew Bible, the "Writings" (*Kethubim*), came from this golden age of literature.

[31]For a recent helpful study of this literature, see Derek K. Kidner, "Wisdom Literature of the Old Testament," *New Perspectives on the Old Testament,* ed. J. B. Payne, pp. 117-130.

[32]A problem regarding historical accuracy arises if it was written in Solomon's time, in view of its detailed conversational content. It may have come from the hand of Job himself.

H. FOREIGN RELATIONS

Because Solomon inherited a land area of empire size and conducted extensive trading, his involvement in foreign affairs became wide-reaching. A clear indication of this is his many marriages to foreign women. Marriages were common seals of foreign alliances. That he had wives from the Moabites, Ammonites, Edomites, Zidonians, and Hittites (I Kings 11:1) suggests that he held alliances with all these people.

1. ALLIANCE WITH EGYPT

A direct statement is made that Solomon made an alliance with Egypt (I Kings 3:1). No doubt Solomon considered this his most important alliance, because Egypt was a major world power. Indeed, that Solomon should have been so honored by this powerful southern neighbor signifies that he held high standing in the world of his day. The alliance was one of the first he made, and the honor accorded by the Pharaoh really must be attributed more to David than to Solomon. In keeping with the importance of the alliance, Solomon built a special house for his Egyptian bride (I Kings 7:8), though there may also have been another reason: II Chronicles 8:11 says that Solomon brought this wife out of the city of David to this special house on Mount Moriah so that she would not live in the city where the ark was housed. He apparently recognized that she did not belong in David's city proper, because of her pagan beliefs.

It was as a result of this marriage that Solomon gained control of Gezer.[33] The Pharaoh had previously seized Gezer, perhaps in an abortive effort to regain Egyptian control in some part of Palestine following David's death. He had killed the inhabitants of the city, but now gave it as a present to his daughter, Solomon's wife (I Kings 9:16). Solomon directly fortified it as one of his defense cities.

2. ALLIANCE WITH TYRE

Another important alliance was made with the Phoenician king, Hiram (ca. 978-955 B.C.). Solomon's wife of the Zidonians was likely a daughter of this ruler. Though this marriage and alliance would not have been as prestigious for Solomon as that involving the Egyptian Pharaoh, it was probably more economically important. The Phoenicians were the merchants of the entire Mediterranean, and their goods would have been of great importance to Israel, especially their valuable cedar for Solomon's extensive building activity. Tyre, rebuilt by the Phoenicians in the twelfth

[33]See p. 227, n. 12.

century, was now capital of the maritime country, which controlled about 150 miles of the Mediterranean coastline north of the Bay of Acre. Phoenicia held colonies at many points around the Mediterranean, and her trade with them and other countries was widely known. Solomon was particularly interested in her cedar, for which he was willing to trade wheat and olive oil (I Kings 5:2-11). It was this same alliance that no doubt led eventually to the joint maritime venture from Ezion-geber, which proved so profitable for Israel.

3. THE HARM OF THE FOREIGN ALLIANCES

Though Solomon's foreign alliances and resulting marriages apparently were economically beneficial to Solomon's kingdom, they were detrimental to the religious condition of both the king and his country. This more than offset the economic advantage, for it prompted God to withdraw His blessing. The marriages brought about the most harm. For a time, Solomon seems to have been able to deal with these marriages without suffering greatly, but then his spiritual state began to decline. God long before had warned that, should Israel have a king one day, that person should be careful to avoid a multiplication of wives, for he would be influenced by them to turn away from Israel's true God (Deut. 17:17). This happened with Solomon. He came in time to give actual worship to the gods of the countries from which these wives came and even to build sanctuaries to at least some of them. The result was that Solomon lost out in his position of power in the latter part of his reign.

I. SOLOMON AND RELIGIOUS CEREMONY

One more matter calls for mention. It concerns Solomon's relation to the priesthood and the religious ceremonies the priests supervised. One thing to note is that he solved David's problem of having two high priests. The Mosaic law called for only one at a time, but during all of David's rule there had been two, Zadok and Abiathar. Solomon deposed the latter (I Kings 2:26, 27). This left Zadok only, who, as noted, probably died soon after so that his son Azariah is listed as Solomon's high priest (I Kings 4:2).

Still more noteworthy is the extent to which Solomon ordered sacrifices to be offered, at least in his earlier years when he followed the Lord closely. Very early in his reign, at the time of his dream when God promised him wisdom, riches, and long life, he offered a thousand burnt-offerings (I Kings 3:4; II Chron. 1:6). This was done at the great altar of the tabernacle at Gibeon (II Chron. 1:5). Then, he returned to Jerusalem; and at the altar David had erected for the tent which housed the ark, he offered peace-offerings and burnt-offerings (I Kings 3:15). At the time of dedicating the temple, he ordered the incredible number of 22,000 oxen and 120,000 sheep as burnt-offerings and peace-offerings (I Kings 8:63, 64; II Chron. 7:5-7). With all of this, of course, God was highly pleased; and because of it Solomon experienced wonderful blessing for a major part of his reign.

16

Solomon the King

The exact relationship between David and Solomon during the period of coregency is not made clear. Normally in such coregencies, the father remained in supreme command as long as he lived, with the son more or less carrying out his directives. This probably was true with David and Solomon also, though the fact that David was bedridden during this time suggests such an arrangement may have been more theoretical than actual. As soon as David died, Solomon began to establish his own position in the kingdom. He began by ridding himself of those who had plotted against him in the attempted coup of Adonijah.

A. CONSOLIDATION OF POWER

1. THE STORY (I KINGS 2:13-46)

Solomon's action in respect to Adonijah himself was prompted by an improper request the older brother made through Solomon's mother, Bathsheba. Adonijah urged her to ask that he be allowed to marry Abishag, who had ministered to David in his dying days. A custom of the day required that a king's concubines become a part of the inheritance of his successor (see II Sam. 16:21). Bathsheba apparently did not see through the strategy of Adonijah, but Solomon did, and asked his mother why she did not simply ask the kingdom for Adonijah (2:22). Then he gave an order to Benaiah, his new commander of the army, to seek out Adonijah and kill him.[1]

Solomon next dealt with Abiathar, the high priest who had served David along with Zadok. Solomon simply told him to leave office and go to his own fields in Anathoth. The dual high priests—Abiathar and Zadok—had been a thorny problem for David all his life. Solomon now solved the problem quickly. He told Abiathar he deserved to die for his part in Adonijah's attempted coronation, but because he had served David many years Solomon would only banish him from office and not take his life. Zadok thus was left alone to serve, and his family continued in the office after him.

Solomon's actions with Adonijah and Abiathar carried ominous overtones for Joab, who had also aided Adonijah. He sought refuge for himself at the horns of the altar (2:28), in the pattern of Adonijah earlier (I Kings 1:50). Solomon had then spared Adonijah's life, but Joab was not to fare as well. David had given explicit instruction that Joab should die (I Kings 2:5, 6), and, moreover, Joab's blame lay deeper than merely having helped Adonijah. He had killed two men in cold blood, Abner and Amasa. Solomon therefore ordered Benaiah to take the man's life.

This left one more to be dealt with: Shimei, who had cursed David and whom David had also instructed Solomon to kill (I Kings 2:8, 9). Solomon at first did not deal so harshly with the man, but warned him that he must always remain in Jerusalem. If he left, he would be slain. Solomon's thinking apparently was that Shimei, who was still a loyalist to Saul's family, could not stir up trouble or insurrection in the country as long as he remained in the capital where he could be watched. When three years had passed, however, and Shimei did leave the city to retrieve two servants who had run away to Philistia, Solomon carried out his father's order and took the man's life. Benaiah was the executioner again.

2. POINTS TO NOTICE

a. The plan of Adonijah

From Adonijah's words to Bathsheba, "Thou knowest that the kingdom was mine, and that all Israel set their faces on me, that I should reign" (2:15), it is evident that he did hope to gain an advantage for the throne even yet by a marriage with Abishag. Perhaps he believed that he had a large enough following among the people so that, if he were permitted to marry this member of David's harem, he would yet be publicly recognized and

[1] It is noteworthy that Solomon did nothing against the other brothers who had sided with Adonijah.

Solomon forced to abdicate. It is doubtful that he did have this strong a following, but, in that he made the request, Solomon saw the implications and ordered him killed. Bathsheba herself must have been rather naive to have been a party to the request, carrying as it did a threat to the rule of her son. It may be that Adonijah recognized her naivete and so used her to make this approach to the king.

b. Abiathar and Zadok

It is likely that Abiathar and Zadok were not the best of friends. Abiathar had been with David longer, having come to him already in his days as a fugitive, while Zadok was inherited as high priest when David became king of all Israel. This could have made Abiathar believe he should be honored above Zadok. He evidently was not, however, for Zadok is always mentioned first in scriptural references and seems to have been given special charge of the ark. That Abiathar was displeased as a result would account for his joining in Adonijah's conspiracy and may also have been a contributing factor in Solomon's finally expelling him.

It should also be noted that the text cites the historical significance of Solomon's expulsion of Abiathar. By so doing he carried out God's warning to Eli concerning his house being deposed (2:27).

c. Joab's due

Joab finally received his just due for his earlier misdeeds. For some reason David had never dealt with Joab as his conduct deserved, but Solomon did. He ordered his life taken, even though Joab fled to the horns of the altar. As noted in Chapter 14, the horns of the altar did provide a place of refuge for an innocent person, but Exodus 21:13, 14 states explicitly that if a man had murdered another deliberately, the altar would not serve to give him safety. Joab apparently fled to the altar, thinking in terms only of his recent association with Adonijah—for this offense he was not liable to death. Solomon had more in mind. David had reminded him that the man had killed two innocent people, and Solomon recognized that the altar did not afford Joab protection on those counts. He properly ordered his death.

d. Solomon's good memory

In respect to Shimei, Solomon remembered what he had told him though three years had intervened. It may be that Shimei, realizing that the king was busy and that three years was a long time to remember a detail, took the chance of leaving the city in hopes that the king had forgotten his word by this time. Solomon had not forgotten, however, and ordered the man killed when he returned.

It might be argued that Solomon should have been more lenient with Shimei, since the man had good reason to leave: to retrieve servants that had run away. It may well be that Shimei's thinking ran in the same vein. He would chance leaving the city for this good cause, thinking that if nothing happened as a result, he could leave again later for some less worthy reasons. He had revealed the kind of man he was when David had left Jerusalem those many years before (no doubt Solomon had witnessed the occasion as a teen-ager), and Solomon took no chance of his taking advantage of leniency at this time. He ordered his life taken.

e. Solomon, a man of decision

All of these actions show that Solomon was a man who could act decisively. In this he seems to have overshadowed his father. David did not always act in this way. He could be too lenient with others, including especially his own family as well as the capable Joab. Perhaps Solomon benefited from observing this weakness in his father. He accomplished two things by these decisions: he served notice to his subjects that he would not tolerate insubordination, and he consolidated his position by removing those who had opposed his coronation.

B. SOLOMON'S FIRST WIVES

1. THE STORY

Altogether, Solomon had as many as 700 wives and 300 concubines. Nothing is known about the great majority of these marriages, and no doubt most were of little significance to Solomon himself. Something is known, however, regarding a few of the earlier ones, which no doubt did mean something to him; and these call for notice. With most of these, as also with many of the later marriages (see I Kings 11:1), political alliances were involved, and this fact is important to bear in mind as they are considered.

The idea of a political marriage had been introduced to Solomon already by David his father. David had made such a marriage for himself when king only of Judah. This was with Maacah, the daughter of Talmai, king of Geshur (II Sam. 3:3; I Chron. 3:2). The country of Geshur was located on the east side of the Sea of Galilee, in Bashan.[2] A treaty with Geshur at this early time had the advantage for David of placing Ish-bosheth between two countries in league, and it also neutralized this important state in David's later struggle with the Aramaean countries of the north.

Further, David had arranged a marriage for Solomon himself with Naamah, princess of Ammon (I Kings 14:21, 31). This marriage must have occurred prior to Solomon's coronation, because Rehoboam, Naamah's

[2] See pp. 40-41.

son, was forty-one years old (I Kings 14:21) at Solomon's death, and Solomon had reigned forty years. He must then have been married to this princess about two years before his crowning, perhaps as a way of giving him standing when the day would come for his assuming the throne.

It is not amiss to notice that apparently Solomon also continued the idea of political marriage with respect to his son, the crown prince Rehoboam. It is known that Rehoboam married Maacah, daughter of Abishalom (I Kings 15:2). Both because Maacah is not an Israelite name and because she introduced into Judah an Asherah pole for worship (I Kings 15:13), it is all but certain that her home country, though unknown, was outside Israel. Also, this marriage must have transpired about the middle of Solomon's rule because Rehoboam reigned only seventeen years and his son Abijam only three years, and still Abijam's son, Asa, was an adult when he came to the throne.

Solomon's most important marriage was with a daughter of the Egyptian Pharaoh. This is attested by the mention of the marriage numerous times (I Kings 3:1; 7:8; 9:16, 24; II Chron. 8:11). The importance arises from the fact that the marriage involved an alliance with a major power of the day, Egypt. All of Solomon's other alliances were with second-ranking powers such as Moab, Ammon, and Edom (I Kings 11:1). In former days, Egypt had permitted alliances and marriages only with major powers like Babylon, Hatti, or Mitanni; and even then it was always a case of a daughter from one of these countries coming to marry a prince in Egypt, never vice versa. But here with Solomon, not only was an alliance formalized by a marriage, but the Egyptian daughter came and married Solomon. No similar instance is recorded. The fact is indicative of two things: that Egypt was now significantly reduced in power from former days (it is known that the twenty-first dynasty, which was now in power, was comparatively weak), and that Israel was now considered a major power, possibly even stronger than Egypt. It is in keeping with these facts that the Pharaoh gave the city of Gezer to his daughter (and so really to Solomon) at the time of the marriage (I Kings 9:16).

The date of this marriage was early in Solomon's rule. This is suggested by its placement (I Kings 3:1) right after the record of Solomon's taking Shimei's life, which was three years after his crowning. Then a direct indication is given that it occurred before completion of the temple (I Kings 3:1), which was in his eleventh year (I Kings 6:38). It apparently happened, then, sometime between Solomon's third and eleventh years. The Pharaoh involved undoubtedly was Siamun, who ruled from 976 to 958 B.C.[3] Solo-

[3]In support of the idea that Siamun had recently seized Gezer from the Philistines, Kenneth Kitchen ("The Philistines," *Peoples of Old Testament Times,* ed. D. J. Wiseman, p. 65) cites a fragmentary bas-relief of this Pharaoh which depicts him slaying a foe in whose hand is an axe of a kind thought to be used by the Philistines.

mon began to rule in 970 and the marriage, therefore, transpired sometime between 967 and 959 B.C. This Siamun was next to the last of the rulers of the twenty-first dynasty.[4]

One other early marriage calls for notice: it was with a young lady from Shunem, described by Solomon in the Song of Solomon. Though ideas concerning the interpretation of the Song of Solomon differ, most expositors are agreed that the story did happen, whether they espouse an interpretation that is purely historical or is historical-typical. This means that at some time (probably early in his reign) Solomon did marry the young lady. The manner of love portrayed, which Solomon and the Shunammite had for each other, suggests people still comparatively young, when vitality and emotion run high. Also, the Shunammite's description of Solomon (5:10-16) is that of a virile young man. And still further, Solomon accompanied the young lady to her own house on one occasion (8:5), and it is not likely that Solomon would have done this later in his life. It is true that Solomon is said already to have sixty other wives and eighty concubines (6:8), which could indicate a later time in his life, but these really were not many in comparison with the total number of wives and concubines he had altogether. It is likely that most of his marriages occurred earlier rather than later in his rule, which suggests that he could have had sixty wives quite early. It is noteworthy that of these sixty, the fresh, beautiful girl from Shunem found first place in his love at the time of writing the book (6:8, 9). This marriage was not a matter of convenience, to formalize a treaty with a foreign country; it was made on the basis of true love.

2. POINTS TO NOTICE

a. Debasement of marriage

God did not intend for marriages to be polygamous or measures of convenience to serve ulterior ends. True marriage is for love and is to endure for the life of the partners. More than one marriage is not to be contracted at a time. Here in Old Testament time, God did permit the rite to be lowered from the level of its original intent. He surely was not pleased with this, but suffered it so to be. Solomon, however, went far beyond all reason in accumulating wives, in his endeavor to gain world status and formalize treaties. In this he was very wrong, and, just as God had warned (Deut. 17:17), the marriages did serve to turn his heart away from God (I Kings 11:4-8).

[4]For an excellent discussion of this marriage and its significance, see Abraham Malamat, "Aspects of the Foreign Policies of David and Solomon" *Journal of Near Eastern Studies* 22 (Jan. 1963), pp. 9-13.

b. The importance of a father's influence

Though David certainly influenced Solomon for good in many ways, he did not in regard to marriage. He married numerous wives himself, and even served the idea of a political end in at least two instances cited. Solomon followed in this pattern and then moved on to increase the wrong of his father many times over. Solomon may have done this without the example of David, but likely he did it in greater degree as a result of that example.

c. Gezer, Pharaoh's gift

In order for Pharaoh Siamun to give the city of Gezer as a gift to his daughter, he had to obtain it first for himself. Egypt had once possessed the whole Philistine region but had lost it when the Philistines settled there at the beginning of the twelfth century. At the time, Gezer had been one of the last cities the Egyptians held, as is evident from a discovery there of a "faience inlay bearing the name of Rameses IX (end of the twelfth century)."[5]

Siamun probably made his campaign to get the city soon after David's death, before Solomon had a chance to consolidate his power. Significantly, it was at this time, too, that Hadad of Edom saw fit to return to Edom from Egypt, where he became a continuing enemy of Solomon (I Kings 11:14-22). Siamun may have had in mind to take over all Israel, but clearly he changed his mind in this. The reason he now gave Gezer to his daughter as a bridal gift was quite possibly that his campaign had proven to be far less successful than he had hoped, and he really had no use for only one city. Solomon's Israel had shown itself to be so strong that, not only did Pharaoh desist from making attack on it, but he gave his daughter to Solomon as wife and granted to her the city he had captured.

C. SOLOMON AND HIS WISDOM

1. THE STORY (I KINGS 3:4-28; 4:29-31; II CHRON. 1:2-13)

a. The bestowal by God

One of the most significant occasions for Solomon took place at Gibeon, some six miles northwest of Jerusalem, early in his reign. It was the occasion when the young king was promised wisdom, riches, and even long life if he would follow God as had David. Solomon went to Gibeon for the purpose of presenting one thousand burnt-offerings. Apparently, he felt an urgent need of seeking God's favor on his reign. He went to Gibeon, rather

[5]See Malamat, "Foreign Policies," p. 13; see also above p. 227, n. 12.

than to David's tent in Jerusalem, because the great brazen altar was there. A large altar was necessary for so many animals to be offered. The importance of the occasion is attested by his taking with him a large number of Israel's leaders (II Chron. 1:2) and certainly many priests and Levites to do the work.

He dreamed as he slept there and heard God bid him make a request for whatever he desired most. Solomon responded first by giving praise that God had honored him in making him king and by admitting that he was in himself incapable of filling the requirements of the position. Then he said that what he wanted most was an understanding heart to judge the people (I Kings 3:9). In other words, he wanted wisdom for his challenging task. God was pleased with this request and said that He would grant not only wisdom, but also wealth, honor, and long life, all gifts Solomon might have asked for. God did make the last one, long life, contingent on Solomon's obedience. When Solomon awoke, he was so impressed that, when he returned to Jerusalem, he offered burnt- and peace-offerings, besides making a feast to all his servants.

b. This wisdom illustrated

In the record of I Kings this account is followed by a story which illustrates the wisdom Solomon received. The story concerns two prostitutes, each of whom had a newborn child. One night, one of the two lay on her child so that it died. The two women came to Solomon, the one asserting that the mother of the dead baby had switched babies during the night, so that she could have the live one. The other mother asserted this was not so but that the live child was hers. To determine who the true mother was, Solomon called for a sword and commanded that the child be divided in two, so that each woman might have half. At this, the true mother protested that she did not want this to be done, whereas the false mother accepted the decision. From these two reactions Solomon knew who the true mother was and gave the child to her. News of this wise action spread through the country and caused the people to respect the wisdom of their king.

2. POINTS TO NOTICE

a. The tabernacle as a "high place"

Historically, "high places" were sacred places of worship for the Canaanite Baal cult. Following the removal of the ark from the tabernacle, however (I Sam. 4:3, 4), and until the building of the temple by Solomon, the Israelites also used high places for worship. Samuel sacrificed at a high place (I Sam. 9:12; cf. I Kings 3:2, 3). These substitute places were approved by God as places of worship during this period of time, but, as soon as the temple was built, they were no longer approved (I Kings 14:22, 23). It is noteworthy that here the very tabernacle (now minus the ark) is called a high place (I Kings 3:4; II Chron. 1:3). Solomon, then, went to the tabernacle as a high place, and God was pleased that he did so.

b. Solomon's commendable action

That Solomon wished to go to Gibeon to offer this large number of burnt-offerings, and take Israel's leaders with him, shows that he was in close and proper relation with God at this time. Since he did not know ahead of time that God would come to him in a dream there, the only reason for his going was to offer the sacrifices. The burnt-sacrifice pictured the full dedication of a person to God, the sacrifice being completely consumed by fire. Solomon, therefore, wanted to demonstrate that he was dedicating himself in this manner and he wanted his leaders to do the same.

c. Solomon's noteworthy humility

That Solomon went to Gibeon at all shows humility on his part, and the request he made shows it even more. It is evidenced not only by his request for wisdom—in place of other attractive gifts—but by his manner in presenting the request. He expressed his heartfelt gratitude that God had given him the position of king and then confessed that he was but a little child, not knowing how to go out or come in, in respect to filling the position adequately (I Kings 3:7). Actually he was not a child in age for, though Josephus says he was but fourteen at the time of his crowning (*Antiq.* VIII. 7. 8), he must have been at least twenty, since Rehoboam had already been born. This was Solomon's way of saying that he was simply incapable of making right decisions, because of immaturity. For this reason he needed wisdom. This was a fine demonstration of humility on his part.

d. Degree of wisdom and wealth indicated

God not only said He would give Solomon wisdom and wealth, but He indicated how much. As to wisdom, Solomon would have more than any person that had either preceded him or would follow (I Kings 3:12). And as to wealth and honor, Solomon would have more than any other king of his day (3:13). The fact that his position did rise to this height is apparent in the attitude of Egypt's Pharaoh toward him. Certainly Solomon had much to anticipate following God's gracious promise that night.

e. Marks of a vision in the dream

What Solomon experienced that night is called a "dream" (*halom*), but it had the marks of a vision. In a dream, a person is normally inert, not able to make a response to God. In a vision, however, a person has sufficient consciousness that he can make an appropriate reply. Solomon did so in this case. He heard God's question and formulated the splendid petition for wisdom.

f. Significance of the peace-offerings

When Solomon returned to Jerusalem, he offered more burnt-offerings and also peace-offerings. The significance of the burnt-offerings has been shown. The reason for the additional peace-offerings now was that they signified thanksgiving. Peace-offerings were presented when one wanted to render praise to God for who He was or for some benefit rendered. Solomon had just received abundant reason for thanksgiving, and therefore, on getting back to Jerusalem, promptly offered the appropriate sacrifices.

D. SOLOMON AND HIRAM OF TYRE

1. THE STORY (I KINGS 5:1-18; 9:11-14; 10:22; II CHRON. 2:3-16; 8:2, 18; 9:10, 21)

Solomon had a friendly relationship with Hiram of Tyre for many years. This is the same Hiram that had already supplied wood and workmen to build David's palace (II Sam. 5:11), for he is specifically said to have been "ever a lover of David" (I Kings 5:1). He must have ruled for more than fifty years, because David's palace certainly was built in the earlier part of his forty-year reign, and it is stated that Hiram aided Solomon at least during the twenty years of his building (I Kings 9:10, 11), and Solomon did not begin until his fourth year (I Kings 6:1). Though Hiram is called merely king of Tyre, it is all but certain that he was the controlling king of all Phoenicia.[6] Tyre was the principal city, having taken over this role from Sidon, and its king was recognized through all the region. His broad power is demonstrated by his ability to negotiate with both David and Solomon concerning Lebanese wood, which belonged to all the country and not merely to Tyre.

Hiram began his friendly relations with Solomon by sending a message of congratulations that Solomon had been enthroned. Solomon replied by asking Hiram to provide wood for building the Jerusalem temple.[7] This made Hiram glad and he entered into an agreement with Solomon. The agreement was that Hiram should supply cedar, fir (possibly pine), and

[6]For background information regarding Phoenicia and the Phoenicians, see Charles F. Pfeiffer, *Old Testament History,* pp. 281-286.

[7]For discussion of the use of Phoenician wood throughout the ancient Near East, see D. R. Ap-Thomas, "The Phoenicians," *Peoples of Old Testament Times,* ed. D. J. Wiseman, pp. 264-265.

algum logs, cutting them and bringing them by raft south to Joppa where Solomon would take charge of them, and Solomon would provide Hiram with wheat, barley, wine, and oil (II Chron. 2:8-10). Solomon also was to send Israelite helpers to assist in cutting the logs; he sent 10,000 per month, alternating on a three-month basis among 30,000 total conscripted laborers (I Kings 5:13, 14). This agreement was put in writing (II Chron. 2:11), and Josephus (*Antiq.* VIII. 5. 3) says that copies of it remained still in the days of Menander (ca. 300 B.C.).

How much Solomon may have planned to build when this arrangement with Hiram was sealed is not indicated, but as it worked out he continued building for a total of twenty years (I Kings 9:10), constructing not only the temple but his palace and other buildings as well. All this time, apparently, Hiram continued to supply wood—and also gold to the amount of 120 talents (I Kings 9:14)—with presumably the same basic arrangement in force.

At the end of the twenty years, Solomon was in debt to Hiram. Evidently his payments of grain, wine, and oil, as well as the help of his own workers, had not balanced out the wood and gold that Hiram had provided. The result was that Solomon sought to pay off the debt by giving Hiram twenty Israelite cities that lay near Phoenician territory.[8] This was agreeable to Hiram until he went to inspect the cities, and then he found that they did not measure up to his expectations. He rejected them and called them the land of Cabul (probably the equivalent of "good-for-nothing").

The debt may have been settled through a further agreement which involved a shipping venture from Ezion-geber to the Indian Ocean. Hiram quite clearly provided both workmen for building the ships and sailors to sail them (since this technology was so well known to the Phoenicians), while Solomon likely provided the capital. The venture was successful, for the ships returned after a journey of three years with gold, silver, ivory, apes, and peacocks (possibly baboons), as well as algum trees and precious stones (II Chron. 9:10, 21). Hiram may have received a large share of the profits until the debt was paid, though no indication of this is given.

2. POINTS TO NOTICE

a. Phoenician-Israelite friendship

Friendly relations existed between Phoenicia and Israel, not only during these years of David and Solomon, but also all during the history of Israel. No doubt the relationship was closer at this time, for one does not read of agreements for wood at other times. Moreover, there is no indication that

[8]This further indicates that Hiram ruled over all Phoenicia, for cities would not have been given merely to Tyre, but to the country.

war ever broke out between the two countries. Wars were frequent with Israel's other neighbors, but not with this one. In fact, in the time of Omri and Ahab, following the division of the kingdom, another formal alliance almost certainly was made. This is evident from the marriage of Ahab with the princess Jezebel from Phoenicia.

b. Solomon's benefits from his father

David's high standing resulted in Solomon's marriage to Pharaoh's daughter (on the basis of political and economic considerations, though not religious), and now Solomon benefited again in this Phoenician alliance. Note that it was Hiram who began the interchange of correspondence with Solomon, because he wanted to congratulate the son of David. This shows that during the lifetime of David a continuing friendly relation had existed, which encouraged Hiram to establish the same sort of relation with the new ruler. This was of major importance to Solomon, for he was to benefit over many years to come.

c. Maintenance of the agreement

One may be sure that David and Hiram had kept true to their agreement, in respect to building David's palace; otherwise their friendship would not have continued. And one may be just as sure that the agreement between Hiram and Solomon was kept also. That they were able to remain in good relation with each other for more than twenty years gives testimony of this. It is true that at the end of the twenty years, Hiram was not pleased with Solomon's payment of twenty cities, but it may be that these were offered in good faith by Solomon. They were, after all, some distance from Jerusalem —being near Phoenicia—and he may not have been familiar with their condition. Just why they did not please Hiram is not indicated. Perhaps they were small and in poor condition. The fact, however, that this disappointment did not cause a break between the two kings shows that in all other respects their interactions had been mutually pleasing.

d. A proper agreement

Sometimes Solomon has been criticized for entering into such an agreement with an unbelieving pagan like Hiram. Scripture says, "Be ye not unequally yoked together with unbelievers" (II Cor. 6:14). The principle does not apply in this case, however. Solomon did not join in a partnership with Hiram to build the temple. Solomon built it and merely purchased material and hired workers from Hiram. Christians and even churches proceed in a similar way today. Every business which supplies material for a church building is not necessarily owned by Christians, though this would be desirable. Solomon's later shipping venture with Hiram was more of a partnership, however, and in relation to that venture this criticism could apply.

e. The resulting marriage

Though no explicit indication is given, it is probable that Solomon's marriage to a daughter of the Zidonians (I Kings 11:1) was a result of this agreement with Hiram. This aspect of the agreement was not good. According to I Kings 11:3, 4, Solomon's heart came to be turned away from God due to foreign marriages; and I Kings 11:5 states directly that Solomon "went after Ashtoreth the goddess of the Zidonians." One need not think that this marriage was unavoidable, in spite of the contractual agreement. David did not marry into Hiram's family, though he held a similar agreement in respect to building his palace. No doubt Solomon could have avoided this marriage if he had so chosen.

E. BUILDING OF THE TEMPLE

1. THE STORY (I KINGS 5:1—6:38; 7:13-51; II CHRON. 2:1—4:22)

Solomon's greatest building achievement was the temple.[9] Its description is given in some detail, and it truly was a magnificent structure. It must have been one of the finest buildings of the Middle East in that time.

a. The years of building

According to I Kings 6:1 (cf. II Chron. 3:2), Solomon began the building in his fourth year, and according to 6:38 it took him seven years. Since he began to rule in 970 B.C.,[10] the years of constructing the temple were 966-959 B.C.

b. The procedure

The building activity involved three areas of work. One was procuring wood from Lebanon. Hiram supplied men to cut logs and Solomon sent conscripted laborers (*mas,* I Kings 5:13) totaling 30,000 men, 10,000 per month, to help. This in itself was a big job, cutting the logs, snaking them down the mountain side, transporting them to the Mediterranean, making them into rafts, and floating them down to the port of Joppa. From there Solomon provided his own help for transporting them to Jerusalem, a distance of about forty-five miles and uphill most of the way.

A second area of work was the procurement of stone. Stone quarries exist all through Palestine, and a large one, called "Solomon's quarries," lies directly under the city of Jerusalem. Some of the stone for the temple

[9]For a description of Solomon's temple in the light of architecture of the day, see Kathleen Kenyon, *Royal Cities of the Old Testament,* pp. 46-50.

[10]See E. R. Thiele, *The Mysterious Numbers of the Hebrew Kings,* pp. 39-52.

may have come from this place. According to I Kings 6:7, the stone was cut to size and squared right at the quarry, so that no sound of hammering was heard at the temple site itself. This would have called for precision in measurement so that a perfect fitting could be made when the stone arrived on location.

A third area of work involved the construction at the temple site, where both the wood and stone had to be put in place, and where the beautiful finishing decor—much of it in gold—was applied. Exact timing would have been necessary to insure that the proper materials arrived on schedule, so that no hindrance would be experienced to slow progress. It may be observed that most of the material David had prepared was for finishing purposes; namely, the 100,000 talents of gold and 1,000,000 talents of silver, besides bronze and iron "without weight" (I Chron. 22:14). David had also prepared some stone and timber, but probably this was not of great amount and likely again primarily for finishing. The great bulk of the construction material certainly had to be brought by Solomon's workers.

c. The workers

All this work called for many laborers. The chief craftsman for skilled work was also named Hiram. He lived in Tyre and came to Jerusalem (I Kings 7:13, 14). As for less skilled workers, there were 30,000 conscripted laborers from Israel that Solomon sent by turn to Lebanon, and there were 70,000 bearers of burdens and 80,000 hewers conscripted from aliens in Israel (I Kings 5:15; II Chron. 2:17, 18). These alien people are called *mas obed,* "conscripted labor slaves" (I Kings 9:21), in distinction from the Israelites, who are called only *mas,* "conscripted labor." Probably the aliens had to work continuously, while the Israelites were called upon for only one month in every three. Over the 150,000 aliens were 3,300 overseers, apparently one overseer to approximately fifty people (I Kings 5:16), and over these in turn were 550 general superintendents (I Kings 9:23).[11] The grand total of workers was 30,000 Israelites, 150,000 aliens, and 3,850 supervisors, or 183,850 men. When one thinks of this number of people laboring over seven years, he gets some idea of the total man-hours required for this remarkable structure.

d. The place of building

The place where Solomon erected this structure was on Mount Moriah, probably the very mountain where Abraham was called upon to sacrifice Isaac (Gen. 22:2). This is very fitting, for Abraham's experience with Isaac foreshadowed the atoning sacrifice of Christ on Calvary, and all the

[11]According to II Chron. 2:18, there were 3,600 alien supervisors; and according to II Chron. 8:10, 250 Israelite supervisors. The same total of 3,850 total supervisors results.

sacrifices to be offered at the temple were to do the same. This was the place also where the threshing floor of Araunah (Ornan) had been located, the place where the plague of David's day had stopped and where David as a result had offered sacrifice (II Chron. 3:1; cf. II Sam. 24:17-25; I Chron. 21:15-28). The location was immediately north of David's northern city wall and is today occupied by Qubbet es-Sakhra, better known as the Dome of the Rock. The cave which is shown within this mosque today could be the place where Araunah and his sons hid themselves from the destroying angel on that memorable occasion (I Chron. 21:20).

e. Differences from the tabernacle

The basic design of the temple was like that of the tabernacle; it had the same two principal rooms, the same types of furniture, and it faced east. It also had numerous differences, and some of the more significant call for notice:

1) The dimensions were twice as large, being ninety feet by thirty feet[12] instead of forty-five by fifteen feet (I Kings 6:2). Two-thirds of it consisted of the Holy Place and this was forty-five feet high (three times the height of the tabernacle), and one-third the Holy of Holies (I Kings 6:20) and this was thirty feet high (twice the height of the tabernacle). The latter was a perfect cube, as in the tabernacle.

2) In front of the Holy Place was a porch, thirty feet by fifteen feet (I Kings 6:3), with two prominent pillars, apparently free-standing. Each pillar was twenty-seven feet high and eighteen feet in circumference (I Kings 7:15-21). One was named Jachin ("He establishes") and the other Boaz ("In him is strength").

3) Both main rooms were entered through solid doors (I Kings 6:31-35), rather than through mere curtains.

4) Chambers surrounded this basic structure, three tiers high, intended for storage (I Kings 6:5-10). The lowest tier was seven-and-a-half feet wide, the next nine feet, and the top ten-and-a-half. This difference was apparently gained by a progressive narrowing of the main wall by eighteen inches at the points where the two upper tiers began.

5) Windows, probably latticed, let natural light into the main structure above the side chambers (I Kings 6:4).

6) Both of the two main rooms were paneled with cedar wood and their floors were planked with pine (or cypress). Walls and doors were carved with flowers, palm trees, and cherubim, and all was overlaid with gold (I Kings 6:15-22).

7) As to furnishings, the temple had ten lampstands, five on each side

[12]Sixty cubits by twenty cubits; the cubit equals about eighteen inches.

of the Holy Place, and ten tables of showbread arranged in the same pattern (II Chron. 4:7, 8, 19).

8) Both the great altar and laver in the court in front of the temple were larger than those of the tabernacle, the altar being thirty feet square and fifteen feet high (II Chron. 4:1) and the laver fifteen feet in diameter and seven-and-a-half feet high (I Kings 7:23-26). The laver held about 10,000 gallons of liquid. Its base was composed of twelve figures of oxen, three facing toward each of the compass points. Besides the main laver, there were ten smaller lavers (I Kings 7:27-39). The stands of these lavers were four-and-a-half feet high and six feet on a side; bowl-shaped lavers that rested on the stands contained about 200 gallons of liquid for washing. Each stand was equipped with wheels for easy movement. The lavers were placed five on the north side and five on the south side of the court.

9) All the items of furniture were certainly new, with the exception of the ark. The ark was the same one that had been used in the tabernacle and was now about 450 years old. Since it was completely covered with gold, both inside and out, it probably was still in excellent condition.

10) In addition to the court of the altar and lavers, there was an outer or great court, apparently completely surrounding the inner court (I Kings 7:9, 12).

2. POINTS TO NOTICE

a. Importance of this temple

Peoples of the day measured how much another people thought of their god by how fine a temple they built to him. The tabernacle had served satisfactorily so long as God's people held only tribal status. But as soon as a national status was achieved, it was appropriate that a fine temple be built. This had been in David's thinking when he had earlier wanted to build such a permanent dwelling—and God was pleased with his intent (I Kings 8:18). God wanted the endeavor postponed at that time, but now that Solomon, a man of peace, was ruling it was appropriate for the permanent dwelling to be constructed. Other people would see and take note that Israelites did think highly of their God.

b. A fine temple

One might think that Solomon became too extravagant in building the temple. Much of it was covered with gold, making its value almost beyond reckoning. However, the Scriptures continually imply divine approval. God clearly was pleased; He desired a fine house to His name. The reason was that He might be magnified all the more in the eyes of both Israelites and foreigners.

c. Contemporary parallels to the temple plan

Some contemporary temples have been found which show notable parallels in plan to Solomon's temple. One dating to the ninth century was discovered at Tell Tainat in Syria, but more recently another was found at Hazor of the Late Bronze period, and still another at Arad, dating to the century of Solomon.[13] All these similarly show an inner room (holy of holies), an outer room (holy place), and a porch with pillars. This does not mean, however, that Solomon's plan was borrowed from other peoples of the day. The plan of the temple was like that of the tabernacle, which had been built before 1400 B.C. in the Sinai Peninsula, well before Israel ever entered Canaan. Moreover, the temple plan was conveyed to Solomon by David, who was guided in conceiving it by the Holy Spirit (I Chron. 28:11, 12). The reason why these parallels exist is likely that the pattern God gave was in general like that being used in the world of the day, with some modifications. Church buildings of today are similar, too, whether of liberal or conservative congregations. Architecture is neutral so far as God's biblical requirements are concerned.

d. A meaningful plan

Though the basic plan was similar to other temples, Solomon's structure was furnished in a way to give an important theological meaning. It pictured God's plan of salvation for sinful man. As one entered the court surrounding the temple proper, he first encountered the great brazen altar, which typified Calvary where Christ paid the penalty of man's sin in dying on the cross. He next encountered the laver, where the priests washed before performing the sacred ceremonies. It typified the cleansing from sin needed by the sinner as he places faith in Christ his Sacrifice. Thus cleansed, he is able to enter the Holy Place for fellowship with God, and here he needs to see the light of God's word for guidance in his Christian life, typified by the lampstands, and to feed on God's word for his daily nourishment, typified by the showbread. He needs also the ministry of prayer and worship, typified by the golden altar of incense. All this, as indicated, is for fellowship with God, who was typified by the ark of the covenant in the adjoining Holy of Holies.

e. Some borrowing from other peoples

Though the general plan of the temple was not borrowed from other peoples of the day, it is all but certain that details, especially pertaining to decoration, were. For instance, Solomon lined the interior walls with cedar

[13]For discussion of the Arad temple, see Yohanan Aharoni, *The Biblical Archaeologist* 31 (1968), pp. 2-32.

wood, all highly carved, and excavation has shown this characteristic to have had a Phoenician background—something quite understandable since Solomon's chief craftsman, Hiram, was from Tyre. Also, the two pillars, Jachin and Boaz, had parallels in Syria, Phoenicia, Cyprus, and even eastward in Mesopotamia in temples of Sargon of the late eighth century. Sometimes such pillars were used to support a roof and at other times they were free-standing, as seems to have been the case with Solomon's temple. The general design of the pillars, particularly in regard to the carved capitals, also had parallels.[14] One need not be surprised that this was true, for in such peripheral matters there was nothing which negated the basic typology and, as noted, such factors are neutral in respect to theological significance.

F. DEDICATION OF THE TEMPLE

1. THE STORY (I KINGS 8:1-66; II CHRON. 5:1—7:11)

When the temple was entirely finished, the ark was brought to it from the tent that David had made in Jerusalem, and then a cloud, representing God's glory, filled the Holy of Holies as it had in the tabernacle. This indicated that the temple was fully ready for service, and it marked the time as appropriate for a great service of dedication. The dedication ceremony consisted of four main parts.

First, Solomon spoke a brief message in the hearing of the people. He began by pronouncing a blessing on those assembled, and all stood to their feet. Then he reminded the people that David had wanted to build the Lord's house, but God had refused permission, promising that David's son would do so. He continued by saying that the Lord had now brought these words to pass by the temple's having been built.

Solomon next offered a lengthy dedicatory prayer. According to II Chronicles 6:13, he mounted a platform specially prepared for this purpose. He had ordered it placed in the court before the great brazen altar. It was seven-and-a-half feet square and four-and-a-half feet high, made of bronze.[15]

The prayer had several main divisions: (1) praise to God for His greatness and faithfulness to promises He had given; (2) a request that God keep His promise to David that his posterity always remain on Israel's throne;

[14]For discussion, see William F. Albright, *Archaeology and the Religion of Israel*, pp. 143-144, or *From the Stone Age to Christianity*, p. 225.

[15]It is called a *kiyor*, the same term used for the laver of the tabernacle (Exod. 30:18, 28) and of the temple (I Kings 7:30, 38). Both objects were empty, container-like items, though their function was entirely different. Albright points out that the same word is used for a similar type of platform pictured on Syrian monuments; see his *Archaeology and the Religion of Israel*, pp. 152-154.

(3) a request that God show favor by recognizing the temple and hearing the prayers of His people made toward it; (4) a catalog of numerous adverse situations—such as defeat by an enemy power, famine, a time of captivity for the people—when the people would have cause to repent of sin and ask for forgiveness; and (5) a request that God should in each such case hear the request and grant forgiveness, since Israel was His specially chosen people.

As Solomon thus prayed, he had bowed on his knees before God, positioned on the raised platform where all could see. His hands had been stretched toward heaven. Having finished, he stood to his feet and then pronounced a blessing on the people: (1) that God would not forget His people, as He had not forgotten them in time past; (2) that God would incline the hearts of all the people to be faithful to Himself; (3) that God would care for His people and hear their petitions when presented; and (4) that the people in turn would give diligence to maintain perfect hearts in the presence of God.

It was probably at the conclusion of this pronouncement of blessing that fire fell from heaven and consumed a sacrifice (burnt-offering) that had been laid on the great altar (II Chron. 7:1-3). Similar fire had fallen to ignite the offering on the altar of the tabernacle years before (Lev. 9:24). Then Solomon ordered sacrifices of peace-offerings to the astounding number of 22,000 oxen and 120,000 sheep.[16] Peace-offerings were appropriate for they represented a spirit of thanksgiving on the part of the people. In order to make possible so many sacrifices, the king sanctified the entire central area of the court before the temple and set up auxiliary altars. The animals were likely sacrificed over the following seven days, while a continuing feast was held. People were present from all Israel and from as far away as "the entering in of Hamath" far to the north. By the eighth day the feast had been completed, and the people in a joyful mood returned to their homes.

2. POINTS TO NOTICE

a. Solomon himself as officiant

It is noteworthy that Solomon himself led in this time of dedication. Though it involved a sermon, prayer, and a pronouncement of blessing, he did not call on a priest or prophet to take the lead. He did it all himself. It was appropriate for him to do so, since he was king. In so doing he also demonstrated confidence that he was himself in a proper relation to God spiritually.

[16]Possibly both sheep and goats, the Hebrew being *tso'n* ("flock"), which normally included both.

b. Solomon's attitude

In all that Solomon did, he demonstrated an attitude of humility and dependence on God. He was concerned that God continue to bless His people, and he recognized that if this were to be the case the people needed to be true in their heart's attitude toward God. And if Solomon wanted this for the people, he must have wanted it for himself as well. One may say, then, that at this point of his reign—eleven years after being crowned—Solomon was yet a fine, God-pleasing monarch.

c. Thinking in big terms

Solomon was a man of big and grand concepts. Some people think in small terms, but this was not true of Solomon. The grandeur of the temple itself was almost beyond description. One may imagine that it came to be reputed in all capitals of the world. And now he sacrificed an incredible number of animals. He had sacrificed as many as one thousand when he had gone to Gibeon early in his reign, but this occasion now dwarfed that one. It has been alleged that the sacrifice of so many animals would have been impossible and that, therefore, the text must be in error. Both I Kings 8:63 and II Chronicles 7:5 agree, however, and the number is quite believable when the occasion is thought of in the way presented above. There were plenty of priests and Levites to do the work; the only area of question concerns space and time. As to space, the temple court could accommodate several altars, and as to time, the seven days would have been ample. Simple arithmetic shows that, though the scene would have been busy, the number indicated could have been offered. One may believe, in fact, that before the festivities started Solomon had figured how many offerings could be presented in the time available and probably let this figure determine the number of animals he had ready.

d. A high-water mark in Solomon's popularity

The people who attended went home in a joyful mood. These would have been influential people, city elders and appointed officials. They were from all parts of the land and even from tribute-paying countries. When they returned home, they would have told of the grand occasion and especially of the splendor of the completed temple. At the focal point of their report would have been the person of Solomon. This would have made him prominent and admired. The time certainly was a high-water mark in Solomon's illustrious reign.

G. GOD'S RESPONSE

1. THE STORY (I KINGS 9:1-9; II CHRON. 7:12-22)

Shortly after the dedicatory ceremonies had been completed, God appeared to Solomon by night with a response to the prayer he had offered. In essence, God stated (1) that He would indeed hear and answer His people in all such situations that Solomon had mentioned, if they would come in humility as they asked for forgiveness and truly put their sinful ways aside; (2) that He would recognize the house built for Him, so that His name would be there for ever and ever and His heart there perpetually; (3) that He would establish Solomon's family as a continuous ruling dynasty, as formerly promised to David, if Solomon would conduct his life as David had his; but (4) that, if Solomon did not, both people and temple would be destroyed, with each becoming "a proverb and a byword among all nations" (II Chron. 7:20).

2. POINTS TO NOTICE

a. God's faithfulness

God is always faithful to His Word, no matter how unfaithful His children are. Here He took opportunity to answer Solomon's prayer. The prayer had been offered in all earnestness by Solomon, and God responded accordingly. He told Solomon that He would truly do the things for which Solomon had asked. This shows that God was pleased with what Solomon had done and said, but it shows even more how gracious God is in that He was willing to respond to Solomon in this tangible manner.

b. God's will made clear

God's response answered Solomon's requests and it also made clear and unmistakable the nature of His will for Israel as a people and Solomon as their king. No one had any excuse for not meeting all the requirements. If the people did not meet them, it was their fault, not God's.

c. Solomon's fall

Though God graciously gave Solomon these wonderful promises and a clear warning, still Solomon failed to live up to God's requirements. For many years he did well. But gradually evil influences took hold of him, and he fell away from the high standard set by God. The result was that God's blessing was eventually withdrawn.

17

Solomon's Power and Fall

Before considering Solomon's decline in power, resulting from his spiritual defection, it is well to notice how great his power became from which he fell. At his zenith of power, he probably surpassed even his illustrious father for a time. He did not hold it, however, and when his position started to slip, it deteriorated quickly.

A. THE HEIGHT OF SOLOMON'S POWER

1. THE STORY (I KINGS 9:10—10:29; II CHRON. 8:1—9:28)

The height to which Solomon's power reached is indicated first by several accomplishments which are cited and then by the illustration of the queen of Sheba's making a long journey just to see this powerful ruler firsthand.

a. Various significant accomplishments

Some of the accomplishments listed in respect to Solomon's power have been noted in other contexts. These need not be discussed again. Our interest here is matters that have not as yet been set forth in appropriate detail.

1) ***The twenty cities*** (I Kings 9:11-13; II Chron. 8:2). It was noted earlier that Solomon gave Hiram twenty cities as payment for his debt of 120 talents of gold, and that Hiram refused them. It should now be added that when Solomon received them back, he improved them and caused more of his people to take up residence in them (II Chron. 8:2). In view of Hiram's refusal it is apparent that they were not attractive population centers, and Solomon clearly wanted to rectify this. Evidently Solomon at this time was taking steps to make his country as fine as possible, a joy to his people. The period in question is indicated by a notice that the twenty years of building had now ended (I Kings 9:10; II Chron. 8:1). This means a total of twenty-four years of Solomon's reign had elapsed; thus it was thirteen years since the temple had been completed.

2) ***A conquest in the north*** (I Kings 9:18; II Chron. 8:3, 4). A significant matter regarding Solomon's power is now noted by the chronicler. He says, "And Solomon went to Hamath-zobah, and prevailed against it. And he built Tadmor" (II Chron. 8:3, 4). The designation *Hamath-zobah* must mean the two adjoining countries, Hamath and Zobah, the former of which was the more northern and had sent tribute to David after he had defeated the latter (II Sam. 8:3, 4, 9, 10). The passage indicates that Solomon marched against both countries and defeated them.[1] This is the only offensive battle indicated for Solomon, but it is a significant one. David had conquered Zobah but never Hamath, which had only sent tribute, thus acknowledging his authority. Then, in keeping with this offensive action by Solomon, he is said to have built Tadmor. The city of Tadmor is well identified with the later Greek and Roman city, Palmyra, located 175 miles northeast of Damascus and directly east of the two countries here in question.[2] It was a center of commercial traffic of the day, as well as a military station. It would have been a logical site for Solomon to seize and fortify, after having taken both countries, Zobah and Hamath, for it provided a natural defense point to the northeast.

Though this type of offensive action is out of keeping with Solomon's ordinary measures as king, the evidence is strong that it did occur, and, if so, he came to hold more extensive control in this northern region than did David his father. Support for this theory is found in II Chronicles 9:26: "And he reigned over all the kings from the river even unto the land of the

[1]Yohanan Aharoni, *Land of the Bible,* p. 275, n. 50, believes this was hardly possible and suggests a textual error of Hamath-zobah for Beth-zobah, finding support in the Septuagint. Abraham Malamat, "Aspects of the Foreign Policies of David and Solomon," *Journal of Near Eastern Studies* 22 (Jan. 1963), p. 7, however, finds no difficulty in accepting the account as completely historical. Merrill Unger, *Israel and the Aramaeans of Damascus,* p. 54, believes that Solomon retaliated against Zobah for having revolted. See also p. 40, n. 22.

[2]The suggestion that a Tamar is here in view is not well supported, but see p. 292, n. 19.

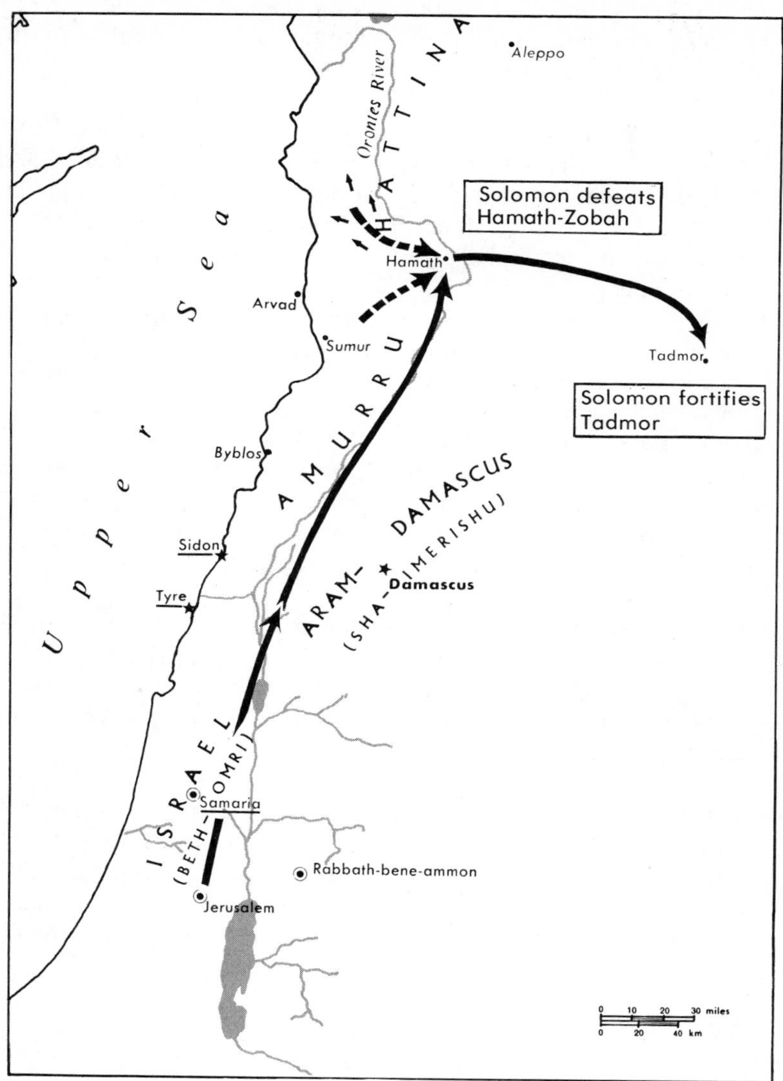

Map 13. The Hamath-zobah Battle

Philistines, and to the border of Egypt." It seems safe to say that, following this action, Israel controlled more territory than at any other time in its history. In his day, Solomon was probably the most powerful and influential ruler in the Middle East.

3) ***Bond service*** (I Kings 9:20-23; II Chron. 8:7-10). As noted earlier, Solomon made bondservants of aliens in his land, to help in his building activity. It may seem rather strange that notice of this should come in the scriptural context indicating his accomplishments, but the probable reason is that bond service contributed significantly to making Solomon's building activity economically possible.

There is a seeming conflict between this notice and an earlier statement in I Kings 5:13. In the present context it is said that Solomon did not make bondservants of the children of Israel, while in I Kings 5:13 it is stated that he did raise "a levy [*mas*] out of all Israel" of 30,000 men to help cut wood in Lebanon. Perhaps those levied from Israel were not made bondservants in the same sense as were conscripted aliens. The difference in mind could be that Israelites had to serve only one month out of three, whereas aliens had to serve continuously. It is also possible that Israelites received some remuneration for their service, while aliens did not.[3]

4) ***Regular sacrifices established*** (I Kings 9:25; II Chron. 8:12-16). A religious note is now added to Solomon's list of accomplishments. He instituted at the new temple the regular sacrifices that had been prescribed in the law and carried on for years at Shiloh and probably at David's temporary tent-sanctuary. This certainly would have been done directly after the completion of the temple, some thirteen years before most of the other events in this list. The sacrifices of every day, of the sabbaths, of the new moons, and the great feasts were included. Also the divisions of the priests and Levites, as designated by David, were put to work in effecting the program. With this done, "the house of the Lord was perfected" (II Chron. 8:16), meaning that everything which had been intended from the beginning was completed and in operation.

5) ***Solomon's wealth*** (I Kings 10:14-27; II Chron. 9:13-27). Still another matter mentioned is that Solomon became very wealthy. His trading is set forth, by which much of this wealth came, as well as the gifts brought by visitors. The result was that he received the incredible income of 666 talents of gold annually and was able to make "silver in Jerusalem as stones" (II Chron. 9:27). From this gold he made many articles. He made 200 large shields (*tsinnah*) of 600 shekels each, and 300 smaller shields (*magen*) of 300

[3]See p. 314.

shekels each. The thought is that these were gold-covered, the framework of the shields being of wood. Such shields would have been used for state occasions (see I Kings 14:27, 28). Then he made all the drinking vessels of gold, as well as all the vessels of the house of the forest of Lebanon (possibly the name of his palace). Perhaps most remarkable of all, he made a magnificent throne of ivory and overlaid it with fine gold. It had six steps, with two carved lions on each step as well as on each side of the seat. The text says that "there was not the like made in any kingdom" (I Kings 10:20; II Chron. 9:19). In summary, "King Solomon passed all the kings of the earth in riches and wisdom" (I Kings 10:23; II Chron. 9:22).

b. Visit by the queen of Sheba

Among Solomon's distinguished visitors was the queen of Sheba. The story of her visit is told in some detail, probably because she was one of the more important of those who came and no doubt the occasion illustrated well what was duplicated often in the visits of others. She may also have journeyed further than any of the other visitors.

She was a Sabean queen from the southern tip of Arabia, the land of Sheba. The country is roughly identified with the modern state of Yemen.[4] Solomon's ships had likely been stopping at ports of this land. In fact, the queen's long journey (some 1200 miles) may have been motivated in part by mercantile considerations. Southwestern Arabia was well known for trade in spice and incense, and this queen may have felt that her business by caravan route was jeopardized by Solomon's merchant fleet.[5]

She came also, as she says, to see Solomon himself, to ask him questions and learn firsthand of his reputed wisdom. Solomon answered her questions and showed her all his buildings and the lavish entertainment schedule he followed. She was greatly impressed, and responded, "It was a true report which I heard in mine own land of thine acts, and of thy wisdom." In fact, she added, "The one half of the greatness of thy wisdom was not told me" (II Chron. 9:5, 6). Having seen and heard all she wanted, she gave Solomon the enormous gift of 120 talents of gold, besides fine spices and precious stones (I Kings 10:10), and Solomon responded by giving her all her desire and gifts out of his royal bounty (10:13). Matters of trade may well have been included in the agreements at which they arrived. The agreements,

[4]Regarding Sabean settlement, cf. William F. Albright, *Archaeology and the Religion of Israel,* pp. 132-135. Modern explorations in Yemen are described by Wendell Phillips, *Qataban and Sheba* (New York: Harcourt, Brace and Co., 1955).

[5]A clay stamp from South Arabia was found at Bethel by James Kelso. It dates from about the time of Solomon, and shows that trade was existent at the time. The stamp was originally about 3 x 4 inches and probably was used to seal bags of cargo. Cf. G. W. VanBeek and A. Jamme, "An Inscribed South Arabian Clay Stamp from Bethel," *Bulletin of American Schools of Oriental Research* 151 (Oct. 1958), pp. 9-16.

however, did not involve the cessation of Solomon's trading activity, for I Kings 10:15, which concerns the period after her visit, states that a part of Solomon's vast revenue came from trading with the spice merchants of Arabia.

2. POINTS TO NOTICE

a. Solomon's God-pleasing life

This list of accomplishments of Solomon shows marked blessing on his life. Since the time involved in respect to at least some of them was shortly after completing the building activity (Solomon's twenty-fourth year), it must be that he was still living in a God-pleasing manner at that point in his reign. As was illustrated by Saul, God's blessing is withdrawn when one turns to disobedient ways. Solomon evidently continued in his faithful conduct before God for more than half of his reign.

b. Possible connection with later defection

Though Solomon did well at this time, it may be that the remarkable degree of power and wealth he then held contributed to his later spiritual downfall. As noted, he probably was the greatest ruler of the Middle East, but this could have fed his human tendency to pride, and pride leads inevitably to a downfall. Pride makes one feel self-sufficient and turns him away from dependence on God. This coupled with other factors soon to be noted could have contributed to the failures of his later life.

c. Significance of the visit of the queen of Sheba

For a queen to travel 1200 miles to visit another ruler, and then give him an enormous gift, proves that the other ruler enjoyed a far-reaching and prestigious reputation. Solomon evidently was well known and highly reputed in faraway countries and capitals.

d. The Ethiopian royal line and the queen of Sheba

The royal family of Ethiopia claimed descent from Solomon and the queen of Sheba. It was asserted that the queen gave birth, as a result of her visit, to Menelik I, the traditional founder of the Ethiopian royal line. This is difficult to prove, but it is also difficult to disprove. Though the queen of Sheba did not come from Ethiopia, it is quite clear that Ethiopia was colonized by Sabeans from South Arabia, crossing the Red Sea. Her descendants could have gone to Ethiopia, and Arabic legends give details regarding the queen who married Solomon. It may be added that Josephus speaks of a relationship which the queen of Sheba had with Ethiopia (*Antiq.* II. 10. 2; VI. 5. 6).

B. SOLOMON'S SPIRITUAL FALL

1. THE STORY (I KINGS 11:1-13)

a. His defection from God

Few men can live with power and wealth and not be affected. No doubt this is the reason Jesus said, "It is easier for a camel to go through the eye of a needle, than for a rich man to enter into the kingdom of God" (Matt. 19:24; cf. Mark 10:25; Luke 18:25). David had succeeded in remaining true to God, in spite of his high position, but Solomon was not David. It is quite clear that he surpassed David in position, but he did not attain David's standard in faithfulness to God, who had permitted all his power and wealth. Indeed, it had been God who was responsible for Solomon's accomplishments. But somehow Solomon forgot this vital fact, as the days of his rule moved on, and he became enamored more of himself and his achievements.

A position of power tends to bring about a wrong use of power. There are clues that Solomon came to use his power wrongly even before the time when the Scriptures note his marked spiritual fall. There had been, for instance, an injustice imposed on both aliens and Israelites in respect to labor conscripted for building. Then Solomon had imposed a taxation program so high that people of the northern tribes came in mass to request relief from his successor Rehoboam (I Kings 12:1-4). Solomon had wanted, among other things, overly lavish food for his entertainments, and he used his power to obtain it in this way—apparently in disregard for hardship imposed. The same wrong use of power is evidenced later by the necessity of Jeroboam's flight from Jerusalem to Egypt (I Kings 11:40). When Solomon learned of God's promise to Jeroboam that ten tribes would be given to him to rule, the king attempted to kill the young man.

The sacred text, however, makes clear that Solomon's fall came mainly as a result of his numerous marriages. That Solomon had so many wives was no doubt in keeping with his general manner of thinking. The temple he built had to be the finest, the sacrifices he offered had to be the greatest in number, the entertainment schedule he followed had to be the most lavish; it follows that he had to have more wives than anyone else. Other kings had a great many, but none are known to have had as many as did Solomon. For instance, it is known that Amenhotep III of Egypt (1414-1378 B.C.) "ordered from the king of Gezer forty 'beautiful women' at forty shekels of silver each. The Pharaoh received thirty young girls as a present from the king of Mitanni, twenty-one from the king of Jerusalem and twenty or thirty from a Syrian prince."[6] At the time when the same ruler married a

[6]Roland de Vaux, *Ancient Israel: Its Life and Institutions,* p. 116.

Mitannian princess, she brought with her 317 young maidens. Another Egyptian Pharaoh, the great Rameses II, fathered 162 children, indicating again a large number of wives. However, none of these approached Solomon's total. The number no doubt speaks of a sensualism on his part, but more of his desire simply for status. He probably seldom if ever saw many of these women.

Several of the marriages were the result of treaties made with foreign countries. Solomon's treaties with Egypt and Phoenicia have been noted. Since mention is made here also of Moabites, Ammonites, Edomites, and Hittites, a special relationship with these peoples is suggested. Regarding the Moabites, Ammonites, and Edomites, however, one can hardly speak of a treaty-relationship, for all three groups were under Solomon's control. David had conquered them and they remained a part of Solomon's empire. Perhaps Solomon merely wanted to solicit their good will by the marriages. The situation was different with the Hittites, however. By Solomon's time, the great Hittite empire in Anatolia had ceased to exist, but pockets of Hittite people continued in various areas to the north of Palestine, and Solomon could well have made an alliance involving marriage with one or more of these groups.

The text reminds us that these were nations of whom God had long before said to the Israelites, "Ye shall not go in to them, neither shall they come in unto you; for surely they will turn away your heart after their gods" (11:2). This is exactly what occurred with Solomon: "When Solomon was old, his wives turned away his heart after other gods" (11:4). The degree to which he turned after these gods is indicated: he "went after Ashtoreth the goddess of the Zidonians" and he built high places "for Chemosh, the abomination of Moab . . . and for Molech, the abomination of the children of Ammon" (11:5-7). It is further stated that he did similarly "for all his strange wives, which burnt incense and sacrificed unto their gods" (11:8). He probably did not go so far as to build high places for these others, for later, when Josiah destroyed the high places such as those built by Solomon, only high places to Ashtoreth, Chemosh, and Milcom (Molech) are mentioned (II Kings 23:13). But Solomon at least gave honor to other deities in some manner. The place where Solomon built these high places is designated as on the mount of corruption (II Kings 23:13), which is known today as the Mount of Offense. This is the southernmost peak of the Mount of Olives to the east of Jerusalem.

b. God's reprimand

As a result of this defection, God appeared to Solomon once again, but this time not to promise blessing. This time the Lord was angry with him (I Kings 11:9) and told him, "Forasmuch as this is done of thee, and thou hast not kept my covenant and my statutes . . . I will surely rend the kingdom from thee, and will give it to thy servant.'' He stated further, however, that for David's sake He would not do this in Solomon's day but in the day of his son, and, further, that He would not take all the kingdom but would leave one tribe to this son (11:11-13). This, of course, took place in the early days of Rehoboam.

2. POINTS TO NOTICE

a. A tragic contrast

When one reads that Solomon actually built high places to false gods at Jerusalem, he cannot help but recall the words of the same man uttered years before at the dedication of the temple: ''LORD God of Israel, there is no God like thee, in heaven above, or on earth beneath, who keepest covenant and mercy with thy servants that walk before thee with all their heart'' (I Kings 8:23); or later, on the same day, his words of admonition to the people, ''Let your heart therefore be perfect with the LORD our God, to walk in his statutes, and to keep his commandments, as at this day'' (I Kings 8:61). Apparently Solomon had forgotten these fine words. Here, near the close of his forty years, he came himself to lead the way in not having a perfect heart toward God and even to worship the false deities.

b. Insufficiency of wisdom

Modern man continues to believe that a trained mind is the main answer to the world's problems. A trained mind is important, but it is not a safeguard against sin. Solomon was the wisest man of his day, but he fell into dire unfaithfulness to God. One would think that, because he was so wise, he would have seen the folly of such action; but, if he did, he was not deterred. The influence of the foreign wives took its toll, and he fell away from the high resolves of his earlier days. Wisdom was not sufficient to keep him from sin.

c. The failure of old age as a guarantee

It is commonly believed that old age leads people to live more sensibly and properly. Young people live and think in radical and innovative ways, but advancing years cause them to settle down to safer, conservative measures. This rule often holds, but not always, and Solomon is a testimony to the fact. It was in his younger years that he was faithful to God. But as the twilight of his life drew on, he gradually fell away. If he had been told twenty years before that he would actually build high places to false gods one day, he no doubt would have declared that an impossibility. But it happened.

d. Gradual defection

Defection of this kind comes as a result of permitting one's mind to be occupied too much with earthly matters and too little with God and His will. Without question, Solomon became very busy as the cares and responsibilities mounted during his reign. He had a far-flung empire to administer, which called for a host of decisions. He had his elaborate building activities to oversee. Then he became involved with international trade and relationships. And further, world-renowned visitors came in increasing numbers and each had to be treated with proper decorum. All of these matters called for attention and time, and apparently Solomon let them claim too much. Time spent in spiritual devotion diminished and no doubt finally ceased altogether. And when this happened, he was in no condition to resist the influence of his many foreign wives, who undoubtedly kept after him to build them places at which to worship their foreign gods.

e. The power of Satan

In the last analysis, of course, one must say that Satan was the mastermind behind Solomon's fall. He is clever and knows how to bring his attack in the most effective manner. It is evident that he worked gradually with Solomon, over a period of many years. Solomon was still doing well after twenty-four years of rule, but in time Satan won out.

f. Solomon's repentance

In the closing chapter of Ecclesiastes, however, there is indication that Solomon came back to a proper relation with God before he died. The Book of Ecclesiastes certainly was written by him,[7] and it sets forth the many ways in which Solomon tried to find satisfaction. The last chapter reveals his thinking at the close of his life. He bids young people: "Remember now thy Creator in the days of thy youth, while the evil days come not" (12:1). By the time that he personally came to this thinking, the days had become late for him, and he had wasted much of his life. In the next to the last verse of the chapter, he writes persuasively, "Let us hear the conclusion of the whole matter: Fear God, and keep his commandments: for this is the whole duty of man" (12:13).

g. The sureness of God's warnings

In His first two appearances to Solomon, God not only had promised great blessing but He had also given clear warning, especially on the second occasion (I Kings 3:14; 9:6-9). God remembered His promises, and Solomon enjoyed remarkable blessings for much of his reign; but now God remembered the warning as well, and He pronounced His sentence of pun-

[7]See especially Eccles. 1:1, 12, 16.

ishment—much of the kingdom would be taken away. It is easy to remember God's promises and forget the warnings, but God remembers both.

h. The reservation of one tribe

In the pronouncement of punishment God told Solomon one tribe would be reserved for his son's rule. The tribe in mind was Judah. This brings questions to mind regarding two other tribes. One is Benjamin: why was no mention made here regarding Benjamin, when much of this tribe also stayed loyal to the southern country (I Kings 12:21; II Chron. 11:3, 23)? The reason probably is that the tribe as a whole did not stay with Judah. The city of Bethel, for instance, at the northern boundary of Benjamin (Josh. 18:21, 22),[8] did not, for Jeroboam even made it one of his two religious centers (I Kings 12:29). The dividing line, the location of which varied in the earlier years of the divided kingdom, evidently passed through the northern part of Benjamin. It was probably for this reason that Ahijah, in promising a division of the kingdom to Jeroboam, spoke of only one tribe being left to Solomon's son (I Kings 11:32, 36). It is significant, however, that he gave Jeroboam only ten pieces of a torn garment, thus symbolizing that he would receive only ten tribes rather than eleven (I Kings 11:30, 31, 35).

The other tribe which presents a problem is Simeon. Simeon was given inheritance in southern Judah, being allotted seventeen cities there (Josh. 19:1-9). If this tribe was within Judah, why was it not considered part of the southern kingdom? The answer is best found in an apparent movement of many (perhaps most) Simeonites, some time prior to the division of the kingdom, north to the region of Ephraim and Manasseh, more particularly northern Manasseh. In both II Chronicles 15:9 and 34:6, Simeon is mentioned along with Ephraim and Manasseh in a way suggesting that all three tribes were then (the time of Asa and following) geographically linked together.[9]

C. SOLOMON'S PUNISHMENT

1. THE STORY (I KINGS 11:14-40)

God not only warned Solomon of what would happen in the days of his son, but he permitted problems to arise for the kingdom while Solomon still

[8]That Bethel is actually included in Ephraim in I Chron. 7:28 suggests that it lay very near the boundary line between the two tribes.

[9]II Chron. 34:6 suggests the location as being more specifically northern Manasseh, in that Naphtali, still farther north, is associated with Simeon. The rationale for Simeon's move lies in Simeon's humbled situation in being assigned only cities when all other tribes had been assigned territories. This humbled status was no doubt related to Jacob's prediction that Simeon would be scattered in Israel (Gen. 49:5-7) and to Simeon's small number upon entering Canaan (only 22,000, the smallest tribe); cf. Leon J. Wood, "Simeon, the Tenth Tribe of Israel," *Journal of the Evangelical Theological Society* 19 (Fall 1971), pp. 221-225.

ruled. Three areas of trouble developed, each of which certainly caused anxiety for the king and a measurable loss of power and influence. The result was that, whereas this man had enjoyed Israel's greatest day of power at the midpoint of his reign, much of this was lost by the close.

a. Hadad of Edom (11:14-22)

The first problem area concerned Hadad of Edom, whose activity served to diminish Solomon's control over the southern part of the empire. Hadad had been the sole survivor of Edom's royal family at the time of Joab's slaughter there in David's reign.[10] Joab had taken six months to cut off "every male in Edom," likely meaning all of the army besides the royal family. At the time, Hadad was still a young lad (*na'ar qatan*). He, along with numerous servants, fled to Egypt, where the Pharaoh welcomed them and gave them asylum.[11] In time he even gave the young man his sister-in-law as wife. A son born to them actually grew up in Pharaoh's house and was among the sons of Pharaoh (11:19, 20). For all this favor, however, Hadad, on learning that David and Joab were dead, returned home.

The text does not state what Hadad did on arriving back in Edom, except that he became an adversary unto Solomon (11:14). He probably became head of his country, though Edom was still under Solomon's control. Once installed, he was in a position to make continual trouble for Solomon, remembering Joab's atrocities. He may not have succeeded in fully removing Edom from Israelite jurisdiction—Solomon's copper and maritime operations from Ezion-geber quite possibly continued for all of his reign—but at least he probably made a strong effort to this end and did cause serious problems. One may believe that Hadad became more successful in these efforts during Solomon's latter days, as God's favor was increasingly withdrawn.

b. Rezon of Damascus (11:23-25)

The second problem area concerned Rezon of Damascus. Like Hadad in the south, this man came to lessen Solomon's control in the north. Rezon had been a supporter of Hadadezer, king of Zobah, whom David had defeated early in his reign (II Sam. 8:3-9). Rezon apparently had escaped unharmed from that battle and then formed a small army to further his personal desire for power. His main prize was Damascus, and he succeeded in becoming ruler there. Damascus had not been a particularly strong center of power before this, but he made it so. He clearly was capable as a military

[10]See pp. 186, 242.

[11]This Pharaoh was likely Siamun, who later gave his daughter in marriage to Solomon; see Ronald J. Williams, "The Egyptians," *Peoples of Old Testament Times,* ed. D. J. Wiseman, pp. 94-95.

figure and gathered an efficient force behind him. He gradually increased the influence of his new center and thus was able to cause serious trouble for Solomon.

No indication is given, however, that Rezon was able to remove Damascus from its provincial status, just as Hadad could not remove Edom from provincial status. Certainly he did not do so before the closing years of Solomon's reign, for it was probably about the middle years when Solomon defeated Zobah and Hamath and fortified Tadmor to the far north. Toward the close of Solomon's rule, however—when God's blessing had been withdrawn from Israel—there can be little question but that Rezon made matters very difficult for Israel's king. The statement that he was an adversary "all the days of Solomon" suggests that he outlived Solomon and so could have made trouble right up until the end of his reign. It may be that effective control by Solomon in both Edom and the Damascus region was all but lost by the time of his death.

c. Jeroboam (11:26-40)

The third problem area concerned Jeroboam, who later became the first king of the northern domain of Israel. Jeroboam was an Israelite; the third problem area, then, arose from within the land. Jeroboam was of the tribe of Ephraim, and his father was an officer under Solomon. While Solomon was having the Millo constructed, along certain broken areas in a wall of Jerusalem repaired (I Kings 9:15; 11:27), he noticed that young Jeroboam was an industrious and talented worker. He therefore placed him in a supervisory position over the work force from the northern tribes.

One day, when on leave from his task, Jeroboam was met by the prophet Ahijah, who tore a new garment into twelve parts and gave Jeroboam ten. He explained that these ten pieces represented ten tribes of Israel over which Jeroboam would one day rule. He told the young man that God would take these tribes away from the domain of Solomon (meaning Solomon's son) because of his unfaithfulness to the Lord in actually worshiping Ashtoreth of the Zidonians, Chemosh of the Moabites, and Milcom (Molech) of the Ammonites. God, however, would leave one tribe (Judah) to the ruler in Jerusalem for the sake of David. Ahijah told Jeroboam, further, that if he like David would be faithful to God, God would bless him in his rule and give him a continuing dynasty.

Solomon somehow learned of Ahijah's words to Jeroboam, perhaps through an indiscretion of the young man, and immediately sought to take Jeroboam's life. One has to wonder why Solomon stooped to such a tactic, wise as he was and with a splendid record in back of him, but he did. What he really tried to do in seeking Jeroboam's life was not only to shed innocent blood, but to circumvent the will of God. Solomon did not succeed, however, for Jeroboam was able to escape to Egypt, in the pattern of Hadad of Edom earlier. The Egyptian Pharaoh, Shishak (Sheshonq I, 940-920 B.C.), gave Jeroboam protection.[12] Jeroboam stayed in Egypt until recalled by the northern Israelite tribes at the time of rebellion against Rehoboam, Solomon's son and successor.

2. POINTS TO NOTICE

a. The reduction of Solomon's power

At the midpoint of his rule, Solomon was the most powerful king of his day. At the close of his rule, the situation had changed drastically. Power both to the south and north had been all but lost. God had permitted major opposition in both directions. The result was that Solomon had little more territory left than Israel proper, though apparently he continued his hold on the Transjordanian countries of Ammon and Moab. With this control gone, much of his source of revenue would have dried up as well, and his wisdom, though still with him, would have lost much of its luster. Solomon no doubt had been very proud of his accomplishments twenty years before, but here at the close of rule, there was little reason for pride.

b. Seriousness of Hadad's opposition

The result of Hadad's opposition was not only that it lost Solomon the full control of a satellite neighbor, but it cut off his southern route for trade. If he maintained his shipping out of Ezion-geber at all, it was probably on a greatly reduced scale, and it is even possible that it stopped entirely before his death.

c. Seriousness of Rezon's opposition

The result of Rezon's opposition was that it cut off all contact with the satellite countries of the north. Damascus was the key to control over Zobah, Hamath, and the fortified city of Tadmor. With full control gone in Damascus, there was no possibility of maintaining supervision in these other areas.

d. Rezon and Hezion

In I Kings 15:18 there is a short list of the kings of Damascus. This list, working backward from Ben-hadad, who waged war with Israel after the division of the kingdom, reads: "Ben-hadad, the son of Tabri-mon, the son of Hezion." These names agree with a similar listing on a votive stele of Ben-hadad I. Albright's reading of Ben-hadad's list is: "Bir-hadad, son of

[12]Ibid., p. 95.

Tab-Ramman, son of Hadyan."[13] Since this list seems to go back to the beginning of the Damascene kingship, it is almost necessary to believe that the Rezon of our story is the same as the Hezion of the list.[14]

e. Solomon's punishment

Solomon's punishment was of a twofold nature. It consisted first in the knowledge that his son would rule only a small part of Israel, and second, in his own loss of much of his power and territory before he died. God did promise Solomon that He would not remove the rule of Israel's tribes from him personally, so long as he lived (I Kings 11:12); but He did not promise that He would not remove Solomon's control over much of the foreign domain. And this is exactly what God did. Solomon himself thus suffered real loss, just as much as did his son after him.

f. Seriousness of fighting God's will

Solomon's sin in actually fighting against God's will was serious. News reached him that Jeroboam was to rule over ten of the tribes. That the news was stated through a prophet should have signified to Solomon that this was God's will, and he should have submitted before it. But instead he tried to kill Jeroboam. This was really an attempt to change what God had said, to challenge God. It was in principle the very same thing that Saul had sought to effect when he tried to take David's life.

D. SOLOMON'S DEATH

1. THE STORY (I KINGS 11:41-43; II CHRON. 9:29-31)

After forty years of rule, Solomon died and was buried in the city of David his father. No details are given regarding his death, but presumably it was peaceful, in keeping with his manner of life. The statement is merely that he "slept" (*shacab,* "lie down, sleep") with his fathers. His age was probably at least sixty, for, as observed, he probably was at least twenty when crowned, having already married Naamah, who had borne him his son, Rehoboam.

The books of I Kings and II Chronicles complement each other in giving source material for Solomon's life. The former states that information is written "in the book of the acts of Solomon" (11:41). The latter says it is contained "in the book of Nathan the prophet [who must have continued

[13]William F. Albright, *Bulletin of the American Schools of Oriental Research* 87 (Oct. 1942), p. 26.

[14]See Merrill Unger, *Israel and the Aramaeans of Damascus,* pp. 56-57.

living on into the reign of Solomon], and in the prophecy of Ahijah the Shilonite, and in the visions of Iddo the seer against Jeroboam the son of Nebat'' (9:29).

2. POINTS TO NOTICE

a. Solomon's regret

Though Solomon's death may have been peaceful, it no doubt was an experience of regret. He had achieved much, but he could have accomplished so much more. There would have been both the haunting memory of how much he had enjoyed twenty years before and the empty recognition of how little remained at the time of his passing. He would have known the reason, too, for God had made this clear from his earliest days. But he had not remembered well; he had forgotten and allowed distracting factors to lead him astray. How he must have wished he had done differently.

b. Forty years of rule

Interestingly, God gave Israel's first three kings the same amount of years for their reigns. They all ruled forty years. It was as though God told them: Here is an identical period of time to reign; what will you do with it? What the three did was quite different. Saul failed almost completely with his period, dying with a disunited country at the mercy of the feared Philistines. Solomon here passed on with regret, for he had enjoyed so much power and opportunity and came to lose so much of it. David alone used his well; taking a people disunited and molding them into a consolidated state, and even forging an empire. He stands out from among the three, as indeed he stands out from all of Israel's history.

BIBLIOGRAPHY

Aharoni, Yohanan. *The Land of the Bible.* Translated by A. F. Rainey. Philadelphia: The Westminster Press, 1962, 1967.

________, and Avi-Yonah, Michael. *The Macmillan Bible Atlas.* New York: The Macmillan Co., 1968.

Albright, William F. *Archaeology and the Religion of Israel.* 3d ed. Baltimore: John Hopkins Press, 1953.

________. *Archaeology of Palestine.* Rev. ed. Harmondsworth: Penguin Books, 1956.

________. "The Biblical Period." In *The Jews: Their History, Culture and Religion,* edited by L. Finkelstein, pp. 3-65. New York: Harper & Bros., 1949.

________. *From the Stone Age to Christianity.* 2d ed. Garden City, NY: Doubleday & Co., Anchor Books, 1957.

________. "The Old Testament World." In *The Interpreter's Bible,* edited by George A. Buttrick, vol. I, pp. 223-271. New York: Abingdon Press, 1952.

________. "Recent Progress in North Canaanite Research." In *Bulletin of the American Schools of Oriental Research* 70 (1938), pp. 151-156.

Anderson, G. W. *The History and Religion of Israel.* London: Oxford University Press, 1966.

Ap-Thomas, D. R. "The Phoenicians." In *Peoples of Old Testament Times,* edited by D. J. Wiseman, pp. 259-287. Oxford: Clarendon Press, 1973.

Archer, Gleason. *A Survey of Old Testament Introduction.* Chicago: Moody Press, 1964.

Armerding, Carl E. "Were David's Sons Really Priests?" In *Current Issues in Biblical and Patristic Interpretation,* edited by Gerald F. Hawthorne, pp. 75-87. Grand Rapids: Wm. B. Eerdmans, 1975.

Baly, Denis. *The Geography of the Bible.* London: Lutterworth Press, 1957.

Barnett, R. D. *Illustrations of Old Testament History.* London: The Trustees of the British Museum, 1966.

Bartlett, J. R. "The Moabites and Edomites." In *Peoples of Old Testament Times,* edited by D. J. Wiseman, pp. 229-259. Oxford: Clarendon Press, 1973.

Barton, G. A. *Archaeology and the Bible.* 7th ed. Philadelphia: American Sunday School Union, 1937.

Breasted, J. H. *A History of Egypt.* 2d ed. New York: Chas. Scribner's Sons, 1912.

Bright, John. *A History of Israel.* 2d ed. Philadelphia: The Westminster Press, 1972.

Bruce, F. F. *Israel and the Nations.* Grand Rapids: Wm. B. Eerdmans, 1963.

Bullinger, Ethelbert W. *Figures of Speech Used in the Bible.* Grand Rapids: Baker Book House, 1965.

Burrows, M. *What Mean These Stones?* New Haven, CT: American Schools of Oriental Research, 1941.

Caird, G. B. "The First and Second Books of Samuel." In *The Interpreter's Bible,* edited by George A. Buttrick, vol. II, pp. 855-1176. New York: Abingdon Press, 1953.

Davis, John. *The Birth of a Kingdom.* Grand Rapids: Baker Book House, 1970.

deVaux, Roland. *Ancient Israel: Its Life and Institutions.* Translated by J. McHugh. New York: McGraw-Hill Book Co., 1961.

Driver, Samuel R. *Introduction to the Literature of the Old Testament.* 5th ed. Edinburgh: T. & T. Clark, 1894.

________. *Notes on the Hebrew Text of the Books of Samuel.* 2d ed. Oxford: Clarendon Press, 1913.

Ewald, Heinrich. *The History of Israel.* Vol. III. London: Longmans, Green, and Co., 1871.

Finegan, Jack. *Handbook of Biblical Chronology.* Princeton: Princeton University Press, 1964.

________. *Light from the Ancient Past.* 2d ed. Princeton: Princeton University Press, 1959.

Fohrer, George. *History of Israelite Religion.* Translated by D. E. Green. New York: Abingdon Press, 1972.

Fosbroke, Hughell. "The Prophetic Literature." In *The Interpreter's Bible,* edited by George A. Buttrick, vol. I, pp. 201-211. New York: Abingdon Press, 1952.

Frankfort, Henri. *Ancient Egyptian Religion.* New York: Columbia University Press, 1948.

________. *Kingship and the Gods.* Chicago: University of Chicago Press, 1948.

Geoff, Beatrice. "Syncretism in the Religion of Israel." In *Journal of Biblical Literature* 58 (1939), pp. 151-161.

Glueck, Nelson. *The Other Side of the Jordan.* New Haven, CT: The American Schools of Oriental Research, 1940.

________. "Transjordan." In *Archaeology and Old Testament Study,* edited by D. W. Thomas, pp. 429-453. Oxford: Clarendon Press, 1967.

Gordon, Cyrus. *The Ancient Near East.* 3d ed. New York: W. W. Norton Co., 1965. Formerly issued as *The World of the Old Testament.* Garden City, NY: Doubleday & Co., 1958.

Gray, George. *Sacrifice in the Old Testament.* Oxford: Clarendon Press, 1925.

Gray, John. *Archaeology and the Old Testament World.* London: Thomas Nelson and Sons, 1962.

Gurney, O. R. *The Hittites.* Rev. ed. Harmondsworth: Penguin Books, 1966.

Harrison, R. K. *Introduction to the Old Testament.* Grand Rapids: Wm. B. Eerdmans, 1969.

________. *Old Testament Times.* Grand Rapids: Wm. B. Eerdmans, 1970.

Hindson, Edward. *The Philistines and the Old Testament.* Grand Rapids: Baker Book House, 1971.

Hitti, Philip. *History of Syria, Including Lebanon and Palestine.* New York: The Macmillan Co., 1951.

Hoffner, H. A. "The Hittites and Hurrians." In *Peoples of Old Testament Times,* edited by D. J. Wiseman, pp. 197-229. Oxford: Clarendon Press, 1973.

Kaufmann, Yehezkel. *The Biblical Account of the Conquest of Palestine.* Translated by M. Dagut. Jerusalem: Jerusalem University Press, 1953.

Keil, C. F., and Delitzsch, F. *Biblical Commentary on the Old Testament.* Vol. V: *Biblical Commentary on the Books of Samuel;* Vol. VI: *Biblical Commentary on the Books of Kings.* Translated by James Martin. Edinburgh: T. & T. Clark, 1891.

Kenyon, Kathleen. *Amorites and Canaanites.* London: Oxford University Press, 1966.

________. *Royal Cities of the Old Testament.* New York: Schocken Books, 1971.

Kidner, Derek K. "Wisdom Literature of the Old Testament." In *New Perspectives on the Old Testament,* edited by J. B. Payne, pp. 117-130. Waco, TX: Word Books, 1970.

Kitchen, Kenneth. *Ancient Orient and Old Testament.* Chicago: Inter-Varsity Press, 1966.

________. "The Philistines." In *Peoples of Old Testament Times,* edited by D. J. Wiseman, pp. 53-79. Oxford: Clarendon Press, 1973.

Lambert, W. G. "The Babylonians and Chaldaeans." In *Peoples of Old Testament Times,* edited by D. J. Wiseman, pp. 179-197. Oxford: Clarendon Press, 1973.

Lewy, J. "Hamat-Zobah and Subat-Hamatu." In *Hebrew Union College Annual* 18 (1944), pp. 443-454.

Liverani, M. "The Amorites." In *Peoples of Old Testament Times,* edited by D. J. Wiseman, pp. 100-134. Oxford: Clarendon Press, 1973.

Malamat, Abraham. "The Aramaeans." In *Peoples of Old Testament Times,* edited by D. J. Wiseman, pp. 134-156. Oxford: Clarendon Press, 1973.

________. "Aspects of the Foreign Policies of David and Solomon." In *Journal of Near Eastern Studies* 22 (Jan. 1963), pp. 1-17.

________. "The Egyptian Decline in Canaan and the Sea Peoples." In *The World History of the Jewish People,* vol. III, pp. 23-38. New Brunswick, NJ: Rutgers University Press, 1971.

________. "The Period of the Judges." In *The World History of the Jewish People,* vol. III, pp. 129-163. New Brunswick, NJ: Rutgers University Press, 1971.

Maly, Eugene. *The World of David and Solomon.* Englewood Cliffs, NJ: Prentice-Hall, Inc., 1965.

Mazar, Benjamin. "The Exodus and the Conquest." In *The World History of the Jewish People,* vol. III, pp. 71-94. New Brunswick, NJ: Rutgers University Press, 1971.

________. "The Historical Development." In *The World History of the Jewish People,* vol. III, pp. 3-22. New Brunswick, NJ: Rutgers University Press, 1971.

________. "The Philistines and Their Wars with Israel." In *The World History of the Jewish People,* vol. III, pp. 164-179. New Brunswick, NJ: Rutgers University Press, 1971.

Mendelsohn, I. "Samuel's Denunciation of Kingship in the Light of the Akkadian Documents from Ugarit." In *Bulletin of the American Schools of Oriental Research* 143 (Oct. 1956), pp. 17-22.

Mendenhall, George. *Law and Covenant in Israel and the Ancient Near East.* Pittsburgh: The Biblical Colloquium, 1955.

Merrill, Eugene. *An Historical Survey of the Old Testament.* Nutley, NJ: The Craig Press, 1966.

Millard, A. R. "The Canaanites." In *Peoples of Old Testament Times,* edited by D. J. Wiseman, pp. 29-53. Oxford: Clarendon Press, 1973.

Moscati, Sabatino. *Ancient Semitic Civilizations.* London: Elek Books, Ltd., 1957.

Murray, John. *Principles of Conduct.* Grand Rapids: Wm. B. Eerdmans, 1957.

Noth, Martin. *The History of Israel.* 2d ed. London: A. & C. Black, 1958.

O'Callaghan, R. T. *Aram Naharaim.* Rome: Pontifical Biblical Institute, 1948.

Oesterley, W. O. E., and Robinson, T. H. *Hebrew Religion.* London: S.P.C.K., 1952.

Olmstead, A. T. *History of Syria and Palestine.* New York: Chas. Scribner's Sons, 1931.

Owen, G. F. *Archaeology and the Bible.* Westwood, NJ: Fleming H. Revell, 1961.

Payne, J. Barton. *An Outline of Hebrew History.* Grand Rapids: Baker Book House, 1954.

________. *The Theology of the Older Testament.* Grand Rapids: Zondervan, 1962.

Pfeiffer, Charles F. *The Biblical World.* Grand Rapids: Baker Book House, 1966.

________. *Old Testament History.* Grand Rapids: Baker Book House, 1973.

Pfeiffer, Robert H. *Introduction to the Old Testament.* New York: Harper & Bros., 1941.

Phillips, Wendell. *Qataban and Sheba.* New York: Harcourt, Brace and Co., 1955.

Pritchard, J. B. *The Ancient Near East in Pictures.* Princeton: Princeton University Press, 1954.

________. *Gibeon, Where the Sun Stood Still.* Princeton: Princeton University Press, 1962.

________, ed. *Ancient Near Eastern Texts Relating to the Old Testament.* Rev. ed. Princeton: Princeton University Press, 1955.

Rainey, A. F. "Gath of the Philistines." In *Christian News from Israel* 17 (Sept. 1966), pp. 31-38.

Ricciotti, G. *The History of Israel.* 2 vols. 2d ed. Milwaukee: Bruce Publishing Co., 1958.

Sags, H. W. F. "The Assyrians." In *Peoples of Old Testament Times,* edited by D. J. Wiseman, pp. 156-179. Oxford: Clarendon Press, 1973.

Schultz, Samuel. *The Old Testament Speaks.* New York: Harper & Bros., 1960.

Schwantes, Siegfried. *A Short History of the Ancient Near East.* Grand Rapids: Baker Book House, 1965.

Scott, R. B. Y. "Weights and Measures of the Bible." In *The Biblical Archaeologist* 22 (1959), pp. 22-40.

Shanks, Hershel. *The City of David.* Washington, DC: The Biblical Archaeological Society, 1973.

Simons, J. *The Geographical and Topographical Texts of the Old Testament.* Leiden: E. J. Brill, 1959.

________. *Handbook for the Study of Egyptian Topographical Lists Relating to Western Asia.* Leiden: E. J. Brill, 1937.

Sinclair, Lawrence. "An Archaeological Study of Gibeah (Tell el-Ful)." In *The Biblical Archaeologist* 27 (May 1964), pp. 52-64.

Smick, Elmer B. *Archaeology of the Jordan Valley.* Grand Rapids: Baker Book House, 1973.

Snaith, Norman H. "The First and Second Books of Kings." In *The Interpreter's Bible,* edited by George A. Buttrick, vol. III, pp. 3-338. New York: Abingdon Press, 1954.

Speiser, E. A. "The Manner of the King." In *The World History of the Jewish People,* vol. III, pp. 280-287. New Brunswick, NJ: Rutgers University Press, 1971.

Thiele, E. R. *The Mysterious Numbers of the Hebrew Kings.* Rev. ed. Grand Rapids: Wm. B. Eerdmans, 1965.

Thomas, D. Winton, ed. *Archaeology and Old Testament Study.* Oxford: Clarendon Press, 1967.

________. *Documents from Old Testament Times.* New York: Harper & Bros., 1958.

Thompson, J. A. *The Bible and Archaeology.* Grand Rapids: Wm. B. Eerdmans, 1962.

Torczyner, Harry. *The Lachish Letters.* London: Oxford University Press, 1958.

Unger, Merrill. *Archaeology and the Old Testament.* Grand Rapids: Zondervan, 1954.

________. *Israel and the Aramaeans of Damascus.* London: James Clarke & Co., Ltd., 1957.

VanBeek, G. W., and Jamme, A. "An Inscribed South Arabian Clay Stamp from Bethel." In *Bulletin of American Schools of Oriental Research* 151 (Oct. 1958), pp. 9-16.

Williams, Ronald J. "The Egyptians." In *Peoples of Old Testament Times,* edited by D. J. Wiseman, pp. 79-100. Oxford: Clarendon Press, 1973.

Wilson, John A. *The Burden of Egypt.* Chicago: University of Chicago Press, 1951.

Wiseman, D. J. *Illustrations from Biblical Archaeology.* Grand Rapids: Wm. B. Eerdmans, 1958.

________, ed. *Peoples of Old Testament Times.* Oxford: Clarendon Press, 1973.

Wood, Leon J. *The Distressing Days of the Judges.* Grand Rapids: Zondervan, 1975.

________. "Ecstasy and Israel's Early Prophets." In *Bulletin of the Evangelical Theological Society* 9 (Summer 1966), pp. 125-137.

________. *A Survey of Israel's Early History.* Grand Rapids: Zondervan, 1970.

Wright, G. Ernest. *Biblical Archaeology.* Philadelphia: The Westminster Press, 1957.

________. *The Old Testament Against Its Environment.* London: S.C.M. Press, 1950.

________, and Filson, F. V. *The Westminster Historical Atlas to the Bible,* Rev. ed. Philadelphia: The Westminster Press, 1956.

Yadin, Yigael. *The Art of Warfare in Biblical Lands in the Light of Archaeological Study.* Translated by M. Pearlman. 2 vols. New York: McGraw-Hill Book Co., 1963.

________. "New Light on Solomon's Megiddo." In *The Biblical Archaeologist* 23 (1960), pp. 62-68.

Young, Edward J. *The Book of Isaiah.* Vol. III. Grand Rapids: Wm. B. Eerdmans, 1972.

________. *An Introduction to the Old Testament.* Grand Rapids: Wm. B. Eerdmans, 1949.

SCRIPTURE INDEX

II Samuel

I Kings

II Kings

I Chronicles

II Chronicles

SUBJECT INDEX